The Praeger Handbook of Victimology

The Praeger Handbook of Victimology

JANET K. WILSON, EDITOR

PRAEGER

An Imprint of ABC-CLIO, LLC

A B C ❖ C L I O

Santa Barbara, California • Denver, Colorado • Oxford, England

Library of Congress Cataloging-in-Publication Data

The Praeger handbook of victimology / [edited by] Janet K. Wilson.
    p. cm.
 Includes index.
 ISBN 978-0-313-35935-4 (hard copy : alk. paper) — ISBN 978-0-313-35936-1 (ebook)
 1. Victims of crimes—United States—Handbooks, manuals, etc. 2. Victims of crimes—United States. I. Wilson, Janet K.
 HV6250.3.U5P73 2009
 362.88—dc22   2009022865

This book is also available on the World Wide Web as an eBook.
Visit www.abc-clio.com for details.

ABC-CLIO, LLC
130 Cremona Drive, P.O. Box 1911
Santa Barbara, California 93116-1911

This book is printed on acid-free paper ∞
Manufactured in the United States of America

Contents

Preface   *vii*

Chronology of Selected Victimology Events   *ix*

Alphabetical List of Entries   *xiii*

Topical List of Entries   *xvii*

The Praeger Handbook of Victimology   **1**

Resource Guide   *319*

Index   *323*

About the Editor and Contributors   *331*

Preface

The crime victim was "rediscovered" in the 1940s. With the coining of the term "victimology" in 1947 came the development of an interdisciplinary field focused on the study of and service to those who fall prey to the criminal offenses of others. The purpose of this book is to provide an overview of the origins and establishment of the field of victimology over the previous 70 years.

This handbook was written with the general public and college or university students in mind. The core of the book features 197 entries written by 95 contributors. Readers are provided an alphabetical and topical list of entries. The alphabetical list reveals the range of entries included in the book; the topical list offers insight into the major areas of focus within the field of victimology and how the entries relate to each other. Within each entry there is an explanation of the concept in light of how it relates to victims of crime. In addition, a suggested reading area is included in which readers may find other relevant sources. Reflecting the interdisciplinary nature of the field of victimology, the contributors who wrote the entries come from 28 states representing 13 academic areas of study (e.g., criminal justice, criminology, gerontology, psychology, sociology, and victim studies).

In addition to the handbook, readers will find a chronology of selected victimology events and a resource guide that includes citations for books, a list of journals, and addresses for Web sites that relate to issues faced by victims of crime. Even the short biographies of the contributors and editor, found at the back of this book, are a resource for those who want to identify professionals who are working in their area of interest. The chronology takes the reader from the first attempts to classify the crime victim in the 1940s, through the active 1980s, which saw the passage of federal legislation extending victims' rights, to today's struggle with policing the use of technology to protect people from such crimes as stalking and identity theft. Those who seek a broad view of the field of victimology are directed to numerous recently published books listed in the resource guide. On the other hand, readers who are interested in additional sources for a narrower topic, for example, child abuse or human trafficking, will also find in the resource guide a selection of journals that include articles pertaining to specific crime victims and Web sites that feature timely victim-related information.

Whether you read this book straight through, from "Abuse: Active and Passive" to the "World Society of Victimology (WSV)," or select entries of interest to you, you will come away with a broader understanding of the perils and struggles, as well as the strengths and achievements, of crime victims and those who advocate for and study them. Hopefully you will recognize what role you can play in this dynamic interdisciplinary field of victimology. Enjoy!

ACKNOWLEDGMENTS

A special thank-you goes to former Senior Acquisitions Editor Suzanne I. Staszak-Silva, who saw the value of this handbook, even before she had to tell me to stop e-mailing her every two weeks asking whether the prospectus had been approved yet. With less than a month before my deadline, and finding myself without an editor, Senior Acquisitions Editor Michael Wilt swooped in to save the day. Thanks, Michael, for your patience in explaining the publishing process to me and ultimately saving me from hours of formatting.

The heart of this book, however, is the contributors. I want to thank each of you for sharing some of the passion that you bring to the study of and service to victims of crime. I had a vision for this book, but you did the work to give it form.

Many thanks are extended to the University of Central Arkansas for the award of a sabbatical to allow me the time to work on this book. To my colleagues in the Department of Sociology, who had to tolerate months of my ongoing countdowns for recruited contributors, submitted entries, edited entries, approved entries, etc., all I can say is that I know just how lucky I am to work where I do.

Finally, I want to thank my family for their enthusiastic support of this project, and, yes, a copy of this book will be up for grabs at next year's "Dirty Santa." Special recognition goes to my daughter, Lia, who may never learn how to tell time for all the occasions when my "couple more minutes" on the computer turned into an hour. Lia, you are my "bringer of good news"!

Chronology of Selected Victimology Events

A chronology of selected events reflecting the development of the discipline of victimology is provided.

1941   Hans von Hentig publishes an article noting the relationship between victims and criminals.

1947   The term "victimology" is coined by Beniamin Mendelsohn, thus earning him the title by many of the "father" of victimology.

1948   Hans von Hentig publishes *The Criminal and His Victim,* in which he provides a typology of victims based on physical, psychological, and social characteristics.

1957   Margery Fry advocates for victim compensation laws, whereby the government would reimburse crime victims.

1958   Marvin Wolfgang publishes *Patterns in Criminal Homicide,* where he reports that 26% of homicides examined were victim-precipitated.

1962   C. Henry Kempe and others publish the article "The Battered-Child Syndrome," chronicling the harm committed by parents and foster parents against children.

1963   New Zealand is the first country to pass victim compensation laws.

1965   California establishes the first victim compensation program in the United States.

1968   Stephen Schafer publishes *The Victim and His Criminal,* in which he provides a typology reflecting victim responsibility for the crime.

1969   The Hate Crimes Prevention Act allows for federal prosecution of those who harm others because of their race, color, religion, or national origin.

1972   The National Crime Survey (later changed to the National Crime Victimization Survey) is designed to supplement the Uniform Crime Reports. This annual survey provides a detailed picture of a select number of personal and property victimizations.

1973   The First International Symposium on Victimology is held in Israel.

1975   The National Organization for Victim Assistance is established, with the mission of advocacy activities, services to victims, and professional development training.

1976   The first scholarly journal on the topic of victimology is published.

1978   Parents of Murdered Children, Inc. is founded. It provides support to parents and other survivors as they deal with their grief and with the criminal justice system.

The National Coalition Against Domestic Violence is formed in an effort to end violence for women and children.

1979   The World Society of Victimology is established.

Lenore Walker publishes *The Battered Woman,* in which she discusses the "cycle of violence."

1980   Mothers Against Drunk Driving is founded to stop drunk driving and assist those harmed by this act.

1981   The Annual National Victims of Crime Week is designated for every April.

1982   The Federal Victim and Witness Protection Act establishes a number of rights for a federal crime victim, including notification of hearings, timely restitution, and fair treatment.

The President's Task Force on Victims of Crime sets forth 68 recommendations at the federal, state, and organizational levels to better serve victims of crime.

1984   The Victims of Crime Act establishes the Crime Victims Fund, which supports victim assistance and compensation programs.

The results of the Minneapolis Domestic Violence Experiment are published, leading, in part, to changes in how police departments respond to domestic disturbances.

A large settlement to the victim in the case of *Thurman v. The City of Torrington* also has an impact on police responses to domestic disputes.

1985   The United Nations adopts the *Declaration of Basic Principles of Justice for Victims of Crime and Abuse of Power.*

1986   The Sexual Abuse Act updates federal law by reclassifying various forms of sexual assault and their penalties.

1988   The Office for Victims of Crime is developed to oversee the Crime Victims Fund and to provide training for service providers, offer victim services, and publish research.

1990   The Crime Awareness and Campus Security Act requires colleges and universities to report crime on and around campus.

The Victims' Rights and Restitution Act mandates specific investigative procedures and victim services to be followed by federal officials when working with crime victims.

The Hate Crime Statistics Act requires the collection of data on crime victimizations that are due to the victim's race, ethnicity, religion, disability, or sexual orientation.

1993   The International Parental Kidnapping Crime Act makes it a federal offense to interfere with parental rights by holding a child outside the United States.

1994   The Violence Against Women Act provides funds to enhance the prosecution of violent crimes against women, as well as support mandatory restitution.

1995   The Jacob Wetterling Crimes Against Children and Sexually Violent Offender Registration Act requires states to establish sex offender registries.

1996   The Federal Anti-Stalker Act focuses on stalking that occurs across state lines or through U.S. mail services.

The Drug-Induced Rape Prevention and Punishment Act provides for enhanced penalties for violent crimes committed when illegal drugs have been introduced to the victim without her knowledge.

Kentucky becomes the first state to provide the Victim Information and Notification Everyday system, whereby victims can call a toll-free number to obtain information about their case and the status of their offender.

2001   The September 11 terrorist attacks lead to changes in U.S. air travel security measures and bring the topic of terrorism to the forefront of national debate.

2002   The Occupational Safety and Health Administration publishes *Workplace Violence,* in which they offer recommendations that both employees and employers can take to protect against workplace violence.

2003   The American Society of Victimology holds its first annual meeting.

2004   The Justice for All Act expands and reinforces the rights of crime victims, including an improvement in DNA collection and testing.

The Crime Victims' Rights Act extends numerous rights to victims in federal proceedings, including the right to be heard at public proceedings, receive timely restitution, and be treated with fairness.

2006   The Adam Walsh Child Protection and Safety Act aims to protect children from violent and sexual assaults, decrease child pornography, and make the Internet more safe for children.

2007   The Rape, Abuse, & Incest National Network expands its services to include the National Sexual Assault *Online* Hotline, which is the first secure Web-based hotline providing live and confidential help to victims.

2008   Facebook, a social networking Web site, adds safeguards in order to protect users from sexual predators and cyberbullies.

Alphabetical List of Entries

Abuse: Active and Passive

Acquaintance Rape

Adult Protective Services (APS)

Advocates

Agent Provocateur

Alcohol and Victimization

Allocution

Alternative Dispute Resolution (ADR)

AMBER Alert

Amir, Menachem

Anatomically Detailed Dolls

Arson

Assault

Battered Child Syndrome

Battered Husband Syndrome

Battered Woman Syndrome

Battery

Belief in a Just World

Blaming the Victim

Bullying

Burglary

Burnout

Bystander Effect

Campus Victimizations

Celebrity Victim

Child Abuse

Child Lures

Child Protective Services (CPS)

Child Witness

Civil Litigation

Community Service

Compensation Programs

Compensatory Damages

Conflict Tactics Scales

Correctional Officials

Corruption

Costs of Crime

Court Appointed Special Advocate (CASA)

Creative Restitution

Crime Prevention

Crime Prevention Through Environmental Design (CPTED)

Critical Victimology

CyberAngels.org
Cybercrime
Cyberstalking
Cycle of Violence
Dark Figure of Crime
Death Notification
Defense Attorneys
Defensible Space
Defounding
Domestic Elder Abuse
Domestic Minor Sex Trafficking
Domestic Violence
Domestic Violence Myths
Elder Abuse
Facilitation
False Allegations
Family Abduction
Family Stress Theory
Family Violence Court
Fear of Crime
Feminist Perspectives on Victimization
Financial Abuse
Fry, Margery
Good Samaritan
Guardian Ad Litem
Hate Crime
Hazing
History of Victimology, Pre-1940s
History of Victimology, 1940s
History of Victimology, 1950s
History of Victimology, 1960s
History of Victimology, 1970s
History of Victimology, 1980s
History of Victimology, 1990s
History of Victimology, 2000 to today
Human Trafficking
Identity Theft
Incest
Infanticide
Institutional Elder Abuse
Insurance Policies

International Crime Victim Survey (ICVS)
International Victimizations
Intimate Partner Violence
Judges
Juries
Kempe, C. Henry
Kidnapping
Larceny-Theft
Learned Helplessness
Lifestyle Theory
Male Rape
Marital Rape
McGruff Campaign
Mediation
Mendelsohn, Beniamin
Mendelsohn's Typologies
Minneapolis Domestic Violence Experiment
Mothers Against Drunk Driving (MADD)
Motor Vehicle Theft
Murder
National Crime Victimization Survey (NCVS)
National Incident-Based Reporting System (NIBRS)
Neglect
Neighborhood Watch Programs
Neutralization Theory
No-Drop Policies
Notoriety for Profit Laws
Operators
Order of Protection
Pain and Suffering Compensation
Parents Anonymous® Inc.
Parole Boards
Pecuniary Damages
Pedophilia
Plea Bargaining
Police Officers
Pornography
Post-Traumatic Stress Disorder (PTSD)

Precipitation

President's Task Force on Victims of Crime, *Final Report*

Primary Victimization

Prison Rape

Prosecuting Attorneys

Provocation

Psychopathology Theory

Punitive Damages

Rape

Rape Myths

Rape Shield Laws

Rape Trauma Syndrome

Rational Choice Theory

Recovered Memories of Sexual Abuse

Reporting Rates

Restitution

Restorative Justice

Retributive Justice

Robbery

Routine Activity Theory

Rule of Thumb

Same-Sex Partner Abuse

Schafer, Stephen

Schafer's Typologies

School Victimizations

Secondary Victimization

Self-Help Justice

Sensationalism

Series Victimizations

Sex Offender Registration

Sexual Assault

Sexual Harassment

Shaken Baby Syndrome

Shelters

Sibling Abuse

Social Exchange Theory

Social Learning Theory

Society for the Prevention of Cruelty to Children (SPCC)

Sociobiology Theory

Sovereign Immunity

Stalking

Statutory Rape

Stockholm Syndrome

Subculture of Violence

Subintentional Death

Supplementary Homicide Report (SHR)

Support Groups

Supreme Court Cases

Symbolic Restitution

Target Hardening

Terrorism

Third-Party Liability

Unfounding

Uniform Crime Report (UCR)

Vicarious Victimization

Victim Bill of Rights

Victim Discounting

Victim Impact Panels

Victim Impact Statement

Victim Information and Notification Everyday (VINE)

Victimization Trends

Victimless Crimes

Victim-Offender Reconciliation Programs (VORPs)

Victimologists

Victimology

Victims' Rights Constitutional Amendment

Victims' Rights Legislation

Victim vs. Survivor

Victim/Witness Assistance Programs (VWAPs)

von Hentig, Hans

von Hentig's Typologies

Widening the Net

Wilson, Mary Ellen

Wolfgang, Marvin E.

Workplace Victimizations

World Society of Victimology (WSV)

Topical List of Entries

Alcohol and Victimization

Alcohol and Victimization

Mothers Against Drunk Driving (MADD)

Victim Impact Panels

Child Abuse and Neglect

Abuse: Active and Passive

AMBER Alert

Anatomically Detailed Dolls

Battered Child Syndrome

Child Abuse

Child Lures

Child Protective Services (CPS)

Child Witness

Court Appointed Special Advocate (CASA)

CyberAngels.org

Domestic Minor Sex Trafficking

Domestic Violence

Family Abduction

Guardian Ad Litem

Incest

Infanticide

Kempe, C. Henry

Kidnapping

Neglect

Parents Anonymous® Inc.

Pedophilia

Shaken Baby Syndrome

Sibling Abuse

Society for the Prevention of Cruelty to Children (SPCC)

Statutory Rape

Wilson, Mary Ellen

Crime Prevention

Crime Prevention

Crime Prevention Through Environmental Design (CPTED)

Defensible Space

McGruff Campaign

Neighborhood Watch Programs

Target Hardening

Criminal Justice System Policies

Allocution
Anatomically Detailed Dolls
Child Witness
Community Service
Defounding
Family Violence Court
No-Drop Policies
Order of Protection
Plea Bargaining
Retributive Justice
Sex Offender Registration
Sovereign Immunity
Unfounding
Victim Impact Statement
Victim Information and Notification
    Everyday (VINE)

**Criminal Justice System
    Representatives**

Correctional Officials
Defense Attorneys
Judges
Juries
Operators
Parole Boards
Police Officers
Prosecuting Attorneys
Victim/Witness Assistance Programs
    (VWAPs)

Domestic Violence

Battered Husband Syndrome
Battered Woman Syndrome
Conflict Tactics Scales
Cycle of Violence
Domestic Violence
Domestic Violence Myths
Family Violence Court
Intimate Partner Violence

Learned Helplessness
Minneapolis Domestic Violence
    Experiment
No-Drop Policies
Rule of Thumb
Same-Sex Partner Abuse
Stalking

Elder Abuse

Abuse: Active vs. Passive
Adult Protective Services (APS)
Domestic Elder Abuse
Domestic Violence
Elder Abuse
Financial Abuse
Institutional Elder Abuse

Fear of Crime

Fear of Crime
Sensationalism
Vicarious Victimization

Financial Issues

Civil Litigation
Compensation Programs
Compensatory Damages
Costs of Crime
Creative Restitution
Insurance Policies
Notoriety for Profit Laws
Pain and Suffering Compensation
Pecuniary Damages
Punitive Damages
Restitution
Symbolic Restitution
Third-Party Liability

Hate Crime

Hate Crime

History of Victimology

History of Victimology, Pre-1940s
History of Victimology, 1940s
History of Victimology, 1950s
History of Victimology, 1960s
History of Victimology, 1970s
History of Victimology, 1980s
History of Victimology, 1990s
History of Victimology, 2000 to today

International Issues

Critical Victimology
Human Trafficking
International Crime Victim Survey
  (ICVS)
International Victimizations
Terrorism
World Society of Victimology (WSV)

Laws and Legal Issues

Allocution
Child Witness
Guardian Ad Litem
Notoriety for Profit Laws
Order of Protection
Rape Shield Laws
Supreme Court Cases
Victim Impact Statement
Victims' Rights Legislation

Mass Media

AMBER Alert
Celebrity Victim
Notoriety for Profit Laws
Pornography
Sensationalism
Vicarious Victimization

Measuring Victimization

Dark Figure of Crime

International Crime Victim Survey
  (ICVS)
National Crime Victimization Survey
  (NCVS)
National Incident-Based Reporting
  System (NIBRS)
Reporting Rates
Series Victimizations
Supplementary Homicide Report (SHR)
Uniform Crime Report (UCR)
Victimization Trends

Restorative Justice

Alternative Dispute Resolution (ADR)
Creative Restitution
Mediation
Restorative Justice
Victim-Offender Reconciliation Programs
  (VORPs)

School Victimizations

Acquaintance Rape
Alcohol and Victimization
Bullying
Campus Victimizations
Hazing
School Victimizations

Service Providers

Adult Protective Services (APS)
Advocates
Burnout
Child Protective Services (CPS)
Court Appointed Special Advocate
  (CASA)
CyberAngels.org
Mothers Against Drunk Driving (MADD)
Parents Anonymous® Inc.
Shelters
Support Groups
Widening the Net

Sexual Assault

Acquaintance Rape
Domestic Minor Sex Trafficking
False Allegations
Incest
Male Rape
Marital Rape
Pedophilia
Pornography
Prison Rape
Rape
Rape Myths
Rape Shield Laws
Rape Trauma Syndrome
Recovered Memories of Sexual Abuse
Sex Offender Registration
Sexual Assault
Statutory Rape

Sexual Harassment

Sexual Harassment

Stalking

CyberAngels.org
Cyberstalking
Stalking

Technology

AMBER Alert
Child Lures
CyberAngels.org
Cybercrime
Cyberstalking
Identity Theft

Terminology

Agent Provocateur
Bystander Effect
Death Notification

Facilitation
False Allegations
Good Samaritan
Post-Traumatic Stress Disorder (PTSD)
Precipitation
Primary Victimization
Provocation
Secondary Victimization
Self-Help Justice
Sovereign Immunity
Stockholm Syndrome
Subintentional Death
Victim Discounting
Victim vs. Survivor
Victimologists
Victimology

Theoretical Applications

Belief in a Just World
Blaming the Victim
Critical Victimology
Defensible Space
Family Stress Theory
Feminist Perspectives on Victimization
Lifestyle Theory
Mendelsohn's Typologies
Neutralization Theory
Psychopathology Theory
Rational Choice Theory
Routine Activity Theory
Schafer's Typologies
Social Exchange Theory
Social Learning Theory
Sociobiology Theory
Subculture of Violence
von Hentig's Typologies

Victimization Types

Acquaintance Rape
Arson

Assault

Battery

Bullying

Burglary

Campus Victimizations

Child Abuse

Corruption

Cybercrime

Cyberstalking

Domestic Elder Abuse

Domestic Minor Sex Trafficking

Domestic Violence

Elder Abuse

Family Abduction

Financial Abuse

Hate Crime

Hazing

Human Trafficking

Identity Theft

Incest

Infanticide

Institutional Elder Abuse

International Victimizations

Intimate Partner Violence

Kidnapping

Larceny-Theft

Male Rape

Marital Rape

Motor Vehicle Theft

Murder

Neglect

Pedophilia

Pornography

Prison Rape

Rape

Robbery

Same-Sex Partner Abuse

School Victimizations

Sexual Assault

Sexual Harassment

Sibling Abuse

Stalking

Statutory Rape

Terrorism

Victimless Crimes

Workplace Victimizations

Victimologists

Amir, Menachem

Fry, Margery

Mendelsohn, Beniamin

Schafer, Stephen

von Hentig, Hans

Wolfgang, Marvin E.

Victims' Rights

President's Task Force on Victims of
   Crime, *Final Report*

Supreme Court Cases

Victim Bill of Rights

Victims' Rights Constitutional
   Amendment

Victims' Rights Legislation

Workplace Victimizations

Corruption

Cyberstalking

Sexual Harassment

Stalking

Workplace Victimizations

The Praeger
Handbook of
Victimology

A

ABUSE: ACTIVE AND PASSIVE. Abuse, whether it pertains to children or elderly, can be broadly classified into active and passive types. Active abuse of children involves acts of violence committed in physical, sexual, or emotional contexts, either to cause injury or deprive someone of her freedom. Physical abuse often affects the emotional, social, and intellectual well-being of children. Passive child abuse, such as neglect, although it does not involve physical force, could cause both physical and emotional injury, such as nonorganic failure to thrive syndrome.[1] This syndrome results from a lack of emotional bonding between the mother and the infant and the infant suffers from starvation and often death. Despite research evidence connecting the physical punishment of children with other forms of family violence, society in general considers slapping, paddling, hitting, and spanking to be "normal" disciplinary practices. Although American states differ on specifics in their legal definitions of sexual abuse of children (e.g., age of consent), all states prohibit the sexual abuse of children.[2] Passive child abuse has also met with a definitional challenge: Which behaviors constitute passive abuse? Moreover, should the focus be on child-related outcomes or on parental behaviors? For example, the courts have dealt with cases in which parents claim religious faith as the reason for denying treatment for their children. At the heart of this debate are two conflicting positions: one says it is not child abuse if parents believe in faith healing, whereas homicide law makes no such exception for prayer. Parents contend that such laws violate their right to freedom of religion and their right of due process because they were not given fair notice that what they were doing was wrong. Many states allow a religious exception when parents fail to seek medical care or physically discipline their children. The penal codes of several states also exclude child neglect if the neglect stems from a financial burden.[3]

Elder abuse, which is similar to child abuse, includes both active and passive abuse of anyone 60 years of age or older.[4] Active abuse is defined as an intentional abusive or neglectful behavior or acts (e.g., physical, sexual, or financial abuse, and neglect) committed for the purpose of harming, deceiving, coercing, or controlling an elderly person. Physical indicators include fractures, broken bones, cigarette burns, abrasions on arms and legs, and bruises, whereas behavioral indicators of physical abuse may include unexplained injuries or implausible explanations, a prior history of similar injuries or suspicious hospitalizations, or a delay in seeking medical care. Passive abuse of elders encompasses unintentional behaviors or acts that may include psychological, social, and financial abuse, or neglect. Passive neglect occurs when the caregiver is unable to fulfill her caregiving obligations due to lack of resources or his own illness, disability, or stress. Unlike in many countries where the laws are clear about who is responsible for the elderly, adult children in the United States are not legally responsible to care for their elderly parents. Due to the lack of any legal standards, U.S. courts have set a standard of "duty of care"[5] between the victim and the caregiver for determining criminal liability.

NOTES

1. Kevin Browne, "The Nature of Child Abuse and Neglect: An Overview," in *Early Prediction and Prevention of Child Abuse,* eds. Kevin Browne, Cliff Davies, and Peter Stratton (New York: John Wiley & Sons, 1988), 15–30.

2. Ola Barnett, Cindy L. Miller Perrin, and Robin D. Perrin, *Family Violence Across the Lifespan: An Introduction* (Thousand Oaks, CA: Sage, 2005), 87–125.

3. John E. B. Myers, *Legal Issues in Child Abuse and Neglect Practice* (Thousand Oaks, CA: Sage, 1998).

4. Lori A. Stiegel, "Washington Report," *Victimization of the Elderly and Disabled* 6 (2003): 19–20.

5. Alison Brammer and Simon Biggs, "Defining Elder Abuse," *Journal of Social Welfare and Family Law* 20 (1998): 285–304.

SUGGESTED READING

Anna S. Lau et al., "What's in a Name? A Comparison of Methods for Classifying Predominant Type of Maltreatment," *Child Abuse & Neglect* 29, no. 5 (2005): 533–51.

SESHA KETHINENI

ACQUAINTANCE RAPE. Acquaintance rape is defined as nonconsensual sexual activity between people who are known to each other. For many years, "stranger" rape was the only rape that was considered actual rape and even then, those cases were difficult to prosecute. Although women historically have been sexually assaulted by people they knew (acquaintance, date, and marital rape), rarely was this viewed as a crime. It was not until the 1970s, that the terms *date, acquaintance,* and *marital rape* even entered our day-to-day lives. However, these types of rapes are more common and less reported than stranger rapes. In fact, some studies show that more than 70% of rapes are committed by someone the victim knows.

From a legal standpoint, this type of rape carries the same penalties as stranger rape (a felony), yet is much more difficult to convince a judge or jury in court. These cases are often defended by the defense of "he said, she said." In the last 20 years, there have been a number of celebrity date rape trials (Michael Tyson, Michael Kennedy Smith) that have raised the profile of this crime.

The definition of consent is at the center of the societal, legal, and cultural controversies surrounding acquaintance rape. While earlier rulings defined not giving consent as physical resistance to the rape, societal and legal response to date rape has gradually shifted to an acceptance that coercion can be verbal including psychological and emotional threats.

The work of Mary Koss and the subsequent attention to this behavior led to actual changes in the law. Across the country, rape laws began to change to reflect a broader cultural understanding of rape. Most states now have provisions that prohibit the use of drugs or alcohol to incapacitate a victim, rendering the victim unable to deny consent.

Young women and those high school-aged are the most vulnerable to acquaintance rape. Women aged 16 to 25 are three times more likely to be raped than other women. Less than one-half of the rapes are reported. We suspect this rate is much higher for acquaintance rape. Moreover, a number of these victims report being assaulted more than once in their lives. Another aspect of this type of behavior is the use of alcohol and drugs.

Victims can suffer from a series of emotional and psychological affects in the aftermath of the rape. These symptoms include anxiety, guilt, nervousness, phobias, substance abuse, sleep disturbances, depression, alienation, sexual dysfunction, and aggression. Moreover, there can be long-term physical affects from the assault.

SUGGESTED READING

Mary Koss and Mary R. Harvey, *The Rape Victims: Clinical and Community Interventions* (Thousand Oaks, CA: Sage, 1991); Callie M. Rennison, *Criminal Victimization, 1998:*

Changes 1997–98 with Trends 1993–98 (Washington DC: Bureau of Justice Statistics, 1999); Robin Warshaw, *I Never Called it Rape: The Ms. Report on Recognizing, Fighting and Surviving Date and Acquaintance Rape,* 2nd ed. (New York: HarperCollins, 1994).

PAMELA JENKINS

ADULT PROTECTIVE SERVICES (APS). Since the 1980s the number of elderly people in the Unites States has grown. Additionally, in the last two decades adult protective services have flourished in order to contest adult and elder abuse and neglect. Adult protective services are a reactive measure to the hundreds of elder and adult abuse cases that occur each day in the United States. Adult protective service agencies bridge the gap between social service agencies and the criminal justice system. They rely on cooperation between personnel in both the criminal justice arena and social service organizations. Adult protection agencies are often connected to health and human service departments and are supported by state legislation.

The primary task of adult protective services centers is investigating cases of abuse, neglect, and exploitation of adults, elderly, and vulnerable persons. An adult protective service investigator, often responding to life-threatening crisis situations, makes key decisions on medical, psychiatric, social, and legal intervention such as filing a protective order, contesting guardianship, or filing criminal charges. Through the investigator's own autonomy and state laws, the investigator collects information and evidence on a case and assesses the best possible outcome for the victim. The ultimate goal is to protect the victim from further maltreatment. Therefore, investigators have the discretion to make decisions involving the living arrangements, health care, nutrition, and financial management of the victim. Depending on the state, these agencies may also be responsible for licensing nursing homes and training social service workers.

The outcome of a victim's case is dependent upon the victim's functioning, the problem bringing the individual to the agency's attention, and any action by a third party that could be deemed harmful to the victim. Refusal of services is a concern for adult protective service investigators. The victim is often dependent on the perpetrator and may fear to report mistreatment and refuse intervention by the adult protective service investigator. The longer the victim refuses assistance the more severe the abuse may become and the less likely she will be to report the maltreatment.

Elder and adult abuse has only recently received attention as a recognized problem. Adult protective services have been established as a reactive measure to elder and adult abuse, neglect, and exploitation; however, more work is needed on both theoretical and applied levels to address the problem and offer working solutions.

SUGGESTED READING

B. Byers and J. E. Hendricks, eds., *Adult Protective Services: Research and Practice* (Springfield, MO: Thomas C. Charles, 1993); M. Lachs et al., "Adult Protective Service Use and Nursing Home Placement," *The Gerontologist* 42 (2002): 734–39; Pamela B. Teaster, *A Response to the Abuse of Vulnerable Adults: The 2000 Survey of State Adult Protective Services* (Washington DC: The National Center on Elder Abuse, 2002); L. Vinton, "Factors Associated with Refusing Services Among Maltreated Elderly," *Journal of Elder Abuse & Neglect* 3 (1991): 89–103.

ANNA E. KOSLOSKI

ADVOCATES. The term "advocate" comes from the Latin word that means to speak for someone else, especially in legal matters for someone who is handicapped because of a lack of information, immaturity, illness, or disability. Thus, one who represents or speaks for another, especially in a legal proceeding, can be called an advocate. Many of those who performed these types of services for others came from earlier movements in the 1960s like civil rights, feminism, and the anti-war movement. In the victim assistance field, originally called the Victim Ombudsman, this term was first applied to the process of helping victims in 1974 when the Fort Lauderdale Florida Police Department Victim Advocate Project was launched.[1] As this project became known throughout Florida and eventually throughout the nation, this term became the standard identifier for those who worked with crime victims, especially from law enforcement agencies. Another type of "victim advocate" was a trained lawyer who represented victims by helping them navigate through the labyrinth of the criminal justice system. Such a program was established in the South East Side of Chicago in 1974.[2]

In the 1970s there were no academies or universities that educated or trained victim advocates. The vast majority of those first victim advocates were victim survivors, volunteers, and a variety of professionals in the helping fields without specific training in victim assistance: social workers, nurses, psychologists, psychiatrists, and lawyers. In those few cases where some training was available, it was usually performed by the victim assistance agency in the form of short-term training in agency orientation; crisis intervention techniques; assistance with compensation applications; death notifications; limited counseling; court companionship; and referrals to medical, psychological, and legal services.

The application of advocacy in the victim field has emerged in two fundamental forms: case advocacy and system advocacy. In both instances the victim is the primary client. With case advocacy there is usually a one-on-one relationship between one victim entity (a person or a group) and an advocate. This form of advocacy is most often found in victim assistance centers and is simple and of short duration. However, with system advocacy there is a class of victims being represented for any number of victims by any number of advocates. This form of advocacy most often emerges as an organized effort to lobby for regulatory, programmatic, or legislative change on behalf of victim needs.

The professional wisdom that has emerged over the last three decades is that advocacy serves as a bridge between victim needs and existing services: social work, psychology, psychiatry, counseling, law, medicine, nursing, etc. Therefore, advocates engage, not only in speaking on behalf of victims in a variety of settings, but also in making referrals to competent professionals on behalf of victims. In order to be an effective advocate, one must be able to establish rapport with victims; understand their behaviors, needs, and the system they must navigate in; and have knowledge about the competence of professionals and service agencies in the community. Finally, a professional advocate must also understand the limits of the advocate's role in helping victims to recover and to insure that their services remain within the realm of their own area of skill, experience, and knowledge.

NOTES

1. John P. J. Dussich, "The Victim Ombudsman: A Proposal," in *Victimology: A New Focus, Vol. II, Society's Reaction to Victimization*, eds., Israel Drapkin and Emilio Viano (Lexington, MA: Lexington Books, 1974).

2. Fredric L. DuBow and Theodore M. Becker, "Patterns of Victim Advocacy," in *Criminal Justice and the Victim*, ed., William F. McDonald (Beverly Hills, CA: Sage Publications, 1976).

SUGGESTED READING

Leo F. Callahan, "The Victim Advocate: Programmed Police Response for Crime Victims," *The Police Chief* April (1975); Mark Ezell, *Advocacy in the Human Services* (Belmont, CA: Wadsworth/Thompson Learning, 2001).

JOHN DUSSICH

AGENT PROVOCATEUR. The term *agent provocateur* is of French origin, denoting a person who is in the employ of law enforcement to entice or provoke another to engage in criminal behavior. In a more general sense an agent provocateur is a person who provokes another to engage in untoward action. The early victimology pioneer and criminologist, Hans von Hentig adapted the term *agent provocateur* to apply to victims of crime. In his studies to understand the criminal-victim dyad, he noted that the victim is often a contributor, and even an instigator, in his own victimization. He sought a more comprehensive understanding of the offender-victim relationship beyond the traditional unidimensional perspective focused on the offender with the victim simply in the wrong place at the wrong time. He expanded on these ideas in his book *The Criminal and His Victim,* published in 1948.

Hans von Hentig created a 13-category victim typology, of which three types display the clearest examples of his agent provocateur. The acquisitive greedy victim is out solely for personal gain and therefore vulnerable to victimization by enterprising criminals. The wanton victim is promiscuous and draws attention, which exposes his or her vulnerability and leads to victimization. The tormentor represents the abusive individual, traditionally a parent, but more recently extended to other familial relationships such as spouse. The victim's contribution can come in the form of either motivation (e.g., arousing, inciting) or function (e.g., precipitation, facilitation). The concept of victim as an agent of provocation has continued to inform the growing field of victimology, with additional study looking at a class of crimes frequently referred to as victim-precipitated crimes.

SUGGESTED READING

Ezzat A. Fattah, "The Vital Role of Victimology in the Rehabilitation of Offenders and Their Reintegration into Society," paper presented at the 12th International Training Course, Tokyo, Japan, 2000; Hans von Hentig, *The Criminal and His Victim* (New Haven, CT: Yale University Press, 1948).

JEFFREY WALSH

ALCOHOL AND VICTIMIZATION. Both experimental and survey research suggest that alcohol may cause violent behavior.[1] The societal focus on alcohol as a cause of violent behavior ignores, however, the role that alcohol can play in victimization experiences. Recent research has shown that victims of violence are often under the influence of alcohol. For example, Lloyd Potter and his colleagues have shown that heavy drinkers have higher rates of physical assault victimization than do light drinkers or nondrinkers.[2] Richard Felson and Keri Burchfield find that victims used alcohol prior to their assault in approximately 20% of reported incidents.[3] They also find that the odds of victimization are over four times higher for those who typically drink four drinks per sitting, compared with individuals who typically consume one drink per sitting. Similarly, the odds of victimization are over three times higher for individuals who drink every day compared with individuals who never drink.

In addition, Felson and Burchfield find that drinking has a larger effect on sexual assault victimization than physical assault victimization.[3] In some ways, this runs counter to popular stereotypes about bar fights, which suggest that physical assault victimization may be most likely during drinking situations. The finding is, however, consistent with stereotypes about non-stranger sexual assault (or date rape situations). Interestingly, Felson and Burchfield also show that males who are assaulted by their female partners are particularly likely to be drinking at the time of the attack.[3] They argue that the drunkenness of the male partners may enable women to use violence, because the male partner would not be in a position to resist. Additionally, the on-average greater strength of male partners may be a deterrent to female use of violence, when the male partner is sober.

One explanation for this increased risk of victimization while drinking has been offered by James Lasley. Lasley argues that drinking routines and activities expose individuals to risky situations.[4] That is, drinking occurs in social contexts (bars and nightclubs) where individuals who are drinking are exposed to motivated offenders who wish to prey on suitable targets. Individuals who appear intoxicated are less likely to be able to defend themselves and therefore make more suitable targets for predatory victimization. A final explanation for the relationship between victimization and alcohol use is suggested by Felson. Felson argues that people who behave in bizarre or annoying ways, such as those who are intoxicated, may motivate others to victimize them by failing to conform to behavior norms.[5]

NOTES

1. Richard B. Felson, Brent Teasdale, and Keri B. Burchfield, "The Influence of Being Under the Influence: Alcohol Effects on Adolescent Violence," *Journal of Research in Crime and Delinquency* 45 (2008): 119–41.

2. Lloyd B. Potter et al., "Non-Fatal Physical Violence, United States, 1994," *Public Health Reports* 114 (1999): 343–52.

3. Richard B. Felson and Keri B. Burchfield, "Alcohol and the Risk of Physical and Sexual Assault Victimization," *Criminology* 42 (2004): 837–59.

4. James R. Lasley, "Drinking Routines/Lifestyles and Predatory Victimization: A Causal Analysis," *Justice Quarterly* 6 (1989): 529–42.

5. Richard B. Felson "Kick 'Em When They're Down: Explanations of the Relationship between Stress and Interpersonal Aggression and Violence," *The Sociological Quarterly* 33 (1992): 1–16.

SUGGESTED READING

Kathleen Auerhan and Robert Nash Parker, "Drugs, Alcohol, and Homicide," in *Studying and Preventing Homicide,* eds. M. Dwayne Smith and Margaret A. Zahn (Thousand Oaks, CA: Sage, 1999); Elizabeth E. Mustaine and Richard Tewksbury, "Specifying the Role of Alcohol in Predatory Victimization," *Deviant Behavior* 19 (1998): 173–99; Maria Testa and Kathless A. Parks, "The Role of Women's Alcohol Consumption in Sexual Victimization," *Aggression and Violent Behavior* 1 (1996): 217–34.

BRENT TEASDALE

ALLOCUTION. Allocution is an oral presentation of a victim impact statement (VIS). The victim allocution, in general, is intended "to allow victims some input in the court's decision in their case by providing a statement of the impact the victimization has had on their lives and their families."[1] Victim allocution allows for victims with limited writing skills to convey the harm done; the emotional, financial, and social costs endured; and a recommendation for appropriate punishment.[2] While all 50 states and the District of Columbia allow written VISs to be presented at sentencing and parole hearings, victim allocutions are allowed only in sentencing hearings and can be limited by the judge's discretion.[3] Given the highly emotional, subjective nature of the allocution, many were initially concerned that it would jeopardize defendants' Eighth Amendments rights. In *Payne v. Tennessee*,[4] however, the U.S. Supreme Court ruled victims had the right to present oral statements in capital cases. Edna Erez and Pamela Tontodonato, furthermore, found that victim allocution did not significantly predict the length of sentence.[5] Erez and Leigh Roeger also found that victims do not necessarily feel better following their allocutions.[6] Some research does indicate that victim allocutions result in harsher sentences when the jury deems the victim "worthy," i.e., a nonminority, wage-earner who is respected in the community.[7] Bruce Arrigo and Christopher Williams still contend that "the practice of submitting a VIS at the time of sentencing in capital trials should be abolished."[8]

NOTES

1. Ezzat A. Fattah, "Victimology: Past, Present and Future," *Criminologie* 33, no. 1 (2000): 17–46, 33.

2. Ida M. Johnson and Etta F. Morgan, "Victim Impact Statements—Fairness to Defendants?" in *Controversies in Victimology*, 2nd ed., ed. Laura J. Moriarity (Newark, NJ: Lexis-Nexis Group, 2008).

3. Douglas E. Beloof, "Judicial Leadership at Sentencing under the Crime Victims' Rights Act: Judge Kozinski in Kenna and Judge Cassell in Degenhardt," *Federal Sentencing Reporter* 19, no. 1 (2006): 36–43.

4. *Payne v. Tennessee*, 111 U.S. 2597 (1991).

5. Edna Erez and Pamela Tontodonato, "The Effect of Victim Participation in Sentencing on Sentence Outcome," *Criminology* 28 (1990): 451–74.

6. Edna Erez and Leigh Roeger, "The Effect of Victim Impact Statements on Sentencing Patterns and Outcomes: The Australian Experience," *Journal of Criminal Justice* 23 (1995): 363–75.

7. Edith Greene, Heather Koehring, and Melinda Quiat, "Victim Impact Evidence in Capital Cases: Does the Victim's Character Matter?" *Journal of Applied Social Psychology* 28, no. 2 (1998): 145–56.

8. Bruce A. Arrigo and Christopher R. Williams, "Victim Vices, Victim Voices, and Impact Statements: On the Place of Emotion and the Role of Restorative Justice in Capital Sentencing," *Crime and Delinquency* 49, no. 4 (2003): 603–26, 618.

SUGGESTED READING

Kathryn Morgan and Brent L. Smith, "Victims, Punishment, and Parole: The Effect of Victim Participation on Parole Hearings," *Criminology and Public Policy* 4, no. 2 (2005): 333–60.

CONNIE FREY

ALTERNATIVE DISPUTE RESOLUTION (ADR). The field of dispute resolution has been dominated by the legal profession for the last century. That is rapidly changing. A very small percentage of all disputes have ever been resolved by litigation, yet the many other methods actually used by people daily are called "alternative dispute resolution." ADR advocates suggest the more accurate name would be "appropriate dispute resolution."

Dispute resolution methods form a continuum with negotiation at one end and verdict at trial at the other. The negotiation end of the continuum is very informal. There are no due process rights since there are no rules to follow. The litigation end is very formal, rule oriented, and due process rights are a large consideration.

Mediation is near the negotiation end since it is also informal. The only rules are those set by the parties. Involving a mediator makes the process somewhat more formal. In mediation the decision still rests with the parties. The mediator serves as a helper who is in charge of the process. Arbitration, near the litigation end of the continuum, is a process very similar to litigation. It is less formal than litigation and the parties can set their own rules. The big difference between it and mediation is that the arbitrator is the decision maker. Once the parties submit the case to the arbitrator, they have no control over the outcome.

Between these extremes are processes such as fact finding, special master, summary jury trial, and other methods more formal than negotiation. All of these result in advice to the parties that is used in their negotiation. Only litigation and arbitration can impose a result. All the other processes are used by the parties in their settlement efforts. Sometimes parties will agree in advance to be bound by the ruling of a special master or fact finder. Litigation and arbitration can look like part of the settlement process because a verdict only reopens negotiations in many cases. Bargaining away the right to appeal a verdict in exchange for a more favorable outcome is common.

Victims of crime are rarely given a role in litigation beyond being called to testify or filing a victim impact statement. Alternative processes can bring the victim to the center of the process. Victim offender dialogue looks very much like mediation. The parties usually meet together with a facilitator. Victims are able to have their questions answered by the only person really able to do so. The opportunity also exists for offenders to do what they can to make things as right as possible with the victim, accepting responsibility for the harm. These processes are so helpful to victims who desire them that 36 states have programs to provide the process in custodial settings either in operation or in some stage of development as of this writing.

Victims of crime who suffer financial harm due to the offense have ways to get compensation from the offender. Courts usually order restitution to be paid, but only a small portion is collected by parole and probation agents. Victims can pursue civil litigation against offenders for damages resulting from the offense. Neither obtaining a civil verdict against an offender nor a restitution order necessarily means the victim receives payment. Collecting a civil judgment is the responsibility of the victim. Victim offender dialogue seeks instead to include any restitution or other claims for damage in the dialogue process. This way, if anything is to be paid or done as part of the agreement, it is more likely that the offender will follow through since the agreement is probably more reasonable than a verdict would be, and it is designed with the offender's active participation.

Where a face-to-face meeting is either impossible or not desired, the dialogue process can be done through facilitated correspondence. This satisfies the victim's need to have questions answered and to have the offender take responsibility. It also allows the offender to do what is possible to make things right.

SUGGESTED READING

Jacqueline M. Nolan-Haley, *Alternative Dispute Resolution in a Nutshell,* 3rd ed. (Eagan, MN: Thomson / West, 2008); Howard Zehr, *The Little Book of Restorative Justice* (Intercourse, PA: Good Books, 2002).

DUANE RUTH-HEFFELBOWER

AMBER ALERT. The AMBER Alert system was first established in 1996 when Dallas-Fort Worth broadcasters teamed with local police to develop an early warning system to help find abducted children. AMBER is officially "America's Missing: Broadcasting Emergency Response." It was originally created and named in memory of Amber Hagerman, a nine-year-old child victim who was abducted and found murdered four days later in Arlington, Texas, in 1996. For those four days there was a massive manhunt underway that utilized television news and radio stations to broadcast the story and capture the community's attention. Since then the AMBER Alert System was born to offer emergency messages broadcast when a law enforcement agency determines that a child has been abducted and is in imminent danger. The broadcasts contain information about the physical descriptions of the child and the abductor, the abductor's vehicle, and geographic location of the abduction, which could lead to the child's quick recovery.

Since the first AMBER alert system was established in 1996, the world of technical communications has expanded greatly to broadcast missing children and abduction of children through the Emergency Broadcast network, traffic signs, wireless phone alerts, e-mails, and Web portals such as www.AmberAlert.com. In 2000, the AMBER Plan was approved by the U.S. House of Representatives in H.R. 605 to initiate a nationwide implementation plan. The AMBER Alert legislation, a national program, was signed by President George W. Bush in 2003. Today the Department of Justice (DOJ) administers the federal mandate that requires each state to implement the AMBER Plan. The Emergency Broadcast System (EBS) guideline was put into place, acting as an alert distribution system for all states to use. Today the AMBER Alert System is a voluntary partnership between law enforcement agencies, broadcasters, and transportation agencies to activate an emergency bulletin in the most serious child-abduction cases. The secondary alert distributors like the National Center for Missing and Exploited Children (NCMEC), founded in 1984, also link their distribution lists with primary alert systems to redistribute alerts and offer additional sources of information and reference data in missing children, sexual exploitation, and the alert systems. Later the wireless industry formed a partnership with the DOJ and NCMEC to distribute alerts of abducted children via text messages to over 200 million subscribers of wireless services.[1] Today all 50 states and Washington DC have created and manage their own AMBER Alert broadcast system.

The AMBER Plan requires local law enforcement to (1) confirm an abduction of a child prior to issue of an alert in order to determine the level of risk to the child such as stranger abduction; (2) assess risk of serious bodily injury or death such as a stranger abduction; (3) obtain sufficient descriptive information about the suspect, vehicle, and missing child in order to enhance law enforcement's ability in recovering the missing child; and 4) adopt 17 years of age or younger as a legal criterion by all states for issuing an alert in order to avoid confusion when multiple alerts are activated across the states and jurisdictions. The Plan also mandates the entry of the AMBER Alert data into the National Crime Information Center (NCIC) system of the FBI to expand the search for an abducted child from local, state, and regional level to the national.[2]

Since the AMBER Plan was implemented nationwide in 2003, a total of 120 alert systems have been established to cover all 50 states. The systems have safely recovered a total of 426 children, a successful rate of 90% since 2002 in the United States.[3] Anecdotal evidence demonstrates that the perpetrators were well aware of the power of the AMBER Alerts. In many cases, the child victims were released quickly after the abductors heard the broadcast of the alerts. NCMEC reports in 2006 and 2007 found that recognizing abductors' vehicles by a police officer or individual from the alert was the most common factor in successful recovery of abducted children.[4]

NOTES

1. Wireless AMBER Alerts Web site, http://www.wirelessamberalerts.org.
2. AMBER Alert Web site, http://www.amberalert.gov.

3. "Department of Justice Conference Highlights AMBER Alert System Success, Finds Way to Enhance Program," Press Release of USDOJ, October 14, 2008, http://www.ojp.gov/newsroom/pressreleases/2008/oaag09002.htm.

4. National Center for Missing and Exploited Children, "2006 and 2007 AMBER Alert Report," http://www.missingkids.com/missingkids/servlet/PublicHomeServlet?Language-Country=en_US&.

SUGGESTED READING

"International Amber Alerts," http://www.internationalamberalerts.com; National Center for Missing and Exploited Children, "International AMBER Alert Plans," http://www.missingkids.com/missingkids/servlet/PageServlet?LanguageCountry=en_US& PageId=1422.

XIN REN

AMIR, MENACHEM. Building on the work of past scholars and his mentor, Marvin Wolfgang, Menachem Amir (1930–) is widely known for his controversial empirical analysis of victim-precipitated rape published in his 1971 book, *Patterns in Forcible Rape*. Examining police records of rape cases occurring between 1958–1960 in Philadelphia, and specifically exploring offender perception of the victim's willingness to perform sexual acts, Amir theorized that an act was victim precipitated when the victim actually agreed or was perceived by the offender to have agreed and did not protest strongly enough to change that perception. Based on this theory it was revealed that 19% of rape incidents in his study were victim precipitated. It was also found that alcohol use and the wearing of revealing clothing or use of risqué language by the victim were significant factors in precipitated rape; that is, these were viewed by the offender as an invitation for intercourse.

While influential, Amir's work has been criticized on a number of fronts including his reliance on police records and misconceptions of the bases for men's behavior as opposed to women's behavior (i.e., social versus psychological). It is also argued that victim precipitation decreases the culpability of the offender and ultimately places the onus on women to prevent rapes from occurring by behaving cautiously so as to not miscommunicate their desires.

Amir is internationally known and respected for his work on this topic and others, and is currently professor emeritus in the Faculty of Law at the Hebrew University of Jerusalem.

SUGGESTED READING

Menachem Amir, *Patterns in Forcible Rape* (Chicago: University of Chicago Press, 1971); Kurt Weis and Sandra S. Borges, "Victimology and Rape: The Case of the Legitimate Victim," *Issues in Criminology* 8, no. 2 (1973): 71–115.

ASHLEY BLACKBURN

ANATOMICALLY DETAILED DOLLS. Anatomically detailed (AD) dolls, also known as anatomically correct dolls, were first utilized in the late 1970s. These dolls, which feature genitalia, are used in the diagnosis and treatment of sexually abused children and can vary considerably in their appearance, from drawn-on genitalia to stuffed or discolored genitalia and the presence of openings for sexual orifices such as the mouth, vagina, or anus on some models.[1] The usage of these dolls became widespread in the 1980s as reporting on and investigations into child sexual abuse cases increased.

Controversy has arisen over the usage of AD dolls to aide in determining child sexual abuse due to design differences among AD dolls, as well as a lack of standardization for interviewing techniques. Additionally, concerns have been raised due to the paucity of research that can accurately depict how nonsexually abused children react to AD dolls.[2] It is believed that children who have had sexual contact will interact with the AD dolls in a more sexual way than children who have not had sexual contact, but as clinicians are usually investigating suspicions of sexual abuse when using AD dolls, normal behavior may lead to false positives.

Although studies have shown that dolls can be used to elicit accurate descriptions of sexual contact in older children, these dolls should not be used with children under five, as research has shown that reports from these children have a large degree of inaccuracy.[3] Memory and suggestibility concerns are additional issues affecting the usage of AD dolls.

NOTES

1. Anne Hungerford, "The Use of Anatomically Detailed Dolls in Forensic Investigations: Developmental Considerations," *Journal of Forensic Psychology Practice* 5 (2005): 75.

2. Gerald P. Koocher et al., "Psychological Science and the Use of Anatomically Detailed Dolls in Child Sexual-Abuse Assessments," *Psychological Bulletin* 118 (1995): 199.

3. Maggie Bruck, Stephen J. Ceci, and Emmett Francouer, "Children's Use of Anatomically Detailed Dolls to Report Genitalia Touching in a Medical Examination: Developmental and Gender Comparisons," *Journal of Experimental Psychology: Applied* 6 (2000): 74.

SUGGESTED READINGS

Mark D. Everson and Barbara W. Boat, "Anatomical Dolls in Child Sexual Abuse Assessments: A Call for Forensically Relevant Research," *Applied Cognitive Psychology* 11 (1997): 55–74; Karen L. Thierry et al., "Developmental Differences in the Function and Use of Anatomical Dolls During Interviews with Alleged Sexual Abuse Victims," *Journal of Consulting and Clinical Psychology* 73 (2005): 1125–34.

TASHA YOUSTIN

ARSON. Arson is the willful or malicious burning of, or attempt to burn, a dwelling house, public building, motor vehicle or aircraft, personal property, etc. Arson affects about 25 out of 100,000 people every year and, compared with other Part I index crimes, arson comes second to last in crime rate.[1] Although victims of arson are not as numerous as victims of other crimes, they differ significantly in the manner in which they are affected. The impact varies depending on the type of arson committed. Over half of arsons involve structures, with single occupant residential homes being the majority of those; the burning of mobile property accounts for another roughly 30%.[2]

There is no "typical" arson victim. The degree of loss and suffering can vary substantially, from minor property loss to death. Loss of property is the most common and most expensive consequence. In 2007, the average arson victim incurred $15,500 in property damage.[3] In addition, victims may need to "reconstruct" their lives (e.g., in the case of a structure fire). Many victims are temporarily displaced, while others are forced to leave communities and relocate. Although relatively uncommon, physical injuries and even death occur as well.[4] Burns can cause extraordinary medical bills and result in lifelong pain and suffering. In addition, while many individuals show great resilience, fire victims, witnesses, and firefighters can suffer short- and long-term grief or traumatic reactions to exposure, including emotional and physical symptoms, potentially exacerbated by the intentionality of the crime.[5]

Motives to commit arson range widely and sometimes are irrational. Victims can be directly or indirectly affected (e.g., owners of neighboring structures, stockholders, etc.) in a variety of ways (e.g., financial, physical, etc.). Most innocent victims are incidental victims who have no relation to the arsonist. Firefighters, as well, can become victims, getting injured while fighting a fire or rescuing another victim.[6] Other times, victims can be closely related to the arsonist (i.e., parents of juvenile vandals), and even the arsonist can be a victim.

In the past decade, the criminal justice system has made efforts to compensate and assist arson victims.[7] Police and firefighters cooperate in investigations to both solve crimes and aid victims, although there is often confusion over who holds jurisdiction once an arson case comes to court. Restitution to victims can be imposed by the courts and arson victims are allowed to speak in court so as to give account of the full impact of the crime. However, relatively few convictions result from arson cases as it is hard to prove. In addition, although victim aid agencies are available to all types of victims, arson victims may not initially realize that they were victimized, as investigators may take days or even weeks to identify arson. This can delay contact between arson victims and victim agencies and hinder aid that is needed.[8]

NOTES

1. U.S. Department of Justice, Federal Bureau of Investigation, "Arson," *Crime in the United States, 2007,* http://www.fbi.gov/ucr/cius2007/documents/arsonmain.pdf.

2. Ibid.

3. Ibid.

4. Ted R. Miller, Mark A. Cohen, and Brian Wiersema, *Victim Costs and Consequences: A New Look* (Washington DC: National Institute of Justice, 1996).

5. Tina Dorn et al., "A Cohort Study of the Long-Term Impact of a Fire Disaster on the Physical and Mental Health of Adolescents," *Journal of Traumatic Stress* 21, no. 2 (2008): 239–42; Peter G. van der Velden et al., "The Effects of Disaster Exposure and Post-Disaster Critical Incidents on Intrusions, Avoidance Reactions and Health Problems among Firefighters: A Comparative Study," *Stress, Trauma and Crisis: An International Journal* 9, no. 2 (2006): 73–93; Sheila Wang, "Traumatic Stress and Thyroid Function," *Child Abuse & Neglect* 30, no. 6 (2006): 585–88; Dian Williams and Paul Clements, "Fire and Behavior: Exploring Intrapsychic Trauma in Arson Survivors," *Issues in Mental Health Nursing* 26, no. 3 (2005): 299–310.

6. Ted R. Miller, Mark A. Cohen, and Shelli B. Rossman, "Victim Costs of Violent Crime and Resulting Injuries," *Health Affairs* 12, no. 4 (1993): 186–97.

7. The American Bar Association Section of Criminal Justice, *Arson Victims: Suggestions for a System Response* (Washington DC: The American Bar Association, 1997).

8. Ibid.

SUGGESTED READING

Jeffrey T. Mitchell, "The Psychological Aftermath of Large- and Small-Scale Fires," in *Trauma Psychology: Issues in Violence, Disaster, Health, and Illness, vol. 1; Violence and Disaster* (Westport, CT: Praeger Publishers, 2007), 231–54; Phyllis N. Stern and June Stern, "Restructuring Life after Home Loss by Fire," *Image: Journal of Nursing Scholarship* 28, no. 1 (1996): 11.

DAISY A. SEGOVIA AND ANGELA M. CROSSMAN

ASSAULT. According to the Bureau of Justice Statistics, assault is defined as "An unlawful physical attack or threat of attack. Assaults may be classified as aggravated or simple . . . The severity of assaults ranges from minor threat to incidents which are nearly fatal."[1] In 2006, 5,110,810 people were victims of assaults according to the National Crime Victimization Survey (NCVS). An estimated 20.7 people over the age of 12 were assaulted for every 1,000 people in the United States.[2]

Male heads of households living alone (27.5) were more likely than female heads of households living alone (16.9) to experience assaults (all rates per 1,000 over the age of 12). Children living in a female-headed household (44.6) were more likely to experience assault in 2006 than those living in male-headed households (30.0). Whites were slightly more likely to report being victims of assault (44.9) than blacks (42.0). Of the 675,960 assaults reported in the 2006 NCVS who received medical care, 11% received medical care at a hospital. Of all assaults in 2006, 56.2% were perpetrated by a non-stranger. The age group that was most likely to experience assaults was those over the age of 65, at 57% (estimate based on less than 10 sample cases). Next in frequency were those in the 20 to 24 age range (48.2%). Of the 5,120,840 total assaults reported in 2006, 237,260 (4.6%) were committed by a relative other than a spouse, parent, or child. Spouses committed 186,980 (3.7%) assaults of this type and 1,803,940 (35.2%) were committed by strangers. Married people (50.9%) were more likely to experience assault than the never married (44.8%).[3]

Those who experience assault are likely to be directed to victims' services agencies by the police officers who interview them if they report the crime. Victims of crime are still treated differently by all levels of the criminal justice system when the crime is a violent one, the offender is known by the victim, or the victim possesses characteristics other than the "ideal" victim.[4] Police responded to calls for incidents of physical assault approximately 80% of the time. Police are "more likely to become involved in first time incidents of physical assaults against women and incidents that involved injury."[5] Crime victims' experience of the criminal justice system has likely improved in the past 20 years, however, with the advent of victim impact statements at trial, mediation, and additional access to victims' service agencies.[6]

NOTES

1. U.S. Department of Justice, Bureau of Justice Statistics, *Criminal Victimization in the United States, 2006 Statistical Tables* (Washington DC: U.S. Department of Justice, Bureau of Justice Statistics, 2008), 131, http://www.ojp.usdoj.gov/bjs/pub/pdf/cvus06.pdf.

2. Michael Rand and Shannan Catalano, *Criminal Victimization, 2006* (Washington DC: U.S. Department of Justice, Bureau of Justice Statistics, 2007), 3, http://www.ojp.usdoj.gov/bjs/pub/pdf/cv06.pdf.

3. U.S. Department of Justice, *Criminal Victimization in the United States.*

4. Rob I. Mawby and S. Walklate, *Critical Victimology: International Perspectives* (London: Sage, 1994).

5. Jana L. Jasinski, "Police Involvement in Incidents of Physical Assault: Analysis of the Redesigned National Crime Victimization Survey," *Journal of Family Violence* 18 (2003): 143–50.

6. Mawby and Walklate, *Critical Victimology.*

SUGGESTED READING

Sandra Walklate, *Victimology: The Victim and the Criminal Justice Process* (Boston: Unwin Hyman, 1989); Sandra Walklate, ed., *Handbook of Victims and Victimology* (Devon: Willan, 2007).

JENNIFER WINGREN

B

BATTERED CHILD SYNDROME. In 1962, C. Henry Kempe, Frederic N. Silverman, Brandt F. Steele, William Droegemuller, and Henry K. Silver coined the term "Battered Child Syndrome."[1] The term refers to a clinical condition in which young children are subjected to physical injuries resulting from nonaccidental injuries inflicted by adults, generally parents or guardians. The injuries range from mild to severe, and often include fatal trauma. In some cases, the clinical manifestations are limited to a single episode of injury, but in most cases, the injuries are from prolonged abuse. Although battered child syndrome may occur at any age, it often involves children younger than three years of age. The diagnosis of the syndrome involves several factors: first, a marked discrepancy between the parent's explanation of the events and the clinical results; second, no new lesions, either of the soft tissue or of the bones, when the child is in a protected environment; and third, subdural hematoma or traumatic brain injury, multiple bone lesions, poor skin hygiene, or soft tissue injuries. More recently, evidence of ophthalmic manifestations (e.g., bruising around the eye, retinal detachments, and conjunctival and subconjunctival hemorrhages)[2] has been documented in these cases. In addition to the physiological aspects in children, the psychiatric factors of parents or caregivers are important when determining whether the injuries were intentional or accidental. Kempe found that parents or caregivers who injured a child often had suffered abuse as children, had a low intelligence, lacked maturity, were in unstable marriages, were sexually promiscuous, suffered from alcoholism, and had committed minor criminal acts. Despite these issues, most of the parents appeared normal.

Researchers have compared the child's psychological suffering with that suffered by battered women (i.e., "battered women syndrome").[3] They posit that battered children, like battered women, suffer from post-traumatic stress disorder. As a result, these children react to certain stimuli differently than the average person. Although the courts have recognized both the physiological and psychological aspects of battered child syndrome, the manner in which they apply it differs. For example, courts have frequently allowed the use of battered child syndrome to prove the intent of the caregiver to commit child abuse, but have rarely allowed it to be used as a justification when children kill their abusers. Courts have allowed children's prior injuries as evidence, despite defendants' arguments that such evidence violated Federal Rule of Evidence 404(b)'s prohibition against using prior wrongs or acts.[4] The courts' primary justification was that such evidence had probative value outweighing any prejudicial effect.

To prevent child abuse, medical and social service agencies should be trained to identify early stages of the syndrome. Intervention programs should provide parenting information and training, develop family skills, and offer social support counseling to prevent the escalation of abuse. Another option is to remove the child, the potential abuser, or both. Agencies such as Court Appointed Special Advocate (CASA) and Lawyers for Children America provide advocacy services. Local family violence and child abuse prevention centers offer parenting classes and intervention services.

NOTES

1. C. Henry Kempe et al., "The Battered-Child Syndrome," *Journal of the American Medical Association* 181 (1962): 17–24.

2. Stephen G. Spitzer, Joseph Luorno, and Léon-Paul Noël, "Isolated Subconjunctival Hemorrhages in Nonaccidental Trauma," *Journal of American Association for Pediatric Ophthalmology and Strabismus* 9 (2005): 53–56.

3. Hope Toffel, "Crazy Women, Unharmed Men, and Evil Children: Confronting the Myths About Battered People Who Kill Their Abusers, and the Argument for Extending Battering Syndrome Self-Defenses to All Victims of Domestic Violence," *Southern California Law Review* 70 (1996): 350.

4. Kristi Baldwin, "Battered Child Syndrome as a Sword and a Shield," *American Journal of Criminal Law* 29 (2001): 59–82.

SUGGESTED READING

Jean Labbe, "Ambroise Tardieu: The Man and His Work on Child Maltreatment a Century before Kempe," *Child Abuse & Neglect* 29, no. 4 (2005): 311–24.

SESHA KETHINENI

BATTERED HUSBAND SYNDROME. In 1977, Suzanne Steinmetz coined the term "battered husband syndrome" to refer to men who were abused by their wives in ways similar to women who were abused by their husbands. In fact, using data from the 1975 National Family Violence Survey, a survey of a representative sample of U.S. households, Steinmetz made the claim that there are as many battered husbands as battered wives in American families. Steinmetz's position came under immediate and intense criticism, and the debate that ensued—known as the gender symmetry debate—continues today.

Those who support the notions of battered husband syndrome and gender symmetry in intimate partner violence point to data from surveys that ask respondents the number of times during a given period (usually the past 12 months) that they have used or been the victims of various acts when attempting to resolve conflicts with their intimate partners. The acts include "tried to discuss the issue calmly," "yelled or insulted," "pushed or shoved," and "hit with something hard." These data usually show that women are as likely as—and sometimes are more likely than—men to report an assaultive act against their intimate partners.

Critics of the battered husband syndrome and gender symmetry point out that only looking at who assaults whom and how many times ignores important factors such as gender differences in the outcome, context, meaning, and motivation for such behavior. For example, given average differences in size and strength between women and men, the same behavior engaged in by a woman against a man—say, a push—is not likely to have the same consequences as when a man engages in that behavior against a woman. Indeed, if one examines injurious outcomes in intimate partner violence incidents, one finds that it is clearly an overstatement to say that as many husbands as wives are "battered," or that women are as "violent" as men. Domestic assaults by men are six times more likely to cause injury than domestic assaults by women. Moreover, research on motivations for assaulting an intimate partner show that men are more often motivated by the desire to punish, intimidate, or control women, whereas women are more often motivated by the desire to retaliate against a man for his past violence or to defend themselves from his violence.

Taking into account such factors as behavioral outcomes and motivations is not to deny that some wives are abusive toward their husbands. However, as sociologist Michael Johnson points out, women rarely engage in the type of intimate partner violence that is frequent and severe enough to warrant escape by their husbands to a shelter or treatment in an emergency room. This type of abuse, which Johnson calls "intimate terrorism," is almost always perpetrated by men as part of a general strategy to control "their" women. In contrast, the intimate violence perpetrated by women is typically less severe and usually results when a conflict between the couple escalates into violence by both parties—what Johnson calls "situational couple violence." When women's use of violence in intimate relationships is decontextualized and labeled "husband battering," the gendered nature of intimate partner violence—that is, the quantitative and qualitative differences between women's and men's violence in intimate relationships—is missed, which can result in inappropriate and even harmful responses by the police, the courts, and social service providers.

SUGGESTED READING

Michael Johnson, *A Typology of Domestic Violence: Intimate Terrorism, Violent Resistance, and Situational Couple Violence* (Boston: Northeastern University Press, 2008); Susan L. Miller, *Victims as Offenders: The Paradox of Women's Violence in Relationships* (New Brunswick, NJ: Rutgers University Press, 2005); Claire M. Renzetti, "The Challenge to Feminism Posed by Women's Use of Violence in Intimate Relationships," in *New Versions of Victims: Feminists Struggle with the Concept,* ed. Sharon Lamb (New York: New York University Press, 1999), 42–56; Suzanne K. Steinmetz, "The Battered Husband Syndrome," *Victimology* 2 (1977): 499–509.

CLAIRE RENZETTI

BATTERED WOMAN SYNDROME. Battered woman syndrome (BWS) is a legal defense that is used to explain why a battered person may kill an abusive intimate partner in self-defense. When first created in the 1970s, BWS, also known originally as battered wife syndrome, was used by defense attorneys to explain how and why a battered woman would kill her husband. At the time, it was deliberately gender specific to address the gender bias in the legal definition of self-defense, which allows that the use of force is justified when a person reasonably believes that *he* is in imminent danger and that force is necessary to prevent great bodily harm or death. This definition was problematic for battered women who sometimes killed their abusive partner after the abuse ended or while he was sleeping. In these circumstances, juries could not apply the case to the legal definition of self-defense because the battered woman did not appear to be in imminent danger or the force exceeded what was necessary to stop bodily injury or death. Over the years BWS has evolved to be more gender neutral allowing any battered individual regardless of gender who is in an abusive relationship and uses self-defense against an abusive intimate partner to invoke this defense. The use of BWS as a legal defense no longer requires a *battered woman* and the batterer does not have to be a husband. Despite the gender neutrality of the terminology, the legal defense is still most often used by battered women.

The BWS outlines the dynamics of an abusive relationship in which the victim is the subject of a constant barrage of severe and increasing violence. As a result of the violence, the victim often exhibits characteristics of post-traumatic stress disorder (PTSD) with depression, sleep disturbances, nightmares, and psychosomatic illnesses. The combination of PTSD and the constant violence renders the victim feeling hopeless and helpless with few options for escape. Once the violence escalates to the point where the victim perceives that she will be killed, the victim may act out violently in self-defense. The totality of these factors explains how the victim perceives that the violence fits within the legal definition of self-defense.

The BWS is a controversial defense because it makes reference to a psychological condition that is not recognized in the Diagnostic and Statistical Manual of Mental Disorders (DSM) or International Classification of Diseases (ICD), two reference manuals used extensively within the medical and mental health professions. Despite the usage of BWS by the courts, there is no consensus in these professions that the violence in an abusive relationship results in a mental condition severe enough to excuse alleged offenders.

SUGGESTED READING

Donald A. Downs, *More Than Victims: Battered Women, the Syndrome Society, and the Law (Morality and Society Series)* (Chicago: University of Chicago Press, 1996); Cynthia K. Gillespie, *Justifiable Homicide: Battered Women, Self Defense, and the Law* (Columbus, OH: Ohio State University Press, 1989); Lenore E. Walker, *The Battered Woman* (New York: HarperCollins, 1980).

BERNADETTE MUSCAT

BATTERY. Battery is in law both a criminal act and a negligent civil act (tort). Battery was defined under the common law as any intentional improper action that caused harm to another person.[1] In criminal law, battery is usually paired with assault. The criminal definition of assault is the threat of bodily harm while battery is the actual harm that occurs. The same harmful physical act could both be a crime and a tort. For example, if a parent punches his child's baseball coach, that act could be the basis for a criminal charge or the coach may pursue a civil case for the nonconsensual contact.

The penalties or punishment for battery differ between the criminal and civil systems. The penalty for battery in civil suits is that the aggressor may be found liable for damages and ordered to financially compensate the victim. The punishment for the crime of battery varies across the different state and federal criminal codes in the United States. Each criminal code sets out criminal penalties (e.g., fines, imprisonment, or both), the levels of battery (e.g., misdemeanor, felony), penalties for recurrence (e.g., second or third charges carry more serious penalties), and aggravating factors (e.g., use of a weapon).

There are different types of criminal battery, which vary between states. Simple criminal battery is the lowest level of the crime and is usually a misdemeanor charge.[2] Aggravated battery is a more serious crime and is often categorized as a felony due to the use of a weapon or the victim suffering serious bodily injury. Sexual battery is defined in some criminal codes as a subtype of sexual assault. Battery that constitutes domestic violence is also often a separate crime in criminal codes with its own specific penalties attached.

Rates of battery become difficult to compare state to state or nationally as various definitions of the crime exist. The Uniform Crime Reporting program by the Federal Bureau of Investigation reports aggravated assault rates as one of its four types of violent crime.[3] Some serious incidents of battery would be included in these statistics. There is overlap in some state definitions of the crime of assault with the common law definition of battery. Often when the term assault is used it is short for both acts of assault and battery.[4]

Some victims of battery experience repeated physical, sexual, or emotional abuse from offenders close to them—family or intimate partners. Battered women, men, or children are victims recognized for the pattern of medical and psychological injuries that they experience with repeated battering.

NOTES

1. *The Guide to American Law: Everyone's Legal Encyclopedia* (St. Paul: West, 1983), 52.

2. Bryan A. Garner, ed., *Black's Law Dictionary*, 8th ed. (Eagan, MN: West, 2004), 162.

3. Federal Bureau of Investigation, "Uniform Crime Reports," http://www.fbi.gov/ucr/ucr.htm.

4. *The Guide to American Law*, 336.

SUGGESTED READING

Jerry K. Daday et al., "Individual, Neighborhood, and Situational Factors Associated with Violent Victimization and Offending," *Criminal Justice Studies* 18, no. 3 (2005): 215–35.

M. ALEXIS KENNEDY

BELIEF IN A JUST WORLD. "A Just World is one in which people 'get what they deserve.'"[1] Thus, "good" people are rewarded while "bad" people are punished. Given all the bad news we hear each day about such violent events as rape, murder, and terrorism, as well as the loss of property from fraud, identity theft, and motor vehicle theft, it may be easier for us to function if we attribute fault to seemingly innocent victims. This leads to victim-blaming. It is easier for us to believe that the victim did some act that led to her harm, than to accept that we are vulnerable irrespective of whether we follow crime prevention guidelines.

Well-meaning friends or family members may ask for the details leading up to an incident, as if it mattered what the victim did leading up to the incident. The victim may start out seeing himself as innocent but then, as others start asking about the victimization, may come to accept some of the responsibility if he was some place he should not have been or had been drinking a bit too much at the time of the incident.

There may be different interpretations of the "innocent victim" depending on the details of the incident. For example, we are desensitized to violence against others but not so much against ourselves or loved ones. The bottom line is that the right and wrong barometer should only be measuring the offender's actions. The victim does not need our judgment; she is dealing with questioning her every move on her own.

NOTES

1. Melvin J. Lerner, *The Belief in a Just World: A Fundamental Delusion* (New York: Plenum Press, 1980), 11.

SUGGESTED READING

Zick Rubin and Letitia Anne Peplau, "Who Believes in a Just World?" *Journal of Social Issues* 31, no. 3 (1975): 65–89.

SARAH LINDAHL-PFIEFFER

BLAMING THE VICTIM. "Blaming the victim," a phrase popularized in the early 1970s by William Ryan in his classic book of the same name, refers to an ideological process that blames victims for their own misfortunes.[1] According to Ryan, the process begins with the assumption that social problems are caused, in part, by the cultural deficiencies of the people who are most likely to be afflicted by the problems. Because victims' behaviors or values are seen as the cause of their problems, victims are expected to change in order to avoid victimization. Those who do not change (or will not change) are then seen as responsible for their own victimization.

Several early victimologists inadvertently engaged in a process of victim-blaming by classifying crime victims according to their degree of responsibility. For example, in the 1950s, Marvin Wolfgang suggested that some victims precipitate criminal homicide by striking the first blow, brandishing a weapon, or initiating violence in some other way with the intention of settling a dispute. According to Wolfgang, it is often the victims' own behaviors that precipitate the tragic chain of events that ultimately leads to their demise.[2]

In 1971, Menachem Amir borrowed from these earlier ideas of victim precipitation and applied them to rape, suggesting that rape victims are not always innocent or passive, but often precipitate their own rapes by behaving in manners that are misinterpreted by offenders as invitations or opportunities to rape.[3] In his book, *Patterns in Forcible Rape*, Amir distinguishes victims' precipitous behaviors into two categories: acts of commission (e.g., getting drunk, going to bars unescorted, accepting rides from strangers, dressing provocatively) and omission (e.g., not resisting strongly enough). Not surprisingly, Amir's ideas of victim-precipitated rape have been immensely criticized over the years for blaming the victim.

While victimologists today rarely engage in such explicit victim-blaming, the ideas that victims do something to precipitate or fail to do something that facilitates victimization are still found within some contemporary explanations of crimes and social problems. Such explanations sustain the illusion that the world is predictable, controllable, and just. By focusing on victims' defects and what they do wrong, a blaming-the-victim ideology reassures nonvictims that a similar fate will not befall them. The ideology also allows nonvictims to avoid feeling guilty for not being more compassionate toward victims of crime and social injustice.

In addition to fulfilling a psychological function, a blaming-the-victim ideology supports dominant American interests, claims Ryan. For instance, by suggesting that poverty is caused by the victims' own deviant cultural norms and values, attentions are diverted away from the structural causes of poverty, such as unemployment, low wages, and discrimination. According to Ryan, blaming the victim becomes an ideal mode of evasion that frees social, political, and economic institutions from any responsibility, and leaves basic social inequities intact.

NOTES

1. William Ryan, *Blaming the Victim* (New York: Pantheon Books, 1971), 9–11.

2. Marvin Wolfgang, *Patterns in Criminal Homicide* (Philadelphia, PA: University of Pennsylvania Press, 1958), 245–64.

3. Menachem Amir, *Patterns in Forcible Rape* (Chicago: University of Chicago Press, 1971), 259–64, 275–76.

SUGGESTED READING

Helen Eigenberg, "Victim Blaming," in *Controversies in Victimology*, ed. Laura J. Moriarty (Cincinnati, OH: Anderson, 2003), 15–24; Doug A. Timmer and William H. Norman, "The Ideology of Victim Precipitation," *Criminal Justice Review* 9, no. 2 (1984): 63–68.

KAREN WEISS

BULLYING. Bullying is an intentional act of aggression that is meant to harm a victim either physically or psychologically. Bullies usually operate alone or in small groups and choose to victimize individuals who they perceive as vulnerable.

Victims may attract bullies by their small stature, younger age, or lower social status. The intent of the bully is to satisfy his own personal needs, such as obtaining money, homework, or simply using intimidation to prove one's power.

Bullying has been observed in children as young as preschool, and is commonly found in elementary, middle, and high schools throughout the world. The prevalence of bullying is large; however, statistics vary greatly with some experts reporting that one in three children are involved in bullying, whereas other experts have found that 60% of all American students have been involved in bullying.

Both males and females engage in bullying. Traditionally males have used physical means to intimidate their victims, whereas females use psychological methods. However, the twenty-first century has seen an increase in physical violence among girls who bully. In fact, sometimes girls post their physically violent bullying scenarios on the Internet.

Both girls and boys are involved in cyberbullying, which is defined as harassment using the Internet, or other digital technologies. Physical and psychological bullying as well as cyberbullying vary in intensity, from mild to severe. Bullying and cyberbullying have led to deaths in some cases with victims having committed suicide. Sometimes, as in the Columbine Massacre, victims of bullying strike back, becoming bullies themselves, killing others.

The myth, that bullies lack self-esteem, has been found to be false. Bullies may be popular, athletic, and intelligent, or they may be the opposite. However, bullies lack empathy and are aggressive. The myth, that victims are weak and small, has been proven false as well. Victims vary in size, shape, and socio-economic and intellectual levels. Victims are sometimes polite rule-followers who signal, in a nonverbal way, their reluctance to fight. Victims may lack social status or social skills.

A study in Stockholm published in 2008 found that students with Attention Deficit Hyperactive Disorder were four times more likely than the average child to be a bully, and 10 times more likely to be bullied. More studies such as this are needed to determine whether there are psychological disorders that may predispose a child to being a bully or victim.[1]

Bullying can lead to problems such as depression, anxiety, decreased academic or work performance, and increased absenteeism. Such issues are found in children and adults, as bullying also occurs at work and in the military.

Dan Olweus, a Swedish psychologist, is considered the father of bully and victim research. In the 1970s he began to study the phenomenon and created anti-bullying educational programs that are integrated in schools throughout the world.[2] In 2008, a meta-analysis of anti-bullying programs found that awareness of the problem increased; however, actual bullying behavior was not significantly reduced.[3]

NOTES

1. Kirsten Holmberg and Anders Hjern, "Bullying and Attention-Deficit Hyperactivity Disorder in 10-Year-Olds in a Swedish Community," *Developmental Medicine & Child Neurology* 50, no. 2 (2008): 134–38.

2. American Psychological Association (APA), "School Bullying is Nothing New, But Psychologists Identify New Ways to Prevent It," APA, http://www.psychologymatters .org/bullying.html.

3. Kenneth W. Merrell et al., "How Effective are School Bullying Intervention Programs? A Meta-Analysis of Intervention Research," *School Psychology Quarterly* 23, no. 1 (2008): 26–42.

SUGGESTED READING

Barbara Coloroso, *The Bully, the Bullied, and the Bystander: From Preschool to High School—How Parents and Teachers Can Help Break the Cycle of Violence* (New York: Harper Collins, 2004); Kipling D. Williams, Joseph P. Forgás, and William von Hippel, eds., *The Social Outcast: Ostracism, Social Exclusion, Rejection and Bullying* (New York: Psychology Press, 2005).

SUSAN LIPKINS

BURGLARY. The "unlawful entry of a structure to commit a felony or theft"[1] is a sterile definition that does not give a person the understanding of the violation felt by victims of home burglary. We expect that our places of business may fall prey to this crime, but there is the assumption that one's home is the safest place on earth. In reality homes are burglarized with far more frequency than commercial establishments. In 2006, victims reported approximately 1,418,423 residential burglaries (67.9% of all burglaries) to police.[2] The majority of these incidents occurred between the hours of 6 a.m. and 6 p.m.[3] when residents are away from the home. Although burglary may happen while the resident is home, it may not necessarily be recorded as such officially but possibly as a "home invasion," since this carries greater criminal penalties. From a victim's point of view, home or not home, his assumptions of safety are severely reduced.[4] On average a homeowner loses $1,243 worth of personal items (41.8% of items taken) of which 82.9% will never be recovered.[5]

Police and victim data indicate that some individuals appear to be more at risk for burglary by their geographic and socioeconomic locations. The most at-risk victims include African Americans, young heads of households, those with incomes below $25,000 a year, those with increasing numbers of people in the residence, and those residing in apartment complexes.[6] As if the items lost were not enough, estimates are that 87.8% of these victims had to miss one to five days of work or school in order to make repairs, install new security devices, work with investigators, etc.[7]

The criminal justice response in home burglary cases does not add much hope to the situation. Officers are often sympathetic to victims but the reality of the situation is that the clearance rate is 12.6%.[8] Possibly due in part to previous experience (direct or secondary), low resolution rates, inability to have stolen items returned, and lack of insurance, many people (49%) elect not to notify the police that a burglary has occurred.[9] Those who do report may do so for any of the following reasons: because they hope to recover the stolen items, because the burglary was a crime and therefore against the law, to stop/catch the perpetrator, or to prevent future incidents. Generally speaking, an officer does respond to the incident, although some jurisdictions may elect to send property crime civilian technicians in lieu of officers so that scenes may be processed. This saves the agency time and does not take active officers away from other priority duties, but may leave the victim feeling that service was less than optimal. The average wait time between calling the police and their arrival appears to be from 11 to 60 minutes,[10] which is typical for property crime-based calls.

NOTES

1. Federal Bureau of Investigation, "UCR Data," http://www.fbi.gov/ucr/ucr.htm.

2. Ibid.

3. U.S. Department of Justice, "NCVS Data," http://www.ojp.usdoj.gov/bjs/cvict.htm.

4. Caroline McGraw and Vari Drennan, "Assessing the Needs of Older Burglary Victims: A Link Nurse Scheme," *British Journal of Community Nursing* 11 (2006): 414–19.

5. Personal account of author during a 1995 internship with the Sault Ste. Marie (Ontario) City Police Department.

6. U.S. Department of Justice, "NCVS Data," African Americans show declining risk around $25,000 a year income and then a dramatic increase as income rises.

7. Ibid.

8. Frank Schmallager, *Criminal Justice Today* (Upper Saddle River, NJ: Prentice Hall, 2009).

9. U.S. Department of Justice, "NCVS Data."

10. Ibid.

SUGGESTED READINGS

Tim Coupe and Max Griffiths, "The Influence of Police Actions on Victim Satisfaction in Burglary Investigations," *International Journal of the Sociology of Law* 27 (1999): 413–31; Mike Maguire, "The Impact of Burglary Upon Victims," *British Journal of Criminology* 20 (1980): 261–75.

MICHELLE RICHTER

BURNOUT. It is estimated that one in three women will experience domestic violence in their lifetime. To assist in dealing with this social problem over 2,000 battered women's shelters and service programs exist today. It is imperative that these shelters be staffed with compassionate, well-qualified workers. Unfortunately, battered women's shelters are known for their high turnover rates, much like other social service agencies.

Burnout is a psychological syndrome that is the result of chronic on-the-job stressors. Christina Maslach describes burnout as having three dimensions: emotional exhaustion, depersonalization (i.e., a negative attitude toward clients, a personal detachment, or loss of ideals), and reduced personal accomplishment and commitment to the profession.[1] Burnout occurs over time and progresses sequentially through each of the above dimensions. Individual, interpersonal, and organizational characteristics contribute to burnout. Sources of burnout include work overload, lack of autonomy, emotional demands, low social support, role ambiguity, and disconnect between work expectations and actual outcomes. Burnout is problematic because it can result in decreased effectiveness, physical and psychological symptoms, and contributes to high levels of turnover in occupations.

Extensive research has documented the presence of burnout among employees within social service occupations (e.g., social work, policing, nursing). Domestic violence advocates, however, have been somewhat neglected in this literature. The few studies that have examined shelter staff find moderate levels of burnout using the Maslach Burnout Inventory—an inventory that has been used extensively within research on burnout.

Moderate levels of burnout have been attributed to individual level variables as well as organizational factors. Vicarious or secondary trauma (i.e., secondarily absorbing the pain of victims), for example, has been cited as a factor contributing to occupational burnout for shelter advocates. Organizationally speaking, lack of time to do one's work contributes to burnout, as does work overload. Lack of resources (e.g., office supplies, computers, money) leads to an inability to complete one's job in a prompt, effective manner, which also increases burnout. Advocates become frustrated when they have to jump over bureaucratic hurdles (e.g., rules that are perceived as unnecessary) when attempting to advocate for victims.

It is also important to take note of what factors help to mediate burnout for domestic violence advocates. Social support (both at home and work), for example, has been cited as a factor in burnout reduction. These findings are mixed. Some studies indicate that high levels of support decrease burnout whereas other studies find no correlation between burnout and social support. The meaningful nature of one's job also helps to buffer the effects of burnout. So, when advocates feel that their job is important and that they are making a difference in women's lives, burnout decreases.

NOTE

1. Christina Maslach, Wilmar Schaufeli, and Michael Leiter, "Job Burnout," *Annual Review of Psychology* 52 (2001): 397–422.

SUGGESTED READING

Stephanie Baird and Sharon Jenkins, "Vicarious Traumatization, Secondary Traumatic Stress, and Burnout in Sexual Assault and Domestic Violence Agency Staff," *Violence and Victims* 18 (2003): 71–86; Lisa M. Baker and Karen M. O'Brien, "Are Shelter Workers Burned Out? An Examination of Stress, Social Support, and Coping," *Journal of Family Violence* 22 (2007): 465–74; Holly Bell, Shanti Kulkarni, and Lisa Dalton, "Organizational Prevention of Vicarious Trauma," *Families in Society: The Journal of Contemporary Human Services* 84 (2003): 463–70.

MICHELLE BEMILLER

BYSTANDER EFFECT. On March 13, 1964, Catherine (Kitty) Genovese was sexually assaulted and murdered in front of her home in Queens, New York. Following the incident, news reports claimed that 38 individuals witnessed the attack but failed to intervene or contact the police.[1] This lack of intervention became a subject of social psychological scrutiny and was eventually termed the *bystander effect*—a phenomenon in which the likelihood that a bystander will intervene in an emergency situation decreases as the number of bystanders increases.

Researchers have conducted a variety of experiments in which medical emergencies,[2] potential fires,[3] and requests for assistance[4] were staged so that both the likelihood of bystander intervention and the length of time it would take bystanders to intervene could be measured. Consistent with the assumptions of the bystander effect, these studies revealed three things. First, as the number of bystanders increased, the likelihood that any one bystander would intervene decreased. Second, time to intervene increased as the number of bystanders increased. Third, bystanders were more likely to intervene when directly asked for assistance.

Three explanations for the bystander effect are prevalent in social psychological literature. The first, audience inhibition, assumes that the risk of embarrassment associated with providing help (i.e., the intervention might fail) impedes bystander intervention. The second, social influence, hypothesizes that when bystanders do not see others providing assistance, they assume the behavioral norm is to remain inactive and, therefore, do not intervene. The third, diffusion of responsibility, presumes that a reduced sense of personal responsibility precludes bystanders from taking action when faced with emergency situations.

NOTES

1. A. M. Rosenthal, *Thirty-Eight Witnesses: The Kitty Genovese Case* (New York: McGraw-Hill, 1964).

2. John M. Darley and Bibb Latane, "Bystander Intervention in Emergencies: Diffusion of Responsibility," *Journal of Personality and Social Psychology* 8, no. 4 (1968): 377–83.

3. Bibb Latane and John M. Darley, "Group Inhibition of Bystander Intervention in Emergencies," *Journal of Personality and Social Psychology* 10, no. 3 (1968): 215–21.

4. Patrick M. Markey, "Bystander Intervention in Computer-Mediated Communication," *Computers in Human Behavior* 16 (2000): 183–88.

SUGGESTED READING

Bibb Latane and John M. Darley, *The Unresponsive Bystander: Why Doesn't He Help?* (New York: Appleton-Century-Crofts, 1970); Bibb Latane and Steve Nida, "Ten Years of Research on Group Size and Helping," *Psychological Bulletin* 89, no. 2 (1981): 308–24.

JENNIFER SCROGGINS

C

CAMPUS VICTIMIZATIONS. In the mid-1980s, civil litigation against universities emerged as a means of addressing unsafe campus conditions that contributed to victimizations. Victims in these cases received large judgments or out-of-court settlements that forced universities to reexamine how to address campus victimizations. One of the more high-profile cases was that of 19-year-old Jeanne Ann Clery who was a freshman at Lehigh University, a private university located in a suburb of Philadelphia, Pennsylvania. On April 5, 1986, while in her dorm room, Jeanne Clery was tortured, raped, and murdered by a fellow student. Jeanne Clery's parents sued the university for negligence and failure to take reasonable action to protect their daughter from foreseeable harm. The university settled out of court for an undisclosed amount that was used by the Clerys to create Security On Campus, Inc.

Created in 1987, Security On Campus, Inc., is an organization dedicated to making legislative changes to raise awareness about violent crime on campus. Within a year, Pennsylvania was the first state to pass campus crime legislation with other states following soon thereafter. The Clerys continued their political activism to ensure that the federal government adopted sweeping legislation including the Student Right to Know and Campus Security Act of 1990. This Act requires that all public and private institutions of higher education publish and distribute an annual report including campus crime statistics, reporting procedures, crime prevention efforts, and security and law enforcement policies. The key requirement involves data collection on murder; forcible and non-forcible sex offenses including rape;

robbery; aggravated assault; burglary; motor vehicle theft; and arrests for violations of liquor, drug, and weapons law violations. Any school found in violation of the Act can be fined or lose access to federal student aid programs.

Within two years, the Campus Security Act was amended to include the Campus Sexual Assault Victims' Bill of Rights under the Higher Education Amendments of 1992. All higher education institutions must comply with the amended law by notifying sexual assault victims about reporting and both on- and off-campus service options, creating sexual assault awareness and prevention programs, imposing campus disciplinary actions, and ensuring victims' basic rights. The latter includes notifying the victim about the availability of reasonable accommodations in academic and on-campus living arrangements, allowing both the accuser (victim) and the accused (alleged offender) to have others present during campus disciplinary proceedings, and acknowledging that both parties shall be informed of the outcome of disciplinary actions.

The Clerys' political advocacy contributed to amendments to the original legislation and expanded university reporting requirements. These 1998 amendments also formally changed the name of the law to honor their daughter and became known nationally as the Jeanne Clery Act. The 1998 Act made two main clarifications: first, campuses must collect data on all student victimizations that occur in school affiliated off-campus housing and on all properties adjacent to the campus. The second clarification requires that schools must report statistics on hate crimes by race, gender, religion, orientation, ethnicity, or disability.

One of the requirements of the Jeanne Clery Act is that both parties be made aware of the outcome of all school judicial proceedings. The law specifically states that compliance with notification of both parties is not a violation of a student's privacy rights under the Family Education Rights and Privacy Act (FERPA). This aspect of the law was challenged in 2000 when an Ohio Federal District Court judge ruled in *United States of America v. Miami University of Ohio*, that campus disciplinary records are student records, which are protected from public release under FERPA.[1] Under the Court's ruling the school was barred from releasing student disciplinary records. This court decision was disappointing for those interested in students' safety because, they argued, students will not know the extent of crime or the school's response to campus crimes without access to these records.

In 1999, the Office of Violence Against Women (OVW) under the U.S. Department of Justice began distributing grants named Reduce Violent Crimes Against Women on Campus Program. These grants support the adoption of comprehensive and coordinated campus-community responses to domestic violence, dating violence, sexual assault, and stalking on-campus. Since its inception until the end of funding authorization in 2011, OVW will distribute approximately $27 million to schools nationwide.

NOTE

1. *United States of America v. Miami University of Ohio*, 91 F. Supp. 2d. 1132 (2000), later reaffirmed in 2002 by the Sixth Circuit Court of Appeals (294 F.3d 797).

SUGGESTED READING

Office on Violence Against Women, "Grants to Reduce Domestic Violence, Dating Violence, Sexual Assault, and Stalking On-campus," Office on Violence Against Women of the U.S. Department of Justice, http://www.ovw.usdoj.gov/campus_desc.htm; Security On Campus, Inc. Web site, http://www.securityoncampus.org.

BERNADETTE MUSCAT

CELEBRITY VICTIM. Approximately 25 million crimes are perpetrated against U.S. residents each year.[1] The majority of these crimes do not become media headlines and most individuals who are victimized do not become household names. However, a small portion are committed against celebrities, and in such cases their victimization receives considerable attention and, often times, becomes a media spectacle.

Numerous cases in which celebrities have been victimized, including the Lindbergh kidnapping, Roseanne Barr's recovered memories of sexual abuse, the murder of fashion designer Gianni Versace, and the assault and subsequent death of popular television anchorwoman Anne Pressly, exemplify the way that attention surrounding victimization changes when it is a celebrity who is victimized. For instance, although there were a substantial number of missing children in the United States in the 1930s, it was the abduction of the son of Charles Lindbergh that drew widespread attention to the problem of kidnapping and led to its classification as a federal crime.[2] Similarly, even though the stories of most victims of sexual abuse remain untold, knowledge of the sexual abuse suffered by Roseanne Barr was rapidly disseminated following her admission that she had been victimized as a child. Finally, the attention surrounding most of the homicides that occur in the United States exists at a relatively local level, and few people become aware of those who were victimized outside of their communities. Inconsistent with this pattern were the murders of Gianni Versace and Anne Pressly; both were quickly placed in the national spotlight and the families of the two victims received an outpouring of compassion from diverse geographical locations.

Other forms of attention surrounding victimization also change when it is celebrities who are victimized. In the case of the Lindbergh kidnapping, the trial phase of the ordeal was deemed "the greatest story since the Resurrection" and large crowds gathered at the courthouse for its duration; very few child abduction cases have received this magnitude of attention since. Moreover, following the death of Gianni Versace, the world watched as police completed a five-month long murder investigation, which eventually yielded more than 700 pages of investigative documents; most murder investigations are not scrutinized by the public as they occur, and it is exceedingly rare for the minutiae of such investigations to appear online.

Mass media plays a role in the increased attention that is paid to celebrity victims. Media exposure to the details of the lives of celebrities has become commonplace, and the consumption of these images has reached an historical high. As such, the lives of celebrities—including their victimizations—have essentially become a readily available form of public property; this has generally not happened to noncelebrities. Because this trend has connected the lives of celebrities to those of noncelebrities, the tragedies that befall them do so in the most public of manners.

NOTES

1. U.S. Department of Justice, *Criminal Victimization in the United States, 2006* (Washington DC: Office of Justice Programs, Bureau of Justice Statistics. NCJ-223436, 2008).

2. U.S. Department of Justice, *National Estimates of Missing Children: An Overview* (Washington DC: Office of Justice Programs, Bureau of Justice Statistics. NCJ-196465, 2002).

SUGGESTED READING

Deborah Jermyn, "'Death of the Girl Next Door:' Celebrity, Femininity, and Tragedy in the Murder of Jill Dando," *Feminist Media Studies* 1, no. 3 (2001): 343–59; Ruth Penfold, "The Star's Image, Victimization and Celebrity Culture," *Punishment and Society* 6, no. 3 (2004): 289–302.

JENNIFER SCROGGINS

CHILD ABUSE. According to the Keeping Children and Families Safe Act of 2003, *child abuse* is any recent act or failure to act on the part of a caretaker that involves death, serious physical or emotional harm, sexual abuse, or exploitation. This includes acts of commission (e.g., hitting the child with an object, burning the child with a cigarette) as well as those of omission (e.g., withholding water, food, sleep, or medical care). *Child neglect,* on the other hand, consists of an act or failure to act that threatens the physical and emotional well-being of the child. For example, the child may not be properly clothed, fed, or supervised. Although it is the most common form of maltreatment, neglect receives far less attention than physical abuse, perhaps because neglect is more difficult to define or recognize than abuse.

What is the incidence of child maltreatment in the United States? The answer to this question depends on the source of the data one uses. Basically, there are two types of data: information from official records prepared by governmental agencies, and self-report survey data collected by social scientists. The National Child Abuse and Neglect Data System, which has collected data since 1990, reported an estimated 905,000 victims of abuse and neglect in 2006, yielding an incidence rate of 12.1 per 1,000 children. In over 80% of the cases the maltreatment was perpetrated by a parent. Sixty-four percent of the cases involved neglect, 16% physical abuse, 9% sexual abuse, with the remainder involving other kinds of maltreatment such as emotional abuse or medical neglect.

Although official statistics such as these are useful, they omit incidents not reported to authorities and therefore underestimate the prevalence of abuse. Further, approximately three-quarters of incidents reported to law enforcement or social services authorities are designated as "unsubstantiated." Though this indicates there was not enough evidence of abuse to take action, it does not mean that abuse or neglect did not take place.

In order to obtain a more complete record of child abuse, social scientists have conducted studies that ask parents to report on their parenting behaviors, including harsh practices that might be considered abusive. These self-report surveys of child maltreatment usually produce much higher rates than those based on cases reported to official agencies as they include the large number of cases that go unreported.

The most widely acclaimed studies of this type are the National Family Violence Surveys. In 1975 Murray Straus, Richard Gelles, and Suzanne Steinmetz[1] conducted a general population survey in an attempt to determine the incidence of parents' physical abuse of their children. Straus and Gelles[2] conducted a second study in 1985. Both studies used the Conflict Tactics Scale (which includes a wide range of aggressive and violent behaviors) to assess violence in families. They found that 3.6% of parents had engaged in violence toward children aged 3 to 17 in 1975, and approximately 2% of parents reported having done so in the 1985 survey. These rates are much higher than official report statistics, and they undoubtedly underestimate the problem as many respondents were probably unwilling to admit to engaging in violence toward their children. The good news, however, is that the rates of child abuse appeared to decline in the years between the two surveys.

It is well established that parents who were abused as children are at risk for abusing their own offspring. Treatment programs for abusive parents usually entail teaching more constructive strategies for managing children's behavior. Although such approaches have value, they are likely to have a limited effect to the extent that they ignore the fact that, at least in many cases, the parent's behavior is indicative of a general antisocial orientation fostered by the inept parenting he received as a child. Abusive parenting is often part of a lifestyle that includes substance abuse, fighting, missing work, mismanaging finances, etc. A truly effective treatment would involve assisting the perpetrator in developing a more responsible lifestyle. Unfortunately, such interventions are likely to be costly in terms of both time and money.

Although childhood exposure to abusive parenting increases the chances that an individual will engage in similar practices with her own children, many abused children grow up to be good parents. Ronald Simons, Leslie Simons, and Lora Wallace[3] review extensive research done in this area and conclude that this positive outcome is most likely to take place when the abused individual was also exposed to an additional, nurturing caretaker or later marries a spouse who encourages caring, competent parenting.

NOTES

1. Richard J. Gelles, "Social Change and Change in Family Violence from 1975 to 1985 as Revealed by Two National Surveys," *Journal of Marriage and Family* 48 (1986): 465–79.

2. Murray A. Straus, Richard J. Gelles, and Suzanne K. Steinmetz, *Behind Closed Doors: Violence in the American Family* (Beverly Hills, CA: Sage, 1980).

3. Ronald L. Simons, Leslie G. Simons, and Lora E. Wallace, *Families, Delinquency, and Crime: Linking Society's Most Basic Institution to Antisocial Behavior* (New York: Oxford University Press, 2004).

SUGGESTED READING

Murray A. Straus, Richard J. Gelles, and Suzanne K. Steinmetz, *Behind Closed Doors: Violence in American Families* (New Brunswick, NJ: Transaction, 2006).

LESLIE GORDON SIMONS

CHILD LURES. Whether in person or via the Internet, sexual predators must have a way to lure the child into a situation where she can be abused. Child lures take the form of meeting children, gaining their initial trust, and engaging them in activities where they can be exploited. The greatest lure is being able to communicate with children. Children have their own culture, including specific language. Adults who sound like adults scare away children or bore them. Predators also use incentives to meet children, such as magic tricks, candy or ice cream, or games. Once the child is initially lured, the predator must continue to gain the child's trust to increase the time spent with the predator. For example, predators often have extensive collections of sought-after video games, to encourage children to spend time at the predator's residence.

Using the Internet rather than direct contact allows the predator to reach more children faster, and with greater convenience. Internet communication involves accessing chat rooms and other areas where children interact. For example, the predator can access video gaming sites and provide tips, ask questions, and gain the friendship of many children at one time. The predator can then approach children individually to see if any respond to initial advances. If that happens, the relationship can be continued; if not, the predator can move to another child. Often, these children are looking for people to talk to, and probably have little to no parental supervision.

Predators can also access personal Web sites like MySpace and Facebook to look for suitable targets. Personal Web sites allow children to exchange photographs and communication with others. Some children also show suggestive photographs of themselves and engage in sexually explicit conversations. Predators access these Web sites looking for children who fit their desired profile. They can then lure them in Internet communication. There are also sites that are more sexually explicit. Two examples of these are hotornot.com and would youhitthis.com. People submit pictures to be placed on these Web sites. Others access the site and rate the pictures. People can also communicate with others and access personal Web pages of those in the pictures. Predators choose children who exhibit some nudity or sexual behavior and attempt to communicate with the child. If the child responds, the predator begins the process of luring and grooming. Initially, this may involve sending pictures. If the child agrees, the predator requests increasingly explicit pictures. If the child is still willing, the predator asks for pictures and movies of the child engaged in sexual activity. This is enhanced when children have access to webcams on their computers. This could also be a part of the grooming process to get the child to agree to meet the predator for sex.

While traditional means of luring a child into a situation where sexual exploitation can happen still remain, the Internet has greatly expanded that threat. To prevent children from inappropriate contact with others, keep computers in public places. If children think they are being watched, they are less likely to engage in reckless behavior. It also means no WiFi laptops that children can carry to a secluded place. It is also important to restrict access to inappropriate Web sites. There are a few programs that are very helpful in this sense. It is necessary to keep up with these, however, because children will find a way to defeat them if given enough time. It is also important to check the child's personal Web pages regularly. This can be accomplished by parents getting their own MySpace/Facebook accounts or using the child's login and passwords to the computer and accounts.

SUGGESTED READING

Maria T. Daversa and Raymond A. Knight, "A Structural Examination of the Predictors of Sexual Coercion Against Children in Adolescent Sexual Offenders," *Criminal Justice and Behavior* 34, no. 10 (2007): 1313–33; Kenneth V. Lanning, *Child Molesters: A Behavioral Analysis* (Alexandria, VA: National Center for Missing and Exploited

Children, 2001); Ernest Poortinga, Craig Lemmen, and Karl Majeske, "A Comparison of Criminal Sexual Conduct," *Journal of Forensic Sciences* 52, no. 6 (2007): 1372–75.

JEFF WALKER

CHILD PROTECTIVE SERVICES (CPS). Child Protective Services (CPS) is a government agency responsible for accepting referrals of child abuse and neglect, investigating those allegations, and initiating attempts to remedy or prevent instances of maltreatment. The Child Abuse Prevention and Treatment Act (CAPTA) mandated federal support to states for the investigation of reports of suspected abuse or neglect and the protection of maltreated children. In addition, CAPTA clearly defined the federal role in child welfare services as one of research, technical support, evaluation, and data collection. Investigation of maltreatment and ensuring the safety of children became the responsibility of states, thus creating CPS agencies across the country. The most recent amendment and reauthorization of CAPTA occurred with the passing of the Keeping Children and Families Safe Act of 2003.

In 2006, over 3 million abuse or neglect referrals involving over 6 million children were made to CPS. More than 60% of those referrals were formally investigated; and, in 30% of those cases, at least one child was found to be the victim of maltreatment. Although federal law mandates minimum standards for establishing legislative definitions of child abuse and neglect, each state creates its own definition, resulting in great variation.

Like abuse and neglect definitions, state mandatory reporting laws also vary greatly. Over 90% of states require professionals such as doctors, educators, and child care providers to report suspected neglect or abuse; though only 25% of states mandate nonprofessionals, such as community members or parents, to report suspected abuse or neglect. Twenty-three states allow reporters to remain anonymous.

Though all states do have some form of disposition classifications in place for investigating reports, each state's disposition policy widely differs on what constitutes a substantiated case of abuse or neglect. A national study concluded that 45% of states dictated high standards of proof, such as material or clear and convincing evidence, to substantiate abuse or neglect reports. Nineteen states required less stringent standards (i.e., probable cause and credible evidence). Nine states indicated no specific standards for substantiation. In 2006, professionals reported almost two-thirds of all substantiated cases.

Child welfare legislation often seeks to establish a balance between maintaining the child's safety and interceding in the family sphere. State and local politics and values on privacy and the family influence each state's definition of abuse and neglect, reporting laws, and standards for disposition. Although all states must comply with basic federal guidelines in establishing a framework to serve children and families who are involved in cases of abuse or neglect, state CPS agencies operate under differing regulations and laws.

SUGGESTED READING

Child Welfare Information Gateway, "How the Child Welfare System Works," U.S. Department of Health and Human Services, http://www.childwelfare.gov/pubs/can_info_packet.pdf; Administration for Children and Families, "Child Protective Services," U.S. Department of Health and Human Services, http://www.acf.hhs.gov/programs/ocs/ssbg/reports/ssbg_focus_2005/cps.html; U.S. Department of Health and Human Services, "National Study of Child Protective Services Systems and Reform Efforts," http://aspe.hhs.gov/hsp/cps-status03/state-policy03.

MELISSA YOUNG-SPILLERS

CHILD WITNESS. The testimony of allegedly abused and neglected children is often crucial. For most children, however, this task is confusing and frightening, and for some even traumatic. These painful emotions can lead to inaccurate or inconsistent statements, recantations, or the inability to testify. In order to minimize this problem most states have established innovative methods of interviewing and taking testimony from child witnesses. For example, most states allow videotaped statements of child witnesses to be viewed in court. Videotaping is less disturbing to children than in-court testimony and also reduces the need for multiple interviews. To prevent children from being disturbed or distracted by video equipment many communities place their cameras out of sight behind one-way glass.

Another means of preventing multiple interviews of child witnesses are laws requiring multidisciplinary investigations of abuse cases (e.g., joint law enforcement-child protective service investigation). Such laws have spawned specialized child abuse investigation centers in which children are interviewed by trained professionals. These interviews are typically observed through one-way glass by interested parties. Professional interviewers are skilled at building rapport with children, helping them relax and feel comfortable, and questioning them in nonleading ways that result in more consistent and reliable testimony.

Most jurisdictions also allow child witnesses to testify via closed circuit television (CCTV). This method allows the child to observe the judge and attorneys from a less intimidating setting and still allows courtroom participants to view the child. This nontraditional procedure was tested in the 1990 Supreme Court case of *Maryland v. Craig*[1] in which the Court ruled that a Maryland statute that approved CCTV testimony was acceptable because it was preceded by a hearing demonstrating that the child would suffer severe emotional damage if required to testify. The Court concluded that in-court and CCTV testimony were equivalent and did not damage a defendant's right to confront and cross-examine witnesses.

Laws of evidence have also been relaxed in most states to allow certain professionals (e.g., social workers, teachers, physicians) to testify about out-of-court statements made to them by children. Normally, such statements would be inadmissible as hearsay. This nontraditional procedure was tested in the 1992 Supreme Court case of *White v. Illinois*[2] in which the Court ruled that prosecutors do not have to produce child witnesses in court if they cannot understand the court process or would likely be traumatized by it. Typically, if the child does not testify, corroboration is needed to support the child's statements.

When children are able to testify in court, a number of procedures have been instituted to minimize their discomfort. In child sexual abuse cases for example, all federal courts and many state courts allow children with limited verbal capacity to demonstrate what happened to them using toys or other props including anatomically correct dolls. Furthermore, most jurisdictions allow child witnesses to observe beforehand the courtroom in which they will testify, sit on the witness stand, speak on the microphone, and even role play possible courtroom scenarios with the prosecutor. Some courts even supply children with books and games that illustrate or demonstrate, "a child's day in court."

NOTES

1. *Maryland v. Craig,* 497 U.S. 836 (1990).
2. *White v. Illinois,* 502 U.S. 346 (1992).

SUGGESTED READING

K. A. Francis, (1994). "Abused Children Should be Spared Having to Confront Abusers in Court," in *Child Abuse: Opposing Viewpoints*, ed. Karin Swisher (San Diego, CA: Greenhaven Press, 1994), 195–202; John E. B. Myers, *Legal Issues in Child Abuse and Neglect Practice* (Thousand Oaks, CA: Sage, 1998); Inger J. Sagatun and Leonard P. Edwards, *Child Abuse and the Legal System* (Chicago: Nelson-Hall, 1995).

THOMAS KELLEY

CIVIL LITIGATION. One of the major ways that crime victims can get reimbursed for their losses is through civil litigation. In other words, crime victims may file civil lawsuits. First-party litigation means that the victim sues the perpetrator directly while third-party litigation means that the victim sues another party for indirectly contributing to the harm suffered by the victim. An example of third-party litigation would be a rape victim suing a landlord or a hotel for failing to provide adequate security.[1]

Civil litigation has several benefits. First, civil litigation gives victims the ability to recover financial losses. For instance, victims can receive compensation for physical injuries, medical costs, economic losses (e.g., stolen property), and pain and suffering.[2] In cases of murder, the victim's family may sue. In some cases, victims have been awarded large sums of money. For instance, a woman who was sexually assaulted at a convention in Las Vegas was awarded $5.2 million.[3] Second, civil litigation affords victims more decision-making power than they typically have in criminal cases. For instance, with a criminal case, the prosecutor generally decides whether to take a case to trial, what evidence to use, and whether to plea bargain. With civil litigation, the victim gets to make these types of decisions: whether or not to pursue a civil suit, which attorney to use, and whether he wants to accept a settlement offer.[4] A third benefit of civil litigation is that the standard of proof is lower than in criminal cases; in civil court, the standard is preponderance of the evidence while in criminal court the standard is proof beyond a reasonable doubt. Thus, it is possible for a defendant who has been found not guilty in criminal court to be found liable in civil court.[5]

Despite its benefits, civil litigation has several weaknesses. First, it may take years for a case to be settled.[6] Second, civil litigation may be an expensive avenue for a victim to pursue.[7] Not only do victims have to pay for attorneys, but also often have to pay filing fees and deposition costs.[8] Some attorneys will take cases on a contingency basis and only charge the victim a fee if the case is won. However, the drawback is that these attorneys are often reluctant to take on such cases unless there is very strong evidence and the offender is able to pay sizeable damages.[9] Third, victims can only sue offenders in cases in which the offender is known. Consider, for example, an incident in which a woman is robbed by an unknown man. Since she is unable to establish the offender's identity, she obviously cannot sue him. Fourth, victims may be revictimized during the civil process. For instance, victims may be forced to reveal personal information about themselves and are subject to cross-examination by the offender's attorney, which can be very disturbing for many victims.[10] Finally, just because a victim wins a judgment against an offender does not mean that she will ever be able to collect any of the money.[11]

NOTES

1. Mario Gaboury, "Financial Assistance for Victims of Crime," National Victim Assistance Academy, http://www.ojp.usdoj.gov/ovc/assist/nvaa99/chap5-1.htm.

2. Ibid.

3. Office for Victims of Crime, "Civil Remedies," U.S. Department of Justice, http://www.ojp.usdoj.gov/ovc/new/directions/pdftxt/chap16.pdf.

4. Ibid.

5. Gaboury, "Financial Assistance."

6. Susan Kiss Sarnoff, *Paying for Crime: The Policies and Possibilities of Crime Victim Reimbursement* (Westport, CT: Praeger, 1996).

7. Gaboury, "Financial Assistance."

8. Sarnoff, *Paying for Crime*.

9. Ibid.

10. Gaboury, "Financial Assistance."

11. Sarnoff, *Paying for Crime*.

SUGGESTED READING

The National Center for Victims of Crime, "Civil Justice for Crime Victims," http://www.ncvc.org/ncvc/main.aspx?dbName=DocumentViewer&Document ID=32318; Office for Victims of Crime, "Civil Legal Remedies for Crime Victims," U.S. Department of Justice, http://www.ncjrs.gov/txtfiles/clr.txt.

SHANNON A. SANTANA

COMMUNITY SERVICE. Community service orders are a form of restitution whereby the work conducted by an offender is provided as a means of repaying his debt to society. In most cases community service is ordered by the sentencing judge and supervised by the probation officer.[1] Most judges prefer that offenders sentenced to complete community service do so at a not-for-profit agency within their local jurisdiction. Offenders may be required to perform any variety of duties, such as street cleaning, routine maintenance of public housing, clean-up activities at parks and other public places, graffiti removal, lawn care for a variety of county or state facilities, or another type of labor that would benefit the community.

Even offenders who are indigent or are unemployed can complete this sanction. Thus, community service provides an alternative for such offenders to pay their debt in a constructive manner that benefits the state as a victim. Further still, skilled laborers and even white-collar workers can provide unique benefits since their specialized skills can be put to use when serving the requirements of their sentence. For instance, medical professionals might be required to provide services to persons in need and those who are disadvantaged. Such services may prove to be even more valuable than fines or other sanctions that might be imposed.

One of the key benefits of community service is that it is a pliable sanction that can be used in a variety of settings and with a variety of outcomes. Indeed, in some criminal cases, a specific victim may not be able to be identified. Rather, the community as a whole may be the victim of an offender's actions. For example, a youth sprays graffiti on a government building and is apprehended, tried, and convicted for defacing a government building. In such a case, punitive measures may not be warranted. Further, it is hard to discern who the exact "victim" might be in such a case. The use of community service provides judges with a sentencing option that can accommodate offenses that lack a clear and specific victim.

Currently, community service is mostly used as an integral condition of probation or parole. Though there may be statutorily prescribed amounts of community service ordered, the amount that is typically required is very subjective and depends on the discretion of the judge. Overall, community service is an effective sanction that benefits the community as a whole since at least some form of compensation is made by the offender. Further, courthouse personnel benefit because community service provides an additional option for sentencing that is low cost and easy to implement. Because of this, communities and victims benefit from the use of community service sanctions through indirect yet tangible means, demonstrating the overall utility of this sanction.

NOTE

1. Dean J. Champion, *Probation, Parole, and Community Corrections*, 4th ed. (Upper Saddle River, NJ: Prentice Hall, 2002).

SUGGESTED READING

Administrative Office of the U.S. Courts, "Community Service," U.S. Courts, http://www.uscourts.gov/fedprob/supervise/community.html; Robert D. Hanser, *Special Needs Offenders in the Community* (Upper Saddle River, NJ: Prentice Hall, 2007).

ROBERT D. HANSER

COMPENSATION PROGRAMS. Violent crime compensation programs provide financial reparations to those victimized and their families. British reformer Margery Fry is credited with the creation of modern compensation programs. In the early 1950s, Fry proposed that restitution be provided through the creation of shelters for battered women, reconciliation between victims and offenders, and programs providing monetary reimbursement to crime victims.[1] The underlying principle was that governments have a fundamental responsibility to protect the welfare of their most vulnerable citizens. As such, society owes recompense to crime victims when that mandate for protection fails them.[2] Fry's efforts led to the establishment in 1963 of the first state-operated victim's compensation fund in New Zealand; in 1964, Britain ratified its own program.

In the United States, compensation programs are the oldest form of victim assistance. First established in California in 1965, programs currently exist in each state, plus the District of Columbia, Virgin Islands, and Puerto Rico.[3] States are responsible for virtually all the administrative costs required to operate their compensation programs. A few states fund them by appropriating tax dollars via legislation. However most require offenders to pay criminal penalties, thereby subsidizing compensation programs without using taxes.[4] Usually this is accomplished in one of three ways: offenders pay fees according to the severity of their crime, a percentage of an offender's fine goes toward victim compensation, or wages owed to inmates working in the prison industry are withheld.[5] Additionally, the Victims of Crime Act of 1984 (VOCA) provides up to 25% of state-level program budgets through assistance grants and federal monies via its Crime Victims' Fund (CVF).[6]

In order to obtain funds, victims must complete an application within one year from the date of the crime and meet several eligibility criteria that restrict who is eligible for compensation; recipients are generally victims of violent crimes who did not provoke their attack, were physically injured, required medical attention, and cannot receive reimbursement through insurance.[7] Typically, victims must exhaust all public and private insurance assets before becoming eligible for compensation program benefits.[8] Many states also require that crimes be reported to the police within 72 hours; victims must then cooperate with authorities during the investigation and prosecution stages.[9]

These restrictions speak to the weaknesses of compensation programs. Most victims fail to meet eligibility requirements. Those who do qualify are forced, however reticent, to assist authorities throughout the criminal process. More troubling is that many victims are unaware of the existence of compensation programs; a problem compounded by the infrequency with which police and courts refer them to such resources.[10] Because many programs lack adequate funding, victims often receive less compensation than they anticipated; that money hardly covers court costs. Such troubles cause many victims to become skeptical of the compensation process.[11] Thus, critics argue that without a more efficient process and improved benefits, the restorative purpose of victims' compensation programs will remain unaccomplished.

NOTES

1. Margery Fry, *Arms of the Law* (London: Victor Gollancz, 1951).

2. Andrew Karmen, *Crime Victims: An Introduction to Victimology* (Belmont, CA: Wadsworth, 1990), 307.

3. National Association of Crime Victim Compensation Boards (NACVCB), "Crime Victim Compensation: An Overview," NACVCB, http://www.nacvcb.org/articles/Overview_prn.html.

4. Karmen, *Crime Victims,* 314.

5. NACVCB, "Crime Victim Compensation."

6. Ibid.

7. Karmen, *Crime Victims,* 313.

8. Washington State Department of Labor & Industries, "About Crime Victims Compensation," Washington State Department of Labor & Industries, http://www.lni.wa.gov/ClaimsIns/CrimeVictims/About/default.asp.

9. Susan S. Siverman, "The Effect of Victim Compensation Programs Upon Conviction Rates," *Sociological Symposium* 25 (1979): 40.

10. Eric J. Fritsch, Tory J. Caeti, and Peggy M. Tobolowsky, "Police Referrals of Crime Victims to Compensation Sources: An Empirical Analysis of Attitudinal and Structural Impediments," *Police Quarterly* 7 (2004): 372.

11. Robert Elias, *The Politics of Victimization: Victims, Victimology, and Human Rights* (New York: Oxford University Press, 1986), 212.

SUGGESTED READING

Susan Herman and Michelle Waul, *Repairing the Harm: A New Vision for Crime Victim Compensation in America* (Washington DC: The National Center for Victims of Crime, 2004); Susan Kiss Sarnoff, *Paying for Crime: The Policies and Possibilities of Crime Victim Reimbursement* (Westport, CT: Praeger, 1996).

RAY MARATEA

COMPENSATORY DAMAGES. Compensatory damages are the sum of money awarded by a civil court to a plaintiff-victim to remedy or "compensate" for actual losses, or damages, suffered. Victims must provide evidence that they experienced an identifiable harm that can be recompensed by a specific sum of money, which can be objectively determined by a judge or jury.

Though similar to judge-ordered "restitution" stemming from criminal conduct, compensatory damages are the result of a civil action for a tort often resulting from a crime. Unlike punitive damages that seek to punish the defendant for illegal conduct as a future deterrent, compensatory damages are designed specifically to provide the victim in a civil action with the money to replace what the victim has lost, but nothing more. Compensatory damages seek to make the victim "whole" again, restoring the economic standing that existed before the illegal act.

Compensatory damages become complicated when the identifiable harm of the victim is not easily quantifiable, such as determining the value of threat to life; emotional distress; pain and suffering; and loss of consortium, reputation, mental capacity, enjoyment of life, etc. Calculations can be very subjective, and often vary tremendously based on judge and jury perceptions and conflicting testimony by both victims and experts.

More easily quantifiable harms include economic losses resulting from medical expenses, lost profits in a business, lost income and potential earnings, repair or replacement of damaged or destroyed property, and legal costs. Perhaps most difficult to calculate are those losses that appear quantifiable, but also involve a victim's emotional loss of something physical or psychological: the death of a loved one; lost limbs, eyesight, or fertility; physical scarring or crippling; or post-traumatic stress disorder.

Compensatory damages are most challenging when long-term impact on the victim is considered. Judgments about whether the life of a healthy child is more valuable than an octogenarian's, whether a supermodel's scar deserves more compensation than a roughneck's, or whether a runner's leg is more valuable than a typist's—all raise complex issues in assigning compensatory damages to victims.

SUGGESTED READING

Andrew Karmen, *Crime Victims: An Introduction to Victimology,* 6th ed. (Belmont, CA: Wadsworth, 2006), 319–22.

CASEY JORDAN

CONFLICT TACTICS SCALES. The Conflict Tactics Scales (CTS) are instruments for identifying domestic violence developed by Murray Straus and his colleagues in the early 1970s. Under the assumption that conflict is an inevitable aspect of life, the purpose of the CTS is to reveal tactics that people use to manage conflicts. After revisions and updates, the CTS have two main versions. The CTS2 includes scales for measuring three tactics of victimization and perpetration that are often used in conflicts between partners in a dating or marital relationship (physical assault, psychological aggression, and negotiation), and scales for measuring injury and sexual coercion. The CTSPC is for measuring different forms of maltreatment of a child by parents, including physical assault, psychological aggression, and non-violent discipline techniques. There are supplementary questions on neglect, sexual abuse, and discipline. In addition, both the CTS2 and the CTSPC have versions for child respondents and for adults to recall tactics used between their parents.

First used in 1972, the CTS have been translated into many languages and widely used particularly to obtain data on physical assaults against an intimate partner. Besides the two National Family Violence Surveys conducted in the United States in 1975 and 1985, the CTS have been used in numerous studies involving participants from diverse cultural backgrounds in the United States and in more than 20 countries around the world.

The CTS have made an important contribution to domestic violence research by enabling researchers to reveal the widespread phenomenon of domestic violence and improve understanding of the problem. Prior to the invention of the CTS, research on violence in families tended to focus on serious forms of violence with the implication that violence in the family was abnormal and grew out of some type of social or personal pathology. Studies using the CTS revealed high incidence of severe physical violence against children and spouses. The first national survey of family violence (1975) revealed that almost 60% of all children under the age of 18 experienced minor and severe violent acts by parents, and that 12% of married adults used violence against their spouses.

While the CTS have been extensively used, the scales have also been criticized. One of the criticisms came from feminist scholars who charged that the design of the CTS was flawed because the scales did not take into account the context and the meaning of violence (e.g., attack or self-defense). Many studies using the CTS showed the sexual symmetry of marital violence, meaning that wives/female partners were as violent as husbands/male partners. These results were contrary to domestic violence statistics, which showed that wives or female partners were often victims of violence by husbands or male partners. To offset this problem, studies using the CTS often added a set of questions asking information about the context and meaning of violence.

SUGGESTED READING

Russell P. Dobash and Rebecca E. Dobash, "The Myth of Sexual Symmetry in Marital Violence," *Social Problems* 39 (1992): 71–91; Murray A. Straus, "Measuring Intrafamily Conflict and Violence: The Conflict Tactics Scales," *Journal of Marriage and the Family* 41 (1979): 75–88; Murray A. Straus et al., "The Revised Conflict Tactics Scales (CTS2): Development and Preliminary Psychometric Data," *Journal of Family Issues* 17 (1996): 283–316.

HOAN N. BUI

CORRECTIONAL OFFICIALS. Correctional officials have long been responsible for the offenders who victimize others but only recently has the field of corrections recognized and accepted its responsibility to the victims of those offenders. Today, their service to crime victims includes protecting them from intimidation and harassment, notifying them of offender status, providing avenues for victim input into release decisions, and collecting restitution.

Correctional agency mission statements have been rewritten to include statements promising to protect public safety and reduce the risk of repeat criminal behavior through incarceration and community supervision decisions based on applicable laws, victims' interests, public safety, and related principles.[1] In addition, crime victims are being asked to join advisory committees and agency boards, become official members of parole boards, and serve as teachers in innovative classes that sensitize offenders to the impact of their offenses.[2]

In 1986, the issue of corrections-based victim services was first raised by the American Correctional Association in a broad policy statement that said victims should be treated with dignity and respect and should be notified about the status of their offender.[3] More recently, many states have adopted victims' rights amendments, legislation, and policies that have enhanced victims' rights and services in adult and juvenile corrections agencies, and paroling authorities. In 1997, the Association of State Correctional Administrators identified 10 core elements for corrections-based victim services as essential to good practice. With these guidelines for good practice, correctional agencies have moved forward creating linkages with victims[4] and giving them a voice in the postsentence phase of their cases.

Victim notification of the release or pending release of convicted offenders is the oldest linkage between correctional agencies and victims. However there is no consistent victim notification system in use across the country. Some correctional agencies notify victims of only certain types of inmate releases whereas others notify victims of changes in offender classification while the offender is still incarcerated. Some notify victims of an inmate's escape whereas others notify victims of an inmate's clemency or death.[5]

Most states have passed laws that either provide for community notification of sexual offender release or authorize the general public or certain individuals or organizations to access sexual offender registries.[6] Correctional agencies play a major role in providing this service by determining when and to where sex offenders will be paroled and by conducting community outreach and public education projects.

Over the past decade the number of educational programs in correctional institutions that involve both offenders and victims has greatly increased. These programs, which reflect a restorative justice philosophy, help offenders understand the devastating impact their crimes have on victims and their families and friends, their communities, and themselves and their own families.[7] They are primarily used in property crime cases or juvenile cases and give the victims an opportunity to engage in a structured dialogue with their offenders who have already admitted their guilt or have been convicted/adjudicated.[8]

Many correctional agencies encourage inmates to fulfill restitution obligations while they are incarcerated. These agencies help increase collections by offering incentives for participation in the form of increased visitation, increased prison commissary visits, and priority enrollment in certain programs.[9]

NOTES

1. Frank Schmalleger and John Ortiz Smykla, *Corrections in the 21st Century,* 2nd ed. (Blacklick, OH: McGraw Hill, 2005), 512.

2. Ibid, 513.

3. Edward Rhine, ed., *Excellence in Corrections: Best Practices* (Alexandria, VA: American Correctional Association Press, 1998), 471.

4. Ibid.

5. The National Center for Victims of Crime, "For Victim Services in Corrections," http://www.ncvc.org.

6. Schmalleger and Smykla, *Corrections,* 515.

7. Kip Kautzky, *Victim Impact Panels: The Restorative Justice Way* (Middletown, CT: ASCA Press, 2000), 141.

8. Schmalleger and Smykla, *Corrections,* 518.

9. The National Center for Victims of Crime, "For Victim Services in Corrections," http://www.ncvc.org, 14.

SUGGESTED READING

American Probation and Parole Association, "Promising Victim-Related Practices and Strategies in Probation and Parole," http://www.appa-net.org; The Association of State Correctional Administrators, "Action Partnerships for Corrections-Based Victims Services," http://www.asca.net.

MARY PARKER

CORRUPTION. As this entry is being written, the governor of Illinois stands arrested and accused of corruption—attempting to sell the senate seat recently vacated by President Barak Obama.[1] Misfeasance of office is only one example of the kinds of corrupt acts committed by public officials that may not have named persons as victims, but neither are they so-called victimless crimes. Following Michael Johnston,[2] corruption is perpetrated for (a) attaining or increasing power, (b) obtaining benefits (e.g., goods, services, and money), or (c) both power and benefits. Further, *unilateral corruption* is perpetrated between or among government officials (e.g., cover-ups, falsification of public records); *transactional corruption* is perpetrated between a government official(s) and a nongovernment person(s) or entity (e.g. extortion, bribery, kickbacks).

The victims of corruption might include persons extorted by a corrupt police officer to avoid traffic citations or by a corrupt building inspector threatening significant delay in the opening of one's business, thus preventing start of any cash flow for the entrepreneur. Somewhat more subtle is the bribery of legislators to select certain vendors, including possibly under-qualified contractors (who, for example, might deliver poorly functioning military weapons). All of us are victimized through higher prices or taxes for all kinds of goods and services and the transportation thereof because the funds for lobbying, bribing, or succumbing to extortion must be recovered by the manufacturer/vendor in the eventual selling price.[3]

An oft-used question asked of recruits in police academies is, "What's wrong with taking a free cup of coffee or a discount on a meal?" A discourse on the economics of police pay today or on the "slippery slope" concept is beyond the scope of this entry; however, the following is suggested: While police officers gather at the free or discount provider, they are not giving equal protection to providers of similar goods and services who do not offer the same free or discounted merchandise.

While documenting the work of the Knapp Commission, the eminent criminologist Lawrence Sherman[4] noted that when corruption in an area reaches an intermediate level of existence, the public becomes emboldened to openly offer bribes because the chances are (a) greater that the bribe will be accepted and a concomitant benefit bestowed than (b) the offer will be rejected and a concomitant penalty (arrest) will be assessed.

When corruption is uncovered, victimization also blankets many totally moral, ethical, and legally acting persons who share some common identifying factor— same uniform, same employer, same occupation (i.e., guilt by association). The public becomes immediately suspicious of other police officers, building inspectors, members of Congress, or whoever they may be when the corruption of one of their own is the subject of the evening news.

Whether unilateral or transactional, corruption involves acts by public officials. When we become suspicious of our public officials, we lose (even more) faith and confidence in those with great power to affect significantly the quality of our lives. In a nationally syndicated column, John Stossel[5] recently wrote, "Government corruption is legal thievery." We come full circle, therefore, to our original question: Who does corruption hurt? *Everyone!*

NOTES

1. Monica Davey, *The New York Times.* December 10, 2008.

2. Michael Johnston, *Political Corruption and Public Policy in America* (Belmont, CA: Wadsworth, 1982).

3. Ibid.

4. Lawrence W. Sherman, *Police Corruption: A Sociological Perspective* (New York: Doubleday, 1974); Johnston, *Political Corruption,* ch. 4.

5. John Stossel, "Government Corruption is Legal Thievery," *Tyler Morning News,* December 20, 2008, 4A.

SUGGESTED READING

William L. Miller, Ase B. Grodeland, and Tatyana Y. Koshechkina, "Are the People Victims or Accomplices? The Use of Presents and Bribes to Influence Officials in Eastern Europe," *Crime, Law and Social Change* 29, no. 4 (1998): 273–310.

PETER W. PHILLIPS

COSTS OF CRIME. The results of criminal activity cause enormous costs for offenders, society, and victims of crime. While the offender costs are often paid for by taxpayers, the costs to victims and society are frequently irreparable and rarely restored. Costs of crime are difficult to measure outside of the financial realm, but crime costs comprise multiple facets, including tangible costs and intangible costs.

Tangible costs include medical expenses, damaged or lost property values, and work-related expenses. Medical expenses include the health costs of treating victims' and offenders' injuries and can range from minimal expenses for a less violent crime to vast expenses for severe and long-term damage from a violent crime. Damaged or lost property value costs may be estimated and possibly be paid for by insurance or through restitution, but victims will be unable to recoup the emotional value of an item. Work expenses include time taken off from work to recover from being victimized; loss of transportation (stolen automobiles); loss of production and output; and possibly loss of a job for missing work due to court time, psychological damage, or even bodily injury.

Tangible costs also include the costs of the criminal justice system itself: police time and activity, prosecution salary and costs, court costs, jury service costs, legal aid, probation services, prison services, and injury compensation costs. The cost of the criminal justice system is contingent on the severity of criminal activity. For example, if an individual is a victim of a violent crime, the trial, sentence, and probation period will be longer for the offender, and will increase the cost of the criminal justice system. Similarly, if the offender is not quickly apprehended, the cost of investigation and police time is greater.

Intangible costs are often the most severe, are difficult to measure, and include costs that will never be recouped. These costs include pain, trauma, fear, lost quality of life, and relationship damage. The pain of crime includes physical and emotional damage. This damage may last a lifetime and is especially detrimental for victims of violent crimes and sexual assaults. Costs to attend to this pain include medical or health care as well as psychological aspects that may call for counseling, therapy, or holistic services.

Victims of crime may also experience post-traumatic stress disorder, which causes flashbacks, violent nightmares, and uncontrollable levels of trauma and fear. Victims of crime may alter their behavior due to the fear of being victimized again. They often become depressed, are afraid to go out of the house, and alter their life patterns. For example, if an individual has been the victim of a burglary, he might not want to live in the same house or be in the house at night. He may move locations, stay with friends and family, or isolate himself from society. This will lead to a decreased quality of life for the victim and might indirectly affect his family and friends.

Of extreme importance is the victim's relationship with intimate others. Depending on the severity of the crime and the emotional damage of the victim, she may internalize her experience out of fear, become quiet and withdrawn, or conversely become aggressive and defensive. Victims often feel as if they are to blame for the incident and sometimes become the recipients of blame or mistreatment from their partners, in particular, rape victims, sexual assault victims, and violent crime victims. At the time when they need others' support and companionship the most, victims find themselves unable to emotionally connect and trust other individuals. Relationships essentially become collateral damage as an indirect, intangible cost of crime.

Victims of crime often experience tremendous losses as a result of being victimized. The most significant cost of crime is the cost of the physical and emotional impact on victims, both direct victims and indirect victims of criminal activity. Though it is possible to place a dollar amount on the tangible costs that are a result of crime, it is much more difficult to price emotional and physical trauma and life alterations. Medical, life, and home insurance may cover tangible costs and sometimes cuts down on direct out-of-pocket costs. However, pain and suffering, lost quality of life, and the loss of intimate relationships are immeasurable. Between the cost of crime for offenders (the criminal justice system) and the cost of crime to victims (public assistance, tangible and intangible costs), crime has been speculated to cost upward of $500 billion a year.

SUGGESTED READING

Bureau of Justice Statistics, *Crime Data Brief: The Costs of Crime to Victims,* (Washington DC: U.S. Department of Justice, 2006); Robert C. Davis and Ellen Brinkman, "Supportive and Unsupportive Responses of Others to Rape Victims: Effects on Concurrent Victim Adjustment," *American Journal of Community Psychology* 19, no. 3 (1991): 443–52.

ALANA VAN GUNDY-YODER

COURT APPOINTED SPECIAL ADVOCATE (CASA). In 1974, the United States Congress enacted the Child Abuse Prevention and Treatment Act,[1] which gave fiscal, human, and technical assistance to states to combat child neglect and abuse. One of the main requirements of the act is the mandatory appointment of a *guardian ad litem* (GAL) that represents the interests of the abused or neglected child in all cases that result in judicial proceedings. The GAL is not required to be an attorney, but most states chose to use attorneys for this advocacy position.

In 1977, Judge David W. Soukup from King County Superior Court in Seattle, Washington, looked for alternatives to using attorneys as GALs due to attorney performance and high fees. Judge Soukup started using community volunteers who made long-term commitments to a child or children.[2] This program is called Court Appointed Special Advocates (CASA) and developed national recognition and adherence. In order to direct CASA's national presence, the National Court Appointed Special Advocate Association was developed in 1982. Currently, there are over 59,000 volunteers that serve 243,000 neglected and abused children and there are more than 900 local program offices throughout the nation.

"The mission of the National Court Appointed Special Advocate (CASA) Association, together with its state and local members, is to support and promote court-appointed volunteer advocacy for abused and neglected children so that they can thrive in safe, permanent homes."[3] These trained CASA volunteers are appointed by judges and usually assigned to only one child for the duration of the child's involvement in the court or welfare system, which allows the CASA to devote more time and consideration to the case than other involved parties.[4] Since CASAs have an unbiased interest in the child's welfare and placement into a safe and permanent home, judges rely on the information presented by CASAs when making legal decisions concerning the child.

CASAs have become very important actors in children's lives as they serve to protect them in a variety of ways. Responsibilities of advocates include listening to the concerns of the child, representation in legal proceedings as a guardian, preparing them for court and welfare proceedings, investigating the child's circumstance, fact finding, monitoring cases, information and resource advising, and mediation. Often, CASA volunteers will interview the child, parents, other family members, teachers, neighbors, friends, social workers, and other relevant people to determine the scope of the neglect and abuse problem and identify the child's needs.[5]

Even though the main function of CASA volunteers is to navigate the children through the criminal justice system and provide criminal justice actors with an impartial and detailed account of the circumstances, they also develop relationships of trust with the children serving as a protective factor in difficult times. Thus far, it appears that CASAs are adhering to their mission of ensuring neglected and abused children are safe and living in permanent homes by enhancing judicial knowledge of the children's situations.[6]

NOTES

1. United States Congress, *Child Abuse Prevention and Treatment Act* (42 USC 5101 et seq; 42 USC 5116 et seq, 1974).

2. National CASA Association, *Annual Report* (Seattle, WA: National Court Special Advocate Association, 2007).

3. National CASA Association, "About Us," http://www.nationalcasa.org/about_us/mission.html.

4. Pat Litzelfelner, "Consumer Satisfaction with CASAs (Court Appointed Special Adcovates)," *Children and Youth Services Review* 30, no. 2 (2008): 173–86.

5. Donald N. Duquette, *Advocating for the Child in Protection Proceedings* (Lexington, MA: Lexington Books, 1990).

6. Victoria Weisz and Nghi Thai, "The Court Appointed Special Advocate (CASA) Program: Bringing Information to Child Abuse and Neglect Cases," *Child Maltreatment* 8, no. 3 (2003): 204–10.

SUGGESTED READING

Sarah Carnochan et al., "Child Welfare and the Courts: An Exploratory Study of the Relationship Between Two Complex Systems," *Journal of Public Child Welfare* 1, no. 1 (2007): 117–36; Barrett J. Foerster, "Children without a Voice," *Juvenile and Family Court Journal* 42, no. 4 (1991): 9–23; Patrick Leung, "Is the Court-Appointed Special Advocate Program Effective? A Longitudinal Analysis of Time Involvement and Case Outcomes," *Child Welfare* 75, no. 3 (1996): 269–84.

MELINDA R. YORK

CREATIVE RESTITUTION. Creative restitution is a process whereby "an offender, under appropriate supervision, is helped to find some way to make amends to those he has hurt by his offense, and to 'walk a second mile' by helping other offenders."[1] During the 1950s, restitution programs existed in the United States, but these programs largely involved financial compensations made by offenders for the crimes they had committed. During the 1950s, Albert Eglash, a psychologist who worked with adults and juveniles in the criminal justice system, was dismayed by a process that was both sterile and ineffective.[2] As a means of creating more effective outcomes for the victim and offender, Eglash expanded restitution beyond mere monetary compensation. Over time, his innovations with restitution processes became known as *creative restitution*, which in turn, has been considered an early predecessor of current day restorative justice practices.[3] Creative restitution has several components.[4] First, this process is one that requires deliberate effort on the part of the offender. Second, the action must have constructive consequences for the victim or society. Third, the constructive aspects of the restitution process should be related to the actual offense.

One example of creative restitution involved a case where a burglar had stolen a prized family heirloom while filching their home. The heirloom was worth a moderate amount of money but had significant sentimental value. The burglar, during the restitution process, offered to not only provide monetary compensation for the item (a requirement of his probation) but also to visit the local pawn shops and black market fences in the area so that item could be located. Within a week, the family's heirloom had been returned intact and the burglar insisted on paying the financial compensation for the loss, though temporary it was. Further, that burglar was later known to provide assistance to other offenders who wished to engage in redemptive forms of restitution, becoming a local advocate for such programs. This example demonstrates how an offender may go well beyond the minimum required in purposeful manner, the goal being grounded more in psychological redemption than the fulfillment of minimal legal requirements. Such programs can alleviate guilt, anxiety, and the tendency for offenders to internalize a negative self-image.[5] In doing so, it is thought that this optimizes the chances of reform and thereby reduces the likelihood of future recidivism.

NOTES

1. Albert Eglash, "Creative Restitution: Some Suggestions for Prison Rehabilitation Programs," *American Journal of Correction* 20 (1958): 20–34, 20.

2. L. Mirsky, "Albert Eglash and Creative Restitution: A Precursor to Restorative Justice Practices," Restorative Justice E-Forum, Dec. (2003), 1–4, http://www.realjustice .org/library/eglash.html.

3. Ibid.

4. Ibid.

5. Ibid.

SUGGESTED READING

Albert Eglash, "Beyond Restitution: Creative Restitution," in *Restitution in Criminal Justice*, eds. Joe Hudson and Burt Galaway (Lexington, MA: Lexington Books, 1975).

ROBERT D. HANSER

CRIME PREVENTION. Crime prevention refers to a broad range of policies and activities directed toward reducing the likelihood that criminal events will occur. Crime prevention efforts are commonly classified according to the public health model of prevention as either primary, secondary, or tertiary.

Primary prevention includes strategies that attempt to address the fundamental causes of crime and victimization. It targets key social institutions such as the economy, family, education, or other entities that are linked in theory to criminal motivation. Primary prevention advocates attempt to direct resources toward strengthening institutions that stabilize communities and give residents a richer balance of legal opportunities for achieving social status and material success. Thus, primary preventions are designed to minimize the number of desperate and alienated people in an area and thereby reduce the likelihood that crime will ever occur.

Secondary prevention includes attempts to reduce crime or control crime victimization with interventions targeted toward controlling the most likely offender groups and reducing easy opportunities to commit crime. Some secondary prevention efforts seek to identify crime-prone groups or individuals and closely monitor the activity of such people to discourage them from engaging in criminal behavior. Other secondary prevention efforts are directed toward controlling physical or social situations that are believed to facilitate crime. Based on the work of Ronald V. Clarke and others, these types of prevention activities are collectively referred to as situational crime prevention. Situational crime prevention includes a broad array of tactics designed to increase the effort required to complete crimes, increase the risks associated with attempting crime, or reduce the benefits associated with completing a crime. Some situational prevention tactics emphasize individual or community awareness that is developed into defensive maneuvers designed to deflect crime. Other popular situational prevention tactics include altering the layout of physical spaces as illustrated by architect Oscar Newman's concept of defensible space in urban design, or as also embedded in the principles of C. Ray Jeffrey's crime prevention through environmental design (CPTED). Problem-oriented policing—an approach that attempts to integrate situational analysis into more proactive law enforcement activities—is also an example of a secondary prevention strategy.

Tertiary prevention generally refers to activities, procedures, or policies designed to control known offenders and keep them from reoffending. Unlike prevention efforts at the primary and secondary stages, prevention at the tertiary stage is most often reactive and designed to contain crime by isolating and incapacitating criminals after offenses have been committed. Many criminologists consider tertiary efforts such as imprisonment to be costly, inefficient strategies of last resort. However, some crime trend analysts such as economist Steven Levitt suggest that strategies involving incapacitation can be highly effective as a means of crime reduction. While the emphasis on tertiary prevention continues to be debated, most agree that tertiary activities are to some extent a necessary element of a comprehensive prevention system.

It is often argued that crime prevention efforts do not actually prevent crime as much as displace crime in time and space. Though prevention efforts may temporarily thwart criminal activity in one time frame or in one location, the criminal is likely to remain motivated to seek out crime opportunities at other times, new places, or using different methods. Several studies of the displacement phenomenon have been undertaken with the result that some measureable displacement has been observed. For example, in evaluations of prevention initiatives directed at street prostitution and drug dealing, David Weisburd and associates found little evidence that criminals moved to new neighborhoods, but they did observe a general diffusion of crime control benefits to surrounding areas. Most available research indicates that prevention efforts can be successful at accomplishing at least temporary reductions in crime while criminals adjust to changing conditions created by prevention strategies.

SUGGESTED READING

C. Ray Jeffrey, *Crime Prevention Through Environmental Design* (Beverly Hills, CA: Sage, 1971); Steven D. Levitt, "Understanding Why Crime Fell in the 1990s: Four

Factors that Explain the Decline and Six that Do Not," *Journal of Economic Perspectives* 18, no. 1 (2004): 163–90; Oscar Newman, *Creating Defensible Space* (Washington DC: U.S. Department of Housing and Urban Development, Office of Policy Development and Research, 1996); David Weisburd et al., "Does Crime Just Move Around the Corner? A Controlled Study of Spatial Displacement and Diffusion of Crime Control Benefits," *Criminology* 44, no. 3 (2006): 549–96.

EDWARD POWERS

CRIME PREVENTION THROUGH ENVIRONMENTAL DESIGN (CPTED).

Crime prevention through environmental design (CPTED) might best be defined as a concept that holds that the physical and social environment in which criminal offending occurs can be manipulated, designed, or altered in an attempt to reduce the frequency or severity of criminal behavior.[1]

CPTED assumes that criminal offending can be reduced by using the physical and social environment to increase the difficulty associated with criminal acts and by increasing the likelihood that offenders will be identified and apprehended. A number of strategies have been suggested to accomplish this goal. Natural surveillance refers to the use of design features to increase the visibility of potential crime targets, thereby reducing their risk of victimization.[2] Territorial reinforcement refers to the use of structural elements and landscape features to provide a sense of ownership and possession over property. Natural access control refers to reducing public access to private areas in an attempt to reduce their vulnerability.[3] CPTED provided a departure from other criminological theories as a result of its focus on crime prevention, its recognition that the physical environment had an influence on criminal offending, and its rejection of punitive crime control policies.[4]

C. Ray Jeffery[5] coined the phrase "crime prevention through environmental design," but many individuals are responsible for making contributions to the concept's growth and development. Elizabeth Wood investigated ways in which neighborhood aesthetics could be altered in order to make residents in public housing developments safer.[6] Jane Jacobs examined how the decline and physical deterioration of urban neighborhoods was related to criminal propensity.[7] Oscar Newman developed and advanced the concept of defensible space.[8] Schlomo Angel argued that human circulation patterns are associated with criminal behavior.[9] Ronald Clarke and others developed the situational crime prevention model.[10] To date, a number of empirical evaluations of CPTED philosophies have been conducted resulting in mixed results.[11]

NOTES

1. Ronald V. Clarke, "Situational Crime Prevention: Its Theoretical Basis and Practical Scope," in *Crime and Justice: An Annual Review of Research*, vol. 4, eds. Michael Tonry and Norval Morris (Chicago: University of Chicago Press, 1983), 225–56; Timothy

Crowe, *Crime Prevention Through Environmental Design: Applications of Architectural Design and Space Management Concepts,* 2nd ed. (Burlington, MA: Elsevier, 2000).

2. Richard H. Schneider, "Introduction: Crime Prevention Through Environmental Design (CPTED); Themes, Theories, Practice, and Conflict," *Journal of Architectural and Planning Research* 22 (2005): 271–83.

3. Ibid.

4. Ibid.

5. C. Ray Jeffery, *Crime Prevention Through Environmental Design* (Thousand Oaks, CA: Sage, 1971).

6. Oscar Newman, *Defensible Space: People and Design in the Violent City* (New York: MacMillan, 1973).

7. Jane Jacobs, *Death and Life of Great American Cities* (New York: Random House, 1961).

8. Newman, *Defensible Space.*

9. Schlomo Angel, *Discouraging Crime Through City Planning* (Berkely, CA: University of California Press, 1968).

10. Clarke, "Situational Crime Prevention."

11. Ralph B. Taylor, "Crime Prevention Through Environmental Design (CPTED): Yes, No, Maybe, Unknowable, and all of the Above," in *Handbook of Environmental Psychology,* eds. Robert Bechtel and Azra Churchman (New York: John Wiley, 2002), 413–26.

SUGGESTED READING

Paul J. Brantingham and Patricia L. Brantingham, eds., *Environmental Criminology* (Prospect Heights, IL: McGraw Hill, 1991); Marcus Felson, *Crime and Everyday Life,* 3rd ed. (Thousand Oaks, CA: Sage, 2002).

JASON JOLICOEUR

CRITICAL VICTIMOLOGY. Rob Mawby and Sandra Walklate developed the critical victimology perspective in the 1990s as a reaction to what they viewed as shortcomings in positivist victimology.[1] According to Walklate, positivist victimology suffers from an "overconcern with the culpable victim to its connections with a functionalist view of society."[2] Walklate also believed that feminist victimology alone was incapable of fully examining the issues of victimization. Gender was an important aspect, but in Walklate's view, it was also necessary to examine parts played by economics and social class.[3]

For Mawby and Walklate, missing from these earlier perspectives is a clear idea of what is "real." According to Mawby and Walklate, "any empirical investigation must take account of a number of processes which contribute to the construction of everyday reality: people's conscious activity, their 'unconscious' activity (that is, routine activities people engage in which serve to sustain, and sometimes change, the conditions in which they act), the generative mechanisms (unobservable and unobserved) which underpin daily life, and finally, both the intended and the unintended consequences of action which feed back into people's knowledge."[4]

Mawby and Walklate define critical victimology as "an attempt to examine the wider social context in which some versions of victimology are interwoven with questions of policy response and service delivery to victims of crime."[5] Walklate believes that it is important to draw on the framework of critical realism in determining our research agenda: "[T]his kind of framework postulates the importance of understanding the process that 'go on behind our backs' which contribute to the victims (and the crimes) we 'see' as opposed to those we do not 'see'. In other words, it ensures that we get beyond the 'mere appearance' of things."[6]

Critical to understanding Walklate's version of critical victimology, is developing an understanding of the term *victim*. Traditional victimological approaches fostered an unquestioning definition of victims, according to Walklate. "These are reflected in the work of those early victimologists whose typologies focused on either the personal characteristics of the victim . . . or the contribution that their behavior made to the commission of a crime . . . Arguably, this way of thinking about the victim reflects an underpinning view that there is a normal person measured against whom the victim somehow falls short."[7] There are "ideal" victims by which others are measured. Victims who do not fit the stereotype of an "ideal" victim are not as likely to receive the recognition and services.[8] There are also "many 'crimes' committed by wealthy or powerful individuals or even by nations [that] are not considered crimes. For example, genocide has occurred and is occurring in some countries, yet we do very little about it. Rape as a weapon of war has been reported in several countries. Abuse of power by those in control is very seldom mentioned as a crime in the media or other sources."[9] Six variables have consistently been found to be related to risk of victimization, "area of residence, class or status, race, gender, age, and marital status."[10]

Mawby and Walklate believe it is important to examine victimization internationally, in order to fully understand it and societal responses to crime and victims of crime. These authors believe that "The common feature of change for primitive societies and/or pre-industrial societies is the way in which the needs of state come to outweigh the needs of the community."[11] Some groups have been marginalized consistently in these cross-cultural comparisons, namely the poor, those who are young, and those who are female.[12]

NOTES

1. Rob I. Mawby and Sandra Walklate, *Critical Victimology: International Perspectives* (London: Sage, 1994), 17–21.

2. Sandra Walklate, "Appreciating the Victim: Conventional, Realist or Critical Victimology" (paper presented at the British Criminology Conference, Bristol), quoted in Sandra Walklate, "Researching Victims of Crime: Critical Victimology," *Social Justice* 17 (1990), 26.

3. Sandra Walklate, "Can There Be a Feminist Victimology?" in *Victimization: Theory, Research, and Policy,* eds. Pamela Davies, Peter Francis, and Victor Jupp (London: Palgrave, 2003) 42.

4. Mawby and Walklate, *Critical Victimology,* 18.

5. Ibid., 21.

6. Sandra Walklate, *Imagining the Victim of Crime* (London: Open University Press, 2007), 48.

7. Sandra Walklate, *Gender, Crime, and Criminal Justice* (Devon: Willan, 2004), 28.

8. Walklate, *Imagining the Victim of Crime,* 28.

9. Harvey Wallace, *Victimology: Legal, Psychological, and Social Perspectives,* 2nd ed. (Boston: Allyn and Bacon), 14.

10. Mawby and Walklate, *Critical Victimology,* 45.

11. Ibid., 68.

12. Ibid., 68.

SUGGESTED READING

Pamela Davies, Peter Francis, and Victor Jupp, *Victimisation: Theory, Research, and Policy* (New York: Palgrave Macmillan, 2003); Tammy C. Landau, *Challenging Notions: Critical Victimology in Canada* (Toronto: Canadian Scholars' Press, 2006); Sandra Walklate, ed., *Handbook of Victims and Victimology* (Devon: Willan, 2007).

JENNIFER WINGREN

CYBERANGELS.ORG. Launched in 1995 as a spin-off of the community-based Guardian Angels group, CyberAngels is a nonprofit online safety education program originally developed to assist individuals confronted with cyber threats.[1] Staffed completely by volunteers dedicated to the task of shielding Internet users from harm, CyberAngels is now one of the most comprehensive online safety education programs in the world. The CyberAngels program routinely collaborates with both public and private organizations in an effort to increase online safety education and support.[2]

In accordance with its mission of "keeping it safe," CyberAngels offers a variety of free services meant to increase individuals' knowledge of online threats and improve online security. Information ranging from cyber security awareness tips to anti-virus software installation procedures is readily available on the CyberAngels Web page, and recent technological advancements have made it possible for CyberAngels to provide virtual safety seminars on bullying, cyberbullying, and gangs to students, parents, and educators.[3] Additionally, CyberAngels volunteers work to locate and restrict access to pornography, report Web sites of a pedophilic nature, and monitor chat rooms to ensure that they remain safe for their users.[4]

CyberAngels is not a law enforcement agency and does not engage in enforcement activity. However, in cases where cybercrimes are uncovered by CyberAngels volunteers, all pertinent information is forwarded to the appropriate national or international law enforcement agency for further investigation.[5] Additionally, through the CyberAngels "Ask an Angel" program, CyberAngels volunteers provide information on laws, rights, and legal options to individuals who believe they have been victimized online.[6]

NOTES

1. CyberAngels, http://www.cyberangels.org.

2. Ibid.

3. Ibid.

4. National Law Enforcement and Corrections Technology Center, "Angels of the Internet," *TechBeat* 3 (2001).

5. Ibid.

6. CyberAngels Web site.

SUGGESTED READING

Berni Dwan, "Nice Kids Need Cyber-Angels," *Computer Fraud and Security* 7 (2001): 7; Erin English, "CyberAngels Unite on the Net," *Network Security* 8 (1995): 8; Scott Scheffler, "Angels of Cyber Space: The CyberAngels Cyber Crime Unit is Watching Over Victims of Internet Crimes," *Law Enforcement Technology* 33, no. 4 (2006): 32–35.

JENNIFER SCROGGINS

CYBERCRIME. Cybercrime generally refers to illegal activities involving the use of computers or computer networks. In the United States, most activities involving computers and computer networks are regulated by The National Information Infrastructure Protection Act of 1996 and subsequent revisions to section 1030 of the U.S. criminal code frequently referred to as "The computer fraud and abuse act" (18 U.S.C. § 1030). International efforts to regulate cybercrime activities include the Council of Europe Convention on Cybercrime and the United Nations World Summit on the Information Society (WSIS).

The criminal activity in cybercrime is commonly focused on theft, vandalism, or some form of forbidden communication. Thefts occur by breaking into protected computer information systems (hacking), by using e-mail systems or spoofed Web sites to trick people into disclosing valuable personal information (phishing), by circulating copyrighted material without permission (piracy), or by using computer networks to conduct confidence games or other forms of fraudulent activity. Vandalism occurs when criminals attempt to destroy information (e.g., through the spread of a computer virus), interrupt the functioning of an established computer network (e.g., denial of service attacks), or when access is used to deface public Web sites. Forbidden communication may include the disclosure of classified government information or corporate trade secrets, transmission of images or other digital materials that are banned from distribution (e.g., child pornography), or using the networks to communicate threats or misinformation for the purposes of terrorizing victims (e.g., cyberbullying). As with other crimes, victims of cybercrime can be governments or government agencies, corporations or privately owned business, and individuals.

Since the early 1990s, computer networks that form the Internet have created an easily accessible virtual place commonly called "cyberspace." As cyberspace continues to expand, more people are using the space for commerce, education, leisure, and other assorted activities. Increased legitimate activity in cyberspace is associated with comparable increases in illegitimate activity as criminals attempt to find victims where they are shopping, working, or otherwise spending their time. The worldwide accessibility of the Internet has made it possible for criminals to interact with a broader range of potential victims than would be possible in a more limited geographically confined physical space. Predators utilize Internet technology as an efficient way to isolate victims and facilitate crimes ranging from financial scams to child sexual abuse. The distant, impersonal nature of cyberspace interactions have also created valued commodities out of formerly less valuable items (e.g., the identity of an average person). Thus, the prevalence of identity theft has risen as a major threat to individuals in developed societies.

Motives for cybercrime vary as broadly as motives for most other types of crime and may include greed, dominance, vengeance, excitement, or attention seeking. Due to the high volume of monetary transactions that have shifted to the Internet, cybercrime has become a lucrative enterprise. The large investments made in the development of online assets have made government and corporate Web sites attractive targets for those who seek to attack these entities. Furthermore, successful attacks on online corporate and government properties can bring heavy publicity to these events and produce instant notoriety for the attackers.

Protecting potential victims from cybercrime presents challenges different from more traditional criminal activity. Cyberspace is practically boundless and thus difficult for authorities to monitor, patrol, and protect. The relative newness of cyberspace along with the diverse backgrounds of people who use the space have resulted in confusion about rules of conduct and jurisdictional disputes surrounding the investigation and prosecution of rule violations. The speed of transactions online and the near anonymity of individuals using cyberspace pose additional obstacles for conventional law enforcement and traditional crime prevention strategies.

In efforts to promote trust in cyberspace commercial transactions, private corporations have been instrumental in the development of strategies for detecting and thwarting online criminal activity. Government law enforcement agencies such as the FBI or INTERPOL have also allocated substantial resources to cyberspace crime prevention. Most prevention efforts have been directed toward educating Internet users and raising awareness about the potential risks involved in cyberspace activity. However, efforts have also been made to develop better reporting mechanisms for cyber offenses (e.g., the FBI's Internet Crime Complaint Center) and to operate proactive task forces that undermine online criminal activity.

SUGGESTED READING

Council of Europe Convention on Cybercrime, http://www.coe.int; Federal Bureau of Investigation (FBI), "The Internet Crime Complaint Center," http://www.ic3.gov/default.aspx; International Criminal Police Organization (INTERPOL), "Information Security and Crime Prevention," http://www.interpol.int/public/TechnologyCrime/CrimePrev; U.S. Department of Justice, "The Cybercrime and Intellectual Property Section," http://www.usdoj.gov/criminal/cybercrime/.

EDWARD POWERS

CYBERSTALKING. Cyberstalking is defined as the use of the Internet, e-mail, or other electronic communications devices to monitor another person.[1] These behaviors include the monitoring of public sites such as Facebook, checking someone's e-mail without permission, threatening someone through cyber mediums, and committing identity theft and sabotage. While many cyberstalking behaviors resemble physical stalking, there are two important differences. First, the identity of the perpetrator is often anonymous and, as a result, cyberstalkers are in the unique position to engage in deception tactics such as assuming a false identity. Second, through the use of electronic communication devices, cyberstalkers do not need to be in close proximity to their targets. However, although the Internet provides opportunities for perpetrators to target strangers, most monitoring transpires between people in a current or past romantic relationship.[2]

The exact prevalence of cyberstalking is difficult to determine because victims are often unaware of such behaviors, but anecdotal data and self-report measures have found that people are more often the targets of cyberstalking than traditional stalking. In addition, the two types of stalking also co-occur. Additionally, unlike physical stalking, which is primarily perpetrated by men,[3] both men and women appear to cyberstalk.[4]

Stalking, defined in a legal context, is the willful, malicious, and repeated harassing of another person, which includes a credible threat with intent to place that person in reasonable fear for his safety or the safety of her family.[5] This definition is difficult to apply to cyberstalking because it requires that victims are aware that they are being stalked and, as a result, experience reasonable fear. However, victims of cyberstalking may not be aware they are being targeted or who is responsible. In addition, it may be more difficult to prove "reasonable fear" because the behaviors are not being performed in person.

Despite these complexities California passed the first cyberstalking law in 1999. Forty-five states mention electronic communications in their harassment or stalking laws, while the remaining states use language that is broad enough to include cyberstalking.[6] In 2000, the Violence Against Women Act added cyberstalking to federal stalking legislation.[7] In 2008, Lori Drew, a woman in California, was convicted of creating a fake MySpace profile and bullying a teenage girl, which led to the victim's suicide. This landmark case suggests that cyberstalking is being considered seriously and legislated as Internet harassment. Future research is needed on the rates and kinds of behavior that comprise cyberstalking, the relationship between cyber and physical behaviors, and gender differences in cyberstalking.

NOTES

1. Brian H. Spitzberg and Gregory Hoobler, "Cyberstalking and the Technologies of Interpersonal Terrorism," *New Media & Society* 4, no. 1 (2002): 71–92.

2. Eileen M. Alexy et al., "Perceptions of Cyberstalking among College Students," *Brief Treatment and Crisis Intervention* 5 (2005): 279–89.

3. Patricia Tjaden and Nancy Thoennes, *Stalking in America: Findings from the National Violence against Women Survey* (Washington DC: National Institute of Justice and Centers for Disease Control and Prevention, 1998).

4. Alexy et al., "Perceptions of Cyberstalking," 279–89.

5. Violence Against Women Grants Office, *Stalking and Domestic Violence, Third Annual Report to Congress Under the Violence Against Women Act, (NCJ 172204)* (Washington DC: U.S. Department of Justice, 1998).

6. National Conference of State Legislatures, "State Computer Harassment or 'Cyberstalking' Laws," http://www.ncsl.org/programs/lis/cip/stalk99.htm.

7. National Institute of Justice, *Domestic Violence, Stalking, and Antistalking Legislation. Annual Report to Congress Under the Violence Against Women Act, (NCJ160943)* (Washington DC: U.S. Department of Justice, 2000).

SUGGESTED READING

Paul Bocij, *Cyberstalking: Harassment in the Internet Age and How to Protect Your Family* (Westport, CT: Praeger, 2004); Jayne A. Hitchcock, *Net Crimes & Misdemeanors:*

Outmaneuvering the Spammers, Swindlers, and Stalkers Who are Targeting You Online (Medford, NJ: CyberAge Books, 2002).

LAUREN REARDON AND CHITRA RAGHAVAN

CYCLE OF VIOLENCE. The term *cycle of violence* refers to the intergenerational transmission of violence. In other words, a childhood history of physical abuse predisposes individuals to the perpetration of violence during adulthood. There is strong evidence, for example, that childhood exposure to abusive parenting increases the probability that individuals will grow up to mistreat their own children. In a review of relevant research, Joan Kaufman and Edward Zigler[1] estimate that 30% of maltreated children grow up to abuse their children while only 2% of parents in the general population engage in child maltreatment. Therefore, parents who were abused as children are 15 times more likely to abuse their offspring than parents who were not themselves victims of child abuse. More recent research by Richard Heyman and Amy Slep[2] continues to find a clear relationship between being abused as a child and perpetrating abuse as an adult.

Exposure to harsh parenting increases involvement in various types of violence besides child abuse. Ronald Simons, Kuei-Hsiu Lin, and Leslie Gordon[3] found, for example, that having experienced abusive parenting predicted subsequent violence toward a romantic partner. Leslie Simons, Callie Burt, and Ronald Simons[4] found that exposure to harsh parenting was related to not only the perpetration of intimate partner violence but sexual coercion by males toward females as well. And, a longitudinal study by Cathy Widom and Michael Maxfield[5] found that being abused or neglected as a child increased the likelihood of arrest for a violent crime by 30%.

Ironically, women who were victims of harsh parenting often grow up to be the victims of violence by their romantic partners. In a meta-analysis of 39 studies, Sandra Stith and others[6] showed that childhood exposure to harsh parenting was a much stronger predictor of being the victim of spouse abuse than was witnessing marital violence between one's own parents. This does not mean that all abused women were abused as children. In fact, over half of abused women were not subjected to harsh treatment by parents. It does appear to be the case, however, that exposure to abusive parents increases the probability of being married to an abusive husband. This pattern is commonly referred to as the "double jeopardy" of women. They escape the violence in their family of origin only to encounter further violence in their marriage. Ronald Simons, Leslie Simons, and Lora Wallace[7] suggest that double jeopardy occurs because women exposed to abusive parenting often engage in delinquent and antisocial behavior. Since people usually affiliate with persons similar to themselves, these women tend to become romantically involved with and marry antisocial men. Unfortunately, antisocial males are at risk for violence toward their romantic partners.

It is important to remember that most abused children do not grow up to become violent adults. For example, although childhood maltreatment is a potent risk factor for becoming an abusive parent, 70% of abused children do not go on to abuse their own children. Research has revealed that abused mothers who do not mistreat their own children either had access to a supportive nonabusive adult as a child or a stable satisfying relationship with a romantic partner in adulthood. In this way the cycle of violence can be broken.

NOTES

1. Joan Kaufman and Edward Zigler, "Do Abused Children Become Abusive Parents?" *American Journal of Orthopsychiatry* 57 (1987): 186–92.

2. Richard E. Heyman and Amy M. Slep, "Do Child Abuse and Interparental Violence Lead to Adulthood Family Violence?" *Journal of Marriage and Family* 64, no. 4 (2002): 864–70.

3. Ronald L. Simons, Kuei-Hsiu Lin, and Leslie C. Gordon, "Socialization in the Family of Origin and Male Dating Violence: A Prospective Study," *Journal of Marriage and Family* 60, no.2 (1998): 467–78.

4. Leslie G. Simons, Callie H. Burt, and Ronald L. Simons, "A Test of Explanations for the Effect of Harsh Parenting on the Perpetration of Dating Violence and Sexual Coercion among College Males," *Violence and Victims* 23 (2008): 66–82.

5. Cathy S. Widom and Micheal G. Maxfield, *An Update on the Cycle of Violence Research in Brief* (Washington DC: U.S. Department of Justice, National Institute of Justice, 2001).

6. Sandra M. Stith et al., "The Intergenerational Transmission of Spouse Abuse: A Meta-Analysis," *Journal of Marriage and Family* 62, no. 3 (2000): 640–54.

7. Ronald L. Simons, Leslie G. Simons, and Lora E. Wallace, *Families, Delinquency, and Crime: Linking Society's Most Basic Institution to Antisocial Behavior* (New York, NY: Oxford University Press, 2004).

SUGGESTED READING

Denise A. Hines and Kathleen Malley-Morrison, *Family Violence in the United States: Defining, Understanding, and Combating Abuse* (Thousand Oaks, CA: Sage, 2005).

LESLIE GORDON SIMONS

D

DARK FIGURE OF CRIME. The "dark figure" of crime, also known as the "hidden figure" of crime, refers to all crimes that are not formally captured in official police data, typically disseminated in the form of the Uniform Crime Reports. The "dark figure" of crime exists for at least two reasons. First, not all crimes that are reported are officially recorded by the police. Donald Black, for example, found that the legal seriousness of the crime, the complainant's preferences, the relational distance between the victim and offender, the complainant's deference, and the complainant's status all influence whether a report is formally recorded.[1] Second, the "dark figure" of crime exists because not all crimes are reported to the police. The National Crime Victimization Survey (NCVS) is used to calculate estimates of the magnitude of the "dark figure" of crime. Based on NCVS data, for example, the Department of Justice estimates that only about 10% of all rapes and attempted rapes are reported each year to the police.[2] Reporting rates for motor vehicle thefts, however, is among the highest.[3] In 2007, NCVS data showed that "46 percent of all violent victimizations and 37 percent of all property crimes were reported to the police, while 66 percent of robbery and 57 percent of aggravated assaults were reported."[4] Data from 2007 also showed that "the percentage of robberies (66%) reported to the police was higher than the percentage of rape or sexual assaults (42%) and simple assaults (41%)."[5] The data, furthermore, showed that only "50 percent of burglaries and 31 [percent] of household thefts were reported."[6]

NOTES

1. Donald Black, "Production of Crime Rates," *American Sociological Review* 35, no. 4 (1970): 733–48.

2. Department of Justice, *Sourcebook of Criminal Justice Statistics* (Washington DC: Department of Justice, 2003).

3. Michael R. Rand, *Criminal Victimization, 2007* (Washington DC: Department of Justice, 2008).

4. Department of Justice, *Violent Crime Rate in 2007 at About the Same Level in 2005* (Washington DC: Department of Justice, 2008).

5. Rand, *Criminal Victimization, 2007*.

6. Ibid.

SUGGESTED READING

Carolyn Rebecca Block and Richard L. Block, 1984. "Crime Definition, Crime Measurement, and Victim Surveys." *Journal of Social Issues* 40, no. 1 (1984): 137–60.

CONNIE FREY

DEATH NOTIFICATION. Death notification represents the process by which people learn of the death of a family member or friend. Because the death notification frequently serves as the first communication about the death of a family member, it can carry enormous emotional significance for the survivors. In this respect, caring and compassionate notifications can help the survivors to begin to engage the layers and meaning of the loss. Conversely, an unprepared or poorly delivered death notification can have the unintended consequences of making the loss more painful or traumatic and can thereby secondarily victimize the survivor(s).

Generally, deaths that involve elements of: (1) suddenness or surprise, (2) a violent end of life, (3) preventability or avoidability, and (4) untimeliness can pose challenges for the notifiers and for those who will receive the tragic news. Contrast the expected death of a long-ill elderly person in a hospital setting with family members gathered around with the death of a teenage driver in a drunk-driving vehicular crash as the parents drive up to the scene. For deaths that occur in medical settings, the personnel and facilities for performing a supportive death notification may be readily available. For nonhospital deaths other first responders such as law enforcement, fire, emergency medical technicians, or clergy may be called upon to deliver a notification.

A core set of seven tasks makes up a caring and compassionate notification regardless of who performs the notification or the setting in which the notification is delivered.[1] First, the notifiers must accurately identify the deceased and the survivors to be notified, taking care to both gather and provide the most accurate information possible. Second the notifiers should make personal contact with the survivors and, if at all possible, avoid performing the notification by telephone or other impersonal means. Third, the survivors are provided with information about the events leading to the death, the injuries that were sustained, and medical treatments provided. Fourth, the actual death notice occurs by telling survivors that death has occurred (using unequivocal terms like *death, died, killed,* etc.). Fifth, a compassionate notification involves supporting survivors' grief reactions and providing immediate emotional or physical assistance. Sixth, some notifiers (e.g., within a hospital or mortuary) will be required to facilitate the survivors' choices about viewing the body shortly after the notification. Finally, notifiers should be prepared to provide information, referral assistance, and follow-up care.

Professionals who regularly perform death notifications should obtain formal training through an academy, professional conferences, or organizations such as Mothers Against Drunk Driving. Notifiers also should develop a personal philosophy about death and should develop ways of dealing with the stresses of death notification so that they and the survivors that they serve do not become secondary victims of the notification process.

NOTE

1. Janice Harris Lord and Alan E. Stewart, *I'll Never Forget Those Words: A Practical Guide for Death Notification* (Burnsville, NC: Compassion Books, 2008).

SUGGESTED READING

Janice Harris Lord, *No Time for Goodbyes,* 6th ed. (Burnsville, NC: Compassion Books, 2006); Alan E. Stewart, "Complicated Bereavement and Posttraumatic Stress Disorder Following Fatal Car Crashes: Recommendations for Death Notification Practice," *Death Studies* 23 (1999): 289–321; Alan E. Stewart, Janice Harris Lord, and Dorothy L. Mercer, "Death Notification Education: A Needs Assessment Study," *Journal of Traumatic Stress* 14 (2001): 221–27.

ALAN STEWART

DEFENSE ATTORNEYS. The defense attorney is charged with the responsibility of protecting the rights of the accused; it is a protection that is guaranteed by law. The right to counsel is constitutionally guaranteed for most, but not all criminal offenses. If the sentence is less than six months, counsel is not guaranteed. We have seen the importance of counsel in many high-profile cases. However, these high-profile cases are really aberrations; they do not reflect the reality of the criminal courts and the defense attorney.

Like the emergence of the court system and the prosecuting attorneys' office, the prominence of the defense attorney can be traced back to the early 1900s.

With urbanization, the office of the prosecuting attorney emerged. There was a corresponding proliferation in the number of defense attorneys. These defense attorneys were politically connected, and it was not uncommon for defense attorneys to "dicker away" jail time for cash. Historians reveal that they were pretty brazen—in that they would stand outside the courtroom with signs pronouncing what type of "justice" they could deliver with cash!

Today, things have changed, but the "politics" of pursuing justice remains. With rare exception, defense attorneys are in effect agent mediators. On the one hand, they are charged with protection of the defendant; on the other hand, they have an allegiance to the court bureaucracy and the courtroom workgroup. Who are the members of the courtroom workgroup? They are judges and prosecuting attorneys and other defense attorneys. The defense attorney recognizes that he has far greater intellectual, professional, and educational ties to the courtroom workgroup, than with the lowly defendant. The defense attorney's role then is to create the impression that justice is "being done," and that the defendant is getting good representation. While doing all of this, the defense attorney's role is to also prepare the defendant for defeat through stage management, and eventually encouraging the defendant to plead guilty. By virtue of the relationship with the courtroom workgroup, defense attorneys learn early on that their clients are at the very least factually guilty. With this allegiance to the workgroup, the defense attorney views the defendant as someone who is here today and gone tomorrow, but the relationship with the courtroom workgroup has to continue.

The point to be made here is that defense attorneys, as members of the workgroup, have stronger ties to the court, and the organizational priorities of the court are not always due process. The defense attorney (working in concert with other members of the workgroup) has two goals, one external and the other internal. Internally, the workgroup is concerned with cohesion—as cases are processed. Externally, the goal is to create the impression that justice is being done. With this practice in mind, crime victims are rarely a concern and are clearly not priorities for the court bureaucracy. As evidence, defense attorneys are notorious for asking for postponements, designed to wear down the victim. In all, we are all victimized by a system that hinges on impression management, with ideals that may not include the principles of justice.

SUGGESTED READING

Abraham Blumberg, "The Practice of Law as a Confidence Game," *Law and Society Review* 1 (1967): 15–39.

ROBERT L. BING

DEFENSIBLE SPACE. Defensible space[1] is a concept that relies on the restructuring of the physical layout of communities so that persons who live in those communities can practice self-help, rather than relying solely on the police for protection. By bringing citizen involvement to bear on the problems of crime, a level of crime prevention remains even when government support wanes or is withdrawn. Since the impact of the area is different for residents and offenders, Oscar Newman believed that the arrangement of space could portray to potential offenders that the space was protected by the residents.

Based on his analysis of public housing, Newman divided space into four areas—public, semi-public, semi-private, and private—based on his analysis of the differing types of space in public housing. Space was divided based on its use. If the space was open to the public for a variety of uses, it was designated public. Space with a limited number of uses was designated as semi-public. As space was restricted to residents, and had fewer uses, it was designated as semi-private. Private space was reserved for residents and used personally by residents and invited guests.

Newman reasoned that as space became more private, individuals would have more ownership of the space and be more aware of who should be in the space and who should not. Increased surveillance by persons living in the community would reduce anonymity, which should lead to a reduction in crime. As space became more private, the knowledge of who was supposed to be in that space and who was not would lead to increased deterrence of criminal activity. By restructuring the layout of public housing from an architectural standpoint, the resulting increase in citizen effectiveness should reduce escape routes used by offenders. In the updated version of Newman's book[2] he noted that serious reductions in crime rates including serious crimes were achieved by reducing pedestrian travel routes, improving lighting, and dividing the complex into separate spaces.

The concept of defensible space, however, is not without its criticisms. Newman was concerned with modifications to the external physical environment, which, in turn, would produce changes to the external social environment. He did little to address the issue of the internal physical environment of the offender. Newman focused his recommendations on lowering the height of buildings; making public areas visible to residents; increasing lighting, fences, and barriers; and installing entry phones. He also advocated the hiring of concierges and porters to assist residents.

Nevertheless, Newman's work was highly influential. Government agencies and architects used his principles in designing the newest and most modern of public housing units across the country. Neighborhoods in major cities such as Atlanta, Georgia, Richmond, Virginia, and St. Louis, Missouri, used defensible space principles in limiting traffic and encouraging resident associations in new subdivisions in an effort to reduce crime and victimization.

NOTES

1. Oscar Newman, *Defensible Space: Crime Prevention Through Urban Design* (New York: Macmilan, 1972).

2. Oscar Newman, *Creating Defensible Space* (Washington DC: U.S. Department of Housing and Urban Development, 1996).

SUGGESTED READING

Robert Ellickson, "Controlling Chronic Misconduct in City Spaces: Of Panhandlers, Skid Rows, and Public-Space Zoning," *The Yale Law Journal* 105, no. 5 (1996): 1165–1248; Ronald V. Clarke, "Situational Crime Prevention: Its Theoretical Basis and Practical Scope," *Crime and Justice* 4 (1983): 225–56.

JAMES W. GOLDEN

DEFOUNDING. Defounding is a discretionary tactic commonly used by criminal justice professionals to decrease the seriousness of an offense through reclassification. The reasons defounding occurs vary, as does its impact on the victim.

First, defounding may occur when there is insufficient evidence to support the original account of a crime. For instance, a police officer is dispatched to a "robbery" at a local convenience store, only to discover that a juvenile shoplifted a candy bar and immediately departed. The proper classification of the incident would be petty larceny (i.e., theft). Of course, the victim who reported the theft may have informed the dispatcher, "I was just robbed." If the officer delicately explains the criminal law distinction, the victim may better appreciate the reasoning behind the defounding.

Second, defounding may be used to reduce criminal charges. This form of "street plea bargaining" occurs when the officer provides leniency to the offender (e.g., reducing the speed on a speeding ticket) without consultation with the prosecutor. This form of defounding is the result of offender cooperation and has little negative impact on the victim (i.e., state, county, etc.).

Third, defounding may occur when police agencies manipulate crime statistics. For instance, if an agency wishes to demonstrate the success of a burglary prevention program, responding officers may reclassify (i.e., defound) the incident as "trespassing." Victims suffer from this deceptive accounting method since valid burglary prevention measures may be hindered (e.g., a homeowner believes that burglary is no longer a problem and is lulled into a false sense of security).

Fourth, defounding occurs when the prosecutor believes that reclassification of a crime will encourage a plea bargain or provide an easy conviction (e.g., reducing a rape charge to sexual assault). The difficulty arises when the victim is not consulted or disagrees with the defounding tactic.

SUGGESTED READING

Richard McCleary, Barbara C. Nienstedt, and James M. Erven, "Uniform Crime Reports as Organizational Outcomes: Three Time Series Experiments," *Social Problems* 29 (1982): 361–72; Eric Pooley and Elaine Rivera, "One Good Apple," *Time,* January 15, 1996: 54.

TOD BURKE

DOMESTIC ELDER ABUSE. Estimates state that between 1 and 2 million adults age 65 or older have been injured, exploited, or otherwise mistreated by someone on whom they depend for care or protection. Further, data show that 1 of 14 incidents of abuse come to the attention of authorities.

Elder abuse, like the other forms of family violence, is often hidden by the day-to-day lives of families. Elder abuse by adult children or caretakers can take many forms including physical abuse, sexual abuse, emotional or psychological abuse, neglect, and abandonment. Some patterns of abuse contain all the elements, but others just one. No matter which element occurs in a situation, the elderly, just like children and victims of intimate partner abuse, find themselves in a context of coercion and control.

The context of coercion and control is defined by an ongoing living situation in which the person who is being victimized does not know when the abuse will occur. Will this be the night she does not receive her supper? Will this be the night her son or daughter beats her before bed? This context produces long-term psychological, emotional, and physical consequences for the elderly, often shortening their lives.

Victimization of the elderly happens more often to women than to men. Older women (67%) are far more likely than men (32%) to suffer from abuse, and slightly more than half of the alleged perpetrators of elder abuse were female (53%).[1] This may, in fact, be due to the longer lives of women but is more likely related to other patterns of victimization of women in our culture. In the 2004 survey, Adult Protective Services (APS) received a total of 565,747 reports of elder abuse of persons age 60 and older, and vulnerable adult abuse for persons of all ages, from all 50 states plus Guam and the District of Columbia—and investigated 461,135 reports. Of that number, APS substantiated 191,908, representing a 16% increase from the 2000 survey.[2]

States usually respond to vulnerable adults who might be abused through the offices of Adult Protective Services, the state agency that sees to the safety of the elderly. Adult Protective Services have jurisdiction over all cases of abuse for persons between 18 and 59; nearly 70% of the caseload involves elder abuse. As with other types of crimes against vulnerable populations, the criminal justice response is mixed. Best practice calls for specialized law enforcement personnel to work with the elderly and that local law enforcement is trained in the specific methods to deal with the elderly.

NOTES

1. Pamela B. Teaster et al., "Abuse of Adults Age 60+: The 2004 Survey of Adult Protective Services" (Washington DC: National Center on Elder Abuse, 2006), 7.

2. Ibid, 6.

SUGGESTED READING

Richard J. Bonnie and Robert B. Wallace, *Elder Mistreatment: Abuse, Neglect, and Exploitation in an Aging America* (Washington DC: National Academies Press, 2002); Lisa Nerenberg, *Elder Abuse Prevention: Emerging Trends and Promising Strategies* (New York: Springer, 2007); Karl Pillemer and David Finkelhor, "The Prevalence of Elder Abuse: A Random Sample Survey," *The Gerontologist* 28 (1988): 51–57; National Center on Elder Abuse Administration on Aging Web site, http://www.ncea.aoa.gov.

PAMELA JENKINS

DOMESTIC MINOR SEX TRAFFICKING. Domestic minor sex trafficking is the human trafficking of children under the age of 18 through commercial sexual activity in the United States. The federal government made the abolition of trafficking a new priority in 2000 with the passing of the Trafficking Victim Protection Act (TVPA). The original focus of the act was on people trafficked into the United States to work in contemporary servitude or slave-like conditions. In the 2005 reauthorization, the TVPA expanded its definition of victims to include domestic minors. Domestic minors are all persons under the age of 18, U.S. citizens or not, who are engaged in commercial sex acts. Commercial sex acts include prostitution, stripping, and pornography, all activities that are illegal in every U.S. state for anyone under 18. Traditionally these victims were referred to as child prostitutes or juvenile delinquents. The TVPA specifies that minors engaged in commercial sex acts should be considered victims of a severe form of trafficking. The act also emphasizes that trafficking victims should be protected rather than punished even if they participated in illegal activities; trafficking victims should not be incarcerated for unlawful acts committed as a direct result of being trafficked.

Although children who are trafficked through prostitution are recognized as victims by U.S. federal law, they are actually being incarcerated and punished for their own sexual exploitation. For example, in Las Vegas, Nevada, 150–200 minors are being arrested and pulled into the juvenile justice system each year for prostitution-related charges.[1] Many of these girls and boys charged with prostitution-related offenses are below the legal age of consent for sex in Nevada. Children as young as 12 are arrested for being involved in prostitution in Las Vegas.

Whereas professionals recognize the exploitation of domestic minor sex trafficking victims, few resources are available to assist these victims.[2] One challenge to helping children out of prostitution is their attachment to their traffickers or pimps. Most children exploited through prostitution have a pimp or trafficker that has forced or coerced them into the commercial sex trade.[3] The juvenile justice system often considers incarceration as an acceptable way to remove domestic minor sex trafficking victims from the physical and psychological control of their traffickers.

Another challenge is that victims require a comprehensive strategy of services to deal with multiple traumas experienced through commercial sexual exploitation.[4] Exploited children need food, clothing, and safe shelter. They also require medical care, psychological and trauma therapy, education, life-skills training, and self-esteem counseling. Very few programs exist in the United States that can address the complex issues faced by children exploited through domestic sex trafficking.

NOTES

1. M. Alexis Kennedy and Nicole Joey Pucci, *Las Vegas Assessment: Identification of Domestic Minor Sex Trafficking Victims and Their Access to Services* (Arlington, VA: Shared Hope International, 2008), 2, http://www.sharedhope.org/dmst/documents/ FINALAssessment_LasVegas_000.pdf.

2. Shared Hope, *National Fact Sheet* (Arlington, VA: Shared Hope International, 2008), 3, http://www.sharedhope.org/dmst/documents/FINAL_FactSheet_National.pdf.

3. Richard J. Estes and Neil Alan Weiner, *The Commercial Sexual Exploitation of Children in the U.S., Canada, and Mexico* (Philadelphia: University of Pennsylvania, 2001), 7, http://www.sp2.upenn.edu/~restes/CSEC._Files/Exec_Sum_020220.pdf.

4. Ibid, 7.

SUGGESTED READING

Michel Dorais and Patrice Corriveau, *Gangs and Girls: Understanding Juvenile Prostitution* (Montreal: McGill-Queen's University Press, 2008).

M. ALEXIS KENNEDY

DOMESTIC VIOLENCE. Domestic violence is one of the most common forms of violence against women, children, and the elderly and is usually performed in the context of a relationship of responsibility, trust, or power. Domestic abuse constitutes all forms of physical and emotional ill treatment, sexual abuse, neglect or negligent treatment, or other exploitation, resulting in actual harm to the victim's health, survival, or development. Although some cultures acknowledge this as a social problem, most of the cultures around the world consider this to be a personal problem.

Intimate partner abuse prevails in all societies around the world. In 48 population-based surveys from around the world, 10–69% of women reported being physically abused by an intimate male partner at some point in their life. Levels of wife beatings are highest when the family norms are the most patriarchal and where institutions such as the state, religious organizations, and legal systems refuse to acknowledge domestic violence and maintain men's superiority over women. Most women who have experienced physical violence generally experience multiple acts of aggression over time.

Attention to domestic violence began in the United States with the women's movement in the 1970s. Cross-culturally, law enforcement agencies uphold patriarchal values by treating wife-killing as less serious than other forms of violence. Such negligence is observed in countries that do not have any laws on domestic violence. In countries where there are no laws against domestic violence and where these crimes are considered under the laws against common assault, fines for such crimes are often a very small amount of money, failing to deter such crimes. Within the United States both decision-making regarding the legal and the economic system and enforcement of such decisions are substantially in men's hands.

Besides intimate partner abuse, child abuse prevails in all societies around the world. Child abuse includes physical, psychological, and sexual abuse as well as neglect. Among individual factors, age and sex play a significant part in the victimization. Although young children are most at risk of physical abuse, adolescent children are at risk for sexual abuse. Boys are victims of beatings and physical punishments more often, whereas girls are at risk for infanticide, sexual abuse, and neglect. Research suggests that women use more physical punishment than men. However, men are far more likely to be the perpetrators of sexual abuse. Factors that contribute to child abuse are unrealistic expectations for children, poor impulse control, stress, and social isolation.

With the increase in the elderly population, abuse of elderly people by their relatives or other caregivers is increasing. Elderly people are especially vulnerable to economic abuse, in which relatives or other caregivers make improper use of their funds and resources. Abusive acts in institutions for the elderly include physically restraining patients, depriving them of dignity and choice over daily affairs, or providing insufficient care.

SUGGESTED READING

Lori L. Heise, "Violence Against Women: An Integrated, Ecological Framework," *Violence Against Women* 4, no. 3 (1998): 262–90; Etienne G. Krug et al., *World Report on Violence and Health* (Geneva: World Health Organization, 2002).

RIFAT AKHTER

DOMESTIC VIOLENCE MYTHS. Numerous myths relating to domestic violence exist. A select few are provided below.

Myth 1: Domestic violence is not a serious social problem. It is difficult to know the real extent of domestic violence because of three factors: the hidden nature of the problem, under-reporting, and the rare identification of domestic violence as a crime. National studies estimate that 3–4 million women are beaten each year in the United States. In 48 population-based surveys from around the world, 10–69% of women reported being physically abused by an intimate male partner at some point in their life. In the United States, 30% of female homicide victims are killed by partners or ex-partners.

Myth 2: Domestic violence occurs only in poor, uneducated, and minority families. Studies of domestic violence consistently have found that battering occurs among all types of families regardless of income, profession, region, ethnicity, educational level, or race. However, the fact that lower income victims more often call police, battered women's shelters, and social services may be due to a lack of other resources. Middle- and upper-class women are less likely to seek assistance because they fear personal embarrassment and damage to their family prestige.

Myth 3: Battered women must have done something to deserve a beating. It is widely believed that the woman's "nagging" or other "unreasonable" provocations (such as refusal to have sex, asking for money, not finishing housework on time, etc.) push the man to lose control. Whatever the perpetrators may claim to have been the "provocation," violence is never an acceptable method of solving conflict in a relationship.

Myth 4: Battered women probably enjoy the abuse; thus they do not leave the perpetrator. Most members of the community fail to understand the difficulties faced by women who wish to leave a violent relationship. Many assume that she stays in an abusive environment because she receives pleasure from the abuse in some way. This is not true. There are many reasons for staying in an abusive relationship, such as fear of retribution, a lack of alternative means of economic support, concern for the children, emotional dependence, a lack of support from the family, an abiding hope that the man will change, stigmatization associated with divorce or living alone (as found in traditional societies), and fear of homicide.

Myth 5: Regret and remorse on the part of the man means he has changed. Although violent men can appear to enjoy the effects of the abuse, they often feel remorseful about their behavior. However, regret and remorse do not indicate change; neither do they mean that he is prepared to renounce the power he has within the relationship.

Myth 6: Violent men cannot control their violence. This misconception allows men to avoid the issue of taking responsibility for their acts of violence. Many men may accept this responsibility once they are taught some strategies for positive change. The crucial issue is that men use violence to control women, and unless men are willing to relinquish this control by working toward changing their beliefs and attitudes about women, then short-term strategies, such as anger management, do very little toward achieving positive and sustainable long-term social change.

SUGGESTED READING

Linda G. Mills, *Violent Partners: A Breakthrough Plan for Ending the Cycle of Abuse* (New York: Basic Book, 2008).

RIFAT AKHTER

E

ELDER ABUSE. Elder abuse encompasses many types of crimes. Elder abuse can take the form of domestic violence between husband and wife or other family members, physical abuse by a caregiver, abuse of a client of a nursing home, sexual crimes, or even street crime or financial crime against an elderly person. Financial crimes can include fraudulent schemes or the overbilling for services in a healthcare facility. Elder abuse also encompasses the neglect of an elderly person. In addition, verbal abuse and even unintentional or intentional communication neglect, such as failure of a caregiver at home or in a nursing home setting to engage in any conversation with an elderly patient, may be included. Although some literature defines elder abuse as encompassing victims age 50 and older, other literature sets the age at 60 or even 65. Some literature categorizes the elderly into the categories of "early old age" (64–74), "advanced old age" (75 and older), and those above the age of 85 (the "old old").[1] Most criminal actions are prosecuted under statutes that encompass crimes that are not specific to elderly victims, such as assault, sexual assault, and fraud; additionally, legislatures in all 50 states have passed elder abuse prevention laws. Although the content of these laws vary, all states have set up reporting systems that involve reporting known or suspected elder abuse to adult protective services agencies. However, state laws differ regarding who is considered a mandatory reporter for purposes of elder abuse.

The Administration on Aging (AoA) is a federal agency that is responsible for policy and planning issues in the area of elder abuse. The AoA reported in its 1998 National Elder Abuse Incidence Study that 236,479 reports of elderly abuse, neglect, and self-neglect were made to adult protective services agencies in 1996; 115,110, or 48.7%, were substantiated after investigation. The majority of these reports (61.6%) were of incidents in which someone else mistreated an elderly person (the remaining were reports of elderly persons neglecting themselves). The types of abuse, from most common to least common, were neglect, emotional/psychological abuse, financial/material exploitation, and physical abuse. Further, the study predicted that there are most likely five abused and neglected elders that are not reported for every one that is reported and substantiated. The AoA found that female elders are abused at a higher rate than males, that those elders ages 80 and over are abused and neglected at two to three times their proportion of the elderly population, and that in 90% of the incidents with a known perpetrator, that perpetrator is an adult child or spouse. The perpetrators of the abuse are most often men in the areas of abandonment, physical abuse, emotional abuse, and financial/material exploitation. Women were more frequently the perpetrators in cases of neglect. Perpetrators are most often in the age group of 41–59, and the majority of perpetrators were white.[2] Any studies of elder abuse that have considered race have suggested that cultural norms and values may influence how abuse is defined. Thus, it is important to develop services that focus on cultural norms that may influence a particular group's incidence of elder abuse, realizing also that once an ethnic group becomes assimilated to its new culture, these norms may change.[3]

Although the elderly, especially those age 65 and over, are generally in the lowest category in terms of general victimization (i.e., street crimes, etc.),[4] the elderly nonetheless are amongst those most fearful of being a victim of crime.[5] The elderly often feel vulnerable to crime as they may not have support systems in place to be able to recover quickly, including emotionally, financially, and physically, from a criminal act.

In addition to mandatory reporting laws and state protective service agencies, changes have occurred in the civil and criminal justice systems in favor of the abused elder. Some states specifically allow the awarding of attorney's fees, damages for pain and suffering, recovery costs, and punitive damages in civil cases in which a defendant is guilty of recklessness, fraud, malice, or oppression. The criminal justice system has created special training programs and investigative techniques in the area of elder abuse, along with specialized courts that deal specifically with the issue of elder abuse. Other suggested but not yet implemented programs include expanding the definition of hate crimes to include elder abuse, publicizing the identity of those who engage in elder abuse, and random unannounced inspections of nursing homes.[6]

NOTES

1. Ezzat A. Fattah and Vincent F. Sacco, *Crime and Victimization of the Elderly* (New York: Springer-Verlag, 1989).

2. Administration on Aging, "The National Elder Abuse Incident Study," http://www.aoa .gov/abuse/report/default.htm.

3. Paulina Ruf, "Understanding Elder Abuse in Minority Populations," in *Elder Abuse: A Public Health Perspective,* eds. Randal W. Summers and Allan M. Hoffman (Washington DC: American Public Health Association, 2006), 51–63.

4. William Pelfrey, Sr. and William Pelfrey, Jr., "Fear of Crime, Age, and Victimization: Relationships and Changes Over Time," in *Current Issues in Victimology Research,* eds. Laura Moriarty and Robert Jerin (Durham, NC: Carolina Academic Press, 1998), 13–29.

5. U.S. Senate, Special Committee on Aging, *Aging America: Trends and Projections* (Washington DC: Department of Health and Human Services, 1991).

6. James Anderson and Nancie Mangels, "Helping Victims: Social Services, Health Care Interventions in Elder Abuse," in *Elder Abuse: A Public Health Perspective*, eds. Randal W. Summers and Allan M. Hoffman (Washington DC: American Public Health Association, 2006), 139–66.

SUGGESTED READING

Lisa Nerenberg, *Elder Abuse Prevention: Emerging Trends and Promising Strategies* (New York: Springer, 2008); Mary Joy Quinn, *Elder Abuse and Neglect: Causes, Diagnosis, and Intervention Strategies* (New York: Springer, 1997).

TINA FRYLING

F

FACILITATION. Facilitation is a term that is applied to situations in which victims are seen as making it easy for criminals to commit crimes against them. For instance, persons who fail to lock the windows in their homes may be blamed for facilitating burglary by providing criminals with easy access into their house. Used in conjunction with two additional ideas—precipitation (i.e., persons do something to cause crime) and provocation (i.e., persons do something to incite crime)—facilitation is part of the broader notion that some victims share responsibility for the perpetration of crime.

Although not as commonly referenced within the victimology literature as precipitation and provocation, the idea of facilitation is implicit within many studies and reports on property crimes such as burglary, motor vehicle theft, and more recently, identity theft. For instance, studies on car theft, sponsored by insurance companies, often focus on the ways in which victims fail to protect their cars, such as leaving the keys in the ignition or not locking car doors. Additionally, studies on identity theft often infer that victims facilitate these crimes by failing to safeguard their personal information, such as neglecting to shred bank statements or using unsecured Web sites when making credit card purchases. The implication in these studies is that it is the carelessness or negligence of victims that enable criminals to steal from them. In fact, by emphasizing how persons can avoid crime, many crime prevention campaigns inadvertently end up blaming victims for not being more careful or cautious and ultimately facilitating their victimization.

SUGGESTED READING

Andrew Karmen, "Auto Theft: Beyond Victim Blaming," *Victimology* 5, no. 2 (1980): 161–74; Andrew Karmen, "Victim Facilitation: The Case of Auto Theft," *Victimology* 4, no. 4 (1979): 361–70.

KAREN WEISS

FALSE ALLEGATIONS. A false allegation of criminal conduct is a serious form of victimization. Persons falsely accused of a crime suffer a loss of reputation and social stigmatization even if exonerated. Defending a false accusation may require an expensive criminal defense.

Accusations of sexual misconduct and abuse are common types of false accusations. According to a study spanning nine years, Eugene J. Kanin found that in the United States, 41% of rape allegations are false. Kanin discovered that most of the false accusers were motivated by a need for an alibi or are seeking revenge against another. And in instances of false allegations, the accused may also be wrongly convicted.

In a study of wrongful convictions, the main cause was faulty eyewitnesses. Other contributors to false convictions are sloppy police work and overzealous prosecution, as occurred in the Duke University lacrosse scandal of 2006. Several white members of the Duke University lacrosse team hired two black strippers to perform at a party. One of the dancers later claimed she was raped by some of the team members. Subsequent investigation revealed that the evidence against the players was insufficient to support a case. The initial police investigation did not establish a rape due in part to inconsistent statements by the accused. Furthermore, DNA test results failed to connect any of the team members to the alleged victim, and the other stripper at the scene later admitted no rape occurred.

Victims of false allegations may suffer long-term financial and emotional consequences as do victims of violent crimes; therefore, laws are in place to punish those who initiate and perpetuate false allegations of criminal conduct.

SUGGESTED READING

Northwestern Law Center on Wrongful Convictions Web site, www.law.northwestern .edu/wrongfulconvictions/; Samuel Gross et al., "Exonerations in the United States, 1989–2003," *Journal of Criminal Law and Criminology* 95, no. 2 (2005): 523–60; Barry Scheck, Peter Neufeld, and Jim Dwyer, *Actual Innocence: Five Days to Execution, and Other Dispatches from the Wrongly Convicted* (New York: Doubleday, 2000).

ROBERT J. MEADOWS

FAMILY ABDUCTION. A family abduction occurs when a family member acts in violation of a legal custody order through failing to return a child or removing a child from a legal custodian. Family abductions account for the vast majority of all child abductions in the United States, although most mass media attention has disproportionately focused on stranger abductions. The dynamics and complexity of this form of abduction are very different than nonfamilial abductions. In many cases, the whereabouts of the child may be known to the custodial parent, although the child may not be returned to the party having custody. For example, many abductions occur following a variety of circumstances related to transitions in family structure, including the dissolution or disruption of a marriage or relationship, a custody battle, or attempts to reconcile. In these cases, perpetrators typically are unhappy with the custodial arrangements and may disregard legitimate custodial rights. Many family abductors have social networks and family ties that aid them either directly or indirectly in the abduction and hiding of the child.

Domestic violence and fear of abuse of a child often complicate these abductions. A survey of prosecutors indicated that four varieties of familial abductions are most common: (a) those involving allegations of domestic violence against the abductor, (b) those involving violence against the other parent, (c) those claiming to be removing their children from the threat of child abuse, and (d) those involving allegations of both domestic violence and child abuse.

Although fathers are the majority of the perpetrators (53%), it is important to note that they are also more likely to be the noncustodial parent. Mothers are 25% of abductors, and the remaining 23% of perpetrators are extended family members or the mother's significant other. However, roughly one-third of all familial abductions are performed by more than one perpetrator. Young children are at higher risk of abduction, perhaps because they are less independent, less vocal, and more easily controlled or concealed. Although earlier studies indicate that whites are more likely to be involved in parental abductions, more recent data indicate that race does not appear to be a significant factor in familial abduction. Within the United States, most children taken by a family member are returned within one month of abduction, and only 6% of children remain missing six months or longer.

Although few parental abduction cases cross international lines, those that do rely upon the Child Abduction Convention (CAC) adopted at the Hague, which is the primary international governing body involved in helping return children who have been taken out of a country by a family member. The CAC was primarily enacted to help facilitate the return of the child to the country of residence rather than to punish the offending parent. In 1993, Congress enacted the International Parental Kidnapping Crime Act, creating federal criminal penalties against abducting parents who flee to non-CAC signatory countries with the intent of keeping the children from the other parent.

SUGGESTED READING

Hague Conference on Private International Law, "The Child Abduction Section," The HCCH—The Child Abduction Section, http://www.hcch.net/index_en.php?act=text

.display&tid=21; Heather Hammer, David Finkelhor, and Andrea J. Sedlak, "Children Abducted by Family Members: National Estimates and Characteristics," Office of Juvenile Justice and Delinquency Prevention of the U.S. Department of Justice, http://www.ncjrs.gov/pdffiles1/ojjdp/196466.pdf; National Center for Missing and Exploited Children, http://www.missingkids.com/.

DAWN C. CARR, MELISSA YOUNG-SPILLERS,
AND GLENN W. MUSCHERT

FAMILY STRESS THEORY. Family stress theory explains victimization as a result of how families handle various stressors. This theory is most often applied to family violence victimization. The foundation of the family stress theory is based on Reuben Hill's ABC-X model.[1] Hill's model describes how the relationship between family stressors (A); individual, family, and community resources (B); and the family's interpretation of the stressor (C) interacts to create a family crisis (X).[2]

Family stressors include a variety of positive and negative life events, such as the birth or death of a family member, marriage or divorce, new job opportunities, and unemployment. Resources are important because they impact the family's ability to cope with the stressor.[3] Families that effectively manage the stressor through available resources are better able to overcome the stressor without violence and victimization. Resources may exist at the individual level (strong coping skills, education, self-control, etc.), within the family system (good communication skills, strong sense of cohesion, etc.), and within the community (supportive friends, community support groups, job training services, etc.). One life event may be interpreted differently by various family units; therefore, the family's perception of the stressor is also important. For example, a new baby may be viewed positively by some families, whereas other families may see a new baby as a financial or emotional burden.

The stressors, resources, and perceptions interact to create a crisis for some families. A crisis is a "period of disorganization that rocks the foundation of the family."[4] It is this crisis stage that can lead to family violence as some family members respond to the situation with violence or other abuse. The birth of a new baby, the addition of a grandparent into the family home, or a sudden medical emergency can all be stressors for the family. Any situation that changes the family dynamic has potential to become a crisis if resources are insufficient and the situation is negatively perceived by the family.

Family members with special needs are at higher risk for family violence. For example, children from unwanted pregnancies or who had a difficult birth, low birth weight, or other early health problems are more likely to be abused by parents.[5] Likewise, children and adults with special emotional or physical needs are at higher risk for abuse.[6] Individuals requiring additional medical care or psychological attention create financial and emotional stressors for the family unit. Violence or neglect may result if the family unit does not have adequate resources (money, time, patience, community services, etc.) to accommodate the special needs of the individual and if the situation is interpreted as a burden on the family unit.

NOTES

1. Reuben Hill, *Families Under Stress* (New York: Harper & Row, 1949).

2. Ibid.

3. Margaret Crosbie-Burnett, "Application of Family Stress Theory to Remarriage: A Model for Assessing and Helping Stepfamilies," *Family Relations* 38 (1989): 323.

4. Bron Ingoldsby, J. Elizabeth Miller, and Suzanne Smith, *Exploring Family Theories* (Los Angeles: Roxbury, 2003), 137–49.

5. Mildred Pagelow, *Family Violence* (New York: Praeger, 1984).

6. Etienne Krug et al., *World Report on Violence and Health* (Geneva: World Health Organization, 2002).

SUGGESTED READING

Pauline Boss and Carol Mulligan, *Family Stress: Classic and Contemporary Readings* (Thousand Oaks: Sage, 2002); Hamilton McCubbin, Marvin Sussman, and Joan Patterson, "Social Stress and the Family: Advances and Developments in Family Stress Theory and Research," *Marriage & Family Review* 6, no. 1/2 (1983).

SUZANNE GODBOLDT

FAMILY VIOLENCE COURT. The 1970s witnessed a movement to raise awareness of the problem of domestic violence. Law enforcement was the first arm of the criminal justice system to begin reforming its practices to better serve victims and decrease recidivism by batterers. This was followed by changes within prosecution, probation, and finally the courts.[1] In the 1980s, the paramount concerns of those involved in the movement were developing shelters and collecting data to better understand the scope of the problem. By the mid-1990s, there was a new focus on treatment programs, case management, and pro-arrest policies. The late 1990s and early 2000s saw the development of the first family violence courts.[2] By the year 2000, there were over 300 jurisdictions in the United States that had some form of family violence court.[3]

According to Susan Eley, family violence courts "have developed out of a recognition that traditional adjudicative approaches were not working particularly well and that a more holistic approach could have benefits to tackling the problem."[4] Courts were often working at cross-purposes, and cases often resulted in conflicting orders.[5] Judges were reluctant to intervene in matters of domestic violence[6]—many held traditional views on the family.[7] Combining cases into one court conserves resources and allows major actors to develop a better under-standing of the underlying issues surrounding domestic violence.[8]

Emily Sack believes there are nine core values that all family violence courts should strive to uphold: victim safety, keeping the victim informed, offender accountability, information sharing and informed decision-making, institutionalized coordination of procedures and services, training and education, judicial leadership, effective use of the justice system, and accountability of courts and programs.[9]

Jurisdictions around the United States employ an endless variety of specialized systems that fall under the guise of family violence courts. These courts, however disparate, share one or more of the following unique features: assignment of cases to a specialized calendar (which is a fundamental feature of a family violence court); screening for related cases; intake units and case processing; and service provision.[10] These specialized courts share one or more of the following key com-ponents: early access to advocacy and services; coordination of community part-ners; a victim and child-friendly court; specialized staff and judges; leveraging the role of the judge; an integrated information system; evaluation and accounta-bility; established protocols for evaluating dangerousness; ongoing training and education; compliance monitoring; and sentencing models.[11]

Three models have emerged from the various specialized courts around the United States: those with a dedicated civil protection order docket; the criminal model; and domestic violence courts with a related caseload, which includes three variations, including an integrated domestic violence court, a unified family court, and a coordinated court.[12]

Strengths of these specialized courts include reduced case backlogs and improved decision-making by court personnel.[13] Another strength is improved consistency in sentencing.[14] Greater judicial oversight of offenders' behavior, greater court access for victims, increased visibility of the problem in the com-munity, and development of expertise in domestic violence cases by judges and prosecutors are a few of the other important strengths of family violence courts.[15]

Critics of family violence courts worry that consistency may not always be a good thing, in that "a consistently unresponsive court or prosecutor will be worse than a system that is only sporadically so."[16] Other weaknesses include burnout by court personnel, increased need for security personnel, judges who may not have the appearance of impartiality, and the fact that these courts may be marginalized, which would undermine the efforts to gain recognition of the problem.[17]

NOTES

1. Susan Keilitz et al., *Specialization of Domestic Violence Case Management in the Courts: Findings from a National Survey* (Williamsburg, VA: National Center for State Courts, 2000).

2. Albert R. Roberts, "Myths, Facts, and Realities Regarding Battered Women and Their Children: An Overview," in *Handbook of Domestic Violence Intervention Strategies: Policies, Programs, and Legal Remedies,* ed. Albert R. Roberts (New York: Oxford University Press, 2002), 3–22.

3. Keilitz et al., *Specialization of Domestic.*

4. Susan Eley, "Changing Practices: The Specialized Domestic Violence Court Process," *The Howard Journal* 44 (2005): 114.

5. Carol Flango, Victor Flango, and H. Ted Rubin, "How are Courts Coordinating Family Court Cases?" National Center for State Courts, http://www.ncsconline.org/WC/Publications/Res_SCtFam_CtCoordFamCasesPub.pdf.

6. Lisa G. Lerman and Naomi R. Cahn, "Legal Issues in Violence Toward Adults," in *Case Studies in Family Violence,* eds. Robert T. Ammerman and Michel Hersen (New York: Plenum, 1991), 73–85.

7. Naomi H. Archer, "Battered Women and the Legal System: Past, Present, and Future," *Law and Psychology Review* 13 (1989): 145–63.

8. Robyn Mazur and Liberty Aldrich, "What Makes a Domestic Violence Court Work? Lessons from New York," *Judges Journal* 42 (2003): 5–11.

9. Emily Sack, "Creating a Domestic Violence Court: Guidelines and Best Practices," Family Violence Prevention Fund, http://endabuse.org/programs/healthcare/files/Final Court_Guidelines.pdf.

10. Dag MacLeod and Julia F. Weber, "Domestic Violence Courts: A Descriptive Study," Judicial Council of California: Administrative Office of the Courts, http://www.courtinfo.ca.gov/programs/cfcc/pdffiles/dvreport.pdf.

11. Sack, "Creating a Domestic Violence Court."

12. Ibid.

13. Eley, "Changing Practices," 121.

14. Charlotte Walsh, "The Trend Towards Specialization: West Yorkshire Innovations in Drugs and Domestic Violence Courts," *The Howard Journal* 40 (2001): 26–38.

15. Amy Karan, Susan Keilitz, and Sharon Denaro, "Domestic Violence Courts: What Are They and How Should We Manage Them?" *Juvenile and Family Court Journal* Spring (1999): 75–83.

16. Stop Violence Against Women, "Specialized Domestic Violence Court Systems," Stop Violence against Women, http://www.stopvaw.org/Specialized_Domestic_Violence_Court_Systems.html.

17. Ibid.

SUGGESTED READING

Angela R. Gover, John M. MacDonald, and Geoffrey P. Alpert, "Combating Domestic Violence: Findings from an Evaluation of a Local Domestic Violence Court," *Criminology & Public Policy* 3 (2003): 109–32; Jane E. Ursel, *Family Violence Courts* (Toronto: University of Toronto Press, 2008).

JENNIFER WINGREN

FEAR OF CRIME. Fear represents an intense emotional response to perceived danger. It is considered a primary, or basic, emotion, meaning that it appears early in life, is recognizable across cultures, and has survival value. In our modern world, one of the most acute sources of fear is crime.

Like many emotions, fear of crime is composed of multiple components. Researchers studying fear of crime generally focus on two related but distinct aspects of fear: emotions and cognition. The emotional component refers to the anxiety elicited by anticipated criminal victimization, whereas the cognitive component generally refers to perceived risk. Early research either utilized risk perceptions as a proxy for emotional response or combined measures of anticipated fear with perceived risk into a single measure. More recently, researchers have begun to examine fear and risk perceptions as distinct concepts and generally find that perceived risk influences anticipated fear of crime.[1]

Research examining demographic differences in fear of crime reveals two fairly consistent patterns: older individuals are more fearful of crime than younger people and women are more fearful of crime than men.[2] Scholars refer to these patterns as the victimization-fear paradox, because the groups of people with the greatest fear of crime are the groups least likely to be victimized. Careful examination of the relationship between age and fear, however, reveals more complex patterns than previously believed. Kenneth Ferraro finds that the relationship between age and fear is curvilinear: fear of crime is greatest for teenagers and very young adults, declines through middle-age, and only increases again during the later stages of old age.[3]

Research continues to find, though, that women are much more fearful of crime than are men despite their lower risk of violent victimization. This apparent contradiction between women's low rates of victimization and their high levels of fear of crime could be explained by fear of rape, which is the only violent crime for which women are more likely to be victimized than are men. Ferraro argues that because any victimization of a woman may potentially involve a sexual assault, women's fear of nonsexual crimes is heavily influenced by their fear of rape.[4] This fear is particularly great among younger women, who also experience the highest rates of rape victimization.[5]

Finally, previous victimization appears to exacerbate fear of crime.[6] Even indirect victimization—the victimization of friends or family— increases both fear of crime and perception of risk.[7]

Research indicates that individuals tend to alter their lifestyles in response to fear of crime and perceived risk of victimization.[8] Ferraro found that perceived risk of victimization causes individuals to constrain their behavior.[9] This included engaging in both "avoidance behavior" (i.e., reducing risky activities) and "defensive behavior" (i.e., target hardening). Generally speaking, avoidance behaviors reduce an individual's exposure to victimization, whereas defensive behaviors make individuals appear less attractive as targets of crime by increasing the risk facing potential offenders.

Some research suggests, however, that the relationship between fear of crime and constrained behavior may not be unidirectional. Allen Liska and colleagues found that fear of crime and constrained behaviors were part of an escalating loop.[10] In other words, fear of crime causes an individual to constrain his behaviors, which, in turn, increases his fear of crime, and so forth. Ferraro questioned these findings.[11] His results suggested that perceived risk increased constrained behaviors, which increased fear of crime; however, he found no evidence that fear of crime then increased constrained behaviors. In contrast, other research has suggested that constraining one's behavior does *not* have an effect on one's fear of crime.[12] This on-going debate suggests the need for longitudinal studies to tease out the nature of the relationship between fear of crime and behavior.

NOTES

1. Kenneth Ferraro, *Fear of Crime: Interpreting Victimization Risk* (Albany, NY: State University of New York Press, 1995); Randy LaGrange, Kenneth Ferraro, and Michael Supancic, "Perceived Risk and Fear of Crime: Role of Social and Physical Incivilities," *Journal of Research in Crime and Delinquency* 29 (1992): 311–34.

2. Ferraro, *Fear of Crime*; Carl Keane, "Evaluating the Influence of Fear of Crime as an Environmental Mobility Restrictor on Women's Routine Activities," *Environment and Behavior* 30 (1998): 60–74; Gary Lee, "Sex Differences in Fear of Crime Among Older People," *Research on Aging* 4 (1982): 284–98; Suzanne Ortega and Jessie Myles, "Race and Gender Effects on Fear of Crime: An Interactive Model with Age," *Criminology* 25 (1987):133–52;

3. Ferraro, *Fear of Crime*.

4. Ibid.

5. Ibid.

6. Ferraro, *Fear of Crime;* Wesley Skogan and Michael Maxfield, *Coping with Crime* (New York: Free Press, 1981).

7. Ferraro, *Fear of Crime;* Skogan and Maxfield, *Coping with Crime.*

8. Ferraro, *Fear of Crime;* Keane, "Evaluating the Influence;" Allen Liska, Joseph Lawrence, and Andrew Sanchirico, "Fear of Crime as a Social Fact," *Social Forces* 66 (1988): 760–70.

9. Ferraro, *Fear of Crime*.

10. Liska, Lawrence, and Sanchirico, "Fear of Crime."

11. Ferraro, *Fear of Crime*.

12. Ralph Taylor, Richard Taub, and Bruce Peterson, "Crime, Community Organization, and Causes of Neighborhood Decline," in *Metropolitan Crime Patterns,* ed. Robert Figelo, Simon Hakim, and George Rengert (New York: Willow Tree Press, 1986), 161–77.

SUGGESTED READING

Mark Warr, "Public Perceptions and Reactions to Violent Offending and Victimization," *Understanding and Preventing Violence, Vol. 4: Consequences and Control,* ed. Albert Reiss and Jeffery Roth (Washington DC: National Academy Press), 1–66.

JACKSON M. BUNCH AND JODY CLAY-WARNER

FEMINIST PERSPECTIVES ON VICTIMIZATION. Feminist theory is a relative newcomer to the field of victimology. It is a product of the resurgence of feminism as a social movement during the 1970s. Beginning in the mid-1970s, feminists critically assessed virtually all academic disciplines, pointing out that historically women were usually excluded from research and theorizing or, if included, were portrayed in sex-stereotyped ways.

Feminist victimology is not a single, unified perspective but rather a group of related perspectives, such as multicultural feminism, standpoint feminism, and postmodern feminism. However, there are several principles that feminist victimologists share more or less. First, feminist victimologists maintain that gender—that is, the socially constructed expectations, attitudes, and behaviors associated with females and males, typically organized dichotomously as femininity and masculinity—is a central organizing component of social life. In other words, gender and gender relations order social life and social institutions in particular ways. Consequently, when one studies any aspect of social life, including victimization, one must consider in what ways it is gendered. For example, one must ask how gender affects frequency and types of victimization. Are females and males victimized at different rates? Are they more or less likely to be the victims of different types of crimes? How does gender impact their victimization experiences?

Embedded in this principle is the assumption that gender is not something natural but rather something social. This is not to deny a biological component to gender but rather a recognition that gender develops through complex interactions between biology and culture and may change over time in response to social actions, opportunities, and experiences. And because gender is socially constructed, it is ascribed social value in society. In American society, as in most other societies throughout the world, one gender (masculinity) is valued over the other gender (femininity). This differential valuing of genders is called sexism, and feminist victimologists maintain that understanding sexism is fundamental to understanding the gendered nature of victimization experiences and both formal and informal responses to victimization.

Although feminist victimologists recognize that males' voices and experiences have historically been privileged over females' voices and experiences, they also point out that not all men are equally privileged in our society, nor are all women equally disadvantaged. More specifically, feminist victimologists maintain that there is no universal male or female experience of victimization that can be described and understood independently of other social locating factors, such as race and ethnicity, social class, age, sexual orientation, and physical ability. Moreover, these factors are not simply additive; rather, they intersect to produce qualitatively different experiences and opportunities that must be studied in their own right. For instance, in studying women's violent victimization experiences, one cannot assume that the experiences and reactions of a sample of white, middle-class women will generalize to all women. One must study a diverse sample of women to determine how race and class intersect with gender to affect victimization experiences and reactions.

One additional principle of feminist victimology that grew out of the feminist movement is a commitment to collective social action to address sexism and promote gender equity. Feminists often disagree on the forms and goals of this activism, but they nonetheless have engaged in various efforts to produce more gender equitable social change (e.g., lobbying for the revision of rape and sexual assault laws to reduce the likelihood that victims will be retraumatized by the legal system if they report the crimes to the police).

Much feminist work in victimology has focused on including women in what has traditionally been male-dominated research. Gender, feminist victimologists point out, is one of the strongest predictors of victimization; males consistently perpetrate more crime, and more serious crime, including violent crime than females do and are more likely to be the victims of these crimes. However, feminist victimological research has shown that females are more likely to be the victims of certain types of crimes, including sexual assault, incest, intimate partner violence, and sexual harassment, and their perpetrators are more likely to be men, particularly men they know. Women are significantly more likely to be victimized by a man they know than by a stranger, whereas men are about equally likely to be victimized by someone they know as by a stranger. Moreover, feminist victimological research has demonstrated that women's victimization by men is far more prevalent than previously suspected. In explaining these findings, feminist victimologists have drawn on research that shows how traditional gender norms reinforce and reward male dominance and control over women and how patriarchal societies such as our own privilege males over females and often blame women for their own victimization. More recent feminist research has examined the connections between victimization and offending by girls and women.

SUGGESTED READING

Daniel J. Curran and Claire M. Renzetti, *Theories of Crime* (Boston: Allyn and Bacon, 2001); Sharon Lamb, ed., *New Versions of Victims* (New York: New York University

Press, 1999); Elizabeth A. Stanko, *Everyday Violence: How Women and Men Experience Sexual and Physical Danger* (London: Pandora, 1990).

CLAIRE RENZETTI

FINANCIAL ABUSE. Financial abuse is a crime that is often committed against the elderly. This type of abuse is difficult to detect and deter because victims often do not report their abuse to law enforcement. There are various forms of financial abuse including misuse of assets; consumer fraud; telemarketer fraud; healthcare fraud; home repair fraud; and getting an older person to sign a deed, will, or power of attorney through deception, coercion, or undue influence.[1] Factors that might increase the likelihood of victimization are social isolation, cognitive impairment, recent loss of a loved one, and at-risk older persons.[2] Warning signs[3] that the elder may be in an abusive situation include the following: they cannot pay bills, there are withdrawals from banks the victim cannot explain, the bank statements no longer come to the victim's home, care of the elder is not commensurate with size of the estate, and they have new "best friends."

Perpetrators of financial abuse include family members, business persons (salesmen, attorneys, caregivers, friends, insurance agents, contractors), and other opportunists motivated by greed.[4] A large portion of financial abuse is committed by family members. "Between one million and two million Americans age 65 or older have been injured, exploited, or otherwise mistreated by someone whom they depend for care or protection."[5] This makes it difficult to detect because monetary transactions are often given by consent to the family member by the victim. The ability to prove financial abuse has occurred can be a challenge when the offender is a family member, particularly if they have been granted power of attorney. Often family members who are also acting as caregivers feel that they are entitled to the victim's resources. Victims are often not willing to report because they are afraid of retaliation and may be embarrassed.[6] Some victims will not report since they fear others will believe they cannot manage their own accounts and may place them in a nursing home. As in other domestic crimes, the victims may be reluctant to turn in family members.[7]

Guardianship is typically used when the victim does not have the capacity to understand the severity of their situation and refuses services.[8] Unfortunately, the power of attorney[9] allows the perpetrator to have access to all of the victim's financial accounts. Victims can get a protective order[10] to help stop the abuse. Civil lawsuits help victims recover stolen assets. Other programs that address financial abuse are Financial Abuse Specialist Teams (FAST).[11] FAST is a rapid-response system made up of members from community and legal services such as adult protective services, public administration/guardians office, and the district attorney's office. The goal is to deter and prevent future financial abuse. In addition to programs like FAST, some police departments like San Diego have developed specialized units that focus on crime against the elderly.[12]

NOTES

1. National Committee for the Prevention of Elder Abuse, "Financial Abuse, 2003," http://www.preventelderabuse.org/elderabuse/fin_abuse.html.

2. Namkee G. Choi and James Mayer, "Elder Abuse, Neglect, and Exploitation: Risk Factors and Prevention Strategies," *Journal of Gerontological Social Work* 33, no. 2 (2000): 5–25.

3. National Committee for the Prevention of Elder Abuse, "Financial Abuse."

4. Bryan J. Kemp and Laura A. Mosqueda, "Elder Financial Abuse: An Evaluation Framework and Supporting Evidence," *Journal of the American Geriatrics Society* 53, (2005): 1123–27.

5. Ellen Alexander et al., "National Victimization Rights Week Resources Guide," Office for Victims of Crime, http://www.ojp.gov/ovc/ncvrw/2006/pdf/overview.pdf.

6. Thomas L. Hafemeister, "Financial Abuse of the Elderly in Domestic Situations," in *Elder Mistreatment: Abuse, Neglect, and Exploitation of in an Aging America,* eds. Richard J. Bonnie and Robert B. Wallace (Washington DC: National Academies Press, 2003), 382–445.

7. Carolyn L. Dessin, "Financial Abuse of the Elderly," *Idaho Law Review* 36, 2000: 203–26.

8. Lisa Nerenberg, *Forgotten Victims of Elder Financial Crime and Abuse: A Report and Recommendations* (San Francisco, CA: Goldman Institute on Aging, 1999).

9. Hafemeister, "Financial Abuse."

10. Dessin, "Financial Abuse."

11. Betty Malks, Christine, M. Schmidt, and Michael J. Austin, "Elder Abuse Prevention: A Case Study of the Santa Clara County Financial Abuse Specialist Team (FAST) Program," *Journal of Social Work* 39, no. 3 (2002): 23–40.

12. Donna J. Rabiner, Janet O'Keeffe, and David Brown, "Financial Exploitation of Older Persons: Challenges and Opportunities to Identify, Prevent, and Address it in the United States," *Journal of Aging & Social Policy* 18, no. 2 (2006): 47–68.

SUGGESTED READING

Conrad Wilkinson and Patricia Wilkinson, "Financial Abuse: A Case Study & Litigation Guide for the Elder Law Attorney," *NAELA Quarterly (National Academy of Elder Law Attorneys)* (2003): 18–21.

DAWANA KOMOROSKY

FRY, MARGERY. Margery Fry (1874–1958) was born into a prominent Quaker family in London, England. She was the great granddaughter of Elizabeth Fry, a well-known prison reformer. Fry studied and worked at Somerville College, a school established for women at Oxford University. The beginnings of her interest in victims can be traced to the South African War (1899–1902), when she began working for victims of war and other forms of violence. Following World War I, she continued her efforts by working for the Friends' War Victims Relief Committee in France. During this time, she began working for penal reform. Fry was a leading advocate for educating prisoners as part of their treatment. In the late 1940s, she was a victim of a purse snatching. It was perhaps this experience that made her realize that victims of crime needed to be compensated for damages but too often were not because the offender was unknown or unable to pay.

In 1953, Fry presented her idea of a publicly funded compensation program to the Howard League for Penal Reform, which she had extensive ties to dating back to the early 1920s. Fry maintained that victims should not be denied compensation even when offenders were not able to compensate their victims. Compensation, in these cases then, should come from public funds. In 1957, she presented her compensation plan to the Magistrates' Association. She died in 1958 before her plan was implemented. Britain, however, established the Criminal Injuries Compensation Scheme in 1964, which provided state-funded compensation programs.

SUGGESTED READING

Enid Huws Jones, *Margery Fry: The Essential Amateur* (London: Oxford University Press, 1966).

CONNIE FREY

G

GOOD SAMARITAN. The term *Good Samaritan* originates from the Biblical parable about compassion for those in need and being a good neighbor. According to the parable, a traveler, a Samaritan, came upon a person who had been robbed, beaten, and left for dead. Unlike other passersby who ignored the man, the Samaritan went to his side, bandaged his wounds, and took him to an inn, paying the innkeeper to take care of the man. The Good Samaritan then graciously left before the victim could thank or repay him for his kindness.

In legal terms, the Good Samaritan is someone who voluntarily comes to the aid of an injured person in an emergency situation or under the imminent threat of danger, or someone who intervenes to prevent another from being harmed as the result of a violent crime.

Unlike most European legal systems, the British and U.S. systems hesitate to legislate Good Samaritan conduct and take the position that a person is not obligated to intervene if the injured or ill person is a stranger or not in a contractual agreement with the victim. Some U.S. states, however, will consider it an act of negligence if a bystander does not at least call for help, has made an initial effort to assist the victim and then did not carry through, or if the victim is being sexually assaulted. Gilbert Guis points out that laws penalizing people for failing to come to the aid of others should be referred to ironically as "Bad Samaritan" laws.

Most U.S. states have enacted Good Samaritan laws to protect those who offer assistance to strangers in need as long as the Good Samaritan is reasonably careful and respectful of the victim's well-being. Such laws are intended to minimize any hesitancy to act a bystander might feel for fear of being sued or prosecuted for causing unintentional injury or death to the victim. In terms of victim compensation, a Good Samaritan is someone who is hurt or killed during an attempt to prevent crime victimization or capture a suspected offender. In all U.S. jurisdictions, victims who are harmed as a direct result of a violent crime are eligible to recover some of the otherwise unreimbursed costs incurred due to their victimization. However, most jurisdictions broaden the category of victims eligible for compensation to include Good Samaritans. The rationale for such compensation is that society is obliged to repay acts above and beyond the normal scope of citizenship and that humanitarianism should be encouraged not discouraged.

SUGGESTED READING

Gilbert Geis, "Crime Victims: Practices and Prospects," in *Victims of Crime: Problems, Policies, and Programs,* eds. Arthur J. Lurigio, Wesley G. Skogan, and Robert C. Davis (Newbury Park, CA: Sage, 1990), 251–68; The National Center for Victims of Crime, "State Compensation laws," http://www.ncvc.org/ncvc/main.aspx?dbName=Advanced Search; Leslie Sebba, *Third Parties: Victims and the Criminal Justice System* (Columbus, OH: Ohio State University Press, 1996).

DOUGLAS F. GEORGE

GUARDIAN AD LITEM. A *guardian ad litem* advocates for the best interests of children who are involved in child-protective proceedings. Over 500,000 children are in the foster care system due to some form of parental abuse or neglect. In 2007, court-ordered *guardian ad litems* represented approximately 234,000 abused and neglected children to ensure no child is lost in an overburdened legal system or languishes in a group or foster home placement.[1]

The court appoints the *guardian ad litem* to avoid allegiance to any of the vested parties. The guardian may be a court-appointed attorney or a trained volunteer who will serve as an independent voice for children in need of protection. The guardian has the authority to investigate the child's background, family relationships, home environment, and any matter related to recommending a disposition to ensure the child's welfare.

The role of the *guardian ad litem* is multifaceted. The guardian will interview caregivers, teachers, and service provides; identify resources to ensure the child's needs are met; serve as the child's voice in court proceedings; and monitor progress with the court's order and conditions.[2] The guardian will work with foster parents, teachers, therapists, medical professionals, and caseworkers to determine what action is in the best interest of the child. Although preferences of the child are considered, the best interests of the child remains focused on the child's physical and emotional needs and a nurturing home environment that promotes healthy growth and development.

NOTES

1. CASAnet, "Ideas for Using Non-Advocate Volunteers to Build Capacity in CASA/GAL Programs," *National CASA Technical Assistance Bulletin* (October 2008): 8.

2. Florida *Guardian Ad Litem* Program, "CASA/*guardian ad litem* Volunteer Training Manual," http://www.guardianadlitem.org/documents/Chapter6ResourceMaterials_001.pdf.

SUGGESTED READING

CASAnet, "Court Appointed Special Advocates CASA/GAL Programs Network," CASAnet, http://www.casanet.org/; Susan Pate, *Evaluation of the Guardian Ad Litem/Advocate Pilot Project* (Portland, ME: University of Southern Maine, Muskie School of Public Service, 2007); John Woodhead, "Guardian Ad Litem." *Journal of Forensic Psychiatry* 5, no. 1 (1994): 5–8.

LAURA PATTERSON

H

HATE CRIME. The term *hate crime* gained prominence in the United States in the 1980s following a number of well-publicized incidents directed against African Americans, Jews, and Asians and in Europe in the 1990s after an outburst of racist and antiforeigner violence. In 1990, the U.S. Congress passed the Hate Crime Statistic Act, which required the U.S. Attorney General to acquire data on hate or bias crimes—defined as a criminal offense committed against a person, property, or society that is motivated, in whole or in part, by the offender's bias against a race, religion, ethnic/national origin group, or sexual orientation group. As a result, for the first time, governmental agencies were making a concerted effort to document and track crimes of hate across a wide array of social categories and crimes.

In 1994, the Hate Crimes Sentencing Enhancement Act expanded the definition of hate crimes to include the victim's disability status and allowed for penalty enhancement, increasing the sentences of offenders convicted of crimes proven to be motivated by prejudice. Although significant, such legislation prohibits only crimes that interfere with federally guaranteed rights such at voting. At the state and local level, the situation is more complicated. The relative legal autonomy of each state means that different states have adopted different forms of hate crime legislation, and a consistent application of the definition of hate crimes across jurisdictions has not emerged. For instance, although most states have hate crime statutes, some states employ penalty enhancement and some do not; conduct considered to be hate crimes in many states may not be covered in the laws of others; and a group protected in the statute of one state may not be protected in the statute of another. More recently, federal legislation has been proposed that would authorize the Department of Justice to assist local authorities in investigating and prosecuting certain hate crimes and make hate crimes not covered in the statutes of some states a federal crime.

Establishing a motive for hate crimes can be extremely difficult, confounding the efforts of the criminal justice system to consistently classify, measure, and respond to hate crimes. The National Crime Victimization Survey (NCVS) has established criteria that must be met in order for a crime to be labeled a hate crime. The victim must believe the offender selected them for victimization because of one or more of the personal characteristics included in hate crimes definition or because the victim was perceived to be associated with a group largely identified by one of these characteristics. In addition, the NCVS requires that corroborating evidence of hate motivation must be present at the incident— the offender used derogatory language, the offender left hate symbols, or the police confirmed that a hate crime had taken place.

The FBI's Uniform Crime Reports is the principal instrument by which data on hate crimes are collected. Although 85% of the U.S. population is now covered in nationally reported hate crime statistics, evidence suggests a staggering number of hate crimes do not come to the attention of law enforcement agencies. In 2006, more than 9,000 hate crimes were reported to the FBI, and the NCVS reports that hate crimes constitute 3% of the total number of violent crime incidents in the United States. According to the NCVS, hate crimes are more likely to be violent, and the most serious kinds of crime—sexual assault, robbery, or simple assault. UCR data indicate that race was the motivation for 51.8% of all hate crimes, followed by religion (18.9%), sexual orientation (15.57%), ethnicity (12.7%), and disability (1.0%).

Proponents of hate crime legislation argue that hate crime statutes are needed because hate crimes more offensively violate society's general concern for the security of all its members, racial and religious harmony, and the collective moral code. Opponents warn that hate crime legislation amounts to the punishment of ideas or "thought crimes," and because the definition and motives for such crimes are open to subjective interpretation, the administration of justice is likely to be inconsistent and uneven.

Established hate groups have increasingly set up Web sites to organize their membership and promote their message. Unlike many countries in Europe, U.S. hate crime legislation does not affect the use of the Internet or other publishing opportunities protected by the Constitution. Watchdog groups like the Southern Poverty Law Center, the Anti-Defamation League, and the National Gay and Lesbian Task Force constantly monitor the activity of hate groups and have come to play an important role in tracking and documenting hate crimes committed by these groups.

The number of local and national advocacy groups seeking to combat hate crimes and support the victims of bias-motivated hate crimes is on the rise. Individuals in these organizations often work to generate resources to support educational programs that promote tolerance, build support systems for hate crime victims, work as liaisons between the victim and the criminal justice system, monitor hate group activity, and collect and report hate crime statistics. A comprehensive assessment of the effectiveness of the efforts of these individuals has yet to emerge, however.

SUGGESTED READING

Nathan Hall, *Hate Crime* (Portland, OR: Willan, 2005); Caroline Wolf Harlow, *Hate Crime Reported by Victims and Police* (Washington DC: Bureau of Justice Statistics Special Report, 2005); Jack Levin and J. McDevitt, *Hate Crimes Revisited* (Boulder, CO: Westview, 2001); Southern Poverty Law Center Web site, http://www.splcenter.org.

DOUGLAS F. GEORGE

HAZING. Hazing is a process based on a tradition that is used by groups to maintain a hierarchy (i.e., a pecking order) or to discipline. Regardless of consent, the rituals require individuals to engage in activities that are physically and psychologically stressful. These activities can be exhausting, humiliating, degrading, demeaning, and intimidating. They result in significant physical and emotional discomfort.[1] Hazing has become more dangerous since the 1990s as rituals have become more sexualized and more aggressive.

Hazing incidents occur among males and females and have occurred in various organizations including athletic teams, school bands, church groups, fraternities, sororities, and police and fire departments. Such groups believe that hazing will increase bonding among teammates. This is a false assumption.

The blueprint of hazing, as defined by Susan Lipkins, illustrates how hazing is learned and spread. It states that the victim, who wants to join the group, is hazed. Once accepted by the group, the victim becomes a bystander and watches as others get hazed. Eventually, the bystander achieves senior status and power and becomes a perpetrator, hazing others. Those who haze usually repeat what was done to them since they believe that they have the right and duty to pass on the tradition. The severity of the hazing ritual increases as perpetrators want to leave their own mark by enhancing the rituals. This may result in increased paddling, increased alcohol consumption, and increased psychological trauma.

An important aspect of hazing is the issue of consent. Often groups claim that there is no coercion and that the individual willingly participated in the activities. However, the definition used here, as well as most of those used in state laws, does not hold the victim liable for participation. This is because the courts acknowledge the psychological pressure that is exerted by the group that hazes. Perpetrators may claim that the victim is able to leave at any time. However, victims report that if they resist or try to exit, the hazing becomes even more painful and dangerous.

Groups that haze emphasize the secret nature of their rituals. Pledges and members must promise never to reveal traditions. This reduces the likelihood that reports of hazing will be given to authorities and is often referred to as the code of silence. Examples of dangerous hazing rituals are paddling, branding, confinement in car trunks or basements, excessive ingestion of water or alcohol, simulating oral sex or performing sodomy, exposure, sleep deprivation, and servitude.

The effects of hazing are frequently underestimated. Each year people die because of hazing; others are hospitalized, and some suffer from post-traumatic stress disorder. Perpetrators and bystanders may be held responsible, resulting in expulsion or jail. Consequences for hazing are changing as states pass tougher hazing laws. Nonetheless, hazing remains widespread, underreported, and increasingly hazardous.

NOTE

1. Susan Lipkins, *Preventing Hazing: How Parents, Teachers, and Coaches Can Stop the Violence, Harassment, and Humiliation* (San Francisco, CA: Jossey-Bass Wiley, 2006), 13.

SUGGESTED READING

Ricky L. Jones, *Black Haze: Violence, Sacrifice, and Manhood in Black Greek-Letter Fraternities* (New York: State University of New York Press, 2004); Susan Lipkins, "Inside Hazing: Understanding Hazardous Hazing," http://www.insidehazing.com; Hank Nuwer, ed., *The Hazing Reader* (Bloomington, IN: Indiana University Press, 2004); Brian Rahill and Elizabeth Allan, "Educating to Eliminate Hazing," http://www.stop hazing.org.

SUSAN LIPKINS

HISTORY OF VICTIMOLOGY, PRE-1940s. The history of victimology before the 1940s is very limited. It can be broken down into the study of the role of the crime victim within the criminal justice system and the academic examination of the crime victim. Three eras define the crime victim's role within the criminal justice system: the Golden Age, the Dark Age, and the Reemergence of the Victim.[1] The Golden Age was the period starting with known recorded history up until the Middle Ages in which crime victims were completely involved in the decision-making process concerning what needed to be done to the offenders. The offended or their survivors were responsible for bringing forth the charges, prosecuting the individuals, and deciding the disposition for offenders. They also received restitution from the offended for the harm incurred.[2]

An artifact of the Golden Age is the Babylonian Code of Hammurabi, dating back some 4,000 years. This early legal code recognized crime victims and the effects from their victimization. It also recognized the responsibility of the state if it failed to apprehend a victim's offender. The code stated,

> If the robber is not caught, the man who has been robbed shall formally declare that ever he has lost before a god, and the city and the mayor in whose territory or district the robbery has been committed shall replace whatever he has lost for him. If it is the life of the owner that is lost, the city or mayor shall pay one maneh of silver to his kinsfolk.[3]

The Dark Age was a period from about the Middle Ages until the twentieth century; the new governments decided that crimes would no longer be against the victims but would be harms against the state. The state assumed complete responsibility for arresting, prosecuting, and punishing the criminal offender. Crime victims no longer had a part in the decision process; they were just pieces of evidence. The crime victim was seen as a witness to the criminal act and would be involved in the criminal justice process only as needed by the state. Crime victims were left to seek justice from offenders in civil court.[4]

In the United States, the treatment of crime victims followed this three-era evolution as well. In colonial times, victims were completely responsible for the apprehension, prosecution, and in many cases disposition of offenders. Up until the mid 1800s there were no public police agents, only sheriffs, who demanded a fee to make arrests. Prosecutors had to be hired to prosecute cases and the victims had a say in the type of punishment that could be dispensed. The sanctions placed upon offenders could include triple damages to crime victims and other punishments as the victims saw fit.[5] However, once public prosecution and the expanded use of public police came into effect in the mid- to late-nineteenth and early twentieth centuries, the role of crime victims was reduced to that of reporters of criminal events and, to a lesser extent, witnesses for the state. The criminal justice bureaucracy excluded victims from having any say in the proceedings and dispositions handed down by the government and excluded restitution to crime victims as part of the criminal justice process. The Reemergence of the Victim is a very recent age. Beginning in the 1960s, the last 40-plus years have seen a complete reversal of the Dark Age, and a new and better Golden Age may be at hand.

The beginning of this reversal can be traced to the early academic work of Edwin Sutherland. Some of the earliest references to crime victims and crime victimization in criminological literature occurred in the first well-known American criminology textbook, Edwin Sutherland's *Criminology* (1924).[6] In this text he included a chapter called simply "The Victims of Crime." This chapter is the first know academic victimological examination of crime victims and their victimization in the United States. This chapter established the various ways crime victims could be categorized or their typologies, the individual and social costs of crime, and the current extent of victimization. Sutherland's initial classification of crime victims first recognized the difference between the victimization of society as a whole and the victimization of individuals. Sutherland proposed that individual victimization occurred in one of two ways: direct victimization (being murdered, raped, etc.) or indirect victimization (having to pay taxes for the criminal justice system or paying higher prices for goods). Sutherland surmised that there were many more indirect victims.

Sutherland's examination of victims of homicide provides similar insight into analyses that are being undertaken today. Sutherland recognized the difference in rates based upon race, gender, age, and ethnic origin. He recognized the problem of domestic homicides and was also the first to report on the interracial nature of homicide. Sutherland found that "the victim and the offender generally belong to the same group, with reference to color, nationality, and age."[7] He even estimated the costs of victimization. Based upon available data in the early 1900s, the estimates of the costs of crime were upwards of $6 billion. Even though this inclusion of the victims of crime was an integral part of his study of American criminology, it would be another 50 or 60 years before the study of crime victims and related issues became part of mainstream criminology. Even Sutherland abandoned his inclusion of the study of crime victims. In later editions of his book, the chapter on the victims of crime was no longer included, and the discussion of the impact of crime upon victims was reduced to just a couple of pages and footnotes, much like the crime victim in the criminal justice system. The study of crime victimization and the crime victim garnered very little support prior to the 1940s.

NOTES

1. Robert A. Jerin and Laura J. Moriarty, *Victims of Crime* (Chicago, IL: Nelson-Hall, 1998); Stephen Schafer, *The Victim and His Criminal* (New York: Random House, 1968).

2. Schafer, *The Victim.*

3. Dale G. Parent, Barbara Auerbach, and Kenneth E. Carlson, *Compensating Crime Victims: A Summary of Policies and Practices* (Washington DC: U.S. Department of Justice, 1992), 54.

4. Schafer, *The Victim.*

5. Elmer H. Johnson, *Crime Prevention: Approaches, Practices and Evaluations* (Westport, CT: Greenwood Press, 1987).

6. Edwin H. Sutherland, *Criminology* (Philadelphia: J. B. Lippincott, 1924).

7. Ibid, 64.

SUGGESTED READING

William G. Doerner and Steven P. Lab, *Victimology*, 5th ed. (Newark, NJ: Lexis/Nexis, 2008); Robert A. Jerin and Laura J. Moriarty, *The Victims of Crime* (Upper Saddle River, NJ: Prentice Hall, 2009).

ROBERT A. JERIN

HISTORY OF VICTIMOLOGY, 1940s. It is generally believed that the role and responsibility of the criminal justice system is to apprehend offenders and protect the rights of victims. Yet for much of history there were no institutions, ideologies, laws on the books, nor legal codes dictating the definitive structure of crime and punishment.[1] Although serious crimes were recognized as unacceptable behavior, it was up to the victim to decide what actions to take against the offender. The understanding that everyone fended for one's self was an integral aspect of the social norm.[2] Offenders might be subject to a philosophy of retribution, which implies that they should suffer in proportion to the degree of harm caused by their actions, or restitution, which implied that the offender should render payment in an amount sufficient to make the victim feel whole again. Either response emphasized the principle of *lex talionis,* i.e., an eye for an eye, and thus constituted something akin to a victim justice system.[3]

Consequently it was the impact of capitalism and social forces driven by a free market economy that contributed to the demise of the victim justice system.[4] Feudal barons of the day, for example, laid claim to all forms of compensation gained through retribution and in doing so provided a lucrative framework for increasing their own status and riches. Crime and criminal acts were now redefined as violations against the state rather than against victims. The victim is then regulated to the status of witness for the state, and the once heralded victim justice system is restructured into the criminal justice system. To this end, the previous emphasis on victims and victimization faded from the public discourse into relative obscurity. It appears that the criminal justice system simply forgot about victims and their best interest and shifted all concerns to the rights of the accused.[5]

Although this state of affairs continued late into the twentieth century, the issue of victims and victimization reemerged into the environs of public discourse sometime during the 1940s. Although the age of modernity ushered in a preoccupation with controlling an ever growing criminal class, several researchers began to examine the broader context of criminal justice as a way to recognize the significance of victimization as an integral part of crime, i.e., events that occur between offenders and victims.[6] However much of the research was not designed to illicit passion for the victim of crime but to structure an epistemology designed specifically to blame the victim. The principle architect of this scholarship was Hans von Hentig, who developed a theory explaining the cause and effects of criminal activity as a form of social interaction occurring between the victim and offender.[7] This activity, which he noted as the criminal-victim dyad, cast the victim in the role of agent provocateur, a rather flamboyant term normally associated with spy novels of the period.[8] Within this social dynamic, the ultimate victim begins the encounter as the aggressor and for some reason ends up the loser in a broader confrontation. This analysis manifested out of a victim typology, which von Hentig used to direct attention to several individuals and groups who were theoretically cast into the framework of the dyad.[9] By virtue of age, gender, sexual practices, mental capacity, and ethnicity, for example, people became victims of crime because of some innate desire to be victimized or because they had direct involvement in the criminal act. Although he attested to the idea that the victim was not always the primary cause of their own victimization, the theory inadvertently or otherwise set the tone for future researchers to follow this same path of theoretical destruction.[10]

In one sense, von Hentig is to be commended for reintroducing the victim back into the public discourse and for recognizing the importance of a victim-based academic orientation. However, it is important to note also that he, like so many others, systematically failed to acknowledge the damage inflicted by offenders, ignored recuperative or rehabilitative efforts for victims, and bypassed other more critical concerns consistent with the needs of victims to attain justice in the aftermath of their experiences. In an attempt to understand the nature of crime causation, this cohort was more concerned with developing empirical studies that revealed how the victim contributed to their own demise.[11] This blame-the-victim strategy set off a major ideological confrontation that gave rise to an epistemology that nearly destroyed the field long before gaining the clarity needed for advanced study.

NOTES

1. William G. Doerner and Steven P. Lab, *Victimology*, 4th ed. (Miamisburg, OH: Anderson Publishing, 2005), 1–3.

2. Ibid, 1–3.

3. Ibid, 2.

4. Ibid, 3.

5. Harvey Wallace, *Victimology: Legal, Psychological, and Social Perspectives*, 2nd ed. (Boston: Pearson Education, 2007), 8.

6. Lawrence E. Cohen and Marcus Felson, "Social Change and Crime Rate Trends: A Routine Activity Approach," *American Sociological Review* 44 (1979), 588–608.

7. Hans von Hentig, *The Criminal and His Victim: Studies in the Sociobiology of Crime* (New Haven, CT: Yale University Press, 1948).

8. Microsoft® Encarta®Online Encyclopedia, "Spy Fiction," http://au.encarta.msn.com.

9. See Bruce Berg, *Qualitative Research Methods for the Social Sciences,* 6th ed. (Boston: Allyn & Bacon, 2007), 207–208, who provides a discussion relating to the relevance of this method in qualitative research. In this respect, a typology is a systematic method used for classifying similar events, actions, objects, people, or places, into discrete groups. Yet constructs of this type are also frowned upon in the social sciences. See, for example, Brian H. Spitzberg and William R. Cupach, "The State of the Art of Stalking: Taking Stock of the Emerging Literature," *Aggression and Violent Behavior* 12 (2006): 64–86, who argued that theoretical models produced by this method are at best, nothing more than categorizations of social phenomenon without the benefit of empirical development. The latter statement reflects a central problem in von Hentig's model, which established categories that he used specifically to blame individuals and groups for their own victimization.

10. See Beniamin Mendelsohn, "The Origin and Doctrine of Victimology," 3 *Excerpta Criminologica* (June 1963): 239–44, who identified the relative culpability of the victim in the criminal act, and Stephen Schafer, *The Victim and His Criminal* (New York: Random House, 1968), who revised the victims' role in their own demise as a form of functional responsibility. As seen in the work of von Hentig, both inevitably validated the cause and effects of victimization as a form of victim precipitation.

11. See Marvin E. Wolfgang, *Patterns in Criminal Homicide* (Montclair, NJ: Patterson Smith, 1958, 1975), who followed this path in the 1950s, and Menachim Amir, *Patterns in Forcible Rape* (Chicago: University of Chicago Press, 1971), who did the same in the 1970s.

SUGGESTED READING

Stanley A. Cook, *The Laws of Moses and the Code of Hammurabi* (London: Adam and Charles Black, 1903); Tracy Tolbert, *The Sex Crime Scenario* (Dubuque, IA: Kendall / Hunt, 2006).

TRACY FAYE TOLBERT

HISTORY OF VICTIMOLOGY, 1950s. Those living in the United States in the 1950s have been referred to as the "silent generation." After the disruptions in their everyday lives and plans for the future that had occurred during World War II, people were trying to establish some normalcy in their existence and achieve personal goals such as having good paying jobs, buying homes, and establishing families. Americans tended to be most concerned about their own immediate needs. Although several movements directed toward reducing the victimization of racial minorities, the poor, and women and children emerged during the 1950s, the achievement of the goals and the changes being sought by these movements in terms of new legislation did not generally materialize until the following decades.

Victimization of Racial Minorities

During the reconstruction period following the Civil War, the southern states, through legislation (Jim Crow Laws) and intimidation, systematically discriminated against the African Americans living in these states. Most of the southern states ignored the provisions of the Fourteenth Amendment to the United States Constitution and of the Civil Rights Act of 1871. This legislation protected the rights of U.S. citizens, even if state governments attempted to infringe on these rights. In 1896, the U.S. Supreme Court ruled in *Plessy v. Ferguson*[1] that the policies of providing "separate but equal" public accommodations and educational programs for members of different races was constitutional. As a result, African Americans were victimized in virtually all areas of their public life—politically, educationally, and socially—well into the middle of the twentieth century.

In the early 1950s, African Americans and other minorities began organizing to secure the rights that they felt were being denied to them. In 1951, a group of African Americans in the United States requested that the United Nations consider their discrimination complaints against the U.S. government. The United Nations did not respond, but this organized effort called attention to the problems that existed and helped to solidify the emerging civil rights movement.[2]

In 1954, the U.S. Supreme Court in *Brown v. Board of Education of Topeka, Kansas*[3] declared that the practice followed in some states of establishing "separate but equal facilities" in school systems was "inherently unequal" and thus unconstitutional. The implementation of the provisions of *Brown v. Board of Education* was not immediate. African Americans continued to be thwarted by local and state officials in their attempts to end their victimization. Leaders of the civil rights movement sought national attention by organizing high-profile events such as the 1955 Montgomery, Alabama, bus boycott and the Selma, Alabama, march. When the mass media revealed the manner in which protesters were arrested, mistreated, and brutalized by police, the public outcries forced federal government officials to take action. This opened the door for new federal legislation directed toward ending the victimization of African Americans and other racial minorities. The passage of the Civil Rights Act of 1964 and the Voting Rights Act of 1965 can be attributed directly to the civil rights movement that began in the 1950s.

Neglect and Abuse of Children

Although the states may define child abuse and neglect somewhat differently, all states and the District of Columbia have enacted legislation protecting children from physical and sexual abuse or neglect. The National Center on Child Abuse and Neglect compiles yearly statistics, gathered from reports submitted by the states, on the amount of abuse and neglect as well as the types of child victimization that occurred and the perpetrators of the victimization.

In addition to defining child abuse, the states have enacted legislation that specifies which professionals (doctors, teachers) are required to report suspected abuse and the procedures to be followed by those professionals who are charged with responding to protect children who have been victimized and are in need of care.

During the 1950s, the extent of child victimization through physical and sexual abuse was being researched, but as with other forms of victimization, it was not until the 1960s and 1970s that major legislation to protect children from abuse was enacted. Numerous research studies focusing on the family completed in the 1950s revealed that a large portion of the victimization of children occurs within the immediate family and that the effects of being victimized can extend throughout a person's life. Research completed in the 1950s also revealed considerable victimization of institutionalized children, those who were sent to orphanages, group homes, or institutions for delinquents.

Victimization in the Juvenile Justice System

In the 1950s a separate juvenile justice system had been in operation in most of the states for almost a half century. Nevertheless, juveniles who were accused of delinquent acts (acts that would be considered criminal if committed by an adult) and those accused of status offenses (acts that would not be illegal if committed by an adult), when arrested and sent to court, were not given the due process rights guaranteed by the U.S. Constitution to adults accused of crimes. Under the doctrine of *parens patriae*, which viewed the judge as acting as a "benevolent parent," judges had almost unlimited discretion to mete out punishments that were often far more severe than would be justified by the severity of the offenses. It was not until the 1960s and early 1970s that the U.S. Supreme Court ruled that juveniles accused of crimes had most of the same rights as adults, including the right to an attorney, to remain silent, to be protected against double jeopardy, and to be judged by the standard of proof beyond a reasonable doubt. When these rights were provided to juveniles, much of their victimization was eliminated.

Summary

In the 1950s many practices existed that contributed to the victimization of minority group members, the poor, and juveniles. Efforts to correct these forms of victimization began to occur in the 1950s, but the mood and focus of the population was such that many citizens preferred to concentrate on their own needs rather than extend support and assistance to those being victimized. Toward the end of the 1950s, the mass media played an important role in informing the general public of the injustices that existed and in motivating citizens to become involved in movements to correct these problems.

NOTES

1. *Plessy v. Ferguson,* 163 U.S. 537 (1896).

2. W. L. Patterson, *We Charge Genocide: The Crime of Government Against the Negro People* (New York: International, 1970).

3. *Brown v. Board of Education of Topeka, Kansas* 347 U.S. 483 (1954).

SUGGESTED READING

Doug Imig, "Building a Social Movement for America's Children," *Journal of Children & Poverty* 12, no. 1 (2006): 21–37.

PETER C. KRATCOSKI

HISTORY OF VICTIMOLOGY, 1960s. The 1960s are remembered as a time of social tumult in the United States. The civil rights movement, the women's rights movement, and the movement to end the war in Vietnam all took to the streets to advance their causes. The Supreme Court under Chief Justice Earl Warren was creating its own revolution in a series of landmark decisions spelling out rights for those accused of crimes. Conservatives reacted to these changes by campaigning for law and order to protect good citizens from rising crime. These wildly disparate elements of the 1960s eventually came together to create a new movement concerned with the rights of victims in the criminal justice system.

The Quiet Revolutionaries: Academics and Professionals Discover Victims

Pediatric radiologist C. Henry Kempe and his colleagues published "The Battered-Child Syndrome" in 1962. The article presented graphic evidence of severe physical abuse of small children committed by their parents. Even before its publication, child advocates were expressing concern about protection of children from abuse. The 1962 social security amendments required states to provide all children in need with child welfare services, including protection and remediation from child abuse. The battered child syndrome brought the weight of the medical establishment to the problem of abused children. The problem was seen as a medical one; the solution was psychological treatment for the offending parent. The focus of social work interventions shifted from families in need of services to children who needed protection from their families.

Similarly, the medical establishment considered that the horrible stories of wife beating emerging from women's groups could be explained by the psychopathology of the brutish abuser and the victim who stayed in the relationship based on her own masochistic needs.

Outside of medicine, actual research into victims of crime was still rare in the 1960s. Sociologists studied criminals, not victims. The few studies that looked at victims focused on the victim's actions in a dyadic relationship that led to the crime. This framework inevitably led to attributing at least part of the crime to the victim rather than to the offender. This victim blame later became a barrier between researchers and the victim advocacy community.

The Emerging Consciousness of Minorities and Women

Both the civil rights and women's rights movements reemerged in the 1960s as challenges to the traditional order of American society, calling attention to the gap between the American values of equality and fairness and the reality of the inability of blacks and women to participate fully in a range of American institutions.

The National Association for the Advancement of Colored People (NAACP) won a major victory with the 1954 U.S. Supreme Court decision in *Brown v. Board of Education of Topeka*,[1] which declared that segregated education was inherently unequal. By the 1960s, however, it became apparent that "all deliberate speed" in implementing the decision was an invitation to postpone desegregation forever. The civil rights movement began a range of nonviolent but highly visible actions in the form of sit ins, marches, and boycotts that called the attention of people outside the south to the injustices of segregation. By successfully creating social change from the grassroots up, rather than from elite decision makers down, the civil rights movement provided the template for every social movement that followed.

The publication of Betty Friedan's book *The Feminine Mystique* is often credited with triggering the second wave of the women's movement in the United States. Friedan articulated the isolation and stultification experienced by women in the middle-class suburban home culture that emerged in the 1950s. Friedan helped found the National Organization for Women, modeled after the National Association for the Advancement of Colored People, to lobby for equal rights for women.

Many of the women who became active in the women's movement were veterans of the civil rights movement. In fact, the refusal of the men leading those organizations to share power with the women who did so much of the actual work was often the motivation for turning to feminist causes. As with the civil rights movement, the women's movement now had both a branch that used traditional political strategies to work for changes in laws and formal structures and a more radical and activist branch that advocated for nothing less than a fundamental reform of society.

One powerful tool for energizing women to advocate for themselves was the consciousness-raising group. When small groups of women started coming together, usually on a weekly basis, to discuss their experiences as women in a patriarchal society, victims of wife beating and rape found for the first time that they were not alone. These victims shared both the harm caused by their abusers and their mistreatment by the criminal justice system.

Law and Disorder: Redefining the Social Contract

Meanwhile, the men of the U.S. Supreme Court were revolutionizing the interpretation of the U.S. Constitution. In a series of decisions, the Court used the due process clause of the post-Civil War fourteenth amendment to rewrite the fundamental relationship between the states and criminal defendants. These decisions restricted police use of evidence gathered without a search warrant (*Mapp v. Ohio*, 1961),[2] required states to pay for legal representation of indigents accused of crimes (*Gideon v. Wainwright*, 1963),[3] and required police to inform suspects of their rights (*Miranda v. Arizona*, 1966).[4] These changes coincided with very real threats to social order. The crime rate rose substantially throughout the 1960s. The civil rights, women's rights, and antiwar movements all challenged the traditional social order. One consequence of the general concern about crime was the establishment of the Law Enforcement Assistance Administration (LEAA) in 1968. Although the LEAA was primarily oriented to improving police response to crime and unrest, it would eventually become a source of funds for new victim services programs.

The law-and-order movement championed the idea that states needed to provide protections for victims of crime in order to balance the protections provided to criminal defendants. In addition to creating the idea of victim rights, reformers argued that the social contract of the state-run justice system created a state responsibility to protect and indemnify members of the society from the harms caused by crime. The first U.S. victim compensation program was established in California in 1965, followed by others in New York and Massachusetts. In general, these programs could pay for medical costs, funeral costs, and wages lost due to crime and participation in the criminal justice system.

Laying the Groundwork for the Victims' Movement

By the end of the 1960s, the elements of the later victims' movement were in place. The civil rights movement had developed tools for grassroots movements to create change. The women's movement had brought to the surface the mistreatment of women victims of violence by the criminal justice system and begun to develop a network to support those victims outside traditional channels. Child abuse was now recognized as a common event not confined to a pathological few. The criminal justice system was being challenged on its mistreatment of victims of crime in its focus on providing due process to defendants. These disparate elements would create new institutions in the coming decade.

NOTES

1. *Brown v. Board of Education of Topeka*, 347 U.S. 483 (1954).
2. *Mapp v. Ohio*, 367 U.S. 643 (1961).
3. *Gideon v. Wainwright*, 372 U.S. 335 (1963).
4. *Miranda v. Arizona*, 384 U.S. 436 (1966).

SUGGESTED READING

C. Henry Kempe et al., "The Battered-Child Syndrome," *Journal of American Medical Association* 181 (1962): 17–24; Frank J. Weed, *Certainty of Justice: Reform in the Crime Victim Movement* (New York: Aldine de Gruyter, 1995).

JOAN CROWLEY

HISTORY OF VICTIMOLOGY, 1970s. The decade 1970–1979 saw the establishment of programs, both grassroots and system-based, dedicated to improving the situation of crime victims. Research emerging from the expanding fields of social and behavioral research, especially sociology and psychology, buttressed the social reforms of the victims' movement. Victimology became a recognized field, with its own journals and conferences. The federal government helped by funding research directly and by establishing requirements for evaluation of programs receiving federal funding.

In 1973, the first wave of the National Crime Survey (NCS, known today as the National Crime Victimization Survey) was fielded. The NCS is a complex rotating panel study of a representative sample of American households. Prior to the inception of the NCS, the only crime statistics available came from the compilation of police reports into the FBI's Uniform Crime Reports (UCRs). By interviewing victims, the NCS provides an estimate of crime patterns independent of police actions. The annual reports of the NCS provide a more accurate estimate of crime trends than the UCR and a more accurate picture of crime victims, including the harm done by crime and victim experiences with the criminal justice system.

Feminist researchers reframed ideas about victims of violence against women. Susan Brownmiller's 1975 book *Against Our Will: Men, Women, and Rape* argued powerfully that rape was a crime of violence used to subjugate women, not a sex crime committed by pathologically driven men. Ann Burgess found that rape victims displayed consistent symptoms that she labeled the rape trauma syndrome. These were a function of the rape, not a reflection of some idiosyncratic pathology of the victim. Similarly, Lenore Walker's first book, *The Battered Woman*, published in 1979, established that women stay in abusive relationships because of the actions of the batterer, not a masochistic desire for punishment. All of these works emphasized that the blame for the violence lay with the perpetrator, not with the victim.

The Women's Movement

The consciousness-raising groups of the women's movement continued to reach victims of violence who had been isolated and unheard before. The first rape crisis centers were established in 1972, as was the first U.S. shelter for battered women. These first programs struggled to raise funds within their communities and were staffed largely by women who had themselves been victims.

In addition to providing services, women began to work to change the legal structures that served more to protect men from women's accusations than to protect women from violence at the hands of men. Rape laws excluded husbands from prosecution and required proof that the victim had resisted to the utmost, even at the risk of her own further injury, in order to overcome the presumption of consent. In Michigan, feminists succeeded in passing a model rape statute in 1975, establishing degrees of sexual assault based on the level of force used and eliminating the spousal exception. Over time, these reforms spread to the rest of the country.

In the area of domestic violence, victim advocates identified two problems hindering effective police intervention. First, since the vast majority of domestic assaults were classified as misdemeanors, officers could not make an arrest unless they observed the crime or the victim had sworn out a warrant. The first warrantless arrest law was passed in Minnesota in 1978, allowing officers to make an arrest based on probable cause, the same standard used in felonies. The second problem was that officers often used their discretion to avoid making an arrest even when an arrest was legal. Activists responded by lobbying to make arrest mandatory in domestic violence situations; the first such law was passed in Oregon in 1977.

Expanding the Federal Role in Protecting Victims: LEAA and CAPTA

The Law Enforcement Assistance Administration (LEAA) was established in 1968 to provide funding to stem the growth of crime in the United States by improving policing and, later, the criminal justice system more broadly. Beginning in 1974, LEAA moved to provide funds for programs serving victims. Many grassroots organizations such as rape crisis centers and domestic violence shelters could now get federal money to expand and stabilize their services.

Based on research showing that a major source of lost prosecutions could be traced to formerly cooperative witnesses dropping out of the process because of mistreatment by the criminal justice system, LEAA also promoted the establishment of victim/witness service programs. These programs were designed to provide notification and support to victims. Although they used many of the ideas developed by the grassroots organizations, their primary function was to facilitate the conviction and sentencing of defendants. LEAA also funded training for police and other criminal justice professionals in working with victims.

Victim-witness programs provided a mechanism for victims to access the victim compensation programs being set up by states. By 1979, at least 28 states had established such programs. Although the programs were initially conceived as social welfare providing help for needy victims, during the 1970s the programs became contingent not on need but on cooperation with the criminal justice system. To many advocates, especially those frustrated with the criminal justice approach to domestic violence, victim compensation appeared to be another way to coerce victims into complying with the needs of the system rather than a compassionate response to the harm caused by crime.

LEAA-funded conferences allowed the development of institutions to facilitate the growth of the new field of victim advocacy. The National Organization of Victim Assistance, the National Coalition Against Domestic Violence, and the National Coalition against Sexual Assault were all established following LEAA-funded conferences. These organizations provided continued training, sharing of ideas, and the establishment of professional identification for advocates. They also facilitated mobilization of efforts for legal and social reforms to better serve victims of crime.

Unfortunately, problems with the scope and performance of LEAA led to its defunding in 1979. Many of the new victim services programs collapsed for lack of money to continue. Although many of the functions of LEAA were taken up by other divisions within the Department of Justice, the end of the 1970s and the early 1980s were lean times for victim services.

While LEAA was funding programs for adult victims of crime, the Child Abuse Protection and Treatment Act of 1974 (CAPTA) established a new mandate for responding to child victims. CAPTA established the National Center on Child Abuse and Neglect (NCCAN) with a mandate to enhance research and training for professionals working with abused children. State funding was made contingent on providing immunity for people reporting child abuse, immediate investigations of reports, and mechanisms for enforcing laws against child abuse. Although the NCCAN was located in the Health, Education, and Welfare department, its requirements for multidisciplinary teams meant that the criminal justice system would be drawn into investigations and legal proceedings involving abused children. The 1978 amendments to CAPTA included provisions emphasizing responding to an expanded definition of child sexual abuse as well as requirements to facilitate adoption when children could not be promptly and safely returned home. The emphasis on investigating allegations moved the response to child abuse away from a social services framework for providing support to troubled families toward the potential criminalization of abusive parents.

New Voices: Survivors of Homicide Victims

Whereas crime victims now had support from victim-witness programs, survivors of homicide victims had no such support unless they had been witnesses to the death of their loved one. Driven by grief and often angered by their treatment by the criminal justice system, survivors began forming groups to support each other emotionally and to advocate for changes to the legal system. These groups included Families and Friends of Missing Persons, founded in 1974, and Parents of Murdered Children, founded in 1978.

Emergence of Conflict:
Lay Advocates and Professionals

The early victim services programs were established by grassroots activists whose expertise and motivations were grounded in their direct experience working with victims of crime. As the programs became more formal and required more funding, the funding agencies required more training and more traditional professionalism in the staff. To the activists, the professionals often seemed to see victims as pathologically harmed and stigmatized. The professionals were often more comfortable working within established structures and protocols than were the advocates. These tensions remain, to a greater or lesser extent depending on the specific circumstances in each community and agency.

SUGGESTED READING

Susan Brownmiller, *Against Our Will: Men, Women, and Rape* (New York: Simon & Schuster, 1975); Lenore E. Walker, *The Battered Woman* (New York: HarperCollins, 1979).

JOAN CROWLEY

HISTORY OF VICTIMOLOGY, 1980s. The 1980s is characterized as a time of marked growth for the victims' rights movement and victimology in general. Historic pieces of legislation were enacted, several federal programs were created, and research on victimology flourished. The 1980s was a conservative time in history, which in more recent times translates to less interest in social service and social science issues, but the law-and-order movement contributed to a focus on victims not receiving justice because offenders were being treated with leniency.[1] The 1980s victims' rights movement focused on offender accountability and vengeance with a focus on street crime versus less tangible crimes like environmental and white-collar crimes.[2] Policies that evolved from this new trajectory allowed for longer and more severe prison sentences that were created under the guise of "helping" victims, though all they really did was to impose a greater burden on the correctional system.[3] Additionally, by the end of the 1980s the United States had soared from being the country with the third highest incarceration rate and severity in punishments to the first—all attributable to the law-and-order movement characterizing individuals as having evil tendencies.[4] At the same time, we see progress toward acknowledging victimizations that were once considered outside the realm of the criminal justice system, such as child abuse, domestic violence, sexual assault, and other interpersonal crimes.

Legislative growth in victimology in the 1980s included the following milestone pieces of legislation: establishment of a national Victim Rights Week (1981), the Victim and Witness Protection Act (1982), and the Victims of Crime Act (1984)-one of the most influential acts for crime victims enacted. On April 8, 1981, President Ronald Reagan proclaimed that the week beginning April 19, 1981, would be Victims' Rights Week as a symbol to victims that federal, state, and local systems should redouble their efforts to provide comprehensive services to crime victims.[5] Each year since 1981 there has been a dedicated Victims' Rights Week with organized celebration efforts by federal, state, and local agencies that work with crime victims. The Victim and Witness Protection Act of 1982 mandated, among other things, that victim impact statements be a standard part of the court process, and it provided guidelines for how victims should be fairly treated by criminal justice personnel.[6] The guidelines in this act were the basis for numerous states' Victim's Bill of Rights.[7] The Victims of Crime Act (VOCA) of 1984 established the Office for Victims of Crime in the Office of Justice Programs within the Department of Justice. It also established the Crime Victims Fund, which supplies money to state compensation programs and local victim services programs.[8] Money from the fund is utilized to support numerous agencies that provide services to crime victims and is often integral to the success of these programs. Two additional pieces of legislation enacted that were specific to children were the Missing Children Act of 1982 and the Missing Children's Assistance Act of 1984. The Missing Children's Assistance Act of 1984 called for the creation of what would ultimately become the National Center for Missing and Exploited Children.[9] As of 2008, every state had the equivalent of a "Victim's Bill of Rights," and this trend began in the 1980s.[10]

Another milestone event in the 1980s was the President's Task Force on Victims of Crime. President Reagan created the task force to explore issues related to crime victimization in 1982. The task force released their findings in 1982 and proposed 68 recommendations on how to improve treatment of and rights for crime victims by criminal justice agencies and other organizations that work with crime victims, such as hospitals, mental health facilities, faith-based organizations, and businesses.[11]

Outside of the United States legislation was created that supported similar rights as those advocated in the United States, including "the right to be notified about and to participate in judicial proceedings, to promptly get back stolen property that was recovered, to be protected from intimidation and harassment, and to receive restitution or compensation."[12] Additionally, in 1985 the General Assembly of the United Nations approved the "UN Declaration of Basic Principles of

Justice for Victims of Crime and Abuse of Power," which articulated that the United Nations formally recognized that there were millions of people in the world who suffered harmful effects from crime and the abuse of power.[13]

In regard to scholarship, there were some interesting developments in the 1980s including the first implementation of International Crime Victim Surveys, which evaluated victimization across countries in multiple continents.[14] Opportunity theory[15] was first introduced and proposed somewhat of an integration of routine activities theory and lifestyle theory. Essentially, opportunity theory suggests that people's lifestyles will bring them or their property into contact with motivated offenders and the lack of capable guardians, thus leading to greater risk of victimization if they live high-risk lifestyles.[16] Additional areas of research that were initiated in the 1980s[17] included investigations into the victims' rights movements both within and outside of the United States. Research conducted in the United Kingdom on victim satisfaction, victim needs, and victim experiences with the criminal justice system may have contributed to or shaped the decision of the British government to provide funding to assist crime victims in various ways.[18] Studies in the 1980s contributed to an understanding that even property crime victims experienced emotional trauma in response to a victimization.[19] It also started to emerge in the 1980s that victims may simply want to be included in the criminal justice process, not to be particularly punitive as legislation enacted in the 1980s may have suggested.[20]

NOTES

1. Ezzat A. Fattah, "Victimology: Past, Present, and Future," *Criminologie* 33, no. 1 (2000): 17–46.

2. Ibid.

3. Ibid.

4. Robert Elias, "Paradigms and Paradoxes of Victimology," http://www.aic.gov.au/publications/proceedings/27/elias.html.

5. William G. Doerner and Steven P. Lab, *Victimology,* 5th ed. (Newark, NJ: Anderson, 2008).

6. Office for Victims of Crime, *New Directions from the Field: Victims' Rights and Services for the 21st Century* (Washington DC: U.S. Department of Justice, 1998).

7. Ibid.

8. Harvey Wallace, *Victimology: Legal, Psychological, and Social Perspectives,* 2nd ed. (Boston, MA: Pearson Education, 2007).

9. Elizabeth Quinn DeValve, "For Adam: The John Walsh Story," in *Icons of Crime Fighting,* ed. Jeffrey Bumgarner (Westport, CT: Greenwood Press, 2008).

10. Andrew Karmen, *Crime Victims: An Introduction to Victimology,* 6th ed. (Belmont, CA: Thomson Wadsworth, 2007).

11. Peggy M. Tobolowsky, *Crime Victim Rights and Remedies* (Durham, NC: Carolina Academic Press, 2001).

12. Fattah, "Victimology," 33.

13. Ibid, 17–46.

14. Ibid.

15. Lawrence E. Cohen, J. Kluegel, and K. C. Land, "Social Inequality and Predatory Criminal Victimization: An Exposition and a Test of a Formal Theory," *American Sociological Review* 46 (1981): 505–24.

16. Fattah, "Victimology," 17–46.

17. Leslie Sebba, "On the Relationship between Criminological Research and Policy: The Case of Crime Victims," *Criminal Justice* 1, no. 1 (2001): 27–58.

18. Ibid.

19. Ibid.

20. Ibid.

SUGGESTED READING

Office for Victims of Crime, "The History of the Crime Victims' Movement in the United States," U.S. Department of Justice, http://www.ojp.usdoj.gov/ovc/ncvrw/2005/pg4c.html.

ELIZABETH QUINN DEVALVE

HISTORY OF VICTIMOLOGY, 1990s. The 1990s brought many changes for victimology and victim services. Political advocacy during this decade strengthened with a more organized and focused agenda. The issues that emerged during this timeframe included expanded funding for victim services, adopting victims' rights, and professionalizing the victim services field.

Funding for Victim Services

The 1990s was a time of increased funding for victim services. One of the more extensive funding packages came with the passage of the federal Violence Against Women Act of 1994 (VAWA). This law provided $1.6 billion in funding over a six-year period. VAWA provided for several provisions under the broad categories of safe streets, safe homes, civil rights, equal justice for women in the courts, national stalker and domestic violence reduction, and protections for battered immigrant women and children. The law also enforced restitution orders, increased penalties for sexual assaults for victims under 16 years old, expanded victim services, increased pretrial detention of the accused, provided mandatory restitution of the convicted, and expanded the ability of victims to use the civil justice system.

Within two years after the passage of VAWA, all 50 states as well as the District of Columbia had crime victim compensation programs to help reimburse victims for the monetary losses they suffered as a result of violent crimes. By 1996, over $525 million worth of fines, penalty fees, bond forfeitures, and special assessments was deposited into the federal Victims of Crime Act (VOCA) Crime Victims Fund. These monies were then allocated to states for victim compensation programs, victim services, and training and technical assistance. That same year, the Office for Victims of Crime (OVC) recognized the need to stabilize state funding of victim service programs, to provide funds for underserved populations, and to improve victims' rights. For the first time in 1997, OVC also provided grants for victim services in Indian Country.

Federal Legislation and Victims' Rights

During the 1990s, the federal government was responsible for passing broad-based legislation to address hate crimes with the enactment of the Violent Crime Control and Law Enforcement Act of 1994 that increased penalties for federal hate crimes due to one's race, color, religion, national origin, ethnicity, gender, disability, or sexual orientation. Congress also addressed child protection with the passage of Megan's Law in 1996, which provided community notification on the location of convicted sex offenders, and the Child Protection and Sexual Predator Punishment Act of 1998, which provided for sentencing enhancements addressing sex crimes against children including using the Internet. In 1998, the Crime Victims with Disabilities Act was passed to gather information on the prevalence of victimization of individuals with disabilities. Finally, Congress passed the Identity Theft and Assumption Deterrence Act of 1998, which outlawed identity theft, increased penalties, and provided information to victims.

The 1990s was also a decade that saw the expansion of victims' rights. In 1991, the U.S. Supreme Court in *Payne v. Tennessee*[1] upheld the right of victims to give a victim impact statement in capital cases. *Payne v. Tennessee* overruled previous cases (*Booth v. Maryland*[2] and *South Carolina v. Gathers*[3]) in which lower courts ruled that victim impact statements were inadmissible during sentencing in a capital case. The U.S. Supreme Court ruling ensured the enforcement of a victim's right to a victim impact statement.

In 1996, the Antiterrorism and Effective Death Penalty Act was adopted, which made restitution mandatory in federal violent crime cases (e.g., domestic violence and sexual exploitation), community restitution available for certain drug offenses, and compensation and services available to victims of domestic and international terrorism, including the military. This Act provided funding for victims and survivors of the Oklahoma City bombing. The same year, the U.S.

Department of Justice through the Office for Juvenile Justice and Delinquency Prevention (OJJDP) enacted the Juvenile Justice Action Plan, which provided recommendations for victims' rights and services for victims of juvenile offenders. The National Domestic Violence Hotline (1-800-799-SAFE) was established in 1996 to provide crisis intervention, information, and assistance.

In 1996, the U.S. House of Representatives and Senate introduced a bipartisan federal Victims' Rights Constitutional Amendment. The Congressional Judiciary Committees held hearings, and Attorney General Janet Reno testified in support of adopting the proposed amendment. During the presidential election that year, both candidates endorsed the concept of the amendment. Hearings were held in Congress throughout the 1990s, but no action was taken. As of 2008, the United States does not have a federal Victims' Rights Constitutional Amendment. Despite the lack of movement at the federal level, the states made strides in this area. By 1995, 48 states had adopted victims' rights legislation through a Victims' Bill of Rights, and within four years, 31 states passed constitutional amendments to protect victims' rights within their borders.

Professionalism and Education

The move to professionalize the field gained momentum in the 1990s with the implementation of professional development seminars and academic programs. In 1995, OVC created the National Victim Assistance Academy (NVAA) model, which provided a 40-hour foundation-level course in victim services. Within three years, nearly 700 practitioners from all 50 states, one American territory, and three foreign countries attended the Academy. The NVAA was evaluated in 2003 and began again with a modified curriculum and format in 2007. The NVAA was the basis for the creation of the State Victim Assistance Academy (SVAA) initiative. The SVAA is a state-based foundation-level program that began in Michigan in 1998. In 1999, OVC created a multiyear grant for the development of SVAAs throughout the United States. As of 2008, approximately 40 states received SVAA funding. The 1990s was also a period when many U.S. universities across academic programs provided victimology course(s) to students. By the end of the decade, a few colleges and universities adopted a comprehensive academic program that offered a degree in victimology or victim services.

NOTES

1. *Payne v. Tennessee* 501 U.S. 808 (1991).

2. *Booth v. Maryland,* 482 U.S. 496 (1987).

3. *South Carolina v. Gathers,* 490 U.S. 805 (1989).

SUGGESTED READING

National Association of VOCA Assistance Administrators Web site, http://www.navaa.org;
    National Coalition Against Domestic Violence Web site, http://www.ncadv.org; Steven
    D. Walker and Dean G. Kilpatrick, "Scope of Crime/Historical Review of the Victims'
    Rights Discipline," in *National Victim Assistance Academy Textbook* (Washington, DC:
    Office for Victims of Crime, 2002).

BERNADETTE MUSCAT

HISTORY OF VICTIMOLOGY, 2000 TO TODAY. The first decade of the
twenty-first century continues to advance the causes of previous decades in terms
of continued funding for victim services, expansion of grants for program development and evaluation, more extensive legislation to assist victims and promote
rights, and greater educational opportunities for those in victim services.

Funding for Victim Services

The federal government renewed its commitment to end sexual assault and intimate partner violence by passing the Violence Against Women Act (VAWA) of
2005. The new legislation builds on earlier versions of VAWA (1994 and 2000) to
bring together existing resources, to promote collaboration to efficiently and
effectively deliver victim services, and to continue the progress made since
VAWA's inception. To meet these goals, VAWA provides funding for existing programs and to develop new services to better assist victims. Funding is also available to improve criminal justice and legal responses to victimization against
women. VAWA (2005) also creates new funding streams for Sexual Assault
Services Programs (the first federal funding for direct services to address sexual
victimization), a National Resource Center on Workplace Responses, housing
resources to ensure that victims have a home, prevention and early intervention
programs to help children who have witnessed intimate partner violence, and
training to improve healthcare practitioner's response to victims. There are provisions that specifically address the needs of American Indian and Alaska Native
women including improved law enforcement response, establishing a tribal registry to track sex offenders and protection orders, and funding for research to
ascertain the prevalence of victimization and program evaluation to determine
access, availability, and effectiveness of service delivery to this target population.

Grant Programs

Many grant programs began in the 1990s and continued into the next decade.
A new grant program was announced in October 2003 by President George Bush
to fund a pilot program called the President's Family Justice Center Initiative

(PFJCI). The Office of Violence Against Women (OVW) awarded more than $20 million to 15 communities nationwide to develop and implement comprehensive services to assist and support victims of intimate partner violence. The PFJCI provides a one-stop-shop approach to victim services by allowing victims to go to a single location for all service needs. The PFJCI brings community and system-based victim advocates, social services, law enforcement, probation officers, medical and mental health professionals, attorneys, and the faith-based community together to help victims. The PFJCI helps victims by improving the efficiency of coordinated service delivery by reducing the fragmentation, eliminating the need to travel, and reducing the amount of time and effort it takes to receive services.

Legislation

During the 2000s, the federal government passed many pieces of legislation to address victimization. Three of the more sweeping legislative accomplishments include the Trafficking Victims Protection Act of 2000, the Justice for All Act of 2004, and the Adam Walsh Child and Safety Protection Act of 2006.

In October 2000, Congress passed the Trafficking Victims Protection Act of 2000 to address trafficking in persons by funding state and local governments, tribal governments, and nonprofit organizations to provide services to victims. The act also provides funding for research, evaluation, training, and technical assistance and grants to enhance services and improve response to victims of trafficking.

The Justice for All Act of 2004 contains several provisions including protecting and enforcing crime victims' rights in federal criminal proceedings. These rights include protection from the accused; notification; presence, participation, and timeliness of public court proceedings; conferring with a government attorney; full and timely restitution; and to be treated with fairness and respect for the victim's dignity and privacy. The act also creates a mechanism for enforcing these rights by allowing the victim or government to file a petition within the court of appeals asserting a violation of the victim's rights. If the court denies relief, the court of appeals must issue a decision within 72 hours of filing indicating on the record in a written opinion why the relief was denied. The act also calls for the elimination of the backlog of DNA samples collected from crime scenes and offenders and to improve and expand the DNA testing capacity of all crime laboratories.

The Adam Walsh Child Protection and Safety Act of 2006 builds on existing legislation by expanding the National Sex Offender Registry to provide information about sex offenders across state lines. The act imposes tough mandatory minimum penalties for serious crimes against children including sex trafficking.

Finally, the act creates regional Internet Crimes Against Children Taskforces that will provide funding to train state and local law enforcement agencies to address child exploitation through the Internet.

Educational Opportunities

In the 2000s, the educational opportunities available to victim service providers and allied professionals expanded. The National Victim Assistance Academy (NVAA), which originally began in 1995, provided a 40-hour foundation-level course in victim services. The original NVAA model was redesigned in 2007 based upon a 2003 formal evaluation of previous NVAA participants. The new NVAA includes three tracks (Foundation-Level Training, Specialized Training, and the Leadership Institute) and was first offered in December 2007 and May 2008.

In 1999, OVC created a multiyear grant for the development of the State Victim Assistance Academy (SVAA) throughout the United States. The SVAA is a collaborative effort between a victim services-based nonprofit or government organization and an academic partner. The SVAA is a week-long course that provides comprehensive foundational and academically based education for victim service and allied professionals. As of 2008, approximately 40 states received SVAA funding.

SUGGESTED READING

Office for Victims of Crime Web site, http://www.ojp.usdoj.gov/ovc; Office for Violence Against Women Web site, http://www.usdoj.gov; Allison Randall and Monica McLaughlin, "The Violence Against Women Act of 2005: Summary Provisions," The National Network to End Domestic Violence, http://www.nnedv.org/docs/Policy/VAWA2005FactSheet.pdf; John Stein and Marlene Young, "The History of the Crime Victims' Movement in the United States," Office for Victims of Crime, http://www.ovc.gov/ncvrw/2005/pg4c.html.

BERNADETTE MUSCAT

HUMAN TRAFFICKING. Although the definition may vary from country to country, most include the following four legal elements to qualify a person for the crime of trafficking in persons: (1) recruiting victims for physical control; (2) by using illegal means of threat, use of force, coercion, abduction, or fraud/deception or abuse of power; (3) for illegitimate profits; (4) through exploitation (sex or labor exploitation, or the harvesting of human organs for sale).[1] The consent of a victim is deemed to be irrelevant to qualify a person for the crime of trafficking in persons when the above illegal means are used to physically control the victim. Recruiting, moving, harboring, or receiving children under age of 18 for any form of exploitation also qualifies a person for the crime of trafficking in persons even in the case of absence of the above illegal means. The United Nations (UN) protocol on antitrafficking in persons has been in force since 2003. The number of member countries that ratified the UN protocol has more than doubled from 54 to 125 out of 155 countries. In response to the UN protocol, the U.S. Congress passed the Victims of Trafficking and Violence Protection Act in 2000, which was reauthorized by President George W. Bush twice in 2003 and 2005. Federal funding is also made available to state and local government agencies to set up 42 special task forces to coordinate regional and local antitrafficking programs and activities.

According to the Trafficking in Persons Report of 2008 by the U.S. State Department, approximately 800,000 people are trafficked across national borders; plus millions are trafficked within their own countries each year. Women and girls count for the majority of victims (80%) trafficked across international borders. Of them, 50% are children under age eighteen.[2] The International Labor Organization estimated that nearly 12.3 million people are in forced labor, bondage, or slavery servitude at any given time.

The most recent report on human trafficking released by the United Nations Office on Drugs and Crime, based on data gathered from 155 countries, offers the first global assessment of the scope of human trafficking and what is being done to fight it. It confirms that the most common form of human trafficking (79%) is sexual exploitation. The victims of sexual exploitation are predominantly women and girls. Surprisingly, in 30% of the countries that provided information on the gender of traffickers, women make up the largest proportion of traffickers. In some parts of the world, trafficking in women is the norm for business enterprise.[3] Worldwide, children make up of 20% of the trafficked population, whereas they make up the majority of trafficked victims in the Mekong River subregion and up to 100% in parts of west Africa. Forced labor and slavery servitude are ranked as the second most common form of human trafficking (18%), although this form of trafficking may have often been ignored by the governmental officials because labor exploitation has not always been deemed illegal in many countries.

Although the world has given a great deal of attention to transnational and cross-border trafficking because of its close association with sex tourism and sexual exploitation against children and women, the data repeatedly show that most trafficking in women and children takes place intraregionally or domestically close to home for the purposes of forced marriage and labors. Those victims unfortunately are often ignored by both law enforcement and local NGOs for any kind of assistance and rescues.

Human trafficking is the fastest growing criminal industry in the world with the total estimated annual profits between $5 and $9 billion. The Council of Europe states that "people trafficking has reached epidemic proportions over the past decade, with a global estimated annual market of about $42.5 billion."[4] The ILO estimated in their 2005 report that forced labor has generated approximately $32 billion a year, with half of this made in industrialized countries and close to one-third made in Asia. The sexual exploitation of women and children as a result of trafficking is estimated to earn $28 billion annually.[5]

Victims of human trafficking suffer various forms of abuse and trauma ranging from rape and sexual assault to physical and psychological threat, fear, and abuse. Although the physical injury can be treated immediately, psychological trauma often takes a long time to heal. Symptoms of post-traumatic stress are similar to those seen in survivors of torture, which include depression, anxiety, hostility and irritability, recurring nightmares and memories of abuse, difficulty concentrating and sleeping disorders, and feelings of apathy or emotional detachment. Rescue and assisting victims of human trafficking requires comprehensive efforts. Currently, the government agencies and NGOs provide various services such as housing assistance, health services, counseling services, job training skills, language and cultural assistance, transportation, and legal aid and immigration services to obtain permanent visas.

NOTES

1. For the international definition of human trafficking see The United Nations Office on Drugs and Crime, *United Nations Convention Against Transnational Organized Crime and the Protocols Thereto* (Vienna: UNODC, 2004), 42–43.

2. U.S. Department of State, *Trafficking in Persons Report 2008* (Washington DC: U.S. State Department, 2008), 7.

3. UNODC, "Global Report on Trafficking in Persons," (Vienna: UNODC, 2009).

4. The Associate Press, "The Council of Europe Says the Human Trafficking Has Reached 'Epidemic Proportions,'" December 5, 2006.

5. P. Bessler, *Forced Labor and Human Trafficking: Estimating the Profits* (Geneva: ILO, 2005).

SUGGESTED READING

Humantrafficking.org Web site, http://www.humantrafficking.org; Office for Victims of Crime Trafficking Efforts Web site, http://www.ojp.usdoj.gov/ovc/help/tip.htm.

XIN REN

I

IDENTITY THEFT. Identity theft is the misuse of another individual's personal information to commit fraud. Although it consists of a variety of acts that have long been criminalized, it was not until 1998 that it became treated as a separate offense with the passage of the Identity Theft and Assumption Deterrence Act. This Act directed the Federal Trade Commission to collect complaint data and to provide information to the public. Although accurate data on the crime are still limited, reports suggest that approximately 6.4 million households (5.5% of U.S. households) reported that at least one member of the household had been the victim of identity theft during the previous six months.[1]

With such high rates of victimization, it is not surprising that the costs of identity theft are very high. The total financial costs are estimated to be over $50 billion a year. Out-of-pocket expenses for consumers amounted to nearly $1.5 billion annually ($740 per victim). Moreover, victims experience a great deal of emotional distress including feelings of anger, helplessness and mistrust; disturbed sleep patterns; and a feeling of diminished security. Much of this distress stems from the hundreds of hours and large sums of money spent trying to resolve the problems caused by the crime.

Consumers aged 24–54; those with higher levels of income, particularly those with incomes greater than $75,000; households headed by women with three or more children; and consumers residing in the Pacific states are at the greatest risk for identity theft.[2] Older persons, particularly those aged 75 and older, and persons in the mountain states are at the least risk for victimization. Educational attainment and marital status have little effect on victimization risk.

Policy makers at federal and state levels have addressed the problem of identity theft by enacting legislation to establish penalties for offenders and by improving protection to consumers and victims. Congress passed the Fair and Accurate Credit Transactions Act (FACTA), which grants consumers the right to one free credit report every year, requires a national system of fraud detection to increase the likelihood that thieves will be caught, requires a nationwide system of fraud alerts to be placed on credit files, and requires lenders and credit agencies to take action before a victim knows a crime has occurred. Lawmakers hope that FACTA and other organizations (e.g., the Identity Theft Resource Center and the Identity Theft Complaint Center) will provide victims with a simple way to protect themselves and to recoup any losses they sustain from this crime.

NOTES

1. Bureau of Justice Statistics, *Identity Theft, 2005* (Washington DC: U.S. Government Printing Office, 2007).

2. Federal Trade Commission, "National and State Trends in Fraud and Identity Theft, January-December 2003," http://www.ftc.gov/bcp/edu/microsites/idtheft/downloads/clearinghouse_2003.pdf.

SUGGESTED READING

Megan McNally and Graeme Newman, eds., *Perspectives on Identity Theft: Crime Prevention Studies* (Monsey, NY: Criminal Justice Press, 2008); U.S. General Accounting Office, *Identity Theft: Prevalence and Cost Appear to be Growing,* Report to Congressional Requesters GAO-02-363 (Washington DC, 2002).

HEITH COPES

INCEST. Incest is defined as marriage or sexual contact between related individuals. Historically, ecclesiastical law prohibited incest because it violated biblical values. This prohibition, which is common across major world religions, was motivated by concerns about regulating marriage and transmission of property as well as preventing inbreeding.

Typically, contemporary criminal and family law prohibits sexual contact without the strict necessity of blood relations (therefore a step-parent who molests a child can be charged under an "incest" statute). Though sibling incest is reported to the police less often than father-daughter incest, several studies assert that brother-sister incest is more frequent than commonly reported and is at least five times more prevalent than parent-child incest.

Criminal codes offer many options for charging interfamilial child sexual abuse, making measurement issues difficult. Nationally, better sources of victimization data include the National Adolescent Survey, which estimates that the prevalence rate for child sexual assault is about 8% and finds that about 22% of those assaults are incestuous (of which about 14% were perpetrated by adult relatives).[1] The U.S. Department of Health and Human Services' publication, *Child Maltreatment,* finds about 55% of all confirmed cases of child sexual abuse are perpetrated by adults related to the child.[2] In the United States, the law rarely if ever punishes consensual sexual relationships among adult relatives, but a strong cultural taboo exists, often based in fears of birth defects if the pair procreates. Contemporary incest concern arose from feminist and child protection movements that brought attention to the psychological and physical harms of incest. The second-wave feminist movement focused on female victims of incest and argued for a "feminist approach" to therapy for victims. Current research explores gender differences between male and female survivors of incest and asserts that findings from female survivors should not be generalized to males.

Measurement of "harm" is hotly debated. For example, recent work has suggested that sibling incest, thought to be less traumatic than parent/child incest, has comparable detrimental impact on participants, such as feelings of isolation and distance from the victim's family. As in other areas of sexual victimization, conclusions are constrained by convenience sampling, which often relies on small clinical or retrospective samples rather than controlled, randomized studies. Therefore, counting incest victims, let alone comparing the experiences of victimization, is deeply problematic.

Family reunification has been another area of debate regarding incest policy. Recidivism data show that intrafamilial child abusers are far less likely to repeat their crimes than other categories of sex offenders or other criminal offenders. Regardless, the best interests of the child may require continued separation from the offender. Separation introduces its own set of complications for victims and their families, who may lose breadwinners or face guilt or other condemnation for "causing trouble" for the family.

NOTES

1. Dean G. Kilpatrick and Benjamin E. Saunders, *Prevalence and Consequences of Child Victimization: Results from the National Survey of Adolescents, Final Report* (Washington DC: U.S. Department of Justice, No. 181028, 2000).

2. U.S. Department of Health and Human Services, Administration on Children, Youth and Families, "Child Maltreatment 2006," U.S. Government Printing Office, http://www.acf.hhs.gov/programs/cb/pubs/cm06/index.htm, Table 3–19.

SUGGESTED READING

Emile Durkheim and Albert Ellis, *Incest: The Nature and Origin of the Taboo* (New York: Lyle Stuart, 1963, 1898).

CHRYSANTHI LEON AND LAURA RAPP

INFANTICIDE. Defined as the unlawful killing of a child under the age of five, infanticide is a subcategory of murder. Official statistics reveal that infanticide accounts for the deaths of approximately 600 American children each year.[1] However, many scholars argue that such statistics underestimate the prevalence of infanticide as they do not account for poor documentation, miscategorization of death, or corpses that are never found.

Children younger than one year of age are the most common victims of infanticide, and the overall risk of infanticide decreases as children grow older.[2] Across all age groups, male children are more likely than female children to be killed.[3] In recent years, infanticide rates have remained relatively stable across all racial groups; white children are killed more frequently than children of other racial groups.[4]

In cases of infanticide, parents are the most common offender (the parental killing of a child is termed filicide), and only 2% of infanticide victims are killed by a stranger.[5] In cases of infant infanticide, mothers are more likely to have committed the crime; fathers are more likely to kill older children.[6] Most infanticides result from the use of physical force.[7]

Although it is a subcategory of murder, there are no federally established punishment criteria for infanticide in the United States; individual states are given the power to determine the penalties they will impose upon individuals who murder children.[8] As such, response to infanticide on the part of the criminal justice system varies widely.[9] Generally, men who commit infanticide are punished more severely than women who commit the same crime, often being sentenced to lengthy periods of incarceration.[10] When women are the perpetrators of infanticide, they are often viewed in a dichotomous light as either mad (psychologically disturbed) or bad (unfit to parent) and treated accordingly.[11] As a result some women are incarcerated for their crimes and others are confined to psychiatric hospitals. The gender, race, and class biases known to exist throughout the criminal justice system are often mirrored in the punishment of infanticide as people of color and the poor often receive more punitive sentences than do their white, wealthier counterparts.[12]

Just as the criminal justice response to infanticide varies, so do social responses. Because the murder of children is a compelling topic, infanticide cases receive high levels of media coverage, particularly when the crime has been perpetrated by the mother of the victim. Often, this coverage focuses on the discord between the culturally defined expectations of motherhood and the reality of infanticide.[13] In these cases, media images often punish mothers for violating the norms of motherhood. There are situations, however, when mothers who have killed their children receive a social outpouring of support. When this occurs, media images paint women as loving mothers who killed as a result of psychosis and, therefore, were intrinsically good mothers in spite of their crimes. Despite the varying media representations of individuals who have committed infanticide, a general sense of loss and disbelief often follows these highly publicized crimes as there appears to be a social consensus that victims of infanticide did not deserve their victimization.

NOTES

1. James Alan Fox and Marianne W. Zawitz, "Homicide Trends in the United States," Bureau of Justice Statistics, http://www.ojp.usdoj.gov/bjs/homicide/homtrnd.htm.

2. Ibid.

3. Ibid.

4. Ibid.

5. Ibid.

6. Janine Jason, Jeanne C. Gilland, and Carl W. Tyler, Jr., "Homicide as a Cause of Pediatric Mortality in the United States," *Pediatrics* 72 (1983): 191–97.

7. Ibid.

8. Dan Maier-Katkin and R. S. Ogle, "Policy and Disparity: The Punishment of Infanticide in Britain and America," *International Journal of Comparative and Applied Criminal Justice* 21, no. 2 (1997): 305–16; Margaret G. Spinelli, *Infanticide: Psychosocial and Legal Perspectives on Mothers Who Kill* (Arlington, VA: American Psychiatric Publishing, Inc., 2002).

9. Elizabeth Rapaport, "Mad Women and Desperate Girls: Infanticide and Child Murder in Law and Myth," *The Fordham Urban Law Journal* 33 (2005): 527–69.

10. Ania Wilczynski, "Images of Women Who Kill Their Infants: The Mad and the Bad," *Women & Criminal Justice* 2, no. 2 (1991): 71–88.

11. Ibid.

12. Ibid.

13. Barbara Barnett, "Medea in the Media: Narrative and Myth in Newspaper Coverage of Women Who Kill Their Children," *Journalism* 7 (2006): 411–32.

SUGGESTED READING

S. E. Pitt and E. M. Bale, "Neonaticide, Infanticide, and Filicide: A Review of the Literature," *Bulletin of the American Academy of Psychiatry and Law* 23 (1995): 375–86.

JENNIFER SCROGGINS

INSTITUTIONAL ELDER ABUSE. Institutional elder abuse occurs within a nursing home or nursing facility while an elder is living in the facility. This type of abuse is perpetrated on the older individuals who cannot protect themselves due to their frailty or health. Different types of abuse that may be inflicted upon the elderly include physical, sexual, emotional, or financial abuse.[1] These incidences of abuse are increasing due to Americans living longer. Families, unfortunately, do not know this abuse is happening because the elderly victim may not be able to tell them due to their frail condition. Many times the elderly have no one to turn to in these situations. During the last 15 years increased incidences of elder abuse led the legal field to begin assisting families with protecting their elders.[2] For example, the federal government has implemented specific amendments to the Older Americans Act. Without legal assistance many families could not receive the help needed for their loved ones. Under federal and state law nursing homes are required to inform and educate their residents on their legal rights.[3] If the residents become unable to make decisions for themselves, then someone is appointed for them. If the facility fails to perform the work within the guidelines of the law, they risk losing their Medicaid or Medicare certification and funding.

The quality of nursing homes and their employed caretakers has been under great scrutiny over the past few years.[4] One main criticism is the lack of staff training and the poor conditions of the facility itself. Many facilities are overrun with residents and understaffed.[5] This has created numerous legal concerns for institutional administrators. For instance, liability can be attached if it can be shown that staff are not competent or there has been a failure to sufficiently train these staff.[6] Enacted in 2001, the Nursing Home Quality Protection Act was set up to give our elderly more personal safety and protection within these nursing homes. The act came about at the urging of consumer and elder advocates, media pressure, and government concerns and was supported by numerous public and private agencies. In a similar manner, the Older Americans Act federally mandates that an ombudsman program exist in every state to meet advocacy needs and to assist with complaints against nursing homes.

NOTES

1. Georgia Anetzberger, "The Reality of Elder Abuse," *Clinical Gerontologist* 28, no. 1–2 (2005): 1–25; L. Rene Bergeron, "Elder Abuse and Neglect: Training Issues for Professionals," in *Encyclopedia of Domestic Violence*, ed. Nicky Ali Jackson (New York: Routledge, 2007), 281–85.

2. Bergeron, "Elder Abuse."

3. National Long Term Care Ombudsman Resource Center, "Ombudsman," National Consumer Voice for Quality Long-Term Care, http://www.ltcombudsman.org/static_pages/ombudsmen.cfm.

4. Bergeron, "Elder Abuse;" Nursing Home Abuse News, "Institutional Elder Abuse," http://www.nursinghomeabuse-news.com/html/institutional.html.

5. Bergeron, "Elder Abuse."

6. Ibid.

SUGGESTED READING

Jeanette M. Daly and Gerald J. Jogerst, "Nursing Home Abuse Report and Investigation Legislation," *Journal of Elder Abuse and Neglect* 19, no. 3–4 (2007): 119–31.

PENNY A. HANSER AND ROBERT D. HANSER

INSURANCE POLICIES. If a person falls victim to burglary, vandalism, larceny theft, motor vehicle theft, or even assaults, they may be faced with damage to their property or personal possessions. Often the victim never comes face-to-face with the perpetrator as the clearance rates for crimes like burglary or larceny theft have fallen to around 12%.[1] To drive in most states individuals must have insurance that may extend to damage to the exterior; however, it may not include contents within the vehicle. This does not mean that the victim will be covered for the exterior damage if they have set a deductible (the amount initially paid by the owner before policy coverage begins) around $250. Most vehicle windows cost between $100 and $200; therefore, the victim is left paying for the damage out of pocket. The situation becomes much more complex in the event of motor vehicle theft.

Unlike car insurance, which is not optional if one wishes to drive, home or renters insurance is another matter. If individuals do decide to take out home policies, the cost is determined by the desired coverage amounts and relative risk. If a home or apartment is located in a high-crime area, then the coverage will be much more expensive and deductibles higher. This context is important, since many victims of burglary and theft live in high-crime areas because they cannot afford to live anywhere else. The cost of a policy, then, may be beyond their means. Data from the National Crime Victimization Survey (NCVS) indicate that as income increases, so does the average dollar loss to crime, so homes with incomes of $50,000–$74,000 suffer an average loss of $846,[2] but these homes are more likely to have insurance policies and may have lower "excess accountable" options.[3] This group has the income available to have the deductible at a lower rate, so if the deductible is $250, the homeowner may recoup $596 of the loss. The $250 loss for this group may appear an inconvenience that may or may not be allowable as a tax deduction. Those families who make less than $7,500 a year are more likely to live in high-crime areas due to economic necessity. These families lose an average of $405 to crime,[4] which appears to be less than the loss of the higher-earning family; however, it is these victims who are often are unable to afford policies or lower deductibles, subsequently paying the full amount of the loss out of an already tight budget.

The fact is that those without policies stand little chance of being helped in terms of recouping losses given that only those who suffer violent crimes may access victim compensation programs.[5] Individuals with the ability to obtain a policy on their home or personal possessions (renters) are often encouraged to set a high deductible since many companies will drop the policy if there are two or more small claims within a given year.[6] One is encouraged to pay for items out of pocket, but that seems counterintuitive to obtaining the policy in the first place. Given the NCVS data on the prevalence of personal loses under $50 and burglary, it would appear that having a homeowners policy does not help the "typical" crime victim at all. If the loss is significant and falls over the deductible, then only a portion can be regained and individuals may face subsequent increases in policy costs. It appears that for home-related loss of possessions and damage associated with crime, there is little benefit to a policy unless there is catastrophic loss.

NOTES

1. Frank Schmallager, *Criminal Justice Today* (Upper Saddle River, NJ: Prentice Hall, 2009).

2. Bureau of Justice Statistics, "Crime and Victims Statistics," U.S. Department of Justice, http://www.ojp.usdoj.gov/bjs/cvict.htm.

3. David Stiehler, "Finding the Best Home Insurance Coverage," Ezine Articles, http://ezinearticles.com.

4. Bureau of Justice Statistics, "Crime and Victims."

5. National Association of Crime Victim Compensation Boards, "Crime Victim Compensation: An Overview," http://www.nacvcb.org/articles/Overview_prn.html

6. Leslie Alderman, "Home Insurance: What You Need to Know," *New York Times* January 27, 2009.

SUGGESTED READINGS

George Galster and Jason Booza, "Are Home and Auto Insurance Policies Excessively Priced in Cities? Recent Evidence from Michigan," *Journal of Urban Affairs* 30 (2008): 502–27; Paul Lashmar, "Look Out, There is a Thief About: Crime, Particularly Burglary, Is Costing the Country More than Ever Before, while an Increasing Number of its Victims Can't Afford Insurance," *New Statesman & Society* 7 (March 25, 1994): 16.

MICHELLE RICHTER

INTERNATIONAL CRIME VICTIM SURVEY (ICVS). The International Crime Victim Survey (ICVS) is a series of surveys investigating the common crime experience of persons age 16 and older living in households in different countries. Using standardized survey methods, the ICVS provides a crime index independent of police statistics and allows comparison of crime rates in different nations, including not only developed countries but also developing countries and countries in transition. So far, the ICVS international working group has collected five waves of ICVS data: 1989, 1992, 1996, 2000, and 2004/2005. By the end of 2005, over 78 different countries participated in the survey, and over 320,000 persons have been interviewed in the course of the ICVS.[1]

The ICVS was launched by a working group of European criminologists in 1987 (Jan van Dijk, Netherlands; Pat Mayhew, England; and Martin Killias, Switzerland) with the sponsorship of the Netherland Ministry of Justice,[2] which led to the first wave of fieldwork in 1989.[3] The main object of the project was to obtain adequate crime statistics beyond official crime data to improve the comparability of crime across different countries. It also aimed to provide some basis for analysis of how crime experiences vary among different sociodemographic groups and across jurisdictions. Fourteen industrialized countries (Australia, Belgium, Canada, England and Wales, Germany, Finland, France, the Netherlands, Northern Ireland, Norway, Scotland, Spain, Switzerland, and the United States) participated fully in the first wave. In addition, three countries (Poland, Indonesia, and Japan) took part in local surveys using the same questionnaire.[4]

With the involvement of the United Nations Interregional Crime and Justice Research Institute (UNICRI), the second wave of the ICVS survey took place in 1992. Eight of the first wave participants plus five other countries, including two eastern European countries (Italy, New Zealand, Sweden, Czechoslovakia, and Poland) fully participated in the second survey.[5] In partnership with the ICVS working group, the UNICRI carried out similar surveys in cities in a number of selected developing countries and countries in transition, with the purpose to "sensitize local governments to the dimensions and extent of crime in their urban areas."[6] The 1992 survey was the first effort to collect credible crime victim data in developing countries, which not only provided information on crime and criminal justice in the developing world but also advanced comparative criminological research and theory. Overall, 30 countries including 11 industrialized countries, 13 developing countries, and 6 countries in transition, participated in the 1992 ICVS survey.[7]

The third ICVS survey was carried out in 1996 to 1997. Besides 11 industrialized countries and 14 developing countries, 20 countries in transition were involved in the survey. The participation of countries in transition provided an opportunity to obtain adequate criminal justice statistics for comparing crime, especially in formerly communist countries[8] in which data were not available to either the national public or to the international community for long periods of time.[9]

The fourth wave occurred in 2000, which encompassed 47 countries, including conventional industrialized countries and countries from Asia, Africa, and Latin America. Some of the 2000 surveys were conducted nationally and others were limited to a main city within a given country.[10]

The most recent ICVS survey took place in 2004/2005. It covered 39 countries in all, consisting of national surveys in 30 countries and regional surveys in 33 capitals or main cities.[11]

The ICVS focuses primarily on respondents' experience with 10 types of common crimes to which the general public is exposed, including car theft, theft from or out of a car, vandalism to cars, motorcycle theft, bicycle theft, burglary and attempted burglary, theft of personal property and pickpocketing, robbery, sexual offences, and assaults and threats. The ICVS questionnaire also investigates victims' experience of reporting crimes to the police, satisfaction with police response, fear of crime, use of social service agencies, general attitudes toward law enforcement, and opinions about punishments.[12]

The findings of the ICVS 2004/2005 survey indicated that on average, in 2004, 15.7% of the population of the 30 participating countries reported victimization for at least one of the ten common crimes. Four countries, Ireland, England and Wales, New Zealand, and Iceland, had the highest overall victimization rates for conventional crime. Overall rates in the United States, Canada, and Australia were below the mean of the European Union. The victimization rates of cities were higher than national rates. About 21.7% of the population living in main cities had been victimized. London had the highest victimization rate; Hong Kong in contrast, had the lowest victimization rate based on the 2004/2005 survey.[13]

NOTES

1. Jan van Dijk, John van Kesteren, and Paul Smith, *Criminal Victimization in International Perspective: Key Findings from the 2004–2005 ICVS and EU ICS. O&B 257*, http://rechten.uvt.nl/icvs/pdffiles/ICVS2004_05.pdf.

2. René van Swaaningen, "Criminology in the Netherlands," *European Journal of Criminology* 3, no. 4 (2006): 463–501.

3. Jan van Dijk, Pat Mayhew, and Martin Killias, *Experiences of Crime across the World: Key Findings from the 1989 International Crime Survey* (Boston: Kluwer Law and Taxation, 1991).

4. van Dijk, Mayhew, and Killias, *Experiences.*

5. Jan van Dijk and Pat Mayhew, *Criminal Victimization in the Industrialized World: Key Findings of the 1989 and 1992 International Crime Surveys* (The Hague: Ministry of Justice, Department of Crime Prevention, 1992).

6. van Dijk and Mayhew, *Criminal Victimization*, 2.

7. van Dijk and Mayhew, *Criminal Victimization*.

8. Annette Robertson, "The Significance of Language, Culture, and Communication in Researching Post-Soviet Crime and Policing," *Journal of Contemporary Criminal Justice* 22, no. 2 (2006): 137–56.

9. Pat Mayhew and Jan van Dijk, *Criminal Victimization in Eleven Industrialized Countries: Key Findings from the 1996 International Crime Victims Survey* (The Hague: Ministry of Justice, WODC, 1997).

10. J. N. van Kesteren, P. Mayhew, and P. Nieuwbeerta, *Criminal Victimization in Seventeen Industrialized Countries: Key Findings from the 2000 International Crime Victims Survey* (The Hague, Ministry of Justice, WODC, 2000).

11. van Dijk, van Kesteren, and Smith, *Criminal Victimization*.

12. Ibid.

13. Ibid.

SUGGESTED READING

Ugljesa Zvekic, "The International Crime (Victim) Survey in the Developing World," *Overcrowded Times* 6, no.5 (1995): 5–7.

YAN ZHANG

INTERNATIONAL VICTIMIZATIONS. This entry will focus on three key forms of international victimization: human trafficking, international war crimes, and international terrorism. The first form, human trafficking, has been found to exist worldwide with victims being transported between countries to meet market demands for any number of services. This is especially true in regard to the illicit sex industry, in which women and children are routinely trafficked from non-affluent nations to the host nation, where the victims work in an underground sex market. Indeed, according to Richard Poulin, during the last 30 years, the rapidly growing sex trade has become highly "industrialized" worldwide.[1]

When considering the international illicit sex trade, it becomes clear that this illicit industry generates profits that add up to billions of dollars.[2] Because of this, a market of sexual exchange has developed in which women and children are essentially indentured into the industry for the sole purpose of meeting the never-ending criminal market demands for sexual services. Because trafficking is an underground organized criminal enterprise, it is difficult to get exact statistics on the extent of the problem. Nevertheless, there has been a general international consensus that over one million persons are trafficked around the world each year.[3] Further, the majority of these victims are thought to come from southeast Asia, with the former Soviet Union being a primary source country that supplies the illegal sex industries in various European nations.[4]

Another form of international victimization is war crimes. Modern-day views and definitions of war crimes emerged in July of 2002 with the establishment of the International Criminal Court (ICC), located in the Hague, Netherlands. The ICC is based on a treaty that includes 108 nations around the world and is established as an independent and permanent court. The ICC is given the charge to try persons who are accused of crimes that warrant international concern, with particular attention to crimes against humanity, various war crimes, and acts of genocide. Further, specific acts during international conflicts have been identified as particularly heinous, such as deliberate attacks against humanitarian relief workers and United Nations peacekeepers, misusing the international truce flag, using poisonous weapons, or using civilians as human shields from the fire of an enemy. Other broader crimes, such as genocide, are under the jurisdiction of this court.

One of the more relevant points regarding the International Criminal Court's role with international victimizations has to do with various rules and procedures that provide a series of rights granted to victims of international crimes. Indeed, these official systems of victim response are the first time in international history that victims have the possibility under statute to present their views and observations before the court. These victim-based provisions allow victims to have their voices heard and to even obtain some degree of reparation, depending on the circumstances. The ICC has likewise developed an international trust fund for victims to provide some degree of economic relief from victimization. According to the ICC, it is the balance between retributive and restorative justice that provides the international agency with the ability to aid victims in achieving some semblance of justice.[5]

Finally, perhaps one of the most publicized types of international victimization would be that related to acts of terrorism. Terrorism is, for the most part, a psychological weapon aimed at both the immediate victims who are harmed by the violent act as well as a much wider audience, with the hope of influencing the behavior among that audience.[6] Indeed, the entire act of terrorism is grounded in the manipulative effort to modify a target group's behavior as a result of threats or actual harm against a small portion of that group's population.[7] With modern-day advances in media technology and reporting as well as the sensationalized forms of portrayal within the news media, terrorists are able to disseminate their threatening messages worldwide. Thus, terrorism is likely to have a multitude of victims that include primary victims harmed by the actual act of violence as well as secondary victims who are indirectly impacted by the violent incident. This means that, in many respects, terrorism is the quintessential form of international victimization since even just one incident has the potential to impact persons throughout the entire global community.

NOTES

1. Richard Poulin, "Globalization and the Sex Trade: Trafficking and the Commodification of Women and Children," *Canadian Women Studies* 22, no. 3–4 (2003): 38–43.

2. Ibid.

3. Francis T. Miko and Grace (Jea-Hyun) Park, *Trafficking in Women and Children: The U.S. and International Response*, Library of Congress, http://fpc.state.gov/documents/organization/9107.pdf.

4. Ibid.

5. International Criminal Court, "Victims Trust Fund," The Hague, The Netherlands, http://www.icc-cpi.int/vtf.html.

6. B. Gaynor, "Terror as a Strategy of Psychological Warfare," http://www.ict.org.il/articles/articledet.cfm?articleid=443.

7. Gaynor, "Terror;" Alex Schmid, "Terrorism as Psychological Warfare," *Democracy and Security* 1 (2005): 137–46.

SUGGESTED READING

Jan Van Dijk, John Van Kesteren, and Paul Smith, *Criminal Victimization in International Perspective: Key Findings from the 2004–2005 ICVS and EV ICS* (Onderzoek en Beleid) (Meppel, Netherlands: Boom Juridische Uitgeuers, 2008).

ROBERT D. HANSER

INTIMATE PARTNER VIOLENCE. The Centers for Disease Control and Prevention (CDC) define intimate partner violence (IPV) as actual or threatened physical or sexual violence or psychological and emotional abuse directed toward an individual with whom the perpetrator has an intimate relationship (i.e., spouse, ex-spouse, current or former boyfriend/girlfriend, current or former dating partner). Intimate partners may be heterosexual, homosexual, bisexual, or transgendered. Such violence includes but is not limited to yelling and insulting, demeaning an intimate partner in front of others, pushing and shoving, slapping, burning, forcing a sexual act against the intimate's will, stalking, threatening to use or actually using a weapon against the intimate, and homicide. IPV, then, is generally conceptualized in terms of a continuum of severity. Research indicates, however, that often the actual act is less significant than the intent of the perpetrator and the effects on the victim. IPV is intended to punish, intimidate, and control the victim, and victims may experience, in addition to physical harm or injury, serious psychological consequences, including fear, depression, lowered self-esteem, and various symptoms of post-traumatic stress disorder (PTSD).

Although some observers have expressed concern with defining IPV broadly, research shows that narrow definitions (e.g., definitions restricted to acts of physical abuse) fail to adequately capture the frequency and diversity of IPV victimization experiences. Although some researchers maintain that women are at least as likely as men to use violence in an intimate relationship—that is, that most IPV is "mutual abuse"—available data show that women are significantly more likely than men to be victims of IPV. Recent data indicate that annually about 1.5 million women and more than 830,000 men are the victims of physical or sexual assault by an intimate partner. Nearly 67% of adult women who are raped, physically assaulted, or stalked are victimized by a current or former intimate. Women are also more likely than men to be killed by a current or former intimate partner.

The mutual abuse argument fails to take into account important differences in women's and men's use of violence in intimate relationships. For example, women's and men's motivations for using violence differ. Women are more likely to use violence, especially severe physical violence, against an intimate partner in self-defense or when they believe they are in imminent danger of being attacked. Studies of women arrested for IPV show that most were previously victimized by their partners. In contrast, men are more likely to use violence against an intimate partner when they perceive themselves losing control of the relationship or when they interpret their partners' words or behavior as challenges to their authority.

SUGGESTED READING

Raquel K. Bergen, Jeffrey R. Edleson, and Claire M. Renzetti, eds., *Violence Against Women: Classic Papers* (Boston: Allyn and Bacon, 2005); Mary Ann Dutton, "Intimate Partner Violence and Sexual Assault," in *Violence: From Theory to Research,* ed. Margaret A. Zahn, Henry H. Brownstein, and Shelly L. Jackson (Cincinnati, OH: Anderson, 2004), 161–76; Claire M. Renzetti, Jeffrey L. Edleson, and Raquel K. Bergen, eds., *Sourcebook on Violence Against Women* (Thousand Oaks, CA: Sage, 2000); Patricia Tjaden and Nancy Thoennes, "Prevalence and Consequences of Male-to-Female and Female-to-Male Intimate Partner Violence as Measured by the National Violence Against Women Survey," *Violence Against Women* 6 (2000): 142–61.

CLAIRE RENZETTI

J

JUDGES. The legal system in the United States is an adversarial system with two parties in "conflict" with each other. Thus, a neutral arbitrator is necessary to impose the law and make decisions in cases in which parties are at conflict. A judge is one such arbitrator who presides over courtroom proceedings and ensures that each side receives fairness in terms of the outcome of the case and the application of the law to the facts that are presented during a proceeding.

The actions of a judge can deeply affect a victim in a criminal case. A judge is responsible for maintaining order in a courtroom, making decisions on rules of evidence and courtroom procedure, and sentencing a criminal defendant who pleads guilty to a crime or is found guilty of a crime during a jury or bench trial. Thus, a judge's decisions affect a victim who may be in the courtroom during any or all of the proceedings. Judges are often called on to make decisions about questions that may or may not be asked of a victim during a criminal proceeding. These questions may be emotionally difficult for a victim to answer. For example, traditionally rape cases often ended up involving questions to the victim that placed the victim on trial, in effect criticizing them for their choice of dress or actions at the time of the rape. Although laws have resulted in the abolition of this type of questioning in many cases, judges often still have the power to limit or allow certain difficult questions based on their probative value and relevance to a proceeding. Judges can further allow or disallow victims to speak freely during sentencing proceedings. Allowing a victim to say everything that is on her mind at sentencing might not be appropriate, and thus a judge can limit a victim's words. However, this may have a chilling effect on the victim, who will feel as though he has not been heard throughout the process. Further, any sentencing should include restitution to the victim. A judge should consider the impact that a pre- or post-release decision of the defendant could potentially have on the victim.

Although traditionally the issue of victims' rights did not focus on the judiciary, judges should ensure that all of a victim's needs are taken care of by some entity during all steps of the criminal justice process. It has only been recently that recommendations for policies and protocol have been issued to the judiciary. These recommendations request that the judiciary ensure that victims are in fact involved in each part of the criminal justice system, including pretrial decisions, bail decisions, trials, plea bargaining, and sentencing.[1] Further, a judge should consider the effect that postponing proceedings will have on a victim. It has also been recommended that judges and other courtroom personnel become educated in the area of victims' rights.

NOTE

1. Office for Victims of Crime, *New Directions from the Field: Victim's Rights and Services for the 21st Century* (Washington DC: U.S. Department of Justice, 1998).

SUGGESTED READING

Howard Abadinsky, *Law and Justice: An Introduction to the American Legal System*, 6th ed. (New Jersey: Pearson, 2008); Christopher P. Banks and David M. O'Brien, *Courts and Judicial Policymaking* (New Jersey: Pearson / Prentice Hall, 2008).

TINA FRYLING

JURIES. Juries can be the most important part of a criminal trial, for if a trial is by jury, the jury will ultimately decide the guilt or innocence of the defendant. The jury, then, is equally important to the victim, as the jury's decision sends a message to the victim as to whether or not the jury believed the victim's testimony and that of the victim's witnesses or the testimony of the defendant and his witnesses.

The jury's decision as to the guilt or innocence of a defendant is called the verdict. Although the Supreme Court has struck down the requirement for the jury's verdict to be unanimous in a criminal trial,[1] many states still require a unanimous verdict. This means that 11 out of 12 jurors could believe a victim's version of the facts, but the jury could not convict the defendant due to one juror's disagreement. Although much has been written about a defendant's right to have a jury that will not improperly convict him, another important aspect is a victim's right to have a jury that will not wrongly dismiss the victim's story as being untrue and fail to convict the person who has done wrong to the victim. A jury is to be chosen from a fair and impartial segment of the community, and both the defense and the prosecution are able to ask questions of the jurors to determine their level of impartiality. Although the defendant is able to assist the defense attorney by participating in a discussion as to whether each jury member seems to be impartial, the victim is generally not as involved with the prosecuting attorney, who makes those decisions alone or sometimes with the help of an officer of the law who may have investigated the case. However, research has demonstrated that the victim's gender and race often has an impact on a jury's ultimate decision.

The role of jurors in criminal cases has shifted over time. Early juries in England were not impartial and did not listen to two sides presenting evidence. Instead, the juries were composed of people who knew something about the case and would then make a decision of the truth of the case based on their knowledge. One issue facing the jury system today that directly affects victims is the concept of jury nullification. Although no laws exist allowing jury nullification, juries may sometimes attempt to "nullify" a provision of the law that they do not agree with by finding someone not guilty even if the facts point to that person's guilt. For example, in a drug possession case in which a person admits to having possessed marijuana, which is illegal, jury members may want to make a statement that they support the legalization of marijuana and may thus find the person innocent in order to demonstrate their lack of support for current drug laws. This type of decision could impact a victim negatively in many ways, including the victim believing that the jury did not believe his testimony, when in fact the jury may instead be attempting to nullify the law.

NOTE

1. See, for example, *Johnson v. Louisiana*, 406 U.S. at 374 (1972).

SUGGESTED READING

Joseph Sanders, "A Norms Approach to Jury 'Nullification:' Interests, Values, and Scripts," *Law & Policy* 30 (2008): 12–45; Mary E. Williams, *The Jury System* (San Diego, CA: Greenhaven Press, 1997); Marian R. Williams et al., "Understanding the Influence of Victim Gender in Death Penalty Cases: The Importance of Victim Race, Sex-Related Victimization, and Jury Decision Making," *Criminology* 45 (2007): 865–91.

TINA FRYLING

K

KEMPE, C. HENRY. C. Henry Kempe was born in 1922 in Breslau, Germany. He immigrated to the United States and attended the University of California Medical School, graduating with his M.D. in 1945. His life's work offers two very distinct and notable contributions. He began his medical career as a virologist working in the area of smallpox vaccination and contributed to the world wide push toward eradication of the disease. His medical career is most widely noted though for his early contribution in exposing the occurrence of child abuse and, with his colleagues, coining the term "battered child syndrome." Prior to Kempe's work, the abuse of children by their parents and caregivers was at worst unnoticed and at best an unspoken reality.

Early pediatric research in the area of childhood injuries conducted prior to the twentieth century, while acknowledging traumatic injuries to children, tended to understate the potential role of the parents or caregivers in the trauma as a possible source of the injuries sustained. Children who presented with abuse-like symptoms usually had their trauma and injuries explained away according to other etiologies and differential diagnoses. The attending pediatrician would typically consider all forms of rare hematological and bone disorders, taking for granted that all parents love their children and would never intentionally harm them. It was not until the mid-twentieth century that parents and caregivers were clearly assigned some responsibility for the injury of the children in their care. In 1959 Henry Silver and Kempe presented a paper at the 69th American Pediatric Society meeting identifying the problem of parental criminal neglect and abuse of children. In 1961 Kempe presented his historic paper to the American Pediatrics Academy and in 1962 it was published in the *Journal of the American Medical Association* with the title of "The Battered Child Syndrome." The paper has been regarded as the single most significant event in creating awareness and exposing the abuse of children.

In the wake of the initial impact of the publication of the paper all states passed laws to set up child protective systems to assist abused and neglected children. Kempe's work went on to change the way injuries and trauma experienced during childhood are identified, examined, and prevented. Kempe later became president of the International Society for Prevention of Child Abuse. He also founded and served as director of the National Center for Treatment and Prevention of Child Abuse and Neglect. For all of Dr. Kempe's tireless efforts in the interest of children he was nominated for a Nobel Prize. Today the Kempe Foundation for the Prevention and Treatment of Child Abuse and Neglect carries on his mission, vision, and his legacy.

SUGGESTED READING

C. Henry Kempe et al., "The Battered Child Syndrome," *Journal of the American Medical Association* 181 (1962): 17–24; Margaret A. Lynch, "Child Abuse before Kempe: An Historical Literature Review," *Child Abuse and Neglect* 9 (1985): 7–15; O. H. Wolff, "Henry Kempe," *Archives of Disease in Childhood* 59 (1984): 688.

JEFFREY WALSH

KIDNAPPING. Kidnapping typically involves seizing or detaining an individual by unlawful force. The term is most often used in reference to missing persons, frequently with regard to children. Thus, the vast majority of research about kidnapping is related to child abductions.

The National Incidence Studies of Missing, Abducted, Runaway and Throwaway Children, or NISMART, was a research project legislated through the 1984 Missing Children's Assistance Act, and its studies provide a rigorous source of data about child abductions. NISMART describes three types of abductions: family, nonfamily, and stereotypical kidnapping, which is a subset of nonfamily abductions. Stereotypical kidnappings, cases in which a nonfamily member takes a child with the intent of physically harming them or extracting a ransom, are a rare variety of abductions that frequently achieve high notoriety. According to the NISMART studies, less than 1% of child abductions are kidnappings. The most recent data indicated that approximately 100 stereotypical kidnappings occurred in 2002 in the United States.

Although kidnappings are relatively rare in the United States, fear of these incidents has stimulated development of public policies to reduce risk or aid recovery.

The best-known policies introduced in the United States to address the kidnapping problem are Code Adam and AMBER Alert. Code Adam policies, named after Adam Walsh, who was abducted from a department store in 1981, are used to help locate missing children, predominantly in public places. For example, many retail stores and other public venues enact a Code Adam by securing entry and exit from their establishment when a child is suspected to be at risk of abduction. As an extension of these plans, similar systems have been utilized in natural disasters, when children are particularly at risk of being abducted. AMBER Alert plans aid in the recovery of kidnapped children. AMBER stands for America's Missing: Broadcast Emergency Response and is named after Amber Hagerman, who was the victim of a stereotypical kidnapping in 1996. Between 1997 and 2005, AMBER alert programs were adopted in all 50 U.S. states and many regions. Although kidnapping incidents are relatively rare in the United States, they nonetheless generate noted concern and policy development.

SUGGESTED READING

Joel Best, *Threatened Children: Rhetoric and Concern about Child-Victims* (Chicago: University of Chicago Press, 1990); Glenn W. Muschert, Melissa Young-Spillers, and Dawn Carr. "'Smart' Policy Decisions to Combat a Social Problem: The Case of Child Abductions 2002–2003." *Justice Policy Journal* 3, no. 2 (2006): 1–32, http:// www.cjcj.org/files/smart_policy.pdf; National Center for Missing and Exploited Children Web site, http://www.missingkids.com/; Andrea J. Sedlak et al., "National Estimates of Missing Children: An Overview," Office of Juvenile Justice and Delinquency Prevention of the U.S. Department of Justice, http://www.ncjrs.gov/pdffiles1/ojjdp/196465.pdf.

DAWN C. CARR, MELISSA YOUNG-SPILLERS,
AND GLENN W. MUSCHERT

L

LARCENY-THEFT. Larceny-theft is defined as the unlawful taking, carrying, leading, or riding away of property from the possession or constructive possession of another.[1] Examples include the theft of bicycles, motorbikes, and motor vehicle parts and accessories, as well as shoplifting, pick pocketing, purse snatching or the theft of any article of property not taken by violence or force.[2] Embezzlement, confidence games, forgery, check fraud, and identity theft are also defined as larceny-theft; however crimes of this type share a special classification based on additional trends such as whether weapons are used in the crime and the value of the items stolen.[3]

Larceny-theft is also a predatory crime of criminal opportunity.[4] In this case, the offender is motivated to steal from an individual or business mainly because he views this entity as the perfect target. The victim, on the other hand, is unaware that they are being targeted by a potential offender, who in some cases fixates on something unique about the victim's own person. Characteristics of this type could be individual body type, personality, apparent vulnerability, carelessness in public, proximity to other people, lack of street knowledge, etc. The target availability of the victim is further magnified when social support networks such as family members, friends, coworkers, etc., are not available to help and warn the victim in times of impending danger. Although it is generally assumed that the police and law enforcement agencies are solely responsible for protecting individuals from this and other types of crimes, the most effective form of protection is applied by those who have the foresight to intervene before the crime is carried out. As long as individuals exist who are motivated to commit predatory criminal acts of this nature, it is important that social support systems are in place to assist intended victims before and, if necessary, after the crime has occurred.[5]

The criminal justice system has responded by improving law enforcement response to larceny-theft crimes, developing constructive legislative doctrines and principles, and enforcing mandatory sentencing laws aimed at reducing the numbers of individuals committing these crimes nationwide.[6] In addition, victim compensation programs are used to restore the victims' sense of justice. The difference between this program and restitution is that rather than demand payment of goods and services directly from the offender, compensation is paid from a public fund, which in the case of larceny-theft may allow the victim to recoup all or some of their financial losses.[7]

NOTES

1. Federal Bureau of Investigation, "Crime in the United States, 2007," U.S. Department of Justice, http://www.fbi.gov/ucr/cius2007/index.html.

2. Ibid.

3. Ibid.

4. Lawrence E. Cohen and Marcus Felson, "Social Change and Crime Rate Trends: A Routine Activity Approach," *American Sociological Review* 44 (1979): 588–608.

5. Tracy Tolbert, *The Sex Crime Scenario* (Dubuque, IA: Kendall / Hunt, 2006).

6. Robert J. Meadows, *Understanding Violence and Victimization,* 4th ed. (Upper Saddle River, NJ: Prentice Hall, 2007); Elsa Chen, "Impacts of 'Three Strikes and You're Out' on Crime Trends in California and Throughout the United States," *Journal of Contemporary Criminal Justice* 24 (2008): 345–70.

7. Meadows, *Understanding Violence,* 247–55.

SUGGESTED READING

David Ormerod and David Williams, *Smith's Law of Theft,* 9th ed. (Oxford: Oxford University Press, 2007); Bambi Vincent and Bob Arno, *Travel Advisory! How to Avoid Thefts, Cons, and Street Scams While Traveling* (Santa Monica, CA: Bonus Books, 2003).

TRACY FAYE TOLBERT

LEARNED HELPLESSNESS. In the course of experimentation on the effects of punishment, Martin Seligman and colleagues discovered that when inescapable aversive stimuli were programmed, animal subjects exhibited an inability to engage in instrumental learning. In a series of experiments Seligman found evidence across species (e.g., dogs, rats, humans, etc.) that if aversive events were inescapable, experimental subjects would eventually show no evidence of escape or avoidance behavior even when the opportunity to escape the punisher was made available.[1] The theory was later broadened to include explanations for the development of depression in some individuals, and Seligman eventually expanded beyond social learning theory, borrowing concepts from attribution theory, to account for some of the cognitive verbal presentations associated with depression.[2]

Lenore Walker utilized the theory as an explanation for why some women remain in battering situations. Walker expounded that learned helplessness theory had "three basic components: (1) information about what should happen (i.e., the contingency), (2) cognitive representation about the contingency (i.e., learning, expectation, belief, perception), and (3) behavior."[3] Walker suggested that women learn that their personal attempts to alter their situation result in punishment and consequently come to believe that they are helpless to change their circumstances.

From a positive perspective, the learned helplessness theory as an explanation of the battered woman's behavior utilized a strong empirical research base. At the time it also provided a strong alternative argument to accusations that these battered women were masochistic and therefore desired the abuse. Critics of the theory argued that the conceptual framework of learned helplessness presented an image of women as weak and powerless. The theory lost favor within the field as victim advocacy groups and victim service providers began looking for alternative theoretical explanations that were more acceptable in title and presented women, the primary victims of battering, as personally and socially more capable. Although some research has questioned the validity of the theory,[4] most published research has for the most part supported learned helplessness as a valid explanation for some behaviors exhibited by battered victims.[5]

NOTES

1. Martin E. P. Seligman and Steven F. Maier, "Failure to Escape Traumatic Shock," *Journal of Experimental Psychology* 74 (1967): 1–9.

2. Lyn Y. Abramson and Martin E. Seligman, "Learned Helplessness in Humans: Critique and Reformulation," *Journal of Abnormal Psychology* 87, no. 1 (1978): 49–74.

3. Lenore E. Walker, "Battered Women and Learned Helplessness," *Victimology* 2, no. 3 (1977): 525–34.

4. Edward W. Gondolf and Ellen R. Fisher, *Battered Women as Survivors: An Alternative to Treating Learned Helplessness*, NCJRS 124935 (Lanham, MD: Lexington Books, 1988).

5. Margaret H. Launius and Carol U. Lindquist, "Learned Helplessness, External Locus of Control, and Passivity in Battered Women," *Journal of Interpersonal Violence* 3, no. 3 (1988): 307–18.

SUGGESTED READING

Donald S. Hiroto and Martin E. Seligman, "Generality of Learned Helplessness in Man," *Journal of Personality and Social Psychology* 31, no. 2 (1975): 311–27.

DAN L. PETERSEN

LIFESTYLE THEORY. Lifestyle theory represents one of the first attempts to explain criminal victimization.[1] Essentially, the lifestyle perspective proposes that variations in risk of victimization across demographic factors are a function of differences in lifestyles.[2] Lifestyle involves daily activities done on a routine basis (e.g., daily work or school routines) or leisure activities. Leisure and routine activities increase the risk of victimization by placing individuals in situations more conducive to criminal activity. Examples of lifestyle factors associated with increased risk for criminal victimization include working away from home, spending more time out at night, and involvement in risky behaviors. Examples of lifestyle factors associated with decreasing the risk of victimization include spending more time at home, living in a household with more adults, and taking precautions to avoid places known for criminal activity.

Lifestyle differences can be explained by individuals' adaptations to their social situation based on social status characteristics.[3] Demographic characteristics such as gender, race, socioeconomic status, and marital status are linked to certain role expectations and structural constraints that lead individuals to engage in specific patterns of behavior. Because different characteristics have different behavioral expectations attached, they also lead to differential risk for criminal victimization.

An important aspect related to lifestyle explanations of victimization are the concepts of victim precipitation and victim provocation. Victim precipitation and provocation are two distinct yet similar terms.[4] Victim precipitation is a social-scientific term and generally refers to actions by the victim that instigate victimization by the perpetrator. Victim provocation is a legal term used by criminal courts and generally refers to the extent to which the accusing party (victim) is criminally responsible for inciting the accused. Victim precipitation implies that the victim did something to cause or hasten another person to act criminally, but it does not necessarily imply blameworthiness on the victim. In contrast, victim provocation has a more serious connotation regarding the level of blame placed on an individual for causing his victimization.

Victim precipitation and provocation can be placed within the overall lifestyle theory framework. Variations in lifestyles can lead to differences in risk for precipitating victimization. Other lifestyle factors typically connected to victimization risk (e.g., time spent away from home, occupation) may increase the likelihood of victim precipitation but do not involve provocation.[5]

A wide range of victimization prevention efforts have utilized concepts from lifestyle theory to aid in reducing crime and victimization.[6] At the institutional level, programs have been developed to alter behavior patterns of would-be offenders and victims. At the individual level, efforts have been made to educate the public about the risks associated with certain lifestyle patterns.

NOTES

1. Robert F. Meier and Terance D. Miethe, "Understanding Theories of Criminal Victimization," *Crime and Justice* 17 (1993): 459–99.

2. Michael J. Hindelang, Michael R. Gottfredson, and James Garofalo, *Victims of Personal Crime: An Empirical Foundation for a Theory of Personal Victimization* (Cambridge, MA: Ballinger, 1978).

3. Meier and Miether, "Understanding Theories," 459.

4. Marvin E. Wolfgang, "Victim Precipitation in Victimology and in Law," in *Questions and Answers in Lethal and Non-Lethal Violence* (Washington DC: National Institute of Justice, NCJ 147480, 1993), 167–83.

5. Lisa R. Muftic, Leana A. Bouffard, and Jeffrey A. Bouffard, "An Exploratory Analysis of Victim Precipitation among Men and Women Arrested for Intimate Partner Violence," *Feminist Criminology* 2 (2007): 327–64.

6. Marcus Felson, "Routine Activities and Crime Prevention in the Developing Metropolis," *Criminology* 25 (1987): 911–31.

SUGGESTED READING

Michael R. Gottfredson, "On the Etiology of Criminal Victimization," *The Journal of Criminal Law and Criminology* 72 (1981): 714–26; Janet L. Lauritson, Robert J. Sampson, and John H. Laub, "The Link Between Offending and Victimization Among Adolescents," *Criminology* 29 (1991): 265–92.

MATTHEW JOHNSON

M

MALE RAPE. There is very little research that addresses the rape of men except for those that occur in prison.[1] Scholarship, and in some jurisdictions laws, on rape typically address only females as victims. What is known is that men (and boys) are victims of rape at the hands of both other men and women. Common beliefs are that when a man is raped by another man, it is by a gay man, although the limited research does not support this. Rape of men, like the rape of women, is typically viewed not as an offense motivated by sex but rather by power and a desire to control another. This fact is supported by the research that shows that sexual assaults of men tend to be more violent and result in more and greater injuries.[2]

Men who are raped are unlikely to report their victimization and unlikely to seek medical or mental health services unless they are severely injured.[3] When they do seek mental health services, it tends to be only after the passage of significant periods of time, with some research suggesting an average of 2 to as many as 16 years.[4] Male rape victims also have fewer specialized services available to them than do women. Many rape crisis service providers do not serve men.[5] Male rape victims fear having their sexuality and masculinity questioned, and the public perceives the rape of heterosexual men as more severe than the rape of either women or gay men.[6]

Because of the low likelihood of reporting or seeking services, there are not reliable estimates of the incidence or prevalence of male rape. The statistics that are available tend to be based either on the few men who report or access medical services or are based on the victimization of boys. Most experts, however, believe that the rape of men is far less common than the rape of women. When assessing rates based on reports and seeking of services, most studies suggest that between 2% and 7% of men will be sexually victimized at some point in life. A few studies have looked at college men, and report rates of men who have been forced or coerced into sex against their will in the range of 14% to 22%.[7]

Consequences for victims include injuries both directly resulting from the rape, accompanying injuries, mental health disturbances, and perceptions of social stigma.[8] Men who are sexually victimized also commonly report sexual dysfunctions, including impotence and questions/concerns about their actual and perceived sexual identities.

NOTES

1. Allen J. Beck and Paige M. Harrison, *Sexual Victimization in State and Federal Prisons Reported by Inmates,* 2007 (Washington DC: Bureau of Justice Statistics, 2008).

2. Michael King, "Sexual Assaults on Men: Assessment and Management," *British Journal of Hospital Medicine* 53 (1995): 245–46; Richard Hillman et al., "Sexual Assault of Men: A Series," *Genitourinary Medicine,* 66 (1990): 247–50.

3. Michael Scarce, *Male on Male Rape: The Hidden Toll of Stigma and Shame* (New York: Insight Books, 1997).

4. Michael King and Earnest Woollett, "Sexually Assaulted Males: 115 Men Consulting a Counseling Service," *Archives of Sexual Behavior* 26 (1997): 579–88; Jayne Walker, John Archer, and Michelle Davies, "Effects of Rape on Men: A Descriptive Analysis," *Archives of Sexual Behavior* 34 (2005): 69–80.

5. Denise Donnelly and Stacy Kenyon, "'Honey, We Don't Do Men:' Gender Stereotypes and the Provision of Services to Sexually Assaulted Males," *Journal of Interpersonal Violence* 11 (1996): 441–48.

6. Kathy Doherty and Irina Anderson, "Making Sense of Male Rape: Constructions of Gender, Sexuality, and Experience of Rape Victims," *Journal of Community and Applied Social Psychology* 14, no. 2 (2004): 85–103.

7. Michelle Davies, Paul Pollard, and John Archer, "The Influence of Victim Gender and Sexual Orientation on Blame Towards the Victim in a Depicted Stranger Rape," *Violence and Victims* 16 (2001): 607–19; Cindy Struckman-Johnson, "Forced Sex On Dates: It Happens to Men Too," *Journal of Sex Research* 24 (1988): 234–41; Richard Tewksbury and Elizabeth Ehrhardt Mustaine, "Lifestyle Factors Associated with the Sexual Assault of Men: A Routine Activity Theory Analysis," *The Journal of Men's Studies* 9 (2001): 153–82.

8. Richard Tewksbury, "Effects of Sexual Assault on Men: Physical, Mental and Sexual Consequences," *International Journal of Men's Health* 6 (2007): 22–35.

SUGGESTED READING

Michelle Davies, "Male Sexual Assault Victims: A Selective Review of the Literature and Implications for Support Services," *Aggression and Violent Behavior* 7 (2002): 203–14;

Michael Scarce, *Male on Male Rape: The Hidden Toll of Stigma and Shame* (New York: Insight Books, 1997).

RICHARD TEWKSBURY

MARITAL RAPE. Rape in marriage is a serious and prevalent form of violence against women. Marital rape is more prevalent than rape by a person who is not a spouse. A study conducted in 1978 revealed that 14% of married women had been sexually assaulted by their husbands, and this rate was two times higher than the rate of nonspousal rape. Although no evidence indicates that this form of violence is confined to particular social groups, research has shown that some groups of women are more vulnerable than others. These include young women, African American women, and women in rural areas.

Marital rape and battering are closely related. Women who are raped by their husbands frequently experience a wide range of violent behaviors, including severe physical violence, violence with weapons, and threats of violence. As a result, some researchers argue that marital rape is an extension of domestic violence. Research has also indicated that compared to batterers, men who batter and rape are particularly dangerous and more likely to inflict severe injuries on their wives.

Despite its seriousness, marital rape was not viewed as a crime until recently. Traditionally, rape laws included a marital exemption, because rape was defined as the forcible penetration of the body of a woman who was not the wife of the perpetrator. The marital rape exemption is rooted in the antiquated view of women as property of men, including fathers and husbands. Ancient laws required married women to oblige their husbands' rulings, including sexual demands, and sexual entitlement in marriage was largely accepted in U.S. courts until recently.

In the late 1970s, attitudes toward rape changed when the women's movement argued for the elimination of the spousal exemption in rape legislations by framing rape as violent rather than sexual. In 1978, John Rideout became the first husband charged with rape while living with his wife. Rideout was acquitted, but the case was widely publicized and brought attention to the concept that rape can exist within the context of marriage. Since the Rideout case, there have been significant advances in repealing spousal exemptions from rape prosecution. By 1993, marital rape had become a crime in all 50 states and the District of Columbia.

Although all states recognize spousal rape as a crime, there are still ways in which spousal rape is treated differently than nonspousal rape. By 2005, 20 states and the District of Columbia had completely removed spousal exemptions from the crime of rape, but in the remaining 30 states some exemptions are still given to husbands, who can be charged with a lesser offense instead of rape. In addition, some states require a shorter reporting period for spousal rape than for nonspousal rape. Moreover, in several states force or threat of force must be used by the spouse whereas only a lack of consent is required for nonspousal rape.

SUGGESTED READING

Jennifer A. Bennice and Patricia A. Resick, "Marital Rape: History, Research, and Practice," *Trauma, Violence, and Abuse* 4 (2003): 228–46; Lisa R. Eskow, "Ultimate Weapon? Demythologizing Spousal Rape and Reconceptualizing its Prosecution," *Stanford Law Review* 48 (1996): 677–709; David Finkelhor and Kersti Yllo, *License to Rape: Sexual Abuse of Wives* (New York: Holt, Rinehart & Winston, 1985); Diana E. H. Russell, *Rape in Marriage* (Bloomington, IN: Indiana University Press, 1990).

HOAN N. BUI

MCGRUFF CAMPAIGN. The McGruff campaign was introduced to the public in late 1979 amidst a broader wave of programs and policies aimed at crime prevention and increased citizen awareness. At the heart of this campaign was an animated, trench coat-wearing dog named McGruff who asked us to help "Take a Bite Out of Crime." The campaign called upon citizens to take individual responsibility for crime reduction (especially with respect to mitigating risk of victimization in burglary and street crimes) while also engaging in collective prevention efforts with fellow citizens and with law enforcement (citizens were encouraged to watch for and report suspicious activity and generally seek to cultivate a more caring community).

The McGruff campaign was relatively effective from the start; diffusion of its messages was rapid and widespread, with people from all walks of life quickly becoming familiar with the campaign and its core messages. Still, critics question whether the campaign has produced the kind of lasting individual risk mitigation strategies and community cohesiveness envisioned by its founders.

As the McGruff campaign approaches its 30th anniversary, it continues to call needed attention to crime, advance crime prevention strategies, and promote citizen involvement in crime reduction. Much of the strength of the McGruff campaign in this regard owes to its consistent attention to its core messages, the retention of McGruff as spokesperson, and the willingness of campaign leaders to adapt to cultural change, innovations in media technology, and shifting concerns about crime (e.g., a greater focus on reducing victimization among children and teens and increased attention to drugs, gun violence, bullying, and Internet safety).

SUGGESTED READING

Garrett D. O'Keefe et al., *Taking a Bite Out of Crime: The Impact of the National Citizens' Crime Prevention Media Campaign* (Thousand Oaks, CA: Sage, 1996); Ronald E. Rice and Charles K. Atkin, eds. *Public Communication Campaigns*, 3rd ed. (Thousand Oaks, CA: Sage, 2001); F. W. Winkel, "Response Generalisation in Crime Prevention Campaigns," *British Journal of Criminology* 27 (1987): 155–73.

BRIAN A. MONAHAN AND MOLLY SWEEN

MEDIATION. Mediation is a conflict resolution process in which a person outside the dispute helps the disputants make agreements that resolve their differences. Decision-making power stays with the parties. The mediator is in charge of the process. There are no rules for mediation other than what the parties agree on.

Mediator practices vary according to culture. Mediation of a typical western business dispute is often done by an evaluative mediator who meets with the parties separately until an agreement is reached. This type of mediator determines how the matter should be resolved and works to sell that idea to the parties. This style is similar to what a court settlement officer does at a settlement conference.

More personal disputes are commonly handled by westerners with a facilitative style in which the mediator assists face-to-face communication. The facilitative style looks very much like counseling.

Most people in the world prefer an indirect style of conflict communication in which the parties speak with a wise person privately and get advice on how to resolve the dispute. One cannot lose face by taking the advice of a wise person. Western mediators are generally valued for their skill and eastern mediators for their wisdom. This difference also means that western mediators are usually trained, whereas eastern mediators usually are not. Trained eastern mediators, however, often utilize a hybrid style useful in cross-cultural situations in which disputants cannot agree on a wise person.

A person serving as a third party needs to know what role to play. A western facilitative style will go nowhere if the parties are waiting to receive advice on what to do. An evaluative approach will not work well when the parties are just looking for help in good communication styles. A would-be mediator needs to discern what the parties are looking for and play the appropriate role.

Once the role is decided mediation always has a similar set of steps. The parties first agree what they want to work on and set ground rules. Then the mediator leads them in a story-telling phase through which they each come to understand the other's point of view. Brainstorming comes next with the parties identifying various ways to resolve the matter. Through a process of elimination, which may include some research, the parties agree on a plan for moving forward together. A follow-up meeting to see how things are going is sometimes scheduled. These steps look different in various mediation styles, but they all are taken in any mediation.

Some mediators focus more on the issues brought by the parties, usually money or other material things, some focus first on hurt feelings, and still others move back and forth between the two as necessary. The western evaluative style seldom delves into feelings, whereas the facilitative style usually does. Eastern mediators assume that feelings are important.

SUGGESTED READING

Peter Lovenheim and Lisa Guerin, *Mediate, Don't Litigate: Strategies for Successful Mediation* (Berkeley, CA: Nolo, 2004); Duane Ruth-Heffelbower, *Conflict and Peace-making Across Cultures: Training for Trainers* (Fresno, CA: Fresno Pacific University, 1999).

DUANE RUTH-HEFFELBOWER

MENDELSOHN, BENIAMIN. Beniamin Mendelsohn (1900–1998), also known as the "father of victimology," was one of the founders of victimization research. Born in Romania, although he would later immigrate to Israel, Mendelsohn was a barrister first admitted to the bar in 1934. Serving his tenure as an attorney, Mendelsohn became interested in the study of victims. Although specializing in criminal defense, he began conducting interviews with victims and witnesses. Mendelsohn realized that the majority of victims had a preexisting interpersonal relationship with their offender. Although the results of his seminal research were first published in 1937, it would be a presentation at a conference in Bucharest at the Romanian Psychiatric Association in 1947 that would catapult him into fame. At the conference, Mendelsohn first coined the term "victimol-ogy." Mendelsohn continued his work on victims, which finally culminated in a typology of criminal victims and their involvement in the offense. Initially, this typology focused on the culpability of the victim and the offender and the extent to which the victim plays a role in their own victimization; however, his later work would extend the theory to include victimizations beyond human control.

SUGGESTED READING

M. Knaper and I. Hurbers, "The Victim and Victimology," *Tilburg Research: Victim Empowerment* 4, no. 1 (2006): 22–23; Beniamin Mendelsohn, "The Origin of the Doctrine of Victimology," *Excerpta Criminologica* 3 (1963): 239–44; Harvey Wallace, *Victimology: Legal, Psychological, and Social Perspectives,* 2nd ed. (Boston: Pearson / Allyn and Bacon, 2007).

TAMMY GARLAND

MENDELSOHN'S TYPOLOGIES. Beniamin Mendelsohn, the father of vic-timology, created a typology classifying the culpability between victims and offenders. Rather than placing blame solely on the offender, this six-category typology focuses primarily on the culpability of the victim and the extent to which the victim plays a role in his own victimization. According to Mendelsohn, the first type is the "completely innocent victim." These individuals are in no way responsible for their own victimization. Instead, these individuals are victimized simply because of the nature of who they are (i.e., a child). Mendelsohn's second category is the "victim with minor guilt." This victimization is perpetrated in some part due to ignorance. Simply, the victim inadvertently placed himself in harms' way. The third category holds that victimization is "voluntary." These victims are as guilty as the offender. They, in essence, assisted in the creation of their own victimization (i.e., a suicide pact). In the fourth type, Mendelsohn holds the victim to be "more guilty than the offender." These are often individuals who provoke or instigate a situation. Mendelsohn's fifth category describes the "most guilty victim." Victims of this type are often those engaged in a criminal act who then become a victim. For instance, an attacker who is killed during an assault would be considered responsible for his own victimization. Mendelsohn's final category is the "imaginary victim." Imaginary victims are those who have not been victimized at all; these individuals fabricate a crime for personal reasons. Filing a false police report would be an example of an imaginary victim.

Mendelsohn's original typology focused on assessing the culpability of the victim; however, Mendelsohn later revised his definition of victimization and culpability. Mendelsohn's expanded typology includes the following: (1) victims of criminals, (2) victims of one's self (i.e., suicide and self-destructive behavior), (3) victims of antisocial behavior on the part of one's social environment (i.e., caste systems, political forces, and genocide), (4) victims of technology (i.e., medical testing), and (5) victims of the natural environment (i.e., earthquakes, hurricanes, and famine). In this expanded typology, Mendelsohn maintained that one's victimization is determined by both endogenous and external environments. One is directly responsible for his own victimization when he harms himself (i.e., suicide) or places himself in such a state that he is likely to attract criminals due to this weakened state (i.e., self-destructive behavior). In contrast, the victim has less control over external factors. It is these external factors that society can work together to eliminate, if possible, and therefore prevent victimization among individuals and groups.

Although Mendelsohn acknowledged that some victims have nothing to do with their own victimization and eventually proposed a means of eliminating factors that lead to victimization, his legacy is one that contributed to placing blame primarily on the victim. Thus, Mendelsohn, along with many of his contemporaries, advanced the idea of victim precipitation.

SUGGESTED READING

William G. Doerner and Steven P. Lab, *Victimology,* 5th ed. (Newark, NJ: LexisNexis, 2008); Helen Eigenberg and Tammy Garland, "Victim Blaming," in *Controversies in*

Victimology, ed. Laura Moriarty (Newark, NJ: LexisNexis, 2008), 21–36; Beniamin Mendelsohn, "Victimology and Contemporary Society's Trends," *Victimology: An International Journal* 1 (1976): 8–28.

TAMMY GARLAND

MINNEAPOLIS DOMESTIC VIOLENCE EXPERIMENT. The Minneapolis Domestic Violence Experiment was conducted by sociologists Lawrence Sherman and Richard Berk with the cooperation of the Minneapolis Police Department. The purpose of the experiment was to determine which police response(s) were most effective in deterring domestic violence offenders from committing repeated acts of domestic assault. The experiment was conducted from March 1981 to August 1982 by officers in two precincts with high rates of domestic violence. When called to respond to a case of misdemeanor domestic assault, officers in these precincts responded with one of three randomly assigned strategies: arresting the offender, requiring the offender to leave the home, or mediating the dispute between the victim and the offender.[1]

Official records and interviews with victims indicated that six months after an incident, offenders who had been arrested were the least likely to commit subsequent acts of domestic violence. Sherman and Berk attribute this result to specific deterrence, which occurs when an individual chooses not to repeat a deviant act out of fear of receiving additional punishment. Based on their findings, Sherman and Berk recommended that police respond to domestic assaults with "a *presumption* of arrest; an arrest should be made unless there are good, clear reasons why an arrest would be counterproductive." However, it is important to note that the authors "do not, however, favor *requiring* arrests."[2]

Policing scholar David H. Bayley suggests that the Minneapolis Domestic Violence Experiment "is undoubtedly the most influential evaluation research ever done."[3] Although a strong statement, there is merit in Bayley's claim. After the dissemination of the experiment's results, cities and states across the United States began to create policies and pass laws requiring (or strongly encouraging) police officers to make an arrest in cases of domestic violence. These mandatory arrest policies were due in part to the substantial influence of Sherman and Berk's research[4] and in part due to policy activism by women's groups seeking to ensure that victims' rights were adequately protected.[5]

The Minneapolis Domestic Violence Experiment has not been without controversy. Sherman and Berk acknowledged that there were a number of potential flaws in the design of the study that could have affected its outcome.[6] Initial results from the replications of the original experiment were inconsistent, with some finding deterrence, some finding no deterrence, and some finding that arrest led to increased incidents of domestic violence.[7] However, a reanalysis of data from the replications later found that arrest was in fact associated with a decrease in repeated offending, arguing in favor of mandatory arrest as a means "for reducing subsequent victimization of women by their intimate partners."[8]

Another concern has focused on victims' preferences for arrest. Not all victims are equally likely to desire arrest as a police response, leading to questions about the extent to which a victim's preferences should be taken into account when an arrest decision is being made.[9]

NOTES

1. Lawrence W. Sherman and Richard A. Berk, "The Specific Deterrent Effects of Arrest for Domestic Violence," *American Sociological Review* 49 (1984): 261–72.

2. Sherman and Berk, "The Specific Deterrent Effects," 270.

3. David H. Bayley, *What Works in Policing* (New York: Oxford University Press, 1998), 223.

4. Lawrence W. Sherman and Ellen G. Cohn, "The Impact of Research on Legal Policy: The Minneapolis Domestic Violence Experiment," *Law & Society Review* 23 (1989): 117–44.

5. J. David Hirschel et al., "Review Essay on the Law Enforcement Response to Spouse Abuse: Past, Present, and Future," *Justice Quarterly* 9 (1992): 247–83.

6. Sherman and Cohn, "The Impact of Research," 117–44.

7. Results summarized in Janell D. Schmidt and Lawrence W. Sherman, "Does Arrest Deter Domestic Violence?" *American Behavioral Scientist* 36 (1993): 601–09.

8. Christopher D. Maxwell, Joel H. Garner, and Jeffrey A. Fagan, "The Preventative Effects of Arrest on Intimate Partner Violence: Research, Policy and Theory," *Criminology & Public Policy* 2 (2002): 69.

9. David Hirschel and Ira W. Hutchison, "The Voices of Domestic Violence Victims: Predictors of Victim Preference for Arrest and the Relationship Between Preference for Arrest and Revictimization," *Crime & Delinquency* 49 (2003): 313–36.

SUGGESTED READING

Joel Garner, Jeffrey Fagan, and Christopher Maxwell, "Published Findings from the Spouse Abuse Replication Program: A Critical Review," *Journal of Quantitative Criminology* 11 (1995): 3–28; Lawrence W. Sherman, Janell D. Schmidt, and Dennis P. Rogan, *Policing Domestic Violence: Experiments and Dilemmas* (New York: Free Press, 1992).

STEPHEN OWEN

MOTHERS AGAINST DRUNK DRIVING (MADD). Mothers Against Drunk Driving (MADD) is a national, nonprofit organization committed to advocacy and victim services for individuals impacted by drinking and driving. MADD was founded in 1980 by Candy Lightner and Sue LeBrun-Green after the death of Candy's 13-year-old daughter Cari in a hit-and-run accident. The driver of the vehicle had been intoxicated. Through her own experience and a continual commitment to fighting drinking and driving, MADD was created. Today, MADD has local chapters organized by county in all 50 states with a central office in Irving, Texas.

MADD's mission statement originally was to assist victims of crimes caused by individuals under the influence of alcohol. Today, their mission statement has expanded to include reducing and preventing underage drinking. Although each chapter is responsible for their own anti-drunk driving campaign, the central mission of MADD is universal: "to stop drunk driving, support the victims of this violent crime and prevent underage drinking."[1] Since MADD's onset the major focus of the organization has been on giving a voice to the victim of a drinking and driving-related offense.

MADD is driven by the need for victims and affected persons to act on their emotions and cope with their loss. MADD offers a 24-hour victim helpline on which individuals can speak to a victim advocate. In addition, they organize a nationwide online chat forum for victims/survivors to speak to other victims/survivors in a safe environment. MADD also provides resources on grieving, injury support, the legal process, and financial recovery for those who have been affected by a drunk driver. Those affected by an incident of drunk driving are often left in anger or rage. MADD, a fitting acronym, offers these individuals an outlet for their emotions through involvement. Through coordinated events such as candlelight vigils, school assemblies, community education, conferences, and workshops, this organization has empowered many victims/survivors to speak out against drinking and driving and offers them a chance to tell their stories.

A second form of empowerment MADD offers bereaved persons is through advocacy. With the support of many elected officials, MADD has successfully witnessed the passage of more than 1,000 local and national laws regarding drinking and driving, including sobriety checkpoints and the 21-year-old minimum drinking age. Through advocacy and a push for reform in how the criminal justice system deals with drinking-and-driving cases, those affected by drunk driving can feel empowered and gain some control in a seemingly complicated and emotional period.

NOTE

1. Mothers Against Drunk Driving, "Mothers Against Drunk Driving (MADD) Mission Statement," Mothers Against Drunk Driving, http://www.madd.org.

SUGGESTED READING

Mac Marshall and Alice Oleson, "MADDer Than Hell," *Qualitative Health Research* 6 (1996): 6–22; John D. McCarthy and Mark Wolfson, "Resource Mobilization by Local Social Movement Organizations: Agency, Strategy, and Organizing in the Movement

Against Drinking and Driving," *American Sociological Review* 61 (1996): 1070–88; Frank J. Weed, "The Victim-Activist Role in the Anti-Drunk Driving Movement," *The Sociology Quarterly* 31 (1990): 459–73.

ANNA E. KOSLOSKI

MOTOR VEHICLE THEFT. According to the National Insurance Crime Bureau and the Federal Bureau of Investigation, a motor vehicle is stolen every 26 seconds in the United States. More than one million vehicles are stolen each year, a trend that has been occurring for several decades. Between 1960 and 2005 there were more than 60 million vehicles stolen in the United States. In 2006, 1.2 million vehicles were stolen, a decrease of approximately 3.5% from 2005. Fortunately, vehicle theft incidents have been decreasing almost every year since the early 1990s with a few exceptions early in the new millennium. Only approximately 13% of vehicle thefts are cleared by arrest annually.

Vehicle theft is the single most expensive property crime in the United States, and the overall costs are continuing to increase as technological developments make motor vehicles more expensive. In 2006 the value of stolen motor vehicles in the United States was approximately $8 billion, with the average value of a stolen vehicle being approximately $6,500. It is important to note that costs and inconveniences of motor vehicle theft are not only experienced by the primary victim but are passed on to all insured drivers through increased insurance premiums in high-theft cities and states and through the need for theft-prevention devices. Further, there are substantial costs extending beyond the value of the vehicle to include the costs to law enforcement, the courts, lost worker productivity on the part of the inconvenienced victim, and lost wages. According to the Bureau of Justice Statistics, the average victim of motor vehicle theft misses between one and five days of work.

Victimization is most likely to occur in urban areas, particularly those in western states. Western states traditionally account for the greatest portion of motor vehicle thefts followed by the south, the midwest, and the northeast. The typical motor vehicle theft victim, unlike victims of most other crimes, is selected in large part based upon features of the vehicle and the environment. Auto thieves target vehicles for the ease of entry and the black market value of their parts. In a recent list of the top 10 most frequently stolen vehicles in the United States, Hondas and Toyotas comprise five of the top spots. Vehicles left running, left with keys in the ignition, or left in areas with poor guardianship are at greatest risk.

One particularly violent and aggressive form of motor vehicle theft is carjacking. A carjacking is characterized by the offender's willingness to steal the vehicle while the owner is present with the vehicle, frequently in the drivers' seat. Carjackers typically use the threat of a weapon or physical force to subdue the victim and demand the vehicle. Carjacking is most common in high-crime areas, at intersections during routine stops, in isolated parking lots, and in residential driveways. The convenience on the part of the offender is that the keys are readily available, and the vehicle, under many carjacking circumstances, is already running. There are several techniques carjackers typically employ in stealing a vehicle. They may bump the victim's vehicle in an effort to get the victim to stop and check for damage, whereupon the victim's vehicle is taken. The offender may indicate to the driver of the target vehicle that there is a problem with the vehicle and that they should pull over. Once the victim pulls the car over, the offender takes the vehicle. Occasionally, offenders will approach a stopped vehicle at an intersection on foot and through the use of threat demand that the victim exit the vehicle; the thief then drives off.

There are several techniques that can be implemented to reduce one's risk of carjacking victimization. It is recommended drivers remain aware of their surroundings at all times, keep windows rolled up and doors locked, carry car keys separately from other keys for easy vehicle entry, and park in well lit areas.

SUGGESTED READING

Insurance Information Institute, "Auto Theft," http://www.iii.org/media/hottopics/insurance/test4/?printerfriendly-yes; National Insurance Crime Bureau, "Vehicles at Risk for Theft," http://www.nicb.org/consumer/index.html; Jeffrey A. Walsh and Ralph B. Taylor, "Predicting Decade-Long Changes in Community Motor Vehicle Theft Rates: Impacts of Structure and Surround," *Journal of Research in Crime and Delinquency* 44, no. 1 (2007): 64–90.

JEFFREY WALSH

MURDER. Murder is the illegal killing of one human being by another. Although "homicide" is often used synonymously with murder, it is a broader term that includes both illegal and legal killings. The latter include slayings by police officers in the line of duty and by private citizens in self-defense.

Universally viewed as the most serious criminal offense, murder is the least common violent crime in developed nations. Expressed as the number of occurrences per 100,000 population, the 2007 murder rate in the United States was 5.6, compared to a robbery rate of 147.6 and an aggravated assault rate of 292.6.[1] In the United States, which has a notably higher murder rate than most developed nations, approximately two-thirds of the murders are committed with a firearm, more often a handgun than a long gun. Knives and other cutting instruments are the most common murder weapons in most European nations. Many researchers assert that the easy availability of firearms to private citizens in the United States is a major factor behind both the high murder rate and the prevalence of guns as murder weapons.

Like most crimes, murder does not occur randomly. Within the United States, rates are higher in the south and west than in the northeast and midwest, and they are typically higher in large cities than in suburbs, small cities, and rural areas. Within cities, murders are further concentrated, so that some neighborhoods rarely experience a murder whereas others are plagued by several each year. Recent research shows that one factor explaining neighborhood differences in the number of murders is the time it takes to transport critically injured victims to a trauma center. Thus, the location of trauma care within a metropolitan area affects whether a violent act becomes a murder or an aggravated assault (an unlawful attack for the purpose of inflicting severe or aggravated bodily injury).

Additionally, an individual's gender, age, and race affect their risk of becoming a murder victim. Men are more involved in violent crimes than women, as both victims and offenders, and their murder victimization rates in 2005 were 9.0 versus 2.3 for women.[2] Infants under 1 year of age are murdered at a higher rate than children between the ages of 2 and 13 years, who have a very low victimization rate. The peak years of risk, however, are from the late teens through the early twenties, after which the chances of becoming a murder victim decrease. In 2005, the murder rate for individuals aged 18–24 years was 14.9 compared to rates of 1.4 for those under 14 and 2.6 for those over 50. African Americans have a very high homicide rate, 20.6, compared to that for whites, 3.3. Among factors that help explain higher murder rates among certain groups in the United States are poverty, residential segregation, and the percentage of female-headed households. Finally, lifestyle choices are also important in explaining murder victimization (and offending), with several cities reporting that well over 50% of murder victims have a prior drug conviction on their records.

NOTES

1. Federal Bureau of Investigation, "Uniform Crime Reports," http:www.fbi.gov/ucr/ucr.htm.

2. Bureau of Justice Statistics, "Homicide Trends in the United States," http://www.ojp.usdoj.gov/bjs/homicide.overview.htm.

SUGGESTED READING

Leonard Beeghley, *Homicide: A Sociological Explanation* (Lanham, MD: Rowman and Littlefied, 2003); Terance D. Miethe and Wendy C. Regoeczi, *Rethinking Homicide: Exploring the Structure and Process Underlying Deadly Situations* (Cambridge: University of Cambridge Press, 2004); M. Dwayne Smith and Margaret A. Zahn, eds., *Homicide: A Sourcebook of Social Research* (Thousand Oaks, CA: Sage, 1999).

JAY CORZINE AND LIN HUFF-CORZINE

N

NATIONAL CRIME VICTIMIZATION SURVEY (NCVS). The National Crime Victimization Survey (NCVS) is a series of surveys collecting data of criminal victimization of persons and households for the crimes of rape, robbery, assault, burglary, larceny, motor vehicle theft, and vandalism in the United States. Using a nationally representative sample of households and rotating panel methods, about 100,000 persons 12 years of age and older living in approximately 50,000 households are interviewed twice each year on the frequency, characteristics, and consequences of criminal victimization. Each person is interviewed seven times at six-month intervals.[1] The NCVS is the primary source of crime statistics, providing information of crimes not reported to the police.[2] Using uniform measures and procedures, the NCVS permits comparisons of crime over time and among and within geographic areas. Since basic demographic information and circumstances surrounding the crimes are also collected, the NCVS also allows estimation and comparison of crime by various subgroups. The current NCVS is sponsored by the Bureau of Justice Statistics (BJS) of the U.S. Department of Justice, with the fieldwork performed by the U.S. Census Bureau.[3]

The NCVS, previously called the National Crime Survey (NCS), was established in 1973 by the Law Enforcement Assistance Administration (LEAA) and administered by the Bureau of the Census.[4] The program was transferred to the Bureau of Justice Statistics in December 1979. Before the NCS, the FBI's Uniform Crime Reporting System (UCR) was the primary source of crime statistics in the United States. Because the UCR is based on crime known to the police, it cannot provide accurate estimates of the true nature of criminal victimization. In addition, police statistics do not provide the demographic and socioeconomic framework essential to understanding the broader impact of crime. The LEAA therefore established the NCS for the purpose of developing more reliable information on estimating national victimization rates and understanding the characteristics of crime victims, including the nature of incidents and how people respond to them. The NCS was originally planned to be operated as a continuous national survey to samples of households (NCS) as well as to commercial establishments (Commercial Victimization Survey). The first wave of the NCS launched by LEAA and the Census Bureau in July 1972, for example, covered a national sample of 72,000 households as well as 15,000 businesses. Data collection for the National Commercial Victimization Survey was suspended in September 1977.[5]

Starting in the early 1980s, the Department of Justice initiated a methodological redesign of the NCS. The redesign was systematically introduced and executed by a consortium of academic and government researchers starting in 1989, which resulted in the final reengineer in 1992, when the NCS was renamed to the National Crime Victimization Survey (NCVS).[6] The redesign used an improved screening questionnaire together with methods to help respondents recall a broader range of incidents. It aimed at obtaining better measures of all crimes with special focus on improving measures of sexual crimes and domestic violence. Comparisons of data before and after the redesign indicated that the redesign draws out more reports of crime for most categories, especially for assault, domestic violence, rape, and sexual attack.[7] Besides the improvement of measurement, the revised NCVS also provides new information on crime incidents including interaction between victims and offenders, situational crime prevention efforts, and perceived alcohol and drug use by offenders.[8]

The NCVS consists of three levels of dataset: household-level, person-level, and incident-level. "The household records contain information about the household as reported by the respondent and characteristics of the surrounding area as computed by the Bureau of the Census. The person record contains information about each household member age 12 years and older as reported by that person or proxy, with one record for each qualifying individual. The incident record contains information drawn from the incident report completed for each household incident or person incident mentioned during the interview."[9] Therefore, the NCVS can be used in studies in which individuals, households, or incidents are the units of analysis.

Because the NCVS uses a nationally representative sample and uses standardized methods and procedures to interview, the NCVS is the primary reliable resource of criminal victimization measurement. It serves as a "model for victimization surveys implemented throughout the world."[10] Although the NCVS has a lot of strengths, the survey is subject to some limitations. The NCVS does not provide information on crimes in which businesses or institutes are victims. Victimization experiences of the homeless are not covered in the NCVS. Juvenile delinquency also receives limited coverage in the NCVS.[11] The NCVS also suffers from many of the methodological problems of surveys, such as instrumentation change, sample size reduction, procedure change over time,[12] and recall errors.

NOTES

1. Inter-university Consortium for Political and Social Research (ICPSR), *National Crime Victimization Survey, 1992–2003* (Ann Arbor, MI: ICPSR, 2004).

2. Robert G. Lehnen and Wesley G. Skogan, *The National Crime Survey: Working Papers,* vol. I: Current and Historical Perspectives (Washington DC: Bureau of Justice Statistics, 1981).

3. ICPSR, *National Crime.*

4. Lehnen and Skogan, *National Crime Survey.*

5. Ibid.

6. Robert M. Groves and Daniel L. Cork, *Surveying Victims: Options for Conducting the National Crime Victimization Survey* (Washington DC: The National Academies Press, 2008), http://www.nap.edu/catalog.php?record_id=12090#toc; Wesley G. Skogan, "The National Crime Survey Redesign," *Public Opinion Quarterly* 54 (1990): 256–72; Bureau of Justice Statistics, "*National Crime Victimization Survey: Questions and answers about the redesign,*" http://www.ojp.usdoj.gov/bjs/pub/pdf/ncsrqa.pdf.

7. Ibid.

8. Ibid.

9. ICPSR, *National Crime.*

10. Callie Marie Rennison and Michael Rand, pp. 17–53, "Introduction to The National Crime Victimization Survey" in *Understanding Crime Statistics: Revisiting the Divergence of the NCVS and the UCR,* eds. James P. Lynch and Lynn A. Addington (New York: Cambridge University Press, 2007).

11. Sherry L. Hamby, "Measuring Gender Differences in Partner Violence: Implications from Research on Other Forms of Violent and Socially Undesirable Behavior," *Sex Roles: A Journal of Research* 52, no. 11–12 (2005): 725–42.

12. Groves and Cork, *Surveying Victims.*

SUGGESTED READING

Sharon L. Lohr and Joanna Liu, "A Comparison of Weighted and Unweighted Analyses in the National Crime Victimization Survey," *Journal of Quantitative Criminology* 10, no. 4 (1994): 343–60.

YAN ZHANG

NATIONAL INCIDENT-BASED REPORTING SYSTEM (NIBRS). The National Incident-Based Reporting System (NIBRS) was created as a result of limitations inherent in the Uniform Crime Reports. After evaluating the Uniform Crime Reports and consulting with law enforcement officials, the Federal Bureau

of Investigation found that the Uniform Crime Report did not offer enough detailed information to provide an accurate description of crime. The NIBRS treats crime as an "incident" and therefore gathers comprehensive data that provide a better measure of crime, criminals, and their victims.

The NIBRS is gathered from data provided by law enforcement. It includes information on the offense, victim, offender, and arrestee and provides data on the following offenses:

> **Group A offenses** (includes information on the offense, property, victim, offender, and arrestee): arson, assault offenses, bribery, burglary/breaking and entering, counterfeiting/forgery, destruction/damage/vandalism of property, drug/narcotic offenses, embezzlement, extortion/blackmail, fraud offenses, gambling offenses, hate crime, homicide offenses, kidnapping/extortion, larceny/theft, motor vehicle theft, pornography/obscene material, prostitution offenses, robbery, sex offenses forcible/non-forcible (includes juvenile victims), stolen property offenses, and weapon law violations.
>
> **Group B offenses** (arrestee data only): bad checks, curfew/loitering/vagrancy, disorderly conduct, driving under the influence, drunkenness, family offenses/nonviolent, liquor law violations, peeping tom, runaway, trespass of real property, and all other offenses.

The main objective of NIBRS was to enhance the quality of crime data. It advances the UCR in numerous ways: level of detail; includes male and female victims of rape; collects information on multiple offenses and multiple victims; provides information surrounding crimes against society (primarily drug-related crime); gathers data via computer from local, state, and national law enforcement; includes data that allow for relationship information between offenses, offenders, victims, and arrests; and provides information on attempted and completed crime. Details available in the NIBRS also provide information regarding crime location, use of weapons, injury, and property loss.

The NIBRS was approved for nationwide use in the late 1980s. Agencies that utilize NIBRS must be certified by the Federal Bureau of Investigation in order to collect and report data for NIBRS. Certified agencies are constantly testing and developing the NIBRS, but only around 16–20% of all crimes are reported using the NIBRS framework. Despite its advances, it has been difficult to make the NIBRS a widespread tool. Agency resources are scarce, and time and devotion necessary to implementing a new data collection tool are limited (this would include updating record management systems and reprogramming current automated systems that do not capture data required by NIBRS).

Other impediments to a nation-wide system involve the perceptions of law enforcement. They report uncertainty of the benefits of switching to the NIBRS, concern for resulting changes in policy (if crime increases), additional time spent by officers either in completing more extensive reports or training involved, subjectivity and relativity of data (especially pertaining to the classification of victims and their involvement/relationships to offender), and inappropriate interpretation by policymakers and key stakeholders.

SUGGESTED READING

Bureau of Justice Statistics, *"Effects of NIBRS on Crime Statistics,"* U.S. Department of Justice, http://www.ojp.gov/bjs/abstract/encs.htm; Bureau of Justice Statistics, "Incident-Based Statistics," U.S. Department of Justice, http://www.ojp.usdoj.gov/bjs/ibrs.htm; Nathan James and Logan Rishard Council, "CRS Report for Congress: How Crime in the United States is Measured," (Washington DC: Congressional Research Service, 2008).

ALANA VAN GUNDY-YODER

NEGLECT. Neglect occurs when a parent, guardian, or caregiver fails to provide for a child's basic needs. These needs are typically classified into four categories: physical (i.e., food and shelter), emotional, medical, and educational. Federal legislation, through the Federal Child Abuse Prevention and Treatment Act (CAPTA), and later the Keeping Children and Families Safe Act of 2003, established minimum child abuse and neglect standards that states must incorporate into their individual child abuse and neglect laws. In their legislative definitions of abuse and neglect, states must include incidents or failure to prevent incidents by a parent or caretaker that result in the serious harm or death of a child or a situation that presents an impending risk of serious harm.

In 2006, over 900,000 children in the United States were determined to be victims of abuse or neglect. Of those children, roughly 66% endured some form of neglect. By law, in most states public figures such as doctors and educators must report suspected abuse or neglect to Child Protective Services (CPS). Following an investigation, children who are deemed to have been neglected may be removed from their home and placed in foster care. CPS in conjunction with the local family court system works with such families to resolve the issues that led to the neglect. In some cases in which neglect is found to have occurred, the child may be allowed to remain living at home. Like families who have had their child removed from their home, families in which neglect is found to have occurred may have to work with CPS and the court system to prevent future incidents of neglect. Although many families are successful at remedying these issues and have their children returned to their care, some are unsuccessful. In these cases, the court may terminate the parents' legal rights to their child and place the child for adoption.

The costs of neglect can be monetary and social. The estimated monetary cost of child abuse and neglect reaches almost $104 billion annually. Outcomes for children who suffer neglect vary based on a number of factors including the physical and developmental age of the child at the time of the incident, the frequency of neglect, and the severity of the neglect. Younger children tend to be most venerable to the effects of neglect. Some children may experience lasting consequences from neglect, while others may experience few or no effects. Young children who experience emotional, physical, or environmental neglect may suffer from depression or withdrawal symptoms. Some older children develop panic disorders, dissociative disorders, and depression or exhibit anger or aggression. Children who are removed from their homes because of abuse or neglect often score lower on cognitive capacity and academic achievement measures than those who had not been removed from their home. Individual characteristics such as optimism, access to positive role models, and self esteem have been linked to more resilient children.

SUGGESTED READING

Child Welfare Information Gateway, "What is Child Abuse and Neglect?" U.S. Department of Health and Human Services, http://www.childwelfare.gov/pubs/can_info_packet.pdf; Child Welfare Information Gateway, "State Statutes," U.S. Department of Health and Human Services, http://www.childwelfare.gov/systemwide/laws_policies/state/; Ching-Tung Wang and John Holton, "Total Estimated Cost of Child Abuse and Neglect in the United States," The Pew Charitable Trusts, http://member.preventchild abuse.org/site/DocServer/cost_analysis.pdf?docID=144.

MELISSA YOUNG-SPILLERS

NEIGHBORHOOD WATCH PROGRAMS. Neighborhood Watch programs, a facet of community crime prevention, encourage neighbors to watch for suspicious activity and to dialogue with police. Neighborhood watch programs began in the 1970s as part of the community policing movement. By 2000, 41% of the United States population lived in a community that had a neighborhood watch program.[1] The federal government promotes it through several agencies and programs, but most neighborhood watch programs are funded locally and depend on donations.[2] Property crime is typically the focus, though some have tried to mobilize neighborhood watch groups for other purposes including the detection of intrafamily violence. Since 9/11, the National Sheriffs' Association has promoted neighborhood watch programs to "empower citizens . . . to work toward the safety of our homeland,"[3] suggesting an attempt to shift the emphasis toward terrorism.

Although the programs are common and popular, the empirical record is unclear. Effectiveness can be measured along several dimensions. Early evaluations found reduced burglary in areas where neighborhood watch programs had been introduced. However, other research found that programs faltered when crime rates decreased[4] and that effectiveness depended on participants "perceived vulnerability."[5]

A 2008 systematic review of the neighborhood watch literature found that some evaluations showed "a reduction in crime, others showed that it was associated with an increase in crime, whereas others provided uncertain results."[6] In addition to measurement and design problems, evaluations generally focus on the entire program rather than its components. Variations by location and implementation further obscure the causes of crime reductions. Recent research has also found that "Criminal Beware!" signs may produce unintended consequences when posted in low-income neighborhoods, such as increased fear of crime and worry about victimization.[7]

Critical scholarship focuses on the social control functions rather than deterrent effects.[8] Scholars of the current trend toward "governing through crime"[9] might consider neighborhood watch programs as another example of citizens' reduced expectations of what the state will do instead encouraging us to monitor ourselves and to remain fearful.

NOTES

1. National Crime Prevention Council, *The 2000 National Crime Prevention Survey* (Washington DC: National Crime Prevention Council, 2001).

2. Katy Holloway, Trevor Bennett, and David P. Farrington, *Crime Prevention Research Review No. 3: Does Neighborhood Watch Reduce Crime?* (Washington DC: U.S. Department of Justice Office of Community Oriented Policing Services, 2008).

3. USA On Watch Web site, http://www.usaonwatch.org/.

4. Betsy Lindsay and Daniel McGillis, "Citywide Community Crime Prevention: An Assessment of the Seattle Program," in *Community Crime Prevention: Does it Work?*, ed. Dennis P. Rosenbaum (Beverly Hills, CA: Sage, 1986), 46–67.

5. Dennis P. Rosenbaum, Dan A. Lewis, and Jane A. Grant, *The Impact of Community Crime Prevention Programs in Chicago: Can Neighborhood Organizations Make a Difference. Final Report; vol. 1* (Chicago: Center for Urban Affairs and Policy Research, Northwestern University, 1987, 1985): 129.

6. Holloway, Bennett, and Farrington, *Crime Prevention,* 21.

7. P. Wesley Schultz and Jennifer J. Tabanico, "Criminal Beware: A Social Norms Perspective on Posting Public Warning Signs" (under review).

8. Eve Darian-Smith, "Neighborhood Watch: Who Watches Whom? Reinterpreting the Concept of Neighborhood," *Human Organization* 52 (1993): 83.

9. Jonathan S. Simon, *Governing Through Crime: How the War on Crime Transformed American Democracy and Created a Culture of Fear* (Oxford: Oxford University Press, 2007).

SUGGESTED READING

Anna Alvazzi del Frate, "Preventing Crime: Citizen's Experiences across the World," *Issues and Reports—United Nations Interregional Crime and Justice Research Institute* 9 (1997): 1–16.

CHRYSANTHI LEON

NEUTRALIZATION THEORY. One of the most important elements in the commission of crime is the psychological process of sanitizing the conscience so that the crime can be accomplished without suffering guilt. Much has been written about the ways that offenders make sense of or account for their criminal acts and related behaviors. Perhaps the most well-known explanation of this process was proposed by Gresham Sykes and David Matza in 1957—what is now referred to as *neutralization theory*. According to Sykes and Matza, when offenders contemplate committing criminal acts, they use linguistic devices to neutralize the guilt associated with committing crime. The most common neutralization techniques that offenders use include denial of responsibility, denial of harm, denial of victim, appeal to higher loyalties, and condemnation of the condemners. The use of neutralization techniques allows offenders to free themselves from the guilt or negative self-image that is associated with their crimes. By holding onto these justifications and bringing them to the foreground when needed, offenders can continue their behavior without the corresponding guilt.

Neutralization theory has found its way into the rationales of numerous criminal justice innovations, including restorative justice conferencing and correctional therapy. Many offender rehabilitation programs are designed to teach offenders, through training and exercises, strategies for overcoming rationalizations and recognizing errors in thinking. The idea is that through changes in thinking and cognitive training, offenders will recognize their responsibilities and apply these lessons when confronting future criminal opportunities. Such programs have been shown to be effective in helping offenders make changes in their lives. Offenders can be taught lessons that change their thinking, and these lessons help them to avoid situations that lead them to crime. Cognitive restructuring programs may prove to be effective in transforming offenders into ex-offenders.

The idea of cognitive restructuring is also consistent with some restorative justice interventions in which offenders sit down with family members, community elders, and their victims in a reintegrative shaming process that often has the explicit aim of undermining offender neutralizations. The social psychological basis behind restorative justice is that it is difficult for offenders to sustain the denial of victim or denial of injury during victim-offender mediation when the offender must directly acknowledge the victims. Similarly, condemnation of condemners is difficult to maintain when the condemners are respectful in their conversations with offenders.

Treatment programs often aim to have offenders take responsibility for their actions and avoid excuse-making. Yet, the relationship between neutralizations and future crime is not clear. Some argue that neutralizations are normal and healthy and that neutralization use should not be seen as evidence of future offending. Instead, it can be seen as the rejection of a criminal identity, which is important for eventual desistance.

SUGGESTED READING

Shadd Maruna and Heith Copes, "What Have We Learned from Five Decades of Neutral-ization Research?" *Crime and Justice: An Annual Review of Research* 32 (2005): 221–320; Gresham Sykes and David Matza, "Techniques of Neutralization: A Theory of Delinquency," *American Sociological Review* 22 (1957): 664–70.

HEITH COPES

NO-DROP POLICIES. No-drop prosecution policies encourage the criminal justice system to take domestic violence cases seriously. Yet, a recent report completed by the National Institute of Justice indicates that prosecution of abusers, without taking offender risk into consideration, does not deter abuse. Given these findings, are these policies beneficial?

Proponents say no-drop policies are beneficial to victims and the justice system. On an individual level, the burden of deciding what to do in abusive situations is taken away from the victim, decreasing offenders' perception that victims were complicit in their arrest. No-drop policies also increase police officer response because police know that cases will be prosecuted. On a structural level, no-drop policies increase victim cooperation, leading to a reduction in case attrition.

Opponents argue that there are unintended consequences of no-drop policies. Re-victimization of victims is one such outcome. No-drop policies take decision-making power away from victims, placing it in the hands of the state. This action implies that victims should not make decisions about their own interests. In an effort to maintain some level of agency, victims' calls to police have decreased, and some women have refused to testify against batterers. This refusal has led to jail time. No-drop policies also contribute to system overcrowding, resulting in a sluggish system.

SUGGESTED READING

Myrna Dawson and Ronit Dinovitzer, "Victim Cooperation and the Prosecution of Domes-tic Violence in a Specialized Court," *Justice Quarterly* 18 (2001): 593–622; Joel H. Garner and Christopher D. Maxwell, *Prosecution and Conviction Rates for Intimate Partner Violence* (Shepherstown, WV: Joint Centers for Justice Studies, 2008); Linda Mills, "Mandatory Arrest and Prosecution Policies for Domestic Violence," *Criminal Justice and Behavior* 25 (1998): 306–18.

MICHELLE BEMILLER

NOTORIETY FOR PROFIT LAWS. Notoriety for profit laws, also known as "Son of Sam" laws, are statutes that serve victims of crimes and protect their rights by prohibiting offenders from financially profiting from a crime. They began when New York serial killer David Berkowitz decided to tell the story of how he murdered several people during 1976 and 1977. Berkowitz's royalties from his story were particularly disturbing in light of the fact that surviving victims continued to suffer physical, emotional, and psychological pain and would relive the incident as it stayed in the headlines. Families of the slain victims were horrified to think that the killer was becoming more infamous and popular, whereas their loved ones were forgotten.

The possibility of David Berkowitz's "tell-all" book deal led to a new breed of laws designed to prevent financial benefit to convicted criminals. Although the law was never applied to Berkowitz personally because it was enacted prior to his conviction, "Son of Sam laws" became the new moniker for *notoriety for profit* laws.

In 1977 the New York Legislature passed a statute stating that the party contracting with the offender to recount the offense must pay all profits to the state that would otherwise be paid directly to the offender. The funds would then be held in escrow to benefit the victims or be contributed to the state's victim compensation fund. The "Son of Sam" laws set a precedent for victims to file civil action against the offenders who could otherwise profit from the sale of a book, film, television show, broadcast, print, recording, live performance, or any other "reenactment" of the crime that they committed. The law was invoked in New York 10 times between 1977 and 1990, including against the convicted killer of John Lennon, Mark David Chapman.

The law was criticized for violating First Amendment rights of free speech, but the point was made that the law did not prohibit telling of the story, only profiting from it. Simon and Schuster, publishers of *Wiseguy* (told by an ex-mobster and the basis for the movie *Goodfellas*), filed suit in 1987 against New York's Crime Victims Compensation Board to overturn the Son of Sam law. In 1991, the case reached the Supreme Court, which overturned the law (8–0) because it was too broad and would have prevented the publication of classics such as *Civil Disobedience* and *The Autobiography of Malcolm X*. The court argued that notoriety for profit laws are not unconstitutional per se but established that they must be crafted carefully so as not to encroach on free speech.[1]

By 2000 more than 40 states had some form of notoriety for profit laws. The concept was tested in 2006 with O.J. Simpson, who received a book deal for *If I Did It*, a "hypothetical" account of how he might have murdered his ex-wife Nicole Brown and Ron Goldman. Because he was found not guilty of murder in criminal court—but liable for their wrongful deaths in civil court—notoriety for profit laws did not apply. Due to public outcry, the book deal was withdrawn, and the rights to the book awarded to the Goldman family as part of their compensatory damages.

NOTE

1. *Simon & Schuster v. NY Crime Victims Board,* 502 U.S. 105 (1991).

SUGGESTED READING

Rudolph Alexander, Jr., "Victims' Rights and the Son of Sam Law: Implications for Free Speech and Research on Offenders," *Criminal Justice Policy Review* 6 (1992): 275–90.

CASEY JORDAN

OPERATORS. 911 operators are essential to the proper functioning of the modern criminal justice system. Although police are often touted as the "gate-keepers" of criminal justice because police action often precedes formal entry into the criminal justice process, the fact is that much police activity is initiated through the work of 911 operators.

Indeed, 911 operators—or dispatchers—hold one of the most complex and stressful jobs in the criminal justice industry. The effective dispatcher must be able to handle a high volume of incoming calls from citizens, collect accurate information (no small feat given the fact that many callers are unwilling or unable to provide all of the necessary information), assess and prioritize calls for service, determine appropriate response needs, dispatch police or other emergency personnel (e.g., fire, EMS, or social services), coordinate multiple ongoing responses, keep meticulous records, regularly communicate with both police officers and administrators, and simultaneously serve the needs of law enforcement, community leaders, and the citizenry.

The complexity and importance of the 911 operator's role is particularly evident in their interactions with crime victims, many of whom are under duress or unable to fully comprehend what has happened when they contact the dispatcher. These interactions present an array of challenges for the 911 operator, who must gather information that is accurate and detailed, set the tone of the interaction, gauge the extent of any ongoing threats to the caller or others, help bring the situation under control, keep the victim calm until appropriate personnel arrive on scene, and manage the victim's expectations regarding the nature and timeliness of police response. Moreover, the dispatcher must do all of this while relaying information to officers in the field and helping to coordinate what may be a multiagency response effort.

SUGGESTED READING

Tod W. Burke, "Dispatcher Stress," *FBI Law Enforcement Bulletin* 64, no. 10 (1995): 1–6; Jim F. Gilsinan, "They Is Clowning Tough: 911 and the Social Construction of Reality," *Criminology* 27, no. 2 (1989): 329–44; S. J. Tracy, "When Questioning Turns to Face Threat: An Interactional Sensitivity in 911 Call-Taking," *Western Journal of Communication* 66 (2002): 129–57.

BRIAN A. MONAHAN AND ANNA E. KOSLOSKI

ORDER OF PROTECTION. An order of protection relies on the petitioner or victim to make her case to support an order detailing no contact between parties. Typically, the petitioner will go to the local courthouse and fill out the appropriate forms for the court to review. If an order is signed, the order is shared with all involved, including law enforcement. The protection is based on the assumption a court order will discourage contact or violent behavior. "Sometimes women may be able to get an immediate short-term emergency protective order, without the abuser bring present, on the basis of their own testimony,"[1] which may be critical in certain cases.

There are many complicating factors in orders of protection: It relies on the victim to report, the court to order, the police to enforce, and the parties to follow. There may be children involved, or housing and financial dependency issues. "Not only can a restraining order cause a woman to feel more powerful and in control, but police are often more supportive of women who get them, possibly because the woman is showing she is serious."[2] Further complicating the relationships of all involved is the fact that police inaction has been shown to lead to continued violence.[3]

The effectiveness of an order of protection largely relies on the respondent following the order, which can include avoiding even indirect contact via e-mail, phone, or through friends. Ultimately, "though respondents often violate their protective order in some way, the orders generally deter repeated incidents of physical and psychological abuse."[4]

NOTES

1. Karen J. Wilson, *When Violence Begins at Home: A Comprehensive Guide to Understanding and Ending Domestic Abuse* (Alameda, CA: Hunter House, 1997), 77.

2. Beverly Ford, *Violent Relationships: Battering and Abuse Among Adults* (Farmington Hills, MI: Gale Group, 2001), 83.

3. Ibid.

4. Ibid, 82.

SUGGESTED READING

Mark Fass, "My Space 'Friend Request' Could Violate Protection Order," *New York Law Journal,* February 14, 2008; Louise Gerdes, ed., *Battered Women* (Farmington Hills, MI: Cengage Gale, 1999).

SARAH LINDAHL-PFIEFFER

P

PAIN AND SUFFERING COMPENSATION. The purpose of "pain and suffering" compensatory damages is to restore victims to their pre-event conditions, to the extent that monetary awards can do so. The definition of "pain and suffering" varies by jurisdiction but often includes bodily harm, including pain, disfigurement, and disability; emotional harm, including depression, anxiety, and embarrassment; and loss of enjoyment of life, including any new limitations on one's lifestyle.[1]

Although compensation can occur via mediations, arbitration, or insurance settlements, civil litigation is the most common method for seeking compensatory damages. Yet it is often difficult for jurors to convert their perceptions of a victim's condition into dollar amounts because legal standards are poorly defined for noneconomic tort damages.[2] Many different factors can impact the amount of monetary awards, including the severity of the injury, attributions of responsibility, and the personality, perceived credibility, and status of litigants and attorneys. Complicating matters further is the fact that there is no objective test to assess the severity of suffering. Juries are usually asked to employ a "reasonable person" standard, defined as what a reasonable person would estimate as fair compensation, when deciding pain and suffering compensation.[3] Yet studies have shown that jury awards for pain and suffering vary widely for injuries that appear to be equally severe. Perhaps as a result, many states have enacted legislative reforms to limit pain and suffering damage awards.

NOTES

1. Roselle L. Wissler et al., "Explaining "Pain and Suffering" Awards: The Role of Injury Characteristics and Fault Attributions," *Law and Human Behavior* 21, no. 2 (1997): 181–207.

2. Mark Geistfeld, "Placing a Price on Pain and Suffering: A Method for Helping Juries Determine Tort Damages for Nonmonetary Injuries," *California Law Review* 83 (1995): 773–852.

3. Wissler et al., "Explaining "Pain and Suffering," 181–207.

SUGGESTED READING

Edith Greene, "On Juries and Damage Awards: The Process of Decision Making," *Law and Contemporary Problems* 5 (1989): 225–46; Paul V. Niemeyer, "Awards for Pain and Suffering: The Irrational Centerpiece of Our Tort System," *Virginia Law Review* 90 (2004): 1401–21.

JASON MANDELBAUM AND ANGELA CROSSMAN

PARENTS ANONYMOUS® INC. Parents Anonymous® was founded in 1969 through the exceptional efforts of a brave mother seeking help to create a safe and caring home for her family. Working in partnership with her social worker, they started a national movement that has brought help, support, strength, and hope to millions of families. Parents Anonymous® Inc. now operates a worldwide network of accredited state and regional organizations that serve thousands annually. Evidence-based Parents Anonymous® programs serve the entire family through free, weekly, ongoing community-based Parents Anonymous® groups co-led by parent group leaders and professionally trained group facilitators. Co-occurring children and youth groups are guided by trained children and youth program workers. Parents Anonymous® groups are not 12-step programs or parent education classes; they are strengths-based mutual support groups. Findings from a recent national evaluation study demonstrated that Parents Anonymous® groups reduce child maltreatment outcomes, increase protective factors, and reduce risk factors in families; parents and children learn new skills, transform their attitudes and behaviors, and create long-term positive changes in their lives.

Parents Anonymous® Inc., in partnership with the National Center on Shared Leadership, implements the Shared Leadership in Action Program to improve national and local policies and practices for families by increasing parent leadership and advocacy skills through training and technical assistance.

Additional information about Parents Anonymous® Inc. and its programs can be found online at http://www.parentsanonymous.org.

SUGGESTED READING

National Council on Crime and Delinquency, *Parents Anonymous® Outcome Evaluation: Promising Findings for Child Maltreatment Reduction (Special Report)* (Oakland, CA: National Council on Crime and Delinquency, 2008), http://www.nccd-crc.org; Parents Anonymous® Inc., *Pathways to Meaningful Shared Leadership* (Claremont, CA: Parents Anonymous® Inc., 2005); Lisa Pion-Berlin and Margaret L. Polinsky, *Parents Anonymous® Research Profile, Number 1* (Claremont, CA: Parents Anonymous®, 2000).

MARGARET L. POLINSKY

PAROLE BOARDS. Parole boards are the release authorities that determine how much of a sentence an offender serves in most states. They vary in size from three to fifteen members, and many of them have special requirements for those eligible to serve on them. Although there is some variation across the country, many parole boards have the authority to rescind an established parole date, issue warrants and subpoenas, grant final discharges, and restore offenders' civil rights.[1] In addition, most parole boards have the statutory authority to either recommend or grant executive clemency in the form of a pardon or commutation of sentence. In states with the death penalty, the parole board often plays a role in determining whether to permit an execution to go forward or to reduce a capital sentence to life imprisonment.

Throughout the 1960s parole release decisions were usually made with few outside constraints. Parole boards were given broad discretion to determine when an offender was ready for release—a decision limited only by the constraints of the maximum sentence imposed by the judge. The gradual adoption of parole guidelines in the 1970s and 1980s represented an attempt to bring greater structure and rationality to the decision to release. Many states that use parole guidelines also include a structured assessment of prisoners' risk. Predicting which inmates may return safely to the community has always been a primary concern of parole boards.[2]

Although there has been considerable movement toward standardizing parole release, there has also been an attempt to open the parole process by providing notice and allowing comment from groups that were previously excluded. Though it varies by state, many parole boards have formal procedures for soliciting comments from prosecutors, law enforcement personnel, judges, and victims. Once the hearing has been completed, the victims and others may be notified of the board's decision and the date of release, if parole has been granted.[3]

The most important linkage between the parole board and victims is the ability of victims or their next of kin to submit a victim impact statement at the time of parole consideration for the individual offender.[4] These statements, whether oral or written, are assertions by the victims and friends or relatives of the victim about the crime's impact on the victim and the victim's family.

In the past two decades the passage of laws requiring victim input at parole has been seen as one of the greatest advances in victims' rights with 43 states now providing this right. The right loses its meaning however if paroling authorities do not notify victims of crime and their families of hearings in advance or do not schedule time during the hearing to allow them to describe the impact of the crime upon their lives.[5]

NOTES

1. Paul F. Cromwell and Rolando del Carmen, *Community Based Corrections,* 4th ed. (Belmont, CA: Thompson Wadsworth, 1999), 214.

2. Todd Clear, George Cole, and Michael Reisig, *American Corrections,* 8th ed. (Belmont, CA: Thomson Wadsworth, 2009), 380.

3. Frank Schmalleger and John Ortiz Smykla, *Corrections in the 21st Century,* 2nd ed. (Blacklick, OH: McGraw Hill, 2005), 513.

4. Howard Abadinsky, *Probation and Parole: Theory and Practice,* 9th ed. (Upper Saddle River, NJ: Pearson, 2006), 233.

5. The National Center for Victims of Crime, *"For Victim Services in Corrections,"* http://www.ncvc.org.

SUGGESTED READING

American Probation and Parole Association, "Promising Victim-Related Practices and Strategies in Probation and Parole," http://www.appa-net.org; Office for Victims of Crime, "Victim Issues for Parole Boards," http://www.ojp.isdoj.gov/ovc.

MARY PARKER

PECUNIARY DAMAGES. Pecuniary damages result from criminal proceedings and can be estimated and monetarily compensated by examining the "out of pocket" losses suffered by the victim. Most likened to "monetary" damages, pecuniary losses refer to the actual amount of money lost by a victim but also include monetary values assigned to other tangible lost items. A stolen car, a broken window, a snatched purse and its contents—all have a monetary value that can be determined with relatively simple market-value research, reliance on an actual receipt or bill, and mathematic computation. Provable losses such as medical expenses, ambulance services, or car rental costs can also be pecuniary.

Pecuniary damages are specific losses that could be recovered by a crime victim if they were able to take action against a defendant in civil court, where the damages would be referred to as "compensatory." Unlike compensatory damages, which can include nebulous losses such as pain and suffering, pecuniary damages are narrowly defined as the monetary equivalent of property taken, destroyed, broken, or otherwise harmed. Many criminal courts offer victims a worksheet on which they may report pecuniary losses in an effort to seek compensation, or "restitution," through a state's victim compensation funds, the purpose of which is to reimburse the actual quantifiable losses suffered by crime victims. Victim compensation funds are often funded by fines and judge-ordered restitution paid by convicted offenders or proceeds realized from police auctions of recovered stolen goods or abandoned property that is never claimed.

SUGGESTED READING

Andrew Karmen, *Crime Victims: An Introduction to Victimology*, 6th ed. (Belmont, CA: Wadsworth, 2006), 319–22.

CASEY JORDAN

PEDOPHILIA. Pedophilia is the sexual attraction to children under 12 years old. The offender is referred to as a pedophile. There are three basic types of pedophiles: fixated, stressed/regressed, and ipso facto homosexuals. Since the fixated pedophile is addicted to having sex with children, he is the least likely to be rehabilitated. Often their motto, which originated with the Rene Guyon Society, "Sex before eight, or it is too late," is one of their strictest abeyances. In fact, the fixated pedophile is no longer attracted to the child once she begins to mature sexually (i.e., grows pubic hair or breasts). The stressed/regressed pedophile responds to some stressful event in her life by dominating sexually over a child. According to official statistics, this type of child sexual abuser has the best chance for rehabilitation. Pedophilia is a variant of heterosexuality, even though the third type of pedophile is called the ipso facto homosexual. The primary motivator for the ipso facto homosexual is the child's age. The ipso facto homosexual is attracted to children of the perpetrator's own gender.

Oral, anal, or vaginal sexual intercourse with any child under 12 years old is legally rape in all jurisdictions within the United States. Gross sexual imposition generally refers to the fondling of a child's erogenous zones (e.g., thighs, buttocks, breasts). Interstate sexual activity is transporting children across state lines for the purpose of sex. We often caution children about looking both ways before crossing the street; 1 in 20 children will be hit by a car before they are 18 years of age. However, statistics show that 1 in 3 girls and 1 in 7 boys will be molested before they are 18. Likewise, we caution children not to talk to strangers, yet over 90% of the time children are molested by someone they know. A difficult balance must be struck; children need to be informed and cautioned about inappropriate sexual touching but not scared away from all touching.

Numerous reforms have been implemented to protect the child witness. Due to the intimidating nature of the courtroom and the fact that children are more suggestible to intimidation by adults, courts in all jurisdictions allow children over five to testify using a videotape and the method of free call so that neither the prosecutor nor defense attorney is using leading or specific questioning styles.

For the victimized child there are both useful evidence gathering and treatment strategies that utilize anatomically correct dolls and art therapy. For the perpetrator, there are treatment strategies offered through both in- and outpatient facilities that use medicine often in conjunction with psychological treatment. In a numbers of states, if the perpetrator does not participate in the treatment offered, he can be sent to a mental hospital for the duration of his prison time and be forced to get the medical and psychological treatment that he refused to participate in while incarcerated.

SUGGESTED READING

Frances P. Reddington and Betsy Wright Kreisel, eds., *Sexual Assault: The Victims, the Perpetrators, and the Criminal Justice System* (Durham, NC: Carolina University Press, 2004).

CHARISSE COSTON

PLEA BARGAINING. Plea bargaining is one of the most controversial manifestations of the criminal courtroom. The practice of plea bargaining affects practically every phase of the criminal justice system; plea bargaining is used as a substitute for jury trials, disposing of almost 90% of criminal cases. Those who favor this type of case disposition argue that without plea bargaining, the entire criminal justice system would collapse under the weight of an excessive caseload. On the other hand, those who oppose plea bargaining argue that the practice erodes the foundation of the judicial system.

In many ways, we are all compromised by the frequency and seclusion of plea bargaining—a process that minimizes the principles of due process and openness. The practice of plea bargaining places emphasis on practical considerations versus legal and procedural matters. For crime victims, there may have been little to no opportunity for input into the plea arrangement. In another observation, plea bargaining forces a defendant to forego his constitutional right against self-incrimination. In order to "strike a deal" with the state, one must admit guilt. Concomitantly, the defendant who elects a jury trial will be punished with a stiffer sentence. The argument put forth by system officials is that the stiffer sentences result from taxing the limited resources and the time of the criminal justice system. In this sense, we are all victims of a system of justice that places a higher premium on organizational considerations.

In the game of plea bargaining, it is frequently the first-time offender who is taken advantage of compared to the repeat offender, who knows the system. The general point is that society, the actual victim, and sometimes law enforcement loses, with respect to plea bargaining because justice is compromised. Only when there are written guidelines and this very pervasive practice becomes public will the system of justice gain credibility.

SUGGESTED READING

Candace McCoy, *Politics and Plea Bargaining: Victims Rights in California* (Philadelphia, PA: University of Pennsylvania Press, 1993); John Rosencrance, "Maintaining the Myth of the Individualized Justice," *Justice Quarterly* 5 (1988): 235–56.

ROBERT L. BING

POLICE OFFICERS. Prior to the 1980s, when the concept of community policing began to impact significantly not only the management of policing specifically but the entire criminal justice apparatus (CJA)[1] generally, crime victims (and others directly involved, such as witnesses) were treated more as objects than as "real people" with real emotions, wants, and needs. Bumper Morgan, as recounted in *The Blue Knight*,[2] time and again emphasized the definition of a good police officer as one who *understands the human condition*—one who has compassion and demonstrates empathy.

As with Rip Van Winkle, it seems the police in particular awoke from a long hiatus of treating victims dispassionately, if not worse. Victims of domestic violence were particularly vulnerable to prejudicial attitudes harbored by the predominantly male, chauvinistic police force of the day. Prior to research such as the Minneapolis Domestic Violence Experiment,[3] the subsequent change in many states' domestic violence (assault/battery) laws, and high-quality sensitivity training in police academies, many police officers appeared totally insensitive to the emotional trauma associated with crime. Many police officers neither recognized nor responded to the psychological implications for the victim(s). This extended to other crimes as well, such as residential burglary with its invasion of privacy in which one's intimate objects are often handled.

In relation to CJA communication, it is pointed out that covert messages often underlie the overt and that nonverbal communication can be as much, if not more, information-laden as the verbal.[4] Therefore, it is imperative that police officers show compassion in their behavior toward crime victims as well as in the words they speak. Demonstrably impersonal attitudes practiced by police officers who believe that such an attitude (1) communicates a so-called "professional approach," or (2) somehow protects them against the psychological impact of continually responding to scenes of inhumanity, are mistaken on both counts. Unfortunately, despite intensive training, departmental policy, and common sense, a few police officers still exhibit authoritarian, condescending, or judgmental attitudes toward crime victims (or certain victims or classes of victims). In "Humor in the Briefing Room," the authors[5] suggest that a certain amount of joking about situations and victims is a form of psychotherapy that helps police officers restore emotional equilibrium and lessens depression induced by the victimization they so often see. A serious problem occurs, however, when victimization is trivialized and the situation or the victim(s) become the brunt of jokes—when these uncomplimentary remarks are overheard or gestures are seen by victims, subjects, and any media representatives who may have arrived on the scene.

Crime victimization increases one's feelings of vulnerability. Therefore, when wittingly or unwittingly the police offend the crime victim, a further victimization occurs. When the police have been perceived as disrespecting the victim, any respect for the police is diminished significantly in the mind of the victim. Feeling compelled to strike back, the only defensive avenue open to the victim then is to "bad mouth" the police through his or her social network, the result being an exponential decrease in respect for and future cooperation with the police by many persons.

Before enlightenment through community policing, victims and witnesses received little feedback regarding their cases until they were telephoned at 8:00 a.m. and told to be in court by 10:00 a.m. the same day. What police and other CJA representatives (e.g., prosecutors and other court personnel) finally came to understand and appreciate was that to engender cooperation of victims and witnesses, especially to increase the amount of information volunteered by those on the periphery who otherwise might never choose to become "involved," the information flow and other forms of related assistance had to be reciprocally equal in quantity and quality. In enlightened case management, periodic reports regarding investigative progress are made to victims with the following benefits to the police:

1. Additional relevant information may be recalled or independently discovered by the victim or witness that previously might not be volunteered because (a) its importance was not recognized or (b) one felt aggrieved by her initial encounter with the police.

2. Rapport with the victim is continually enhanced, which leads to more complimentary word-of-mouth publicity and eventually better community relations.

3. Higher regard for the police may develop over time, leading to a quantitative and qualitative increase in information flow (criminal intelligence), higher case solution rates, and possibly to lower crime rates—all of which lead to greater citizen satisfaction with the police, a particularly important goal in minority neighborhoods where the perceived incidence of victimization by police is the highest.

NOTES

1. Peter B. Kraska, *Theorizing Criminal Justice: Eight Essential Orientations* (Long Grove, IL: Waveland, 2004), 7. "Criminal justice *apparatus*" is used rather than the usual

"criminal justice *system*" to acknowledge those who perceive criminal justice in America as a non-system.

2. Joseph Wambaugh, *The Blue Knight* (London: Little, Brown and Company, 1972).

3. Lawrence W. Sherman and Richard A. Berk, "The Specific Deterrent Effects of Arrest for Domestic Assault," *American Sociological Review* 49, no. 2 (1984): 261–72.

4. Wayne W. Bennett and Karen M. Hess, *Management and Supervision in Law Enforcement,* 5th ed. (Belmont, CA: Wadsworth / Thomson Learning, 2007), ch. 4; Stan Stojkovic, David Kalinich, and John Klofas, *Criminal Justice Organizations: Administration and Management,* 4th ed. (Belmont, CA: Thomson Higher Education, 2008), ch. 4.

5. Mark R. Pogrebin and Eric D. Poole, "Humor in the Briefing Room," *Journal of Contemporary Ethnography* 17, no. 2 (1988): 183–210.

SUGGESTED READING

Mary Finn et al., "Dual Arrest Decisions in Domestic Violence Cases: The Influence of Departmental Policies," *Crime and Delinquency* 50 (2004): 565–89; B. Payne, Bruce Berg, and Jeff Toussaint, "The Police Response to Elder Abuse," *Policing* 24 (2001): 605–25.

PETER W. PHILLIPS

PORNOGRAPHY. Pornography can be described as sexually explicit material primarily intended for sexual arousal. Typically, pornography is accessed through print media, videos, movies, television, phone, and the Internet. Although the literature has been mixed, there is some evidence to suggest that pornography plays a role in some incidents of sexual assault. William Marshal[1] found that 53% of sex offenders had viewed pornography before committing sexual assault, and previous studies by Neil Malamuth and James Check[2] reveal that college men exposed to violent pornography were more prone to interpersonal violence and showed more aggression toward women. Pornography supporting rape myths can lead to sexual aggression. Joetta Carr and Karen VanDeusen[3] found that pornography, along with other predictive factors such as negative gender-based attitudes and heavy alcohol use, plays a role in sexual aggression among college males.

The Internet has provided a new outlet for those with an interest in all aspects of pornography.[4] Pornographic material is readily available to all ages of Internet users through pop-up advertisements, Web sites, Internet searches, and e-mail.[5] The Internet can also be used to produce and distribute child pornography and expose children to pornography with the intent to pursue them to exchange pornographic material.[6] Offenders often find their victims through "kids only" chat rooms in which children often reveal personal information about themselves.[7]

Often pornography offenses are not known to the police. These offenses comprised 0.03% of crimes known to the police between 1997 and 2000.[8] Incidents occur within the home among both adults and children. In 2000, law enforcement arrested 1,713 offenders for Internet-related crimes that involved the possession of child pornography.[9] Among those arrested, 80% possessed pornography depicting graphic sexual images and 83% possessed images depicting prepubescent children. One in five offenders arrested for possession of Internet child pornography was in the possession of images of children as the victims of bondage, rape, and torture. Many individuals arrested for child pornography were males over the age of 25.[10]

The FBI has created the Innocent Images program that focuses on computer-facilitated child sexual abuse. In this program, coordinators from the Office of Victims of Crime help address the needs of the victim. Additionally, FBI field divisions employ Crimes against Children Coordinators who work closely with local law enforcement, investigators, and prosecutors. The OJJDP created Internet Crimes against Children (ICAC)[11] through their Missing Children's Program in 1998. This program assists state and local law enforcement officers by providing skills, equipment, and resources to respond to ICAC offenses.[12]

With increased use of technology, pornography continues to be a challenge for law enforcement. The use of violent pornography has been linked to sexual assault and child abuse and exploitation. Since victims often do not report to police, it is difficult to detect and therefore apprehend offenders. Through Innocent Images and Crimes against Children Coordinators law enforcement is making great efforts to prevent further crimes and abuses stemming from the use of pornography.

NOTES

1. William L. Marshall, "Pornography and Sex Offenders," in *Pornography: Research Advances & Policy Considerations,* eds. Dolf Zillman and Jennings Bryant (Hillsdale, NJ: Lawrence Erlbaum, 1988), 185–214.

2. Neil M. Malamuth and James V. P. Check, "Sexual Arousal to Rape Depictions: Individual Differences," *Journal of Abnormal Psychology* 92 (1983): 55–67.

3. Joetta L. Carr and Karen M. VanDeusen, "Risk Factors for Male Sexual Aggression on College Campuses," *Journal of Family Violence* 19, no. 5 (2004): 279–89.

4. Philipe Bensimon, "The Role of Pornography in Sexual Offending," *Sexual Addiction & Compulsivity* 14, (2007): 95–117.

5. Stephan C. Dombrowski, Karen L. Gischlar, and Theo Durst, "Safeguarding Young People from Cyber Pornography and Cyber Sexual Predation: A Major Dilemma of the Internet," *Child Abuse Review* 16 (2007): 153–70.

6. OVC Bulletin, "Internet Crimes Against Children," U.S. Department of Justice Office of Justice Programs, Office for Victims of Crime, http://www.ojp.usdoj.gov/ovc/publications/bulletins/internet_2_2001/welcome.html.

7. National Center for Missing and Exploited Children, "Child Pornography Fact Sheet," http://www.missingkids.com/missingkids/servlet/PageServlet?LanguageCountry=en_US&PageId=2451.

8. Melissa Wells et al., "Defining Child Pornography: Law Enforcement Dilemmas in Investigations of Internet Child Pornography Possession," *Police Practice and Research* 8, no. 3 (2007): 269–82.

9. National Center for Missing and Exploited Children, "Child Pornography."

10. Juvenile Justice Bulletin, "Child Pornography: Patterns from NIBRS," Office of Justice Programs, Partnerships for Safer Communities, http://www.ncjrs.gov/pdffiles1/ojjdp/204911.pdf.

11. Ibid.

12. National Center for Missing and Exploited Children, "Child Pornography."

SUGGESTED READING

Eva J. Klain, Heather J. Davies, and Molly A. Hicks, "Child Pornography: The Criminal Justice System Response," March 2001, NCJ 201355; Diana E. H. Russell, *Dangerous Relationships: Pornography, Misogyny, and Rape* (Thousand Oaks: Sage, 1998).

DAWNA KOMOROSKY

POST-TRAUMATIC STRESS DISORDER (PTSD). Victims of post-traumatic stress disorder (PTSD) suffer recurring and distressing recollections of a traumatic event. The victim may re-experience psychological or physiological reactivity when exposed to any cue of the original event. A sufferer may consciously or unconsciously attempt to avoid any such stimuli resulting in (1) a general numbing of responsiveness or (2) a heightened arousal or hyper-vigilance to other people and the environment. The DSM IV (Diagnostic and Statistical Manual) codes PTSD as an anxiety disorder (Code 309.81).[1] The affliction is common, with an estimated 7.8% of Americans suffering PTSD some time in their lives.[2]

Historically, post-traumatic stress was linked to the trauma of war. PTSD symptoms have been identified in the literature from the Civil War.[3] "Shell shock" and "battle fatigue" described soldiers from the world wars with PTSD symptoms.[4] The term, "post-traumatic stress disorder" was not coined until 1980 following research with veterans from the Vietnam War, the Gulf War, and other war zones.[5] More recently, studies have examined the trauma experienced by crime victims. In fact, it is estimated that 28% of all crime victims will suffer from PTSD, and an even higher number (51%) of those with high contact with the criminal justice system will report crime-related PTSD symptoms.[6]

Various theories seek to explain the persistence of PTSD symptoms in individuals exposed to trauma. Learning theory emphasizes the conditioning that becomes associated with traumatic event-related cues. Information processing theories focus on the absence of "completion" for incorporating new information (created by the traumatic event) into one's existing beliefs. According to memory formation theories, traumatic experiences may result in fragmented memories that are situationally encoded. These fragments may be too susceptible to memory accessibility due to strong cues from the event and, thus, overwhelm the victim.[7] Psychobiological theories have involved the neurobiological system in the study of PTSD. The amygdala and the hippocampus process and contextualize information from the traumatic event activating cortisol release, which can change brain structure.[8]

NOTES

1. American Psychological Association, *Diagnostic Criteria from DSM-IV* (Washington DC: American Psychiatric Association, 1994).

2. NetWellness, "Anxiety and Stress Disorders," http://www.Netwellness.org/health topics/anxietya/ptstress.cfm.

3. Ibid.

4. Brain Injury Resource Center, "Post Traumatic Stress Disorder," http://www.head injury.com/faqptsd.htm.

5. NetWellness, "Anxiety."

6. Robert J. Meadows, *Understanding Violence & Victimization*, 2nd ed. (Upper Saddle River, NJ: Prentice Hall, 2001), 9–10.

7. Matthew T. Feldner, Candice M. Monson, and Matthew J. Friedman, "A Critical Analysis of Approaches to Targeted PTSD Prevention: Current Status and Theoretically Derived Future Directions," *Behavior Modification* 31 (2007): 80–116.

8. Ibid.

SUGGESTED READING

Carol S. Fullerton and Robert J. Ursano, eds., *Posttraumatic Stress Disorder: Acute and Long-Term Responses to Trauma and Disaster* (Washington DC: American Psychiatric Press, 1997); National Institute of Mental Health, "Post-Traumatic Stress Disorder (PTSD)," http://www.nimh.nih.gov/health/topics/post-traumatic-stress-disorder-ptsdindex.shtml; Larry Rosenbaum, "Post-Traumatic Stress Disorder: The Chameleon of Psychiatry," *Nordic Journal of Psychiatry* 58 (2004): 343–48.

BARBARA HART

PRECIPITATION. According to the victim precipitation theory, victimizations result from a number of precipitating factors such as the victim's behavior, lifestyle interactions, and associations, especially in situations in which deviance and criminality flourish. Victim precipitation can be active or passive, depending on the role or behavior of the victim.

Active precipitation refers to situations in which victims provoke violent encounters or consciously place themselves in positions in which violence or confrontation may occur. Those who frequent areas prone to high crime activity or hang out with deviant types are more likely to be victimized than those who choose safer environments or associate with more stable people. A gang member killed in a retaliatory killing by another gang is an example. Victims of homicide may contribute to their own deaths by their associations or deeds such as dealing drugs or participating in violence.

Passive precipitation occurs when a victim unknowingly provokes a confrontation with another. An unsuspecting lover who is assaulted by his or her partner's estranged spouse would be considered a passive victim, especially if the suitor had no knowledge of the spouse. People victimized because of their religious beliefs, sexual orientation, or racial background are considered passive victims. These victims of hate crimes often are unaware of the intended aggression directed toward them, as evidenced by the victims of the bombing of the Oklahoma City Federal Building in 1995 and the thousands killed on September 11, 2001. The government was the target, and the victims were unaware of the intended aggression.

SUGGESTED READING

Jeffrey Fagan, Elizabeth S. Piper, and Yu-Teh Cheng, "Contributions of Victimization to Delinquency in Inner Cities," *Journal of Criminal Law and Criminology* 78 (1987): 586–613; James R. Lasley, "Drinking Routines/Lifestyles and Predatory Victimization: A Causal Analysis," *Justice Quarterly* 6, no. 4 (1989): 529–42; Ali H. Mokdad et al., "Actual Causes of Death in the United States, 2000," *Journal of the American Medical Association* 291, no. 10 (2000): 1238–45.

ROBERT J. MEADOWS

PRESIDENT'S TASK FORCE ON VICTIMS OF CRIME, *FINAL REPORT.* President Ronald Reagan called for the creation of the President's Task Force on Victims of Crime in 1982. The Task Force was composed of a nine-member commission consisting of attorneys, police, a psychiatrist, and the president of a Christian broadcast agency.[1] A review of the literature on crime victims' issues was performed, and interviews were conducted with crime victim service providers as well as crime victims. The significance of this Task Force is that it was the first serious review of the effects of crime and the treatment of crime victims by the federal government. The Task Force thoroughly reviewed "the current state of things" and provided specific recommendations to both improve treatment of crime victims and to assist crime victims in becoming more a part of the deciding body for what happened to them and "their" cases. The results of their research culminated in a 144-page report outlining 68 recommendations on how to improve services to crime victims on the federal and state levels.[2] The report included specific recommendations to criminal justice agencies as well as hospitals, mental health facilities, faith-based organizations, schools, and other private sector agencies.

The 68 recommendations that were offered focused on six core areas: recognition/validation of the psychological effects of victimization, protection of crime victims from revictimization, assistance efforts and programs for crime victims, participation of crime victims including their rights to be informed, information proliferation on crime victimization, and legal and procedural issues surrounding crime victimization. Specifically, in regard to recognition/validation of the psychological effects, the Task Force suggested sensitivity training for police, prosecutors, judges, and hospital, mental health, and ministry personnel both to prevent against harming crime victims and to better understand the effects of victimization.[3]

The Task Force suggested that victims be protected against unnecessary appearances in court and intimidation and harassment from defendants. They also stated that communications with counseling personnel be privileged, that victims' input be included in all judicial processes, and that new charges incurred by parolees be dealt with severely.[4]

Assistance recommendations focused on funding for victims services by the federal government, counseling to be provided both to the victim and their families, that employer's provide leave and programs to crime victims, no incurred costs due to the victimization, and that property be returned to victims quickly.[5]

The Task Force recommended that studies be conducted on the effects of victimization and a national center for information for crime victims be established. Legal and procedural recommendations focused on allowing for all evidence to be presented in trials and parole hearings, that bail be strictly monitored, that restitution be ordered, that victims be considered and included in all elements of a trial and parole hearing by all criminal justice agents, that a constitutional amendment be created for crime victims, and that background checks be mandated for persons wanting to work with children.[6]

State victims' bills of rights, as well as the Crime Victims Rights Act of 2004, echo a number of these recommendations and discussion continues on a constitutional amendment.

NOTES

1. Peggy M. Tobolowsky, *Crime Victim Rights and Remedies* (Durham, NC: Carolina Academic Press, 2001); President's Task Force on Victims of Crime, "Final Report," Office for Victims of Crime, http://www.ojp.usdoj.gov/ovc/publications/presdntstskforcrprt/welcome.html.

2. President's Task Force on Victims of Crime, *Final Report*.

3. Tobolowsky, *Crime Victim Rights.*

4. Ibid.

5. Ibid.

6. Ibid.

SUGGESTED READING

Office for Victims of Crime, *New Directions from the Field: Victims' Rights and Services for the 21st Century* (Washington DC: U.S. Department of Justice, 1998).

ELIZABETH QUINN DEVALVE

PRIMARY VICTIMIZATION. The specific acts of victimization and the direct experience of those acts are what entail primary victimization.[1] In addition, the victim's own perception of the act and the manner by which they cope with the act perpetrated against them also describes the experience of primary victimization. Further, primary victimization includes the experiences that the victim has when interacting with others in public and private as they explain their victimization and receive feedback from persons external to the victimization.[2] In this regard, the victim's interaction with the criminal justice system can be seen as the extended effects of primary victimization.[3] According to Uli Orth, when criminal proceedings have a negative impact on the victim or cause psychological harm to the victim, the result is what is commonly referred to as secondary victimization.[4]

Further, it is important to distinguish between primary victims and secondary victims. Secondary victims tend to be family or friends of the victim who experience a sense of trauma due to their knowledge or witnessing of the primary victim's experience.[5] Though not to minimize the experiences of the secondary victim, it is the primary victim who actually has the action perpetrated against their person.[6]

The experience of primary victimization can have a variety of effects on the victim. There are the obvious physical effects that may take a toll on the victim if there has been physical assault. The victim may experience a degree of pain and suffering or possible disfigurement, whether it be temporary or permanent. In addition, victims are likely to have psychological difficulties due to their victimization, depending on the degree of victimization that has occurred.[7] It is quite normal for victims to report feelings of depression, anxiety, or fear after being exposed to a traumatic event. Some victims may experience symptoms of post-traumatic stress disorder. Naturally, this has an adverse impact on the person's overall quality of life, and this can negatively affect their social relationships with friends, family, and coworkers.[8]

In addition, victims may suffer financial difficulties due to theft or property damage. A financial effect may also be felt if the victim is in need of medical attention due to physical injuries or trauma.[9] The victim may experience a loss or drop in income due to the aftermath of the crime and a corresponding loss in future earning potential, particularly if the victim experiences a decline in future work output. As a result, victims may pursue private legal assistance, which is costly and runs the risk of generating further disappointment.

NOTES

1. James Dignan, *Understanding Victims and Restorative Justice* (Berkshire, UK: McGraw-Hill, 2005).

2. Ibid.

3. Ibid.

4. Uli Orth, "Secondary Victimization of Crime Victims by Criminal Proceedings," *Social Justice Research* 15, no. 4 (2002): 313–25.

5. Diane M. Daane, "The Ripple Effect: Secondary Sexual Assault Survivors," in *Sexual Assault: The Victims, the Perpetrators, and the Criminal Justice System*, eds. Francis P. Reddingtion and Betsy W. Kreisel (Durham, NC: Carolina Academic Press, 2005), 77–106.

6. Ibid.

7. Sandra Walklate, ed., *Handbook of Victims and Victimology* (Devon, UK: Willan, 2007).

8. Ibid.

9. Dignan, *Understanding Victims*.

SUGGESTED READING

National Organization for Victim Assistance (NOVA), "The Trauma of Victimization: How to Get Help After a Victimization," NOVA, http://www.trynova.org/victiminfo/victimization help/thetrauma.html.

ROBERT D. HANSER

PRISON RAPE. Prison rape is the sexual assault of an incarcerated individual by either another inmate or correctional institution staff member. The full range of sexual acts is included in a definition of prison rape, including forced vaginal, anal, and oral sex, as well as unwanted sexual touching. Research documenting prison rape reports a wide range of rates of incidence, including studies that have found no instances to those that report rates as high as 20% of inmates.[1] More recently, the first national study of prison rape has shown that approximately 4.5% of all prison inmates report some form of sexual victimization while incarcerated. Of all victimizations, 2.1% of inmates are victimized by another inmate and 2.9% are victimized by a staff member.[2] In juvenile detention centers a rate of 16.8 allegations for every 1,000 juveniles was reported to authorities. Additionally, inmates in jails report higher rates of victimization (3.2% overall, 2.9% of men and 5.1% of women). The numbers of instances reported by inmates are higher than those reported by correctional authorities; only about 14–25% (depending on type of victimization) of all official reports of victimization are substantiated by investigations.[3]

Although all prison and jail inmates may be susceptible to sexual victimization while incarcerated, research has shown that male inmates most vulnerable are those who are younger, white, of smaller physical size, first-time offenders, property offenders, and those who are mentally ill, intellectually challenged, and perceived to be gay, bisexual, or transgendered. Women inmates at highest risk of victimization are those with a history of sexual victimization, mental illness, and those least familiar with correctional culture.

In recognition of the problem of prison rape, in 2003 Congress passed the Prison Rape Elimination Act. This federal legislation required the completion of a national study to identify facilities with high rates of rape, funded independent research, and created the National Prison Rape Elimination Commission (NPREC). This commission was charged with completing a comprehensive study of the dynamics, characteristics, and consequences of prison rape and establishing operational standards for prisons, jails, juvenile facilities, and immigration detention centers that will advance the prevention, effective intervention, provision of effective medical and mental health services, and encourage the prosecution and punishment of perpetrators. Additionally, many states have also established offices in their departments of corrections to study and address the prevention, intervention, and services for prison rape.

Studies of inmates show that sex and sexuality are complex issues in prison, and instances of sexual violence are viewed differently than in free society. Rape is seen as something that many victims bring onto themselves and something that all inmates have a responsibility for avoiding and averting. Inmates work to control the sexual violence in their institutions and to establish a safe environment, based on values, beliefs, and norms unique to the correctional setting.[4]

NOTES

1. Gerald Gaes and Andrew Goldberg, *Prison Rape: A Critical Review of the Literature* (Washington DC: National Institute of Justice, 2004).

2. Allen J. Beck and Paige M. Harrison, *Sexual Victimization in State and Federal Prisons Reported by Inmates,* 2007 (Washington DC: Bureau of Justice Statistics, 2008).

3. Allen J. Beck, Paige M. Harrison, and Devon B. Adams, *Sexual Violence Reported by Correctional Authorities, 2006* (Washington DC: Bureau of Justice Statistics, 2007).

4. Mark Fleisher and Jessie Krienert, *The Culture of Prison Sexual Violence* (Washington DC: National Institute of Justice, 2006).

SUGGESTED READING

Allen J. Beck and Paige M. Harrison, *Sexual Victimization in Local Jails Reported by Inmates, 2007* (Washington DC: Bureau of Justice Statistics, 2008); Christopher Hensley, ed., *Prison Sex: Practice and Policy* (Boulder, CO: Lynne Rienner, 2002); Human Rights Watch, *No Escape: Male Rape in U.S. Prisons* (New York: Human Rights Watch, 2001).

RICHARD TEWKSBURY

PROSECUTING ATTORNEYS. The prosecuting attorney is one of the most powerful individuals in the criminal courtroom. Although the police have the power to invoke the criminal sanction, the prosecuting attorney has the power to drop the case or to prosecute to the fullest extent of the law. The prosecuting attorney may proceed with a case for symbolic reasons, or he may drop the case because of insufficient evidence or problems related to the collection of the evidence by police. The point to be made is that he has an enormous amount of discretion.

The office of the prosecuting attorney emerged in the early 1900s. With urbanization, the court system became more formal. With the formalization of the court system emerged the use of full-time prosecuting attorneys. As full-time prosecutorial staff developed, the court no longer had sole responsibility to issue arrest warrants, etc., and the decision to prosecute was transferred to the district attorney's office. Not surprisingly, during the early 1900s, the prosecuting attorney or the district attorney was also actively involved in political corruption. It was not uncommon for prosecuting attorneys to strike deals with defendants resulting in reduced charges or sentences for "monetary payoffs." In fact, many of the prosecuting attorneys would make decisions based upon politics overlooking violations of criminal law by some constituents.

Today, it is common knowledge that the discretion continues. It is prosecuting attorneys' responsibility to initiate criminal proceedings against the defendant; this discretionary power is subject to few limitations and may sometimes put the prosecuting attorney in the position of making major decisions without specific policies and guidelines. Most of the research on the prosecuting attorney focuses on the broad discretion and his penchant for prosecutorial overcharging for an offense in order to gain a conviction by inducing a guilty plea. With an indictment, there may be several counts (or offenses) that are related to a particular charge, say possession of an ounce of heroin. Overcharging, then, is integral to plea bargaining because it establishes the "asking price" in negotiation.

There are some prosecuting attorney offices that are actively involved in programs that protect the victim; these programs may be called restorative justice, a type of punishment that requires direct community involvement, designed to meet the needs of the victim. Almost every office in the country maintains a desire to protect the rights of the victims of crimes. Many of these offices have moved toward victim impact statements and others have implemented victim assistance and victim notification programs. The state of California, for example, has a penal reform code that favors the victim. The code requires the system to notify victims of all hearings and final dispositions. The truth, however, is that these notification programs are not always adhered to by system officials. On the other hand, the data do show that there are potential therapeutic benefits for the victim when allowed to make a statement at trial.

SUGGESTED READING

Mark S. Umbreit, *Victim Meets Offender: The Impact of Restorative Justice and Mediation* (Monsey, NY: Willow Tree Press, 1994).

ROBERT L. BING

PROVOCATION. Provocation is a mitigating factor that reduces the degree of blame or punishment. The partial defense under English common law requires three elements: the wrongfulness of the instigating insult, the heat of passion, and the timing of the killing. According to the Model Penal Code, an intentional homicide committed in "sudden heat of passion" as the result of "legally adequate provocation" may reduce the offense to voluntary manslaughter.[1]

Provocation requires an offensive act by a victim that incites the offender's retaliatory response. The act must evoke a violent emotion causing a "reasonable person" to lose control and must occur during the "heat of passion," without time for emotions to cool. The defense is more likely to excuse culturally ingrained challenges to male honor or acts resulting from mutual combat.

Inspired by notions of shared responsibility, victimologists have studied the role victims play in the genesis of crime. Arguably, "offender" and "victim" designations may misrepresent the dynamics involved an incident. Hans von Hentig notes that a closer look may reveal a victim as an *agent provocateur,* without whom the act would not have occurred.[2] Early victimologists, Beniamin Mendelsohn, Menachem Amir, Stephen Schafer, and Marvin Wolfgang, argue an analysis of victim-offender dyads offer insights into crimes as situated transactions. These efforts produced several typologies, which underscored varying degrees of victim facilitation, precipitation, and provocation.

NOTES

1. Model Penal Code § 210.3.1b (1985).

2. Hans von Hentig, "Remarks on the Interaction of Perpetrator and Victim," *Journal of Criminal Law, Criminology and Police Sciences* 31(1940): 305.

SUGGESTED READING

Alan W. Mewett, "Murder and Intent: Self-Defense and Provocation," *Criminal Law Quarterly* 27, no. 4 (1985): 433–49; William I. Torry, "Social Change, Crime, and Culture: The Defense of Provocation," *Crime Law and Social Change* 36, no. 3 (2001): 309–25.

LAURA PATTERSON

PSYCHOPATHOLOGY THEORY. Stereotypes about mental illness incorporate notions of violent behavior and unpredictability. In fact, research suggests that the stigma associated with a mental illness is largely due to these stereotypes of individuals with psychiatric disorders.[1] An unintended consequence of the deinstitutionalization movement for persons with mental illness and the closures of public psychiatric hospitals has been the high proportion of individuals with mental illness being left without services. This vacuum of services has been filled by the criminal justice system. As a result, there has been an increase in the number of specialty dockets devoted to people with mental illness (mental health courts) and increased need for psychiatric services in jails and prisons across the country.[2] This is a process known as the criminalization of the mentally ill.

Accordingly, much research attention has been paid to the role of people with mental illness in the commission of violence.[3] One of the major attempts at understanding why people with mental illness have a somewhat higher likelihood of violence is referred to here as psychopathology theory. Psychopathology theory is the idea that it is something about the disorder itself that is causing individuals to be violent. Such theorizing focuses on aspects of the disorder, such as hallucinations, delusions, and medication noncompliance, as causes of violent behavior.

One prominent example of this kind of theorizing is given by Bruce Link and colleagues, who focus on threat/control-override delusions (TCO delusions).[4] TCO delusions are a special type of delusions typically experienced by individuals with schizophrenia spectrum disorders. These delusions involve perceived threats to the individual's safety or the override of the individual's ability to control their own behaviors. When confronted with these delusions of threat or the inability to control one's own behavior, persons with mental illness are more likely to engage in violence.

On the other hand, recent research by Eric Silver and his colleagues have shown that individuals with psychiatric disorders have a higher risk of victimization than do individuals without such disorders.[5] Psychopathology theory may help us understand why individuals with mental illness are at this higher risk of victimization. Specifically, highly symptomatic individuals with psychiatric disorders may prompt stereotypes of mentally ill individuals as dangerous, unpredictable, and violent. Thus symptoms of psychopathology may serve as cues for individuals in proximity to the disordered person. These symptoms activate stereotypes of dangerousness and a corresponding need to protect oneself from that perceived danger. Preemptive attempts by nondisordered individuals to control the disordered individual may then result in the victimization of people with mental illness, as these attempts at control often involve physical control of the person. That physical control may inadvertently escalate to victimization. In fact, this approach is consistent with a theory of conflicted social relationships put forth by Eric Silver. Silver argues that people with mental illness are more likely to be involved in social relationships that involve conflict. It is these conflict filled relationships that explain why people with mental illness are victimized at higher rates than nondisordered individuals.[6]

NOTES

1. Bernice A. Pescosolido et al., "The Public's View of the Competence, Dangerousness, and Need for Legal Coercion of Persons with Mental Health Problems," *American Journal of Public Health* 89 (1999): 1339–45.

2. Nancy Wolff and Wendy Pogorzelski, "Measuring the Effectiveness of Mental Health Courts: Challenges and Recommendations," *Psychology, Public Policy, and Law* 11 (2005): 539–69.

3. John Monahan, "Mental Disorder and Violent Behavior: Perceptions and Evidence," *American Psychologist* 47 (1992): 511–21.

4. Bruce G. Link et al., "Real in Their Consequences: A Sociological Approach to Understanding the Association between Psychotic Symptoms and Violence," *American Sociological Review* 64 (1999): 316–32.

5. Eric Silver et al., "Mental Disorder and Violent Victimization in a Total Birth Cohort," *American Journal of Public Health* 95 (2005): 2015–21.

6. Eric Silver, "Mental Disorder and Violent Victimization: The Mediating Role of Involvement in Conflicted Social Relationships," *Criminology* 40 (2002): 191–212.

SUGGESTED READING

Virginia Aldigé Hiday et al., "Criminal Victimization of Persons with Severe Mental Illness," *Psychiatric Services* 50 (1999): 62–68; Virginia Aldigé Hiday et al., "Impact of Outpatient Commitment on Victimization of People with Severe Mental Illness," *American Journal of Psychiatry* 159 (2002): 1403–11.

BRENT TEASDALE

PUNITIVE DAMAGES. Punitive damages are awarded in lawsuits to punish defendants and deter defendants and others from committing similar future acts. They are defendant-focused, distinguished by law from damages that compensate victims. Several well-publicized, large punitive award judgments, including

$79.5 million in 1991 against Phillip Morris[1] and $5 billion in 1994[2] against Exxon Mobile,[3] have led to concerns that punitive damages are excessive and unpredictable. However, research suggests that punitive damages are awarded in a minority of cases and tend not to be large.[4]

Indeed, the Supreme Court ruled that punitive damages, based on the reprehensibility of a defendant's conduct, must be reasonable,[5] recommending a single-digit (no more than nine-to-one) punitive to compensatory damages ratio.[6] There is a tendency to award punitive damages that do not exceed compensatory damages (a ratio of less than one-to-one). The Supreme Court also ruled that jurors can consider harm to victims to evaluate reprehensibility of conduct.[7]

State laws govern punitive damages, and possible reforms are intensely debated due to concerns about how juries award them. Possible reforms include eliminating or limiting these awards and delegating them to judges. However, some research suggests that mock jurors tend to increase compensatory damages when punitive damages are eliminated,[8] and judges and mock jurors typically award similar punitive damages.[9] Reformers also propose splitting (bifurcating) the compensatory and punitive trial phases to address concerns that victim characteristics unduly influence punitive awards.[10] Yet, research suggests that jurors can separate evidence relevant to compensatory and punitive damages without bifurcation.[11]

NOTES

1. Bill Mears, "Court Tosses Punitive Damages against Big Tobacco," *CNN.com*, 20, February, 2007.

2. Robert Barnes, "Justices to Examine Punitive Damages in Exxon Oil Spill," *Washington Post*, October 20, 2007, http://www.washingtonpost.com.

3. Adam Liptak, "Damages Cut against Exxon in Valdez Case," *The New York Times*, 26 June 2008, http://www.nytimes.com.

4. Marc Galanter and David Luban, "Poetic Justice: Punitive Damages and Legal Pluralism," *American University Law Review* 42 (1993): 1393–463.

5. *BMW of North America, Inc. v. Gore*, 517 U.S. 559 (1996).

6. *State Farm Mutual Automobile Insurance Co. v. Campbell et al.*, 538 U.S. 408 (2003).

7. *Philip Morris USA v. Williams*, 549 U.S. 346 (2007).

8. Edith Greene, David Coon, and Brian Bornstein, "The Effects of Limiting Punitive Damage Awards," *Law and Human Behavior* 25, no. 3 (2001): 217–34.

9. Jennifer K. Robbennolt, "Punitive Damage Decision Making: The Decisions of Citizens and Trial Court Judges," *Law and Human Behavior* 26 (2002): 315–42.

10. Michelle Chernikoff Anderson and Robert J. MacCoun, "Goal Conflict in Juror Assessments of Compensatory and Punitive Damages," *Law and Human Behavior* 23 (1999): 313–30.

11. Edith Greene, William Douglas Woody, and Ryan Winter, "Compensating Plaintiffs and Punishing Defendants: Is Bifurcation Necessary?" *Law and Human Behavior* 24, no. 2 (2000): 187–205.

SUGGESTED READING

Corinne Cather, Edith Greene, and Robert Durham, "Plaintiff Injury and Defendant Reprehensibility: Implications for Compensatory and Punitive Damage Awards," *Law and Human Behavior* 20, no. 2 (1996): 189–205; Joni Hersch and W. Kip Viscusi, "Punitive Damages: How Judges and Juries Perform," *The Journal of Legal Studies* 33, no. 1 (2004): 1–36; Cass R. Sunstern et al., *Punitive Damages: How Juries Decide* (Chicago: The University of Chicago Press, 2002).

MICHELLE WEST AND ANGELA CROSSMAN

R

RAPE. Estimates of rape rates vary according to the survey methods used to gather data. The FBI's Uniform Crime Reports (UCR) program relies on police agencies to report incidences of rape. However, research indicates that levels of rape reported in the UCR significantly undercount actual rates. In order to be included in the UCR, a rape must both be reported to police and recorded by the policing agency. The UCR definition is also a relatively restrictive definition: "Forcible rape, as defined in the Uniform Crime Reporting (UCR) Program, is the carnal knowledge of a female forcibly and against her will. Assaults and attempts to commit rape by force or threat of force are also included; however, statutory rape (without force) and other sex offenses are excluded."[1]

Rape is often not reported to police because of the intimate nature of the crime, the stigma attached to the crime, the belief that reporting will not result in police intervention, and protection of the offender. Victimization surveys record much higher rates compared to the UCR data.

A comparison of annual rape risk data from the two most comprehensive victimization surveys reveals some disparity in rates.[2] The National Crime Victimization Survey (NCVS) found an annual rape rate of 0.26 women per 100 in 1995.[3] However, the National Violence Against Women Survey (NVAWS) found an annual rate of 0.87 women per 100 for the same year.[4] Both surveys indicated that women are most likely to be raped by a friend/acquaintance, followed by an intimate partner.

According to the NVAWS, 17.6% of women reported being a victim of a completed or attempted rape in their lifetime.[5] Of those women, 21.6% were younger than 12 when they were first raped, and 32.4% were between 12 and 17.[6] Rape victimization also varies by race and ethnicity. Of all racial categories surveyed in the NVAWS, American Indian/Alaskan Native women were the most likely to have experience rape and had a rate around twice as high as white women.[7]

The NVAWS also found a relationship between early victimization and subsequent victimization.[8] Women who reported being raped prior to the age of 18 were twice as likely to report being raped as an adult.[9] Nearly one-third (31.5%) of female rape victims reported being injured during their most recent rape.[10] The risk of injury increased when the offender was a current or former intimate relation.[11]

A major obstacle to reporting rape to police is the prevalence of rape myths. Examples of rape myths include that rape takes place primarily between strangers, forced intercourse between intimates is not rape, and if women do not fight back, no rape has occurred. Research indicates that men are more likely than women to find rape victims at fault for the incident.[12] Furthermore, victims who know their offender are more likely to be blamed.[13] A study of college-aged women found that women whose experiences corresponded to a rape myth were less likely to label their victimization a rape, even if the act met the legal definition.[14]

NOTES

1. Federal Bureau of Investigation, "Uniform Crime Report," Federal Bureau of Investigation, http://www.fbi.gov/ucr/05cius/offenses/violent_crime/forcible_rape.html.

2. Ronet Bachman, "A Comparison of Annual Incidence Rate and Contextual Characteristics of Intimate-Partner Violence Against Women from the National Crime Victimization Survey (NCVS) and the National Violence Against Women Survey," *Violence Against Women* 6 (2000): 839–67.

3. Bachman, "A Comparison," 852.

4. Ibid.

5. Patricia Tjaden and Nancy Thoennes, *Full Report of the Prevalence, Incidence, and Consequences of Violence Against Women: Findings From the National Violence Against Women Survey* (Washington DC: National Institute of Justice, 2000), iii.

6. Ibid.

7. Tjaden and Thoennes, *Full Report,* 22.

8. Tjaden and Thoennes, *Full Report,* iv.

9. Ibid.

10. Ibid.

11. Ibid.

12. Amy Grub and Julie Harrower, "Attribution of Blame in Cases of Rape: An Analysis of Participant Gender, Type of Rape, and Perceived Similarity to the Victim," *Aggression and Violent Behavior* 13 (2008): 396–405.

13. Ibid.

14. Zoe D. Peterson and Charlene L. Muehlenhard, "Was It Rape? The Function of Women's Rape Myth Acceptance and Definitions of Sex in Labeling Their Own Experiences," *Sex Roles* 51 (2004): 129–44.

SUGGESTED READING

Rebecca J. Macy, "A Research Agenda for Sexual Revictimization: Priority Areas and Innovative Statistical Methods," *Violence Against Women* 14, no. 10 (2008): 1128–47.

BENJAMIN PEARSON-NELSON

RAPE MYTHS. Rape myths are false beliefs that promote the ideas that sexual aggression is natural, normal within relationships, and justifiable under certain circumstances. Rape myths also perpetuate the ideas that victims want to be raped, deserve to be raped, or "ask for it." According to Martha Burt, rape myths fall into one of four main categories: (1) nothing happened, or women lie about rape to cover up infidelity; (2) no harm was done, especially when victims have previously engaged in consensual sex with their offenders; (3) she wanted it, or women secretly want to be forced and can prevent rape if they really want to; and (4) she deserved it, or women who get raped have done something that contributes to their victimization.[1]

In combination with these four categories of myths, the idea that men cannot control their sexual urges once they have been excited during foreplay not only excuses rapists for sexual aggression due to their presumed biological drives, but it blames women for provoking men's desires by their seductive behaviors. For instance, rape myths suggest that women are responsible for rape when they have behaved "inappropriately," such as getting drunk, going to bars alone, inviting men to their homes, or initiating kissing. Rape myths also suggest that women are responsible for rape when they do not aggressively resist an attack. The implication is that someone who does not fight back to the point where there is evidence of a struggle must have subconsciously wanted to be forced.

The ideas inherent in rape myths, especially the ideas that women enjoy being forced or deserve what happened, are commonly invoked by accused rapists during trials to deny the severity of injury or the victim's innocence. By drawing on rape myths, blame is redirected toward victims, who are portrayed as having intentionally misled, manipulated, or seduced the men into raping them. Rape myths are so entrenched within popular culture that they sometimes factor into decisions made by police or prosecutors working on rape cases. For instance, Lisa

Frohmann found that prosecutors were less likely to take on rape cases when a victim admitted to having flirted with an offender prior to an incident, allowed him into her home, consented to some sexual acts, or was intoxicated at the time of the assault.[2] In each of these situations, the victims are seen as having shared responsibility for their rapes.

Even victims themselves sometimes invoke rape myths as they try to make sense of their unwanted sexual experiences. For instance, victims may excuse sexually aggressive boyfriends for not being able to stop prior to penetration, or they may blame themselves for sending the "wrong messages" or for being too drunk to resist rape.[3] The fact that the persons most harmed by rape myths—rape victims themselves—invoke many of these myths, underscores the pervasiveness of these ideologies within the culture. In fact, rape myths have been so normalized in the ways that people define and conceptualize rape and its victims that it has taken a concerted effort by anti-rape advocates and educators over the years to begin to dispel the ideas inherent in these ideologies.

NOTES

1. Martha R. Burt, "Rape Myths and Acquaintance Rape," in *Acquaintance Rape: The Hidden Crime,* eds. Andrea Parrot and Laurie Bechhofer (New York: John Wiley & Sons, 1991), 251–69.

2. Lisa Frohmann, "Discrediting Victims' Allegations of Sexual Assault: Prosecutorial Accounts of Case Rejections," *Social Problems* 38 (1991): 213–26.

3. Karen G. Weiss, "Boys Will Be Boys and Other Gendered Accounts: An Exploration of Victim Excuses and Justifications for Unwanted Sexual Contact and Coercion," *Violence Against Women* (forthcoming, 2009).

SUGGESTED READING

Martha R. Burt, (1980). "Cultural Myths and Supports for Rape," *Journal of Personality and Social Psychology* 38, no. 2 (1980): 217–30; Kimberly A. Lonsway and Louise F. Fitzgerald, "Rape Myths in Review," *Psychology of Women Quarterly* 18 (1994): 133–64.

KAREN WEISS

RAPE SHIELD LAWS. Rape shield laws are court rules designed to restrict the introduction of evidence in rape cases regarding a victim's sexual history, reputation, or past sexual conduct.[1] Prior to the passage of rape shield laws, irrelevant information about a victim's sexual history was often introduced in rape cases in order to raise doubt about a victim's conduct or chastity. Historically, the law considered the sexual reputation of a woman to be relevant to the legitimacy of her rape allegation.[2] A chaste woman's allegation was considered more truthful because it was believed that she would have refused the defendant's sexual advances. However, an allegation from an unchaste woman was considered less convincing because it was believed that she likely consented to the defendant's advances and then lied about the consent afterward to claim that she was raped.[3]

Recognition that rape victims were often reluctant to inform law enforcement about their victimization, because of the humiliation that they were subjected to during the legal process, led states to adopt rape shield laws in order to reduce the practice of discrediting victims by discussing past sexual conduct. States enacted such laws beginning in the 1970s; now every state (and the District of Columbia) has some form of a rape shield law.[4] Such laws vary, ranging from the least restrictive, in which evidence of a victim's sexual conduct can be admitted if proven relevant to the case, to the most restrictive, which prohibits any information about a victim's sexual history unless it involves a prior relationship between the victim and the defendant.[5] By not permitting irrelevant information about a victim's sexual history in a criminal trial, the intent of rape shield laws is to ensure a fairer trial and help improve how victims are treated during the legal process.

Rape shield laws are frequently challenged within the courts. For example, an appellate court overturned a conviction of sexual assault by ruling that e-mail correspondence between the defendant and the victim was improperly excluded as evidence within the original trial. The defense argued that content within the e-mails illustrated the victim's consent.[6] In a more recent case involving a young male offender convicted of criminal sexual penetration of a young female victim, the state supreme court ruled that the lower court erred by not allowing the defense counsel to question the female victim about a prior sexual encounter between the two individuals, and the resulting punishment by her parents, to establish a motive for why she would fabricate the rape allegation.[7] These cases demonstrate how rape shield laws are continually contested within courts and how the sexual history of a rape victim may still be used as evidence if it is proven to be relevant to the defense.

NOTES

1. The National Center for Victims of Crime, "Rape Shield Laws," The National Center for Victims of Crime, http://www.ncvc.org.

2. Michelle J. Anderson, "From Chastity Requirement to Sexuality License: Sexual Consent and a New Rape Shield Law," *George Washington Law Review* 70 (2002): 51.

3. Ibid.

4. The National Center for Victims of Crime, "Rape Shield Laws."

5. Cassia Spohn and Julia Horney, "The Law's the Law, But Fair Is Fair: Rape Shield Laws and Officials' Assessments of Sexual History Evidence," *Criminology* 29 (1991): 137–61.

6. *People v. Jovanovic,* 263 A.D.2d 182, 700 N.Y.S.2d 156 (N.Y. App. Div. 1st Dep't 1999).

7. *State of New Mexico v. Stephen, F.* (144 N.M. 360, 188 P.3d 84, 2008).

SUGGESTED READING

Heather D. Flowe, Ebbe B. Ebbesen, and Anila Putcha-Bhagavatula, "Rape Shield Laws and Sexual Behavior Evidence: Effects of Consent Level and Women's Sexual History on Rape Allegations," *Law & Human Behavior* 31 (2007): 159–75; A. E. Taslitz, *Rape and the Culture of the Courtroom* (New York: New York University Press, 1999).

JESSICA P. HODGE AND HOLLY JACOBS

RAPE TRAUMA SYNDROME. Rape trauma syndrome was first identified by Ann Burgess and Lynda Holmstrom in their classic article, which described various commonalities among survivors of rape victimization.[1] During the time that these authors introduced this term, the clinical diagnosis of post-traumatic stress disorder (PTSD) did not officially exist within the DSM-IV.[2] In current times, the symptoms of rape trauma syndrome are considered similar, if not identical, to the symptoms listed in the DSM-IV-TR for PTSD.[3]

PTSD describes a series of symptoms in which the victim's response to the experienced traumatic event involves intense fear, helplessness, or horror. The victim is likely to psychologically reexperience the traumatic event, while exhibiting persistent symptoms of anxiety or increased arousal that were not present before the rape.[4] Furthermore, victims tend to have difficulty falling asleep and may have persistent nightmares related to the victimization. Displays of hypervigilance and exaggerated startle responses are also common.[5] Last, it is very common for victims to avoid stimuli that are connected with the source of trauma or that remind the victim of the traumatic experience.[6]

Rape trauma syndrome consists of physical, emotional, and behavioral symptoms that are related to a life-threatening and psychologically damaging sexual victimization.[7] The trauma from rape tends to be comparable to any other life-threatening event, regardless of the level of violence actually used during the attack.[8] A great number of victims report fear of extreme bodily harm, such as mutilation or death, during their experience. These victims also report the existence of symptoms such as nausea, startle responses, insomnia, and nightmares.

According to Burgess and Holstrom, rape trauma syndrome is divided into two phases.[9] The first phase, known as the acute phase, can last anywhere from several days to weeks. During this phase, victims experience reactions to the realization of their experience, which tend to occur within a matter of hours. During the acute phase, there are two types of reactions common among victims of rape trauma syndrome. The expressive reaction results in visible signs of trauma, such as crying, restlessness, or tenseness. Conversely, the controlled reaction results in the masking of feelings, with the victim appearing to be calm or without emotion.

The second phase, referred to as the reorganization phase, tends to last considerably longer, spanning anywhere from several months to several years.[10] During this phase, victims contend with the need to regain structure and order within their lives and the provision of some control.[11] Intermediate effects that often emerge during this phase may include a disruption and change in the victims' lifestyle, such as moving houses or changing jobs, increased dependence on family or friends, and fear of going out or being alone. During this phase, the victim may feel anger, especially toward the offender, and may also feel anger toward family or friends, or the legal system—if the victim does not feel that some sense of justice was meted out against the offender.[12]

NOTES

1. Ann W. Burgess and Lynda L. Holstrom, "Rape Trauma Syndrome," *American Journal of Psychiatry* 131 (1974): 981–86.

2. Diane M. Daane, "Victim Response to Sexual Assault," in *Sexual Assault: The Victims, the Perpetrators, and the Criminal Justice System*, eds. Francis P. Reddington and Betsy W. Kreisel (Durham, NC: Carolina Academic Press, 2005), 77–106.

3. American Psychiatric Association, *Diagnostic and Statistical Manual of Mental Disorders* (Arlington, VA: American Psychiatric Association, 2000).

4. American Psychiatric Association, *Diagnostic*.

5. Daane, "Victim Response;" American Psychiatric Association, *Diagnostic*.

6. Ibid.

7. Burgess and Holstrom, "Rape Trauma;" Daane, "Victim Response."

8. Daane, "Victim Response."

9. Burgess and Holstrom, "Rape Trauma."

10. Ibid.

11. Ibid.

12. Daane, "Victim Response."

SUGGESTED READING

Maureen W. Groer et al., "Inflammatory Effects and Immune System Correlates of Rape," *Violence and Victims* 21, no. 6 (2006): 796–808.

ROBERT D. HANSER

RATIONAL CHOICE THEORY. Rational choice theory is often used to explain why offenders commit crime. According to the rational choice theory, offenders make rational decisions to commit crimes by weighing the costs and benefits associated with that crime.[1] Consequently, crimes will be deterred if the costs of committing the crime outweigh the benefits. Punishments enforced by the criminal justice system are one of the costs associated with committing crimes. According to

Cesare Beccaria, punishments are most effective at deterring crime when they are swift, severe, and certain.[2] Therefore, the criminal justice system must ensure that punishments are likely to occur, happen quickly after the crime is committed, and are harsh enough to make potential offenders choose not to commit the crime.

Having laws and a criminal justice system available to punish criminal offenders is just one way to have an impact on the rational choice to commit a crime. Victims, or potential victims, can also affect the likelihood of victimization by increasing the costs associated with crime. Victims can increase the costs of crime by making it more difficult for the crime to occur. Making offenders work harder at committing a crime increases the risk that they will be caught and ultimately punished. Therefore, although rational choice theory primarily focuses on the offender, it also has implications concerning victim responsibility for the crime and suggestions for prevention strategies.

According to Andrew Karmen, there are five levels of victim responsibility, depending on how much blame falls on the victim for the crime.[3] Innocent victims are ideal crime victims who share no responsibility for the crime and took every reasonable precaution to prevent victimization from happening.[4] Victim facilitation involves a victim who unwillingly made it easier for a crime to occur.[5] For example, a victim may have left her car unlocked, making it an easier target for motor vehicle theft. Victim precipitation occurs when a victim significantly contributed to the criminal event, whereas victim provocation involves victims who were more responsible for the crime than the offenders.[6] This person may have actually provoked a fight but ended up with more injuries and therefore is declared the victim. Finally, fully responsible victims are pseudo-victims, because no victimization actually took place.[7] Someone committing insurance fraud or filing a false police report against an ex-spouse for assault represents a fully responsible victim.

Victim responsibility is an important issue because it influences how victims are perceived by society, how victims are treated within the criminal justice system, and how victims will be compensated in the civil court system.[8] Victims can take an active role in prevention, which decreases the level of victim responsibility. Prevention strategies for victims involve precautions taken at the individual level and within the environment. People can influence the rational choice of offenders by making themselves and their property less attractive to offenders. Some strategies for victimization prevention include target hardening, avoiding dangerous people and places, incorporating security measures on personal property, and studying self-defense techniques.[9]

NOTES

1. Cesare Beccaria, *On Crimes and Punishments* (Indianapolis: Hackett, 1986), 105.

2. Beccaria, *On Crimes and Punishment.*

3. Andrew Karmen, *Crime Victims: An Introduction to Victimology* (Belmont: Thomson Wadsworth, 2007): 445.

4. Karmen, *Crime Victims*.

5. Ibid.

6. Ibid.

7. Ibid.

8. Harvey Wallace, *Victimology: Legal, Psychological, and Social Perspectives* (Boston: Pearson, 2007), 403.

9. Robert Meadows, *Understanding Violence and Victimization* (Upper Saddle River, NJ: Pearson, 2007), 291.

SUGGESTED READING

Jan van Dijk, "Understanding Crime Rates: On the Interactions between the Rational Choices of Victims and Offenders," *British Journal of Criminology* 34 (1994): 105; Sharon Lamb, *The Trouble with Blame: Victims, Perpetrators, and Responsibility* (London: Harvard University Press, 1999), 244; Douglas Setter, *One Less Victim: A Prevention Guide* (Victoria, BC: Trafford, 2004), 128.

SUZANNE GODBOLDT

RECOVERED MEMORIES OF SEXUAL ABUSE. The issue of recovered memories of sexual abuse has been polarizing in the legal, clinical, and academic worlds. Although Sigmund Freud originated the idea of recovering memories in the late 1800s with his theory of repression,[1] it was not until the 1980s that recovered memories of sexual abuse gained notoriety. Recovered memories of sexual abuse refers to the process of individuals experiencing sexual abuse, usually in childhood, forgetting the incident(s), and at a later time "recovering" those memories, generally through therapy. Claims of abuse arising from recovered memories have led to lawsuits against alleged abusers, as well as against therapists who "implanted" false memories of abuse.

At the heart of the controversy over recovered memories is the discussion of whether or not traumatic events from childhood can truly be forgotten, as well as the issue of false memories. Even though opponents to recovered memories suggest that victims of traumatic events rarely forget their experiences, even after desperately trying to do so, most researchers believe that it is possible to experience amnesia brought on by a traumatic event, although the rate at which this occurs in the general population is unknown.

Currently there are four possible explanations offered for the observed forgetting of memories: repression, dissociation, ordinary forgetting, and false memories.[2] The possibility of false memories being "recovered" creates additional concerns, particularly in the legal arena, because researchers have established that it is possible to plant false memories and that it is difficult to distinguish between true recovered memories and false recovered memories without additional evidence.[3]

NOTES

1. Joseph Sandler and Peter Fonagy, eds., *Recovered Memories of Abuse: True or False* (London: Karnac Books, 1997), 164.

2. Chris R. Brewin and Bernice Andrews, "Recovered Memories of Trauma: Phenomenology and Cognitive Mechanisms," *Clinical Psychology Review* 18 (1998): 949.

3. D. Stephen Lindsay and J. Don Reed, "'Memory Work' and Recovered Memories of Childhood Sexual Abuse: Scientific Evidence and Public, Professional, and Personal Issues," *Psychology, Public Policy, and Law* 1 (1995): 846.

SUGGESTED READING

Elizabeth F. Loftus, "Planting Misinformation in the Human Mind: A 30–year Investigation of the Malleability of Memory," *Learning & Memory* 12 (2005): 361–66; Kenneth S. Pope and Laura S. Brown, *Recovered Memories of Abuse: Assessment, Theory, Forensics* (Washington DC: American Psychological Association, 1996).

TASHA YOUSTIN

REPORTING RATES. Estimations of victimization rates for a population as large as the United States require extensive resources, careful planning, and accurate measurements. Thus, data containing such information are limited. Most reported estimates of victimization in the United States are based on the National Crime Victimization Survey (NCVS). Rates of victimization have also been assessed using self-report panel data from the National Youth Survey and Monitoring the Future studies.[1] Internationally, commonly used data for estimating rates include the British Crime Survey (BCS) and the International Crime Victimization Survey.

Victimization rates are calculated by dividing the number of victimizations by the population over a designated period and are typically weighted to maintain population estimates.[2] The NCVS collects longitudinal information by surveying the same households every six months for a three-year period. The BCS is a cross-sectional design, administering surveys periodically to different samples each time.

Obtaining accurate estimates of something as personal as criminal victimization presents a number of challenges. A number of methodological issues have been found to affect overall rates of victimization. First, differences in reference periods can lead to biased estimates, because respondents' capacities for remembering specific instances weakens over time. There is general agreement that a one-year recall avoids serious problems with memory decay.[3] Second, the manner in which multiple victimizations are recorded has an impact on overall victimization rates.[4] For example, the NCVS does not include "series incidents" in overall victimization rates, which leads to underestimation.

Third, surveys such as the NCVS include a number of follow-up questions when respondents report victimizations. This can lead to lengthy interviews when multiple victimizations are reported, causing fatigue for the respondent. Bias in reporting rates may occur when respondents alter their responses to questions in subsequent interviews to avoid extended questioning.[5] Fourth, different survey methods have been associated with differences in reported rates of victimization. Commonly used techniques, such as face-to-face interviews, computer-assisted interviews, and telephone interviews, can have an impact on rates in certain circumstances.[6] For example, domestic violence estimates may be underreported in household phone surveys, where offenders are often near the victims. Finally, the wording of questions can influence rates of victimization. Narrowly worded screening items tend to miss legitimate victimization experiences, whereas overly broad definitions can result in the inclusion of trivial events as forms of victimization.[7]

Based on victimization surveys such as the NCVS, property crimes are experienced more often than personal crimes.[8] The most commonly reported property crimes are incidents involving theft of items or money worth less than $50. The least common property crime based on victimization surveys is motor vehicle theft. Among violent crimes, the most common incidents are simple assaults involving minor or no injury. The least commonly reported violent crime is sexual assault, followed by robbery. These differences are generally stable across demographic factors (e.g., gender, race, and marital status), but the magnitude may vary depending on the type of crime and victim characteristics.

NOTES

1. L. Edward Wells and Joseph H. Rankin, "Juvenile Victimization: Convergent Validation of Alternative Measurements," *Journal of Research in Crime and Delinquency* 32 (1995): 287–307.

2. Bureau of Justice Statistics, "Criminal Victimization in the United States, 1999 Statistical Tables" (Washington DC: National Institute of Justice, NCJ 184938, 2001).

3. Scott Menard, "The 'Normality' of Repeat Victimization from Adolescence through Early Adulthood," *Justice Quarterly* 17 (2000): 543–74.

4. Mike Planty, "Series Victimization and Divergence," in *Understanding Crime Statistics: Revisiting the Divergence of the NCVS and UCR*, eds. James P. Lynch and Lynn A. Addington (New York: Cambridge University Press, 2006), 156–82.

5. Timothy C. Hart, Callie Marie Rennison, and Chris Gibson, "Revisiting Respondent 'Fatigue Bias' in the National Crime Victimization Survey," *Journal of Quantitative Criminology* 21 (2005): 345–63.

6. Roger Tourangeau and Madeline E. McNeeley, "Measuring Crime and Crime Victimization: Methodological Issues," in *Measurement Problems in Criminal Justice*

Research: Workshop Summary, eds. John V. Pepper and Carol V. Petrie (Washington DC: The National Academies Press, 2003), 10–42.

7. Martin D. Schwartz, "Methodological Issues in the Use of Survey Data for Measuring and Characterizing Violence against Women," *Violence Against Women* 6 (2000): 815–38.

8. Shannan M. Catalano, "Criminal Victimization, 2005" (Washington DC: National Institute of Justice, NCJ 214644, 2006).

SUGGESTED READING

Janet L. Lauritson, "Social and Scientific Influences on the Measurement of Criminal Victimization," *Journal of Quantitative Criminology* 21 (2005): 245–66; James P. Lynch and Lynn A. Addington, eds. *Understanding Crime Statistics: Revisiting the Divergence of the NCVS and UCR* (New York: Cambridge University Press, 2006).

MATTHEW JOHNSON

RESTITUTION. Typically, restitution is thought of as a form of monetary payment that an offender is ordered to pay to a victim for a crime that has been committed against that victim. However, restitution can include both monetary reimbursements and in-kind services.[1] Beyond the simple monetary payment for damages incurred by the victim, other restitution models include the community service model, the victim-offender mediation model, and the victim-reparations model.[2]

Community service models require offenders to complete a given number of hours of community service as a means of compensating for the damages against victims and as a means of offsetting judicial expenses.[3] Victim-offender mediation brings the victim and the offender together for reconciliation.[4] The use of alternative dispute resolution may occur with a third-party arbiter overseeing the process to ensure that victims are compensated and that offenders are accountable. Crime Victims Reparations Acts existing in many states support programs in which victims are provided with direct financial payment for injuries that are claimed. In these cases, reparations might include medical expenses, loss of earnings, and other related losses that are affiliated with the criminal offense.

There are some notable advantages to implementing restitution programs within a given jurisdiction. Among these is the fact that victims are given some sort of compensation for their loss. This is much superior to having the offender simply incarcerated, without any possibility of repaying the victim. Furthermore, restitution programs allow offenders to defray some of the costs that are incurred by the criminal justice system. Another benefit to the use of restitution is that offenders are made accountable for their actions.

Despite the advantages, there are also some disadvantages to the use of restitution. First, restitution models that call for offender-victim mediation processes may run contrary to the desires of the victim. Indeed, many victims may not want to meet their perpetrator. In such cases, the wishes of the victim should remain primary: this means that face-to-face restitution may be impractical. Furthermore, not all injuries are quantifiable, and it may be difficult to attach any particular value to a given crime. This is especially true for violent crimes such as rape or murder. In such cases, no amount of restitution may be equitable to the loss incurred by the victim.

Overall, it would appear that restitution programs are fairly successful: recidivism rates tend to go down when restitution efforts are made part of the offender's sentence.[5] Furthermore, many victims and community members have indicated satisfaction with restitution programs, as well as with other types of restorative approaches.[6] This has especially been true when restitution is compared with sentencing schemes that are largely punitive in nature.[7] Although it is by no means a judicial panacea, restitution does provide a sentencing option that provides some form of tangible benefit for victims, rather than leaving them empty-handed as many other sentencing approaches might do.

NOTES

1. Christopher Bright, "Restitution," Prison Fellowship International, http://www.restorativejustice.org/intro/tutorial-introduction-to-restorative-justice/outcomes/restitution.

2. Dean J. Champion, *Probation, Parole, and Community Corrections,* 4th ed. (Upper Saddle River, NJ: Prentice Hall, 2002).

3. Ibid.

4. Ibid.

5. Ibid.

6. John Doble, "Attitudes to Punishment in the US—Punitive and Liberal Opinions," in *Restorative Justice and the Law,* ed. Lode Walgrave (Portland, OR: Willan, 2002), 111–32.

7. Ibid.

SUGGESTED READING

Hanoch Dagan, *The Law and Ethics of Restitution* (Cambridge: Cambridge University Press, 2004).

ROBERT D. HANSER

RESTORATIVE JUSTICE. Restorative justice is a response to crime that seeks to balance the needs of crime victims, criminal offenders, and the communities to which they belong. This justice perspective is unique in that it respects victims, traditionally the forgotten component of the criminal justice system. The restorative framework holds offenders accountable to their victims, but it often allows the community to take an active role in the justice process.

Albert Eglash, credited for coining the phrase *restorative justice* in 1977, identifies three types of justice that are often juxtaposed with the restorative ideal.[1] The
first, retributive justice, is a foundation for punishment and a perspective that views
crime as simply the violation of the law. The second, rehabilitative justice, is based
on therapeutic treatment of offenders but also views the state as the victim. In this
view the emphasis is on accountability through punishment, with a focus on the
treatment needs of the offender. The third, restorative justice, is a restitution-based
system and an alternative to both retributive justice and rehabilitative justice.
Restorative justice, with roots in biblical principles, differs from the previous two
paradigms in that crime is viewed as a violation of people and relationships, and it
concentrates on the harmful outcomes of offenders' actions. In this process, victim,
communities, and offenders are actively engaged in a process of justice whose
main objectives are to restore, repair, and promote healing.

Justice paradigms provide the framework through which societies determine
the fundamental principles, their relative importance, and the desired outcomes of
justice policies and practices. Fundamental to restorative justice is the principle
that key stakeholders include both primary and secondary victims. Primary
victims, sometimes called "direct victims," are those who are directly harmed by
an offender's criminal behavior and often suffer physical injury, monetary loss,
and emotional anguish. Although the effects of victimization vary, two common
needs that victims encounter are the need to reclaim an appropriate sense of control of their lives, because victimization is in itself an experience of helplessness,
and the need to have their rights justified. Secondary victims are "indirect
victims," who are indirectly harmed by the offender's actions, and this category
can include both the victim's and offender's family members and the community
at large.

The tenets of restorative justice have surfaced in diverse cultures and locations and
on national and international forums, which has led to the development of numerous
associations whose objectives are to advance restorative justice proponents and
practitioners' desire to share experiences, innovations, and outcomes. In numerous
jurisdictions across the United States, restorative policies and ideals serve a repara-
tive and supplemental role within existing justice practices. The restorative process
seeks to right the wrong that has been committed and to repair the damage that
victims, offenders, and communities have encountered. Common examples include
restitution, community service, and victim-offender conferencing.

NOTE

1. Albert Eglash, "Beyond Restitution: Creative Restitution," in *Restitution in Criminal Justice,* eds. Joe Hudson and Burt Galaway (Lexington, MA: D.C. Heath, 1977),
91–2.

SUGGESTED READING

James Dignan, *Understanding Victims and Restorative Justice* (New York: Open University Press, 2005); Clifford K. Dorne, *Restorative Justice in the United States* (Upper Saddle River, NJ: Prentice Hall, 2008); Debra Heath-Thornton, "Restorative Justice," in *Encyclopedia of Crime and Punishment*, ed. David Levinson (Thousand Oaks, CA: Sage, 2002), 1388–89.

DEBRA HEATH-THORNTON

RETRIBUTIVE JUSTICE. The goal of retributive justice is to restore balance in the social order by punishing criminals in a way that is proportionate to their crimes. The criminal justice system in the United States is based on retributive justice, as reflected in a sentencing structure that assigns punishment according to the severity of the crimes committed. The Christian Bible contains a well-known reference to retributive justice: "an eye for an eye, and a tooth for a tooth." This phrase reflects the core assumption that perpetrators should experience harm that is equal to that experienced by their victims. The eighteenth-century philosopher Immanuel Kant expanded on this assumption in advocating that criminals should receive their "just deserts"— punishment that they justly deserve. Kant argued that just deserts were warranted because the state has a responsibility to uphold the rule of law against individuals who fail to practice self-restraint, who violate the rule of law, and who give themselves an unfair advantage over others.[1] Because the offenders freely choose to commit crimes, they must expect and accept punishment.

Difficulties emerge, however, when trying to enact retributive justice. Experimental studies find that victims are likely to overestimate the amount of harm done to them, thereby overestimating the amount of punishment necessary to make things fair.[2] Perpetrators, in contrast, are likely to underestimate the amount of harm that their wrongdoing did to the victim. Thus, offenders are more likely to think that the punishment enacted by the victim is unfair. This leads to escalating tensions between victims and offenders.[3]

Although retributive justice may appear to be victim-focused, its underlying goal is actually to take the focus away from the victim. This is accomplished by shifting attention toward the state, which is ultimately responsible for upholding the rule of law. The state is motivated to seek "just deserts" in order to decrease the likelihood of vigilantism. As a result, retributive justice can be thought of as "vengeance curbed by the intervention of someone other than the victim and by principles of proportionality and individual rights."[4] Consistent with this philosophy, retributive justice does not take into account victims' desire to forgive perpetrators or extend mercy, although victim impact statements are sometimes used in the sentencing phase of criminal trials.

A common critique of retributive justice is that it is too heavily focused on punishment. Indeed, retributive justice does not seek to rehabilitate offenders, nor does it attempt to restore the relationships between victims, offenders, and their communities, as does restorative justice.[5] Despite this criticism, retributive justice receives widespread support. In survey research, people typically fit punishments to crimes. An exception to this is that typically disadvantaged groups, such as minorities and low-income individuals, often deviate from the principles of retributive justice and assign less severe punishments than do respondents who are white or have higher incomes.[6] Additionally, people report that punishing the offender is more important than victim compensation.[7] Therefore, retributive justice may have more public support than does restorative justice.

NOTES

1. Jeffrie Murphy and Jules Coleman, *Philosophy of Law* (Boulder, CO: Westview Press, 1990), 120–24.

2. Lee Ross and Andrew Ward, "Psychological Barriers to Dispute Resolution" in *Advances in Experimental Social Psychology,* ed. Mark Zanna (New York: Academic, 1995), vol. 27, 255–304.

3. Jeffrey Z. Rubin, Dean G. Pruitt, and Sung Hee Kim, *Social Conflict: Escalation, Stalemate, and Settlement* (New York: McGraw-Hill, 1994).

4. Martha Minow, *Between Vengeance and Forgiveness* (Boston: Beacon Press, 1998), 11.

5. Kathleen Daly, "Revisiting the Relationship between Retributive and Restorative Justice" in *Restorative Justice: Philosophy to Practice*, eds. Heather Strang and John Braithwaite (Aldershot, England: Ashgate / Dartmouth, 2000), 33–54.

6. V. Lee Hamilton and Steve Rytina, "Social Consensus on Norms of Justice: Should the Punishment Fit the Crime?" *The American Journal of Sociology* 85.5 (1980): 1117–44.

7. R. Hogan and N. P. Emler, "Retributive Justice" in *The Justice Motive in Social Behavior*, eds. M. J. Lerner and S. C. Lerner (New York: Academic Press, 1981), 125–44.

SUGGESTED READING

John Darley, "Just Punishments: Research on Retributional Justice," in *The Justice Motive in Everyday Life*, ed. Michael Ross and Dale T. Miller (New York: Cambridge University Press, 2002), 314–33; Neil Vidmar, "Retribution and Revenge," in *Handbook of Justice Research in Law*, eds. Joseph Sanders and V. Lee Hamilton (New York: Kluwer Academic / Plenum, 2001), 31–64.

KATIE JAMES AND JODY CLAY-WARNER

ROBBERY. Robbery is defined as the taking and carrying away of personal property of another by force or threat of force. There are two categories of robbery: armed and unarmed. *Armed robbery* occurs when a weapon is used, which may include a gun, knife, or club, to name a few. *Unarmed robbery*, also called "strong-arm" robbery or "mugging," occurs when the suspect obtains valuables from the victim by using intimidation, hands, feet, etc. Street criminals often resort to strong-arm tactics to intimidate victims to turn over their valuables, including wallets, jewelry, purses, money, clothing, etc.

It is important to note that robbery is not burglary or theft. Too often, victims inform a police officer that they have been "robbed," when their house has been burglarized or an item has been taken from their garage. This becomes an important victimization distinction, because robbery is a crime against a person, whereas *burglary* (the breaking and entering into a home or office) and *theft* (the taking and carrying away of personal property of another) are crimes against property.

There are a number of classifications of robbery, including street, carjacking, home invasion, and commercial. The vast majority of robberies (approximately half of all robberies) are *street robberies*. The victim and suspect are more likely to be strangers. Victims of street robberies vary greatly. They may include young, lower-income males, or women, the elderly, and immigrants. What each of these groups has in common is the appearance of vulnerability to street criminals.

Carjacking occurs when a person's vehicle is taken from the victim by force or threat of force. Victims are often selected according to convenience rather than via a well-thought-out criminal plan.

Unlike street robberies and carjackings, *home invaders* often plan their attacks. Suspects may or may not know the victims, but victim selection is rarely random. For example, a group of home invaders may target victims who are entering their homes—knowing that they carry large sums of money from their place of employment. They will use some strategy to gain entry into the home (e.g., waiting for victims to unlock the front door and then forcing their way into the home); forcing victims to surrender their valuables.

Commercial robberies (i.e., robbery of a business) may or may not be planned. Victims may be selected based on the suspect's financial need (e.g., suspect needs money to buy drugs), demeanor (e.g., suspect is intoxicated, mentally ill, etc. at the time of the robbery), or knowledge of business (e.g., suspect knows the business location and income potential).

The victim of a robbery may experience fear, physical suffering, and personal loss (e.g., money). Signs of post-traumatic stress disorder, including flashbacks, nightmares, isolation, and other psychological conditions, are not uncommon.

Depending on the victim, the criminal justice system (and society as a whole) often treats robbery victims differently. For instance, the police may treat a prostitute who was the victim of a robbery quite differently than a clerk who was held up at a convenience store.

SUGGESTED READING

Wayne W. Bennett and Karen M. Hess, *Criminal Investigation,* 5th ed. (New York: Wadsworth, 1998), 278–305; James N. Gilbert, *Criminal Investigation,* 6th ed. (Upper

Saddle River, NJ: Pearson, 2004), 242–73; Richard T. Wright and Scott H. Decker, *Armed Robbers in Action* (Boston, MA: Northeastern University Press, 1997).

TOD BURKE

ROUTINE ACTIVITY THEORY. Developed by Lawrence Cohen and Marcus Felson[1] during the late 1970s, *routine activity theory* is a criminological theory that is frequently used to explain crime and victimization. Routine activity theory is actually an outgrowth of another criminological theory—rational choice. Rational choice theory assumes that the offender chooses to commit criminal activity based on free will. In other words, the offender uses a strategic thinking process to evaluate the risks, including the type of offense committed, the selection of the victim, and the chances of apprehension. If the rewards of committing the crime outweigh the consequences of apprehension, the offender will likely commit the criminal act.

According to Cohen and Felson, crime and victimization is based on three criteria: (1) a suitable target, (2) an absence of capable guardians, and (3) a motivated offender. Each of these variables will be explained as it relates to the victims' actions and prevention strategies.

A *suitable target* can be a person or object. Offenders select their targets based on victim vulnerability. To determine victim selection, offenders often examine victim location, habits, behaviors, lifestyle, living condition, and social interactions. For instance, assume that an offender wishes to burglarize a home that provides easy entry, substantial valuables, and minimal chances for apprehension. Before committing the burglary, the offender will likely note the home owner's daily routine (e.g., when does the home owner leave for work?), security measures taken (e.g., does the home owner lock all doors?), etc. To minimize victimization, home owners may alter their departure times and travel routes and secure all doors and windows prior to leaving the home.

Capable guardians are people or objects that serve to deter criminal activity. These may include concerned neighbors, watchful parents, crime prevention strategies (such as locking devices, security alarms, effective lighting, etc.), and patrol officers. According to Cohen and Felson, victimization is greater when capable guardians are lacking or nonexistent. In the prior example, the potential for victimization may be reduced if the home owner properly secures the home, if a dog barks when strangers approached, or if neighbors report suspicious activity to the police (e.g., "Neighborhood Watch").

Motivated offenders are individuals who are not only capable of committing criminal activity but are willing to do so. Motivation varies. For instance, one burglar may be motivated by the sheer excitement of the act. Another may commit criminal activity for need of money to support a drug addiction. In the latter situation, offenders may believe that they have nothing to lose. The rewards from committing the burglary are greater than the risk and consequences of apprehension. An individual need not fully understand the motivation of an offender to take preventive measures to minimize victimization. This may include any of the preventive strategies previously noted, as well as environmental awareness (i.e., knowing surroundings, neighbors, etc.) and developing a crime prevention plan in the event of victimization.

NOTE

1. Lawrence Cohen and Marcus Felson, "Social Change and Crime Rate Trends: A Routine Activities Approach," *American Sociological Review* 44 (1979): 588–608.

SUGGESTED READING

Elizabeth Groff, "Simulation for Theory Testing and Experimentation: An Example Using Routine Activity Theory and Street Robbery," *Journal of Quantitative Criminology* 22 (2007): 75–103; Richard Tewksbury and Elizabeth Mustaine, "College Students' Lifestyles and Self-Protective Behaviors: Further Consideration of the Guardianship Concept in Routine Activity Theory," *Criminal Justice and Behavior* 30 (2003): 302–27; Majid Yar, "The Novelty of Cybercrime: An Assessment in Light of Routine Activity Theory," *European Journal of Criminology* 2 (2005): 407–27.

TOD BURKE

RULE OF THUMB. For centuries the physical punishment of women by men was well within social norms. Representative of this unofficial acceptance of domestic violence is the bygone concept of the "rule of thumb," which permitted the rod as long as it was no bigger than the abuser's thumb. Moreover, casual attitudes toward "disturbances at home" facilitated systematic inadequacies in the legal response to domestic violence.

Historically, law enforcement officers were cautioned against creating a police problem when only a family problem existed; instead, standard procedure was to "pacify the parties," refer them to community agencies, and arrest only "as a last resort."[1] In the 1980s the law became a bit more progressive; under the "stitch rule," arrests were sanctioned if the injuries to the victim were serious enough to require sutures.[2]

Through the years, the courts have also taken a somewhat cavalier attitude toward the abuse of women. With the creation of family courts, where the goal is to "preserve the family"—not to punish an offense—the criminal justice system sent the message that violence against women was not worth the time and attention of a criminal court.[3] It was not until 1984, with the landmark class-action suit *Thurman v. City of Torrington*,[4] that the U.S. criminal justice system began taking serious action in cases of intimate partner violence.[5]

Today, with the implementation of pro-arrest and no-drop policies, there have been substantial increases in the number of intimate partner violence cases that reach the court system. However, popular mandatory arrest policies have led to a rise in arrests of women during domestic dispute calls, some of whom are victims trying to defend themselves.[6]

NOTES

1. Deborah Rhode, *Justice and Gender* (Cambridge, MA: Harvard University Press, 1989), 239.

2. Nicky Ali Jackson, *Encyclopedia of Domestic Violence* (New York: Routledge, 2007).

3. Elizabeth Pleck, *Domestic Tyranny: The Making of Social Policy against Family Violence from Colonial Times to the Present* (Oxford: Oxford University Press, 1987).

4. *Thurman v. City of Torrington*, 595 F. Supp 1521 (D. Conn. 1984).

5. R. Emerson Dobash and Russel P. Dobash, *Women, Violence, and Social Change* (New York: Routledge, 1992).

6. Joann Belknap, *The Invisible Woman: Gender, Crime, and Justice* (Belmont, CA: Thompson/Wadsworth, 2007).

SUGGESTED READING

Susan A. Lentz, "Revisiting the Rule of Thumb: An Overview of the History of Wife Abuse," *Women and Criminal Justice* 10, no. 2 (1999): 9–27.

TARA N. RICHARDS

S

SAME-SEX PARTNER ABUSE. In many ways, intimate partner violence in gay and lesbian relationships is similar to that which occurs in heterosexual relationships. Victims may experience verbal threats, physical assault, stalking, emotional abuse, and coerced sexual activity. Studies of same-sex intimate partner violence have produced varying results. For instance, research on lesbian partner abuse has found rates of physical violence ranging from 8% to 60%; research on gay male partner abuse has found rates of physical violence ranging from 11% to 44%. However, a recent large-scale survey of gay and lesbian persons found that, overall, they "experience physical and sexual violence at similar frequencies to heterosexual people."[1]

The dynamics underlying intimate partner violence are also similar regardless of sexual orientation. Gay and lesbian intimate partner violence is driven by the batterer's desires for power and control, and often proceeds following a cycle of violence. Just as heterosexual victims are often reluctant to leave violent relationships, so too are gay and lesbian victims.[2]

Despite the previously described similarities, there are at least three ways in which gay and lesbian intimate partner violence differs from heterosexual violence. First, homophobia within society can complicate victimization, especially when a victim is not "out" to family, friends, coworkers, and so on. Victims may not report violence if they fear that doing so will expose their relationship and reveal their sexual orientation. Abusers may also threaten to reveal a victim's sexual orientation. Second, victims may fail to report violence if they fear police bias against homosexuality.[3] Research has found that police response does not vary based on sexual orientation, although responses do differ between gay male and lesbian incidents.[4] Third, members of the gay and lesbian community and service providers are often underinformed about same-sex partner abuse. Further education of community members and service providers is necessary to ensure that victims' rights are protected and that adequate victim resources are provided.[5]

NOTES

1. Susan C. Turell, "A Descriptive Analysis of Same-Sex Relationship Violence for a Diverse Sample," *Journal of Family Violence* 15 (2000): 288.

2. Linda M. Peterman and Charlotte G. Dixon, "Domestic Violence between Same-Sex Partners: Implications for Counseling," *Journal of Counseling & Development* 81 (2003): 40–7.

3. Tod W. Burke, Michael L. Jordan, and Stephen S. Owen, "A Cross-National Comparison of Gay and Lesbian Domestic Violence," *Journal of Contemporary Criminal Justice* 18 (2002): 231–57.

4. April Pattavina et al., "A Comparison of the Police Response to Heterosexual versus Same-Sex Intimate Partner Violence," *Violence Against Women* 13 (2007): 374–94.

5. Burke, Jordan, and Owen, "A Cross-National Comparison," 231–57.

SUGGESTED READING

Tod W. Burke, "Male-to-Male Gay Domestic Violence: The Dark Closet," in *Violence in Intimate Relationships: Examining Sociological and Psychological Issues*, ed. Nicky Ali Jackson and Giselé Casanova Oates (Boston: Butterworth-Heinemann, 1998), 161–79; Nicky Ali Jackson, "Lesbian Battering: The Other Closet," in *Violence in Intimate Relationships: Examining Sociological and Psychological Issues*, ed. Nicky Ali Jackson and Giselé Casanova Oates (Boston: Butterworth-Heinemann, 1998), 181–94; Beth Leventhal and Sandra E. Lundy, eds., *Same-Sex Domestic Violence: Strategies for Change* (Thousand Oaks, CA: Sage, 1999).

STEPHEN OWEN

SCHAFER, STEPHEN. István Schäfer (1911–1976) was born in Budapest, Hungary.[1] At age 15, while reading his father's book on criminal law, he discovered that victims were hardly mentioned.[2] This observation was to become the seed that ultimately grew into his final passion. Eighteen years later Stephen Schafer earned his Doctor of Jurisprudence at the University of Budapest in 1933.[3] Subsequently he practiced law for about 14 years, eventually earning his *Habilitation* as a qualified professional teacher in 1947. In the years that followed, he became involved in many aspects of the criminal justice process: juvenile delinquency, prisons, the bar association, law reform; at the same time, he was suffering prosecution from the Hungarian Communist regime, which ultimately lead to his resignation from the University of Budapest and his many other positions. In 1956, during the pro-Stalinist political turmoil and the Hungarian Uprising, he left Budapest with his wife Lili and son Andrew and entered England as a refugee. There he found odd jobs to help him survive financially while teaching criminology in the evenings at the Polytechnic of London.[4] In spite of these hardships, with the influence of Sara Margery Fry[5] and support from the British Home Office, he studied restitution, and in 1960 he managed to publish the first hardbound book on a victim topic in the English language, *Restitution to Victims of Crime.*[6]

After joining the Criminology Department of the Florida State University in 1961, he conducted an extensive victim study, with the assistance of the Florida Department of Corrections, and included many of his findings in what was to become the first victimology textbook completely dedicated to crime victims, *The Victim and His Criminal: A Study in Functional Responsibility* in 1968. Subsequently he was invited to teach at the Ohio State University and then Northeastern University, where he remained until his untimely death. In 1970 an expanded version of his earlier restitution book was published under the title *Compensation and Restitution to Victims of Crime.* In 1973 he was one of the key persons who promoted the First International Symposium on Victimology in Jerusalem, Israel, with the organizer Israel Drapkin. Three years later, he organized the Second International Symposium on Victimology in Boston, Massachusetts in the United States. However, he died July 29, 1976, just 38 days prior to the Symposium. His students and colleagues made his dream a reality from September 5 to 11, 1976. Just one year later, an enlarged version of his earlier work, renamed *Victimology: The Victim and His Criminal,* was published in 1977. These last two books had a major impact on the emerging field of victimology in the United States. The earliest courses taught at universities used these books because they were among the first in the English language to cover this new discipline of victimology.

NOTES

1. Miklós Lévay, "ESC Criminology in Europe," *Newsletter of the European Society of Criminology* 2, no. 2 (2003): 14.

2. Emilio Viano, "Pioneers in Victimology," *Victimology: An International Journal* 1, no. 2 (1976): 223–25.

3. Richard Knudten, "Stephen Schäfer," *American Sociological Association Footnotes* (1977): 6.

4. Ibid.

5. Viano, "Pioneers."

6. Leslie T. Wilkins, "Unofficial Aspects of a Life in Policy Research (1999)," http://www.essex.ac.uk/psychology/overlays/policyresearch.htm.

SUGGESTED READING

Stephen Schafer, *Compensation and Restitution to Victims of Crime*, 2nd ed. enlarged (Monclair, NJ: Patterson Smith, 1970); Stephen Schafer, *Victimology: The Victim and His Criminal* (Reston, VA: Reston Publishing, 1977).

JOHN DUSSICH

SCHAFER'S TYPOLOGIES. Thirty-one years after Beniamin Mendelsohn began studying the victim-offender relationship and 20 years after Hans von Hentig published his criminology book, *The Criminal and His Victim,* Stephen Schafer published his first victimology book, *The Victim and His Criminal: A Study in Functional Responsibility* in 1968, using an ironic reversal of von Hentig's book title. This first victimology textbook was clearly about victims, and the focus was mainly about the victims' responsibility for their victimizations. In 1977, in a much expanded later edition of this book, called *Victimology: The Victim and His Criminal*, Schafer presented his seven-victim typology. For Schafer, each victim type identified a special characteristic that made her or him responsible for the crime that ultimately victimized them. These are Schafer's seven types:

1. *Unrelated Victims*. These victims had no relationship with their offenders prior to the crime. For these victims, the criminal was entirely responsible for the decision to commit a crime; they were entirely innocent.

2. *Provocative Victims*. The behavior of these victims caused their offenders to react so that a crime occurred; thus, these victims shared a significant amount of the responsibility for the crime.

3. *Precipitative Victims*. These victims did something inappropriate because of where they were, how they were dressed, the way they acted, or what they said; thus, their responsibility was only negligible.

4. *Biologically Weak Victims*. These victims had physical characteristics that made them obviously vulnerable to their offenders; thus, they had no responsibility for the crime. Examples are the young, the old, the sick, or the handicapped.

5. *Socially Weak Victims*. These victims had social characteristics that made them vulnerable to their offenders; thus, they had no responsibility for the crime. Examples are the isolated, immigrants, or minorities.

6. *Self-Victimizing Victims*. These victims engaged in deviant and criminal behaviors in which they were partners with the offenders; thus, these victims were totally responsible. Examples are prostitutes, drug users, drunks, and gamblers.

7. *Political Victims*. These victims were persons who opposed those in political power and were abused so as not to upset the offender's political dominance. Thus, they are not responsible for their victimization.[1]

It is interesting that Schafer, being mindful of Mendelsohn's victim types based on their levels of culpability and von Hentig's victim types based on their vulnerability, chose to base his seven victim types on degrees of "functional responsibility." He did not care for the speculative nature of these two other typologies and chose, instead, to link his typology to theory and to empirical observations that he had made and that could be realistically applied to the assignment of functional responsibility. His opinion was that the key issue of assigning responsibility had utility in making judgments about crime. Schafer claimed that responsibility had to be understood as functional because it was essential for maintaining social order.

NOTE

1. Stephen Schafer, *Victimology: The Victim and His Criminal* (Reston, VA: Reston, 1977), 45–47.

SUGGESTED READING

Stephen Schafer, *The Victim and His Criminal: A Study in Functional Responsibility* (New York: Random House, 1968).

JOHN DUSSICH

SCHOOL VICTIMIZATIONS. Reports on various forms of adolescent violence, ranging from physical assaults among students to youth fatally wounding their teachers and classmates, are now common.[1] The increase in school violence is linked to the notable spike in adolescent violence during the 1990s. In 1996 alone, 37% of all violent crime arrestees were under the age of 18, yet this group only comprised about 25% of the U.S. population at the time.

Although the concern has been with violence, property crimes are the most common occurrence at school.[2] Thefts, in particular, were notably high in 1992, with 100 occurring per 1,000 students between the ages of 12 and 18. This rate dropped substantially, to less than 50 per 1,000 students by 2005. Younger youth (12- to 14-year-olds) were more often victims than were older adolescents (15- to 18-year-olds). Surprisingly, there are no substantive differences in reports of thefts at school among white, black, and Hispanic students.[3]

Next to theft, students commonly report being bullied at school. Being bullied ranges from verbal harassments, such as being called names or insulted, to physical forms of violence, including being pushed or shoved. Overall, 28% of 12- to 18-year-old students reported that they were bullied at school in 2005, with the majority or 79% reporting that the bullying occurred inside the school building.

Most were verbally harassed by classmates (19%); few reported more serious forms of bullying that entailed physical violence (9%). Contrary to popular belief, only a small proportion of bullied students (8%) indicated that they were harassed at school on a regular or daily basis. Older students were less likely to report being bullied than were younger ones, and white students were more likely to experience bullying than their black or Hispanic counterparts.[4]

Simple assaults or fights are also a source of concern when considering school violence. However, the percentage of students involved in physical fights at school remained relatively stable between 1993 and 2005, averaging at approximately 20% during this time. Students in lower grades (i.e., ninth graders) were more likely to report being in physical fights at school than those in higher grades (i.e., twelfth graders). Furthermore, male students were more likely than female students to be involved in physical altercations, and Asians students were less likely than all other racial or ethnic groups to fight in school. Teachers, like students, also face intimidation and injury at school. During the 1993–1994 school year, nearly 12% of teachers were threatened with injury or physically attacked at school by a student. Fortunately, this proportion declined to 7% by 2005.[5]

Because schools are community institutions, they are largely affected by the dynamics of the neighborhoods in which they are situated. The organization (or lack thereof) of their surrounding neighborhoods often have an impact on the school environment.[6] During the 2005–2006 academic year alone, 86% of public schools reported that at least one crime had occurred in their school. Compared to private school students, public school students are consistently more likely to report that there are gangs, guns, and drugs present at school.[7] Consequently, public school students are nearly twice as likely to report being violently victimized at school than are private school students.[8] Urban teachers are also twice as likely as those in suburban, rural, or town schools to experience violence.[9]

Although the previously described victimizations are far more common, attention has focused invariably on fatalities at school. School-associated violent deaths of students, staff, and nonstudents fluctuated between 57 and 30 from 1992 to 2006. Most of these were homicides of students between the ages of 5 and 18. The number of such deaths was particularly high between 1992 and 1999, ranging from 28 to 34 per year. Not until 2000 did these figures drop below 20 per year.[10]

In response to school violence, various efforts have been undertaken to prevent and reduce its occurrence. Schools are inundated with anti-violence programs, including peer mediation, mentoring programs, and anti-violence courses. Metal detectors and police officers are now a common feature in many schools. Most schools have adopted zero-tolerance policies, by which students can be suspended or expelled for perpetrating acts of violence at school.[11] Importantly, the peak number of school shootings during the 1990s resulted in state and federal efforts to prevent school victimization, such as the U.S. Department of Health and Human Services and Substance Abuse and Mental Health Services Administration's multimedia initiative to increase public awareness about bullying and its consequences.[12]

NOTES

1. David S. Jackson, "A Room Full of Doom," *Time*, May 24, 1999, 65; Eric Pooley, "Portrait of a Deadly Bond," *Time*, May 10, 1999, 26.

2. Kathryn A. Chandler et al., *Students' Reports of School Crime: 1989 and 1995* (Washington DC: United States Departments of Education and Justice, 1998).

3. Rachel Dinkes et al., *Indicators of School Crime and Safety: 2007* (Washington DC: United States Departments of Education and Justice, 2007).

4. Ibid.

5. Ibid.

6. Denise C. Gottfredson, *Schools and Delinquency* (New York: Cambridge University Press, 2001).

7. Chandler, *Students' Reports of School Crime*; Dinkes, *Indicators of School Crime*.

8. Ibid.

9. Dinkes, *Indicators of School Crime*.

10. Ibid.

11. Gottfredson, *Schools and Delinquency*.

12. Dan Olweus, *Bullying Is NOT a Fact of Life* (Washington DC: United States Department of Health and Human Services, 2003).

SUGGESTED READING

Delbert S. Elliot, Beatrix A. Hamburg, and Kirk R. Williams, eds., *Violence in American Schools* (New York: Cambridge University Press, 1998).

TOYA LIKE

SECONDARY VICTIMIZATION. Secondary victimization is recognized as effects of a criminal victimization on the family and friends (loved ones) of a primary or direct victim—the person to whom the criminal event occurred.[1] Secondary victimization is also referred to as secondary victims or indirect victims.[2] However, secondary victims are not limited to those who have interpersonal relationships with the primary victim. First responders to a crime scene (police, emergency medical technicians, forensic evidence technicians, fire fighters) also experience trauma as a result of all that they are exposed to in their jobs.[3] Furthermore, secondary victims have been classified into four distinct categories, including the traditional groupings of family and friends and adding associates of the victim and the entire community in which the victimization occurred.[4]

There is a lot of support for the finding that secondary victims often suffer from effects of victimization that are similar to those of primary victims, including both psychological and financial difficulties.[5] People who identify as family or friends of a crime victim often report psychological disturbances, including anger, guilt, helplessness, depression, fearfulness, a need for revenge, a loss of security, grief, shame, and fear.[6] Some secondary victims, particularly family and friends of murder victims, may also experience post-traumatic stress disorder.[7] Criminal victimizations can be particularly devastating to those who have lost someone as the result of a homicide. Not only do these secondary victims have to deal with the grief of losing someone, they may also be revictimized by the agents of the criminal justice system, who may be reticent to share information with them or keep them updated as to the progress of a case.[8] Secondary victims identified as emergency responders may suffer psychological disturbances from the trauma of responding to multiple victimizations and seeing humans in such negative states on a consistent basis.[9] Members of the community and associates of a primary victim may experience a loss in their belief in a "just world" after seeing the effects of the criminal victimization.[10]

Financially, secondary victims may suffer if the primary victim has a loss in income that is the result of an inability to return to work because of the psychological and physical effects of the victimization or because of the time that is needed to participate in the judicial process.[11] Additionally, if the murder victim was the primary or significant breadwinner in the family, the financial health of a family may be severely affected. Costs incurred to attend counseling or in response to a physical injury may not be covered by crime victim compensation programs or insurance; thus the money brought into the family may have to be diverted elsewhere to take care of these new expenses. This point is particularly salient for those who have lost items as a result of nonviolent crimes, because victim compensation programs do not cover losses from property crimes.[12]

NOTES

1. Andrew Karmen, *Crime Victims: An Introduction to Victimology* (Belmont, CA: Thomson Wadsworth, 2007).

2. Ibid.

3. Ibid.

4. Paul J. Becker, Arthur J. Jipson, and Alan Bruce, "The Pinto Legacy: The Community as an Indirect Victim of Corporate Deviance," *The Justice Professional* 12 (2001): 305–26.

5. Courtney E. Ahrens and Rebecca Campbell, "Assisting Rape Victims as They Recover from Rape: The Impact on Friends," *Journal of Interpersonal Violence* 15, no. 9 (2000): 959–86; Karmen, *Crime Victims*.

6. Ahrens and Campbell, "Assisting Rape Victims."

7. Martie P. Thompson, "Homicide Survivors: A Summary of the Research," in *Victims of Crime*, 3rd ed., eds. Robert C. Davis, Arthur J. Lurigio, and Susan Herman (Thousand Oaks, CA: Sage, 2007), 109–24.

8. Brian Williams, *Working with Victims of Crime: Policies, Politics, and Practice* (London: Jessica Kingsley, 1999).

9. Cheryl Regehr and Ted Bober, *In the Line of Fire: Trauma in the Emergency Services* (New York: Oxford University Press, 2005).

10. Elizabeth A. Stanko, "Victims R Us: The Life History of 'Fear of Crime' and the Politicization of Violence," in *Crime, Risk and Insecurity: Law and Order in Everyday Life and Political Discourse*, eds. T. Hope and R. Sparks (London: Routledge, 2000), 12–20.

11. Leslie W. Kennedy and Vincent F. Sacco, *Crime Victims in Context* (New York: Oxford University Press, 1998).

12. Karmen, *Crime Victims*.

SUGGESTED READING

Arthur J. Lurigio, Wesley G. Skogan, and Robert C. Davis, *Victims of Crime: Problems, Policies, and Programs* (Newbury Park, CA: Sage, 1990).

ELIZABETH QUINN DEVALVE

SELF-HELP JUSTICE. Motivated by beliefs that justice cannot be obtained through official institutions, members of some communities "take the law into their own hands" and dispense punishments, at times lethal, through informal mechanisms.[1] Commonly termed "vigilantism," these actions express dissatisfaction with normal channels of law and social control. Victims are usually persons who have violated important norms that are held by the larger community or by powerful segments of it. The San Francisco Committees of Vigilance and the lynching of African Americans in the postbellum South are historical examples. Contemporary self-help justice examples in the United States include communities' extralegal efforts to remove drug dealers and sex offenders and to maintain racial homogeneity. In the following, we discuss two types of self-help justice: lynching and defended neighborhoods.

Lynching, the extralegal execution of suspects by a "mob" of three or more persons, was a relatively frequent form of informal social control from 1880 to 1930. Jay Corzine, Lin Huff-Corzine, and Candice Nelsen[2] found that nineteenth-century lynchings in Louisiana were similar to the "self-help" justice that Donald Black described in his 1983 article, "Crime as Social Control."[3] In brief, the first 20 years of the lynching era revealed numerous examples of whites lynching blacks, interracial mobs lynching blacks and whites, and blacks lynching blacks. Lynching circumstances were often described as ones in which a serious crime, e.g., murder or rape, had been committed in a rural area having little regular law enforcement. Alleged perpetrators were often brought before the victim to be sure the right person had been apprehended. At the turn of the twentieth century, lynchings began to be used by whites to maintain the lower caste status of blacks.

Defended neighborhoods are defined by Gerald Suttles as "[t]he residential group which seals itself off through the efforts of delinquent gangs, by restrictive covenants, by sharp boundaries, or by a forbidding reputation."[4] Most large cities have neighborhoods with a reputation for maintaining close surveillance of outsiders and an attitude toward them that hovers between mistrust and hostility. In some cases, a single racial or ethnic group dominates these neighborhoods, and informal social control is partially maintained by criminal organizations, e.g., the Mafia in Italian American areas or street gangs in other neighborhoods. There is some evidence that robberies and other street crimes are reduced in defended neighborhoods, but the sharp boundary between residents and outsiders can sometimes lead to tragedies. Counterevidence indicates that vigilante or self-help justice increases violence in "defended" neighborhoods where gangs rule the streets. As a means to maintain and expand control over drug markets, gangs may become involved in protracted disputes involving several homicides.

Generally, groups resort to self-help justice more often if they cannot realize strongly shared values through legitimate channels or if they believe that the criminal justice system is biased or unresponsive. Perhaps the best way to reduce the level of self-help justice in the contemporary United States is to ensure that all citizens have equal access to the police and courts.

NOTES

1. Donald Black, "Crime as Social Control," *American Sociological Review* 48, no. 1 (1983): 34–45.

2. Jay Corzine, Lin Huff-Corzine, and Candice Nelsen, "Rethinking Lynching: Extralegal Executions in Louisiana," *Deviant Behavior* 17, no. 2 (1996): 133–57.

3. Black, "Crime as Social Control."

4. Gerald D. Suttles, *The Social Construction of Communities* (Chicago: University of Chicago Press, 1972), 21.

SUGGESTED READING

Judith N. DeSena, *Protecting One's Turf: Social Strategies for Maintaining Urban Neighborhoods* (Lanham, MD: University Press of America, 1990); Margaret Vandiver, *Lethal Punishment: Lynchings and Legal Executions in the South* (New Brunswick, NJ: Rutgers University Press, 2006).

LIN HUFF-CORZINE AND JAY CORZINE

SENSATIONALISM. The mass media disproportionately cover violent personal crimes.[1] Such coverage routinely typifies racialized, nonwhite suspects[2] and white, female victims,[3] suggesting "journalistic assessments of newsworthiness firmly grounded in long-standing race and gender typifications."[4]

Crimes occurring in suburbs receive disproportionate coverage in relation to urban crimes, both in terms of frequency and prominence. Suburban crime stories frequently lead newscasts and are typically longer than their urban counterparts. They are also more likely to be presented using live location reports, a more expensive production package, underscoring the importance that media gatekeepers place on them.[5]

These typified portrayals affect consumers' attitudes toward crime and punishment. Exposure to presentations of racialized suspects substantiates negative attitudes toward racialized minorities and engenders support for punitive crime control such as mandatory sentencing and capital punishment.[6] Likewise, media overrepresentation of white, middle-class female victims has led to the misconception that this group comprises the majority of violent crime victims[7] and leads to a disproportionate level of fear among this group.[8]

NOTES

1. Ray Surette, "Predator Criminals as Media Icons," in *Media, Process, and the Social Construction of Crime*, ed. Greg Barak (New York: Garland, 1994).

2. Franklin D. Gilliam, Jr. and Shanto Iyengar, "Prime Suspects: The Influence of Local Television News on the Viewing Public," *American Journal of Political Science* 44, no. 3 (2000): 560–73.

3. Ted Chiricos, Sarah Eschholz, and Marc Gertz, "Crime, News and Fear of Crime: Toward an Identification of Audience Effects," *Social Problems* 44 (1997): 342–57.

4. Richard J. Lundman, "The Newsworthiness and Selection Bias in News about Murder: Comparative and Relative Effects of Novelty and Race and Gender Typifications on Newspaper Coverage of Homicide," *Sociological Forum* 18, no. 3 (2003): 357–86.

5. Danilo Yanich, "Crime Creep: Urban and Suburban Crime on Local TV News," *Journal of Urban Affairs* 26, no. 5 (2004): 535–63.

6. Gilliam et al., "Prime Suspects."

7. Samuel Walker, Cassia Spohn, and Miriam DeLone, *The Color of Justice: Race, Ethnicity, and Crime in America*, 4th ed. (Belmont, CA: Thompson / Wadsworth, 2007).

8. Chiricos et al., "Crime, News and Fear."

SUGGESTED READING

Kathryn Russell, *The Color of Crime: Racial Hoaxes, White Fear, Black Protectionism, Police Harassment, and Other Macro Aggressions* (New York: New York University Press, 1998).

TERRY GLENN LILLEY

SERIES VICTIMIZATIONS. Series victimizations generally pertain to reports of multiple victimizations, within a specified time frame, that are experienced by the same individual.[1] The term "series victimizations" is often associated with the technique used by the National Crime Victimization Survey (NCVS) to handle instances of repeat victimization. Currently, the NCVS identifies series victimizations when a respondent reports at least six victimizations that are similar, but separate in nature, over the six-month recall period and when the respondent is unable to provide details about each specific event. Because detailed information is limited to the most recent incident, series victimizations are not included in overall rates of victimization.

Although methodological problems have been cited regarding the use of NCVS series incidents to measure multiple victimization, a sizeable portion of published research is based on such information.[2] Given the limited number of large-scale, population-based data sources on victimization, alternatives for studying multiple and repeat victimization are typically limited to one of two studies. First, the British Crime Survey (BCS) has been used to study series victimizations, but it is based on cross-sectional data and uses a method of recording series incidents that is similar to that used by the NCVS. Others have utilized long-term self-report panel data, particularly the National Youth Survey, to measure multiple victimizations.

Multiple victims represent a small percentage of all victims, but they account for the majority of incidences.[3] One common misconception among the lay public is that experiencing multiple instances of victimization over a short time span is attributed to bad luck. Several studies have found that the extent of series incidents varies across crime types, because multiple victimization is more likely for personal or violent crimes (particularly domestic violence) than for property crimes.[4]

Despite the lack of empirical research comparing repeat victims with repeat offenders, victimologists have often reported substantial overlap between chronic victims and offenders.[5] However, most reports of similarities are based on comparisons between victims and offenders in general, without accounting for differences between one-time and repeat victims, and one-time and repeat offenders. One of the few studies to examine systematically the differences between these four groups found some differences in repeat offenders and repeat victims.[6] However, the study was based on a sample of adolescents in Australia, limiting generalizations to other populations.

The police play an important role in dealing with multiple victimizations incidents.[7] Since the 1970s, police departments have paid increasingly more attention to their role in repeat victimizations. By implementing programs and policies to reduce rates of multiple victimizations, offenders have fewer opportunities for criminal behavior, victim satisfaction increases, and overall rates of crime are reduced. Examples of general strategies used to reduce repeat victimizations include intervening after a first-reported victimization, when the circumstances are related to high risk of multiple incidences, focusing on "hot spots" of chronic victimization, notifying victims of community resources such as domestic violence shelters, and educating the public on reducing individual risk for victimization through changes in daily routines.[8]

NOTES

1. Michael Planty and Kevin J. Strom, "Understanding the Role of Repeat Victims in the Production of Annual U.S. Victimization Rates," *Journal of Quantitative Criminology* 23 (2007): 179–200.

2. Ibid.

3. Scott Menard, "The 'Normality' of Repeat Victimization from Adolescence through Early Adulthood," *Justice Quarterly* 17 (2000): 543–74.

4. Maureen Outlaw, Barry Ruback, and Chester Britt, "Repeat and Multiple Victimizations: The Role of Individual and Contextual Factors," *Violence and Victims* 17 (2002): 187–204.

5. Abigail A. Fagan and Paul Mazerolle, "Repeat Offending and Repeat Victimization: Assessing Similarities and Differences in Psychosocial Risk Factors," *Crime and Delinquency* Prepublished July, 16, 2008, DOI: 10.1177/0011128708321322.

6. Ibid.

7. Graham Farrell, "Progress and Prospects in the Prevention of Repeat Victimization," in *Handbook of Crime Prevention and Community Safety*, ed. Nick Tilley (Cullompton, UK: Willan, 2005), 145–72.

8. Graham Farrell and William Sousa, "Repeat Victimization and Hot Spots: The Overlap and Its Implications for Crime Control and Problem-Oriented Policing," in *Repeat Victimization*, eds. Graham Farrell and Ken Pease (Monsey, NY: Criminal Justice Press, 2001), 221–40.

SUGGESTED READING

Janet L. Lauritson and Kenna F. Davis Quinet, "Repeat Victimization among Adolescents and Young Adults," *Journal of Quantitative Criminology* 11 (1995): 143–66.

MATTHEW JOHNSON

SEX OFFENDER REGISTRATION. Sex offender registration is the legal requirement that individuals who have been convicted of sex crimes provide their personal information (name, birth date/age, address, physical description, and other information that varies by state) to public officials who post this information (and a photograph) on a publicly accessible Web site.[1] The stated purpose of sex offender registration is to allow community members to know the identities and whereabouts of sex offenders so that they may protect themselves and their children from victimization.

Sex offender registration began in 1994 when Congress enacted the Jacob Wetterling Act, requiring convicted sex offenders to record their addresses with local law enforcement agencies. Megan's Law in 1996 amended the Wetterling Act, by allowing the dissemination of registry information directly to the public. In 2006 the passage by Congress of the Adam Walsh Sex Offender Registration and Notification Act expanded the number of registered sex offenders to whom public disclosure applies, lengthened the duration of registration periods, and created the national sex offender registry.

Some states register all persons convicted of any sex crimes, but some states list only those sex offenders who are clinically evaluated as being high risk for recidivating. Additionally, on sex offender registries in some states, there are distinctions drawn between sex offenders and sexual predators (those individuals determined to be predatory and at highest risk of victimizing others). Also, some universities also maintain their own sex offender registries, listing students, faculty, and staff who are convicted sex offenders.[2]

The number of sex offenders who are registered increases daily. There is no well-established number of known registrants, although it is believed that, at the start of 2009, there were between 650,000 and 700,000 individuals registered in the United States. More than 90% of these individuals are men. Juveniles are included in some sex offender registries. The length of time that an individual remains on the registry varies by state law, although most often registration is for either 20 years or lifetime.

Sex offender registration is accompanied by a number of additional consequences for offenders, some of which are legal requirements and some of which are social consequences that result when community members learn of an offender's status as a registered sex offender. The most common legal accompaniment of registration is a restriction on where a registered sex offender may live. Residential restrictions laws are present in most states (and in many local communities) and prohibit sex offenders from living within a specified distance (usually 500 to 2,500 feet) from "child congregation locations." These are most often defined as schools, day care centers, playgrounds, public parks, and, occasionally, school bus stops. As a result of such laws, many registered sex offenders have difficulties finding and maintaining affordable and legal housing.[3] Additionally, research shows that registered sex offenders also experience a range of collateral consequences, including difficulties with employment, loss of family and social relationships, harassment and assault, and a persistent sense of stigmatization and vulnerability.[4]

NOTES

1. Richard Tewksbury, "Effects of Sexual Assault on Men: Physical, Mental and Sexual Consequences," *International Journal of Men's Health* 6 (2007): 22–35.

2. Richard Tewksbury and Matthew Lees, "Sex Offenders on Campus: University-Based Sex Offender Registries and the Collateral Consequences of Registration," *Federal Probation* 70, no. 3 (2006): 50–56.

3. Richard Tewksbury, "Exile at Home: The Unintended Collateral Consequences of Sex Offender Residency Restrictions," *Harvard Civil Rights—Civil Liberties Law Review* 42 (2007): 531–40; Paul Zandbergen and Timothy C. Hart, "Reducing Housing Options for Convicted Sex Offenders: Investigating the Impact of Residency Restriction Laws Using GIS," *Justice Research and Policy* 8, no. 2 (2006): 1–24.

4. Jill S. Levenson, "Collateral Consequences of Sex Offender Residence Restrictions," *Criminal Justice Studies* 21 (2008): 153–66; Jill S. Levenson and Leo P. Cotter, "The Effects of Megan's Law on Sex Offender Reintegration," *Journal of Contemporary Criminal Justice* 21 (2005): 49–66; Richard Tewksbury and Matthew Lees, "Perceptions of Punishment: How Registered Sex Offenders View Registries," *Crime & Delinquency* 53 (2007): 380–407; Richard Tewksbury and Matthew Lees, "Perceptions of Sex Offender Registration: Collateral Consequences and Community Experiences," *Sociological Spectrum* 26 (2006): 309–34.

SUGGESTED READING

Jill Levenson, Kristin Zgoba, and Richard Tewksbury, "Sex Offender Residence Restrictions: Sensible Crime Policy or Flawed Logic?" *Federal Probation* 71, no. 3 (2007): 2–9; Richard Tewksbury and Jill Levenson, "When Evidence Is Ignored: Residential Restrictions for Sex Offenders," *Corrections Today* 69, no. 6 (2007): 54–57.

RICHARD TEWKSBURY

SEXUAL ASSAULT. Although legal definitions vary from state to state, sexual assault is defined as forced sexual intercourse (i.e., oral, vaginal, or anal) against a person's will. Whether it is homosexual, prison, date, spousal, stranger, gang, or interspecies sexual assault, these actions are synonymous with rape. Statistics report that one in three women now 18 years of age or younger will be the victim of sexual assault. Because of differing legal definitions of sexual assault, the frequency and scope of its occurrence are difficult to identify precisely; however, victimization reports indicate that its numbers are actually four times higher than police data indicate.

Research indicates that about 90% of the rapes that occur do so between people who know one another. Crime statistics generally indicate that the closer the personal relationship is between victims and perpetrators, the less likely the law is to prosecute. This is evidenced by the 70% unfounding rate of cases of sexual assault (those cases that are thrown out of court because of the lack of evidence). Ninety-five percent of rapists, who notably are between 15 and 24 years of age, do not ejaculate. Because most men do not ejaculate, the search for causes of rape has shifted from rape as sex to the motivator of rape as power, dominance, and degradation. The majority of rapes that occur happen between people from the same social, economic, and racial backgrounds. Researchers often use an ecological approach when explaining sexual assault. They tend to examine the culture's traditional roles of men and women, how gender roles were adapted into the family, the influence of peer groups, and individual differences when determining an offender's motivation for rape.

Attempts to explain basic truths that are accepted without scientific support are called myths. There are a number of sexual assault myths including the following: all women want to be raped (assumption: men do it in the name of their masculinity, so women have it done in the name of their femininity); no woman can be raped against her will (assumption: if a woman does not escape, it is somehow her fault); she was asking for it (this shifts the blame for what happened onto the female); men have uncontrollable sex drives (most men do not rape); and if you are going to be raped, you might as well relax and enjoy it (assumption: it makes light of the physical violation of rape).

Victims of sexual assault are thrown into a crisis situation. Rape crisis centers for victims of rape were formed beginning in the early 1970s and have one-on-one as well as group and telephone counseling, using others who have been victimized to let the victim know that she is not alone. In most jurisdictions there is a triage program offered free of charge to victims in all area hospital emergency rooms. The triage program is initiated by the police, who take and file a report of the incident and transport the victim to the hospital. There nurses and doctors gather evidence for successful prosecution, and rape crisis counselors offer emotional support and provide the victim with toiletries and a clean set of clothes.

After the occurrence of rape, the victim will have her defenders and blamers. The victim defenders assert that no victim should ever be blamed for what has happened to her. These defenders support rape awareness and support groups for women. They want to teach would-be victims how not to be victim-prone. However, there are those victim blamers who look at her past criminal and social records (rape shield laws prohibit sexual interactions with anyone else besides the perpetrator from being entered into court testimony), drug use, and possible motivations with the assumption that she did something wrong. Instead of minimizing the risks, it is assumed that she heightened them by acting provocatively, negligently, or deliberately. Bad judgment is not a crime. Sexual assault is a crime.

SUGGESTED READING

Susan Brownmiller, *Against Our Will: Men, Women, and Rape* (New York: Random House, 1975); Diana E. H. Russell and Rebecca M. Bolen, *The Epidemic of Rape and Child Sexual Abuse in the United States* (Thousand Oaks, CA: Sage, 2000).

CHARISSE COSTON

SEXUAL HARASSMENT. Sexual harassment is a form of sex discrimination in violation of Title VII of the Civil Rights Act of 1964. It is a widespread problem. A survey conducted by the U.S. Merit Systems Protection Board in 1994 indicated that more than 40% of female workers and 19% of male workers reported experiences of unwanted sexual attention, but only 6% of those experiencing sexual harassment took formal action. In 2007, the Equal Employment Opportunity Commission (EEOC) received nearly 13,000 complaints about sexual harassment, and 16% of those complaints were filed by male workers. In the educational setting, research by the American Association of University Women in 2001 and 2005 indicated that 81% of students at the secondary level and 62% of college students reported being sexually harassed. Although a higher proportion of younger girls experienced this form of victimization, male and female college students were harassed equally but in different ways.

Traditionally, sexual harassment was considered a personal issue and a private problem. The term "sexual harassment" was coined in 1975 by a group of feminists led by legal scholar Catherine McKinnon, but early court cases had difficulty finding support for the claim of sexual harassment as a form of sex discrimination under the Title VII of the Civil Rights Act of 1964. In 1980, the EEOC formulated guidelines defining sexual harassment to address the confusion resulting from different understandings of sexual harassment.

Under the EEOC guidelines, sexual harassment is defined as unwelcome sexual advances, requests for sexual favors, or other verbal or physical conduct of a sexual nature under the following conditions: (1) submission to such conduct is made a term or condition of an individual's employment; (2) submission to or rejection of such conduct by an individual is used as the basis for employment decisions affecting such individual; or (3) such conduct has the purpose of interfering with an individual's work performance or creating an intimidating, hostile, or offensive working environment. These guidelines reflect two broad categories of sexual harassment. *Quid pro quo* harassment involves threat of job-related consequences, a form of "sexual bribery" or "sexual coercion" with promise for benefits. The more common form of sexual harassment is *hostile environment*, which involves sex-related verbal or physical conduct that is unwelcome.

Since the original EEOC guidelines, changes have been made to sexual harassment law. In 1993, the EEOC extended the meaning of hostile environment to include offensive, sex-related conduct that is not specifically sexual in nature, such as gender harassment. The Supreme Court ruled that schools had the power to discipline students when they used obscene, profane language or gestures that could interfere with the educational process *(Bethel School District No. 403 v. Fraser)*[1] and that private citizens could collect damage awards when teachers sexually harassed their students *(Franklin v. Gwinnett County Public Schools)*.[2]

In 1997, the U.S. Department of Education issued policy guidance on sexual harassment, including Title IX's requirements in this area. Despite changes in the law, in part because of a heavy burden of proof required by law, very few victims of sexual harassment go forward to file complaints.

NOTES

1. *Bethel School District No. 403 v. Fraser*, 478 U.S. 675 (1986).
2. *Franklin v. Gwinnett County Public Schools*, 503 U.S. 60 (1992).

SUGGESTED READING

Catherine Hill and Elena Silva, *Drawing the Line: Sexual Harassment on Campus* (Washington DC: American Association of University Women—Educational Foundation, 2005); Donald E. Maypole and Rosemarie Skaine, "Sexual Harassment of Blue Collar Workers," *Journal of Sociology and Social Welfare* 9 (1982): 682–95; Catherine McKinnon, *Sexual Harassment of Working Women* (New Haven, CT: Yale University Press, 1979).

HOAN N. BUI

SHAKEN BABY SYNDROME. The National Center for Shaken Baby Syndrome (NCSBS) defines shaken baby syndrome (SBS) as "a term used to describe the constellation of signs and symptoms resulting from violent shaking or shaking and impacting of the head of an infant or small child."[1] SBS was first formally described in 1972 by pediatric radiologist John Caffey, who referred to the syndrome as "whiplash shaken infant syndrome."[2]

Studies suggest that most perpetrators of SBS are male.[3] The perpetrators are typically the child's parents or caregivers such as the mother's boyfriend. Other risk factors for shaking include substance abuse, social isolation, and lack of social support among the perpetrators.[4]

Several factors may place an infant at greater risk for SBS. One of these factors is being male.[5] According to James Peinkofer, male infants have a 60% greater risk of being shaken than female infants.[6] A second risk factor for SBS is being young.[7] Although children as old as four or five years of age can be victims of SBS, most victims are under one year of age.[8]

Research suggests that the most common trigger of shaking is the baby's crying.[9] Researchers believe that the intent of the perpetrators of SBS is generally not to harm the child, but rather to control the child's behavior, make the child subservient, or to provide discipline.[10]

According to the NCSBS, 1,200 to 1,400 children are killed or injured annually as a result of shaking in the United States.[11] The NCSBS warns, however, that this may be an underestimate, because many cases of SBS go undetected.

The various charges and penalties that perpetrators of SBS are subject to depend partly on the state in which the abuse occurred. For instance, when victims of SBS die from their injuries, the perpetrator may be charged with first- or second-degree murder, reckless or negligent homicide, or manslaughter. When victims of SBS survive the shaking, the possible charges against the perpetrator include felony assault of a child, reckless endangerment, felony child abuse, battery, or child endangerment. Because many of these charges are felonies, the perpetrator often faces considerable prison time. Some cases of SBS are resolved through plea bargains. For instance, there have been cases in which perpetrators of SBS have plea-bargained the sentence from murder to reckless homicide, resulting in sentences of probation.[12]

SBS has a high mortality rate: approximately 25% of all SBS victims die. The children who survive SBS often have lifelong health problems, such as motor deficits, seizures, developmental delays, or blindness.[13] These children may thus need special assistance, including long-term medical care and special education.

Another issue affecting victims of SBS is parental rights. If a child's parent is convicted of SBS, the perpetrator's spouse may seek to terminate legally the perpetrator's parental rights. Family members can also request restraining orders against perpetrators of SBS to limit the contact that a perpetrator can have with the victim and the victim's family. Finally, in some situations, victims of SBS may be removed from their homes and placed in foster care. Some of these children may eventually be adopted.[14]

NOTES

1. The National Center on Shaken Baby Syndrome Web site, http://www.dontshake.org.

2. Stephen Lazoritz and Angela Bier, "Historical Perspectives," in *The Shaken Baby Syndrome: A Multidisciplinary Approach*, ed. Stephen Lazoritz and Vincent J. Palusci, (Binghamton, NY: Haworth Press, 2001), 9–18.

3. James R. Peinkofer, *Silenced Angels: The Medical, Legal, and Social Aspects of Shaken Baby Syndrome* (Westport, CT: Auburn House, 2002).

4. W. Hobart Davies and Molly Murphy Garwood, "Who Are the Perpetrators and Why Do They Do It?" in *The Shaken Baby Syndrome: A Multidisciplinary Approach*, ed. Stephen Lazoritz and Vincent J. Palusci, (Binghamton, NY: Haworth Press, 2001), 41–54.

5. Halim Hennes, Narendra Kini, and Vincent J. Palusci, "The Epidemiology, Clinical Characteristics and Public Health Implications of Shaken Baby Syndrome," in *The Shaken Baby Syndrome: A Multidisciplinary Approach*, ed. Stephen Lazoritz and Vincent J. Palusci, (Binghamton, NY: Haworth Press, 2001), 19–40.

6. Peinkofer, *Silenced Angels*.

7. Ibid.

8. Hennes, Kini, and Palusci, "The Epidemiology."

9. Peinkofer, *Silenced Angels*.

10. Davies and Garwood, "Who Are the Perpetrators."

11. The National Center on Shaken Baby Syndrome.

12. Peinkofer, *Silenced Angels*.

13. Hennes, Kini, and Palusci, "The Epidemiology."

14. Peinkofer, *Silenced Angels*.

SUGGESTED READING

William Brooks and Laura Weathers, "Overview of Shaken Baby Syndrome," in *The Shaken Baby Syndrome: A Multidisciplinary Approach*, ed. Stephen Lazoritz and Vincent J. Palusci (Binghamton, NY: Haworth Press, 2001), 1–7; Sara H. Sinal et al., "Is Race or Ethnicity a Predictive Factor in Shaken Baby Syndrome?" *Child Abuse and Neglect* 24, no. 9 (2000): 1241–46.

SHANNON A. SANTANA

SHELTERS. Shelters for victims of crime have a unique history. Victims of stranger crimes often have little need for shelter away from their residence, but it is the victims of non-stranger violent crime that have led to the creation of shelters across the country and the world. These victims are often women, children, and the elderly. The creation of shelters for family members who are targets from other family members is a recent concept.

Historically, refuges from harm have existed. In early Western civilization, a few women fled their violent homes for a convent, often being prescribed to convert in the process. However, late sixteenth-century wealthy benefactors in Italian commercial city-states pioneered lay-administered refuges that addressed problems specific to women; the *Casa delle Malmaritate* (House of Unhappily Married Wives), in Florence, allowed women some shelter from relationships from their families.

Cultural understanding of crime victims became part of the national and international discourse, reaching a peak in the 1970s. At the same time, through the efforts of both feminist scholars and activists, domestic violence was brought to the attention of communities in the United States and Europe. It was not that domestic violence was a new problem; it was that it was an unrecognized problem.

Beginning in the 1970s in England, the shelter movement spread quickly throughout Europe and the United States. In the United States, shelters usually are developed as part of the initial crisis intervention. A woman, and often her children, leave their abusive partners and stay at a shelter for four to six weeks, until other resources are identified. Recently, shelters in the United States developed more long-term transitional housing.

Shelters for battered women in the United States were originally designed to have undisclosed locations in order to protect women from their abusive partners.

However, in recent years, some shelters have opted out of secrecy for more open locations. Furthermore, some shelters have restrictions about who can stay at their shelters, such as age restriction of male children in their residence.

Shelters for battered women are not the only shelters created for victims of crime; they are, however, the most well known. Other types of housing are possible for victims of crime—the state and local government run housing alternatives for children who are abused or neglected by their families (such as group homes and foster homes), and there are numerous state and nongovernmental shelters for teenage runaways, who are often abused by their custodial parents. Homeless shelters are also filled with individuals who have been victims of stranger crime on the streets and violence from their families.

SUGGESTED READING

Susan Schechter, *Women and Male Violence: The Visions and Struggles of the Battered Women's Movement* (Cambridge, MA: South End, 1982); Albert L. Shostack, *Shelters for Battered Women and Their Children: A Comprehensive Guide to Planning and Operating Safe and Caring Residential Programs* (Springfield, IL: Charles C. Thomas, 2001).

PAMELA JENKINS

SIBLING ABUSE. Sibling abuse is a type of victimization that is much more common than many people may realize. Research has demonstrated that sibling abuse of one sort or another may occur in over half of all families across the United States.[1] This type of abuse is often not recognized by family members for the abusive behavior that it is. This may seem unusual because one would expect family members to be aware of the victimization that occurs in their own household. However, this phenomenon has less to do with observing the behaviors and more to do with the means by which families may choose to define those behaviors.[2] Indeed, family members may explain away instances of sibling abuse, treating such behavior as if it were a natural part of growing up or something that will subside over time as the youngster grows older. Because of this, sibling abuse is seldom recognized for what it is and this allows it to continue unchecked.

There are multiple types of sibling abuse, including physical, emotional, and sexual abuse. Physical abuse between siblings can include any form of hitting, kicking, biting, or striking that one can imagine.[3] Emotional abuse might include the use of verbal degradation, continuous teasing, or perhaps torturing the victim's pet.[4] Lastly, sexual abuse includes any type of sexual activity in which the child is under the age of consent.[5] However, the incidence of sibling sex abuse is complicated and difficult to discern because the actors may have differing motivations, with some instances being the outcome of simple sexual experimentation, whereas other occurrences may be the result of exploitative abuse.[6]

Official responses to sibling abuse can vary depending on the circumstances. In cases where the legal guardian fails to protect one child from abusive behavior of his or her sibling, the victimized child may be removed from the home.[7] Likewise, depending on the age of the sibling who commits the act, the juvenile justice system may adjudicate the youthful perpetrator, resulting in probation in most cases, but also including some type of institutionalization if intensive treatment is warranted.[8] Naturally, if the perpetrator is a juvenile, there is the likelihood that he or she will, at some point, return to the family-of-origin. If this does occur and the victim of the abuse also lives in the home, the legal caretakers incur a responsibility to prevent further abuse once the family is reunited.

Victims of this type of crime, when discovered, are typically provided with some type of counseling or psychotherapeutic intervention. These types of interventions can range from standard counseling and play therapy to assertiveness training that teaches the youth how to thwart the actions of abusive perpetrators. In some cases, family therapy or other forms of intervention that include the entire family may be a required to aid the victim, the family system, and the perpetrator so that future incidents can be prevented.

NOTES

1. Ola W. Barnett, Cindy L. Miller-Perrin, and Robin D. Perrin, *Family Violence across the Lifespan*, 2nd ed. (Thousand Oaks, CA: Sage, 2004).

2. Harvey Wallace, *Family Violence: Legal, Medical, and Social Perspectives*, 4th ed. (Boston: Allyn & Bacon, 2005).

3. Barnett, Miller-Perrin, and Perrin, *Family Violence*.

4. Ibid.

5. John Pesciallo, "Understanding Sibling Incest," Walla Walla College, http://www.bmi.net/jgp/USI.htm.

6. Ibid.

7. Barnett, Miller-Perrin, and Perrin, *Family Violence*.

8. Robert D. Hanser, *Special Needs Offenders in the Community* (Upper Saddle River, NJ: Prentice Hall, 2007).

SUGGESTED READING

Shelley Eriksen and Vickie Jensen, "All in the Family? Family Environment Factors in Sibling Violence," *Journal of Family Violence* 21, no. 8 (2006): 497–507.

ROBERT D. HANSER

SOCIAL EXCHANGE THEORY. Social exchange theory is a common theoretical approach that views society as a complex system of resource trading ("exchanges") between individuals and other entities that comprise a society. Resources that are exchanged may be any combination of goods or services that are considered valuable by the parties involved in the exchange, including real property, labor, emotions, time, or information. Variations of social exchange theory focus on exchanges occurring among and between all levels of social organization, including between individuals, between individuals and groups, between groups, and so forth. Social exchange theory can be used to explain a broad range of phenomena, including the origins of society, the nature of power, the maintenance of social networks, and the resiliency of personal relationships.

The modern origins of social exchange theory can be traced historically to Jeremy Bentham's development of utilitarian microeconomics in the latter part of the eighteenth century. Social exchange theory also has roots in the anthropological studies of gift rituals in pre-industrial societies, such as illustrated by Bronislaw Malinowski's ethnographic work among Trobriand islanders in the early part of the twentieth century. However, it was not until 1958 that the concepts of rational social exchange found formal theoretical expression, with sociologist George Homan's article "Social Behavior as Exchange." According to Homans, humans sustain exchanges with others as long as the exchanges are perceived to be fair and rewarding compared to available alternatives. Homans viewed individual exchanges as the basis of society, with the sum total of these interactions creating social structure.

In 1962, Richard Emerson developed power-dependence theory as an extension and modification of Homan's exchange theory. Power-dependence theory posits that power is a characteristic of relationships that resides in the dependency of one exchange partner on another. The more dependent that one partner in an exchange is on another, the more power the other has over the dependent. Emerson recognized that dependency is not only a function of individual preferences but also a function of social networks, which provide alternative sources of reward and thus serve to balance power by reducing isolation and dependency. Emerson's work, along with Peter Blau's influential 1964 book *Exchange and Power in Social Life*, helped develop a dynamic social exchange theory that is centered on power and embedded in social network analysis.

During the 1980s and 1990s theoretical insights continued to build with regard to power use and power imbalances in exchange relationships. For example, Samuel B. Bacharach and Edward J. Lawler employ concepts of social exchange, power, and dependency as a theoretical frame in analyses of bargaining, negotiating, and conflict resolution. Linda D. Molm similarly has expanded the social exchange and power-dependency perspectives by examining coercive power, as opposed to more balanced reciprocal exchanges.

The social exchange theory is a useful framework for understanding many types of crime and victimization, but especially those types of incidents that involve abuse of power or psychological coercion. Application to such subjects as domestic violence, workplace bullying, child abuse, sexual assault, terrorism, and other common victimization topics is obvious. Additional policy applications, such as support for best practices in mediation and other forms of dispute settlement, are also well founded.

SUGGESTED READING

Peter Blau, *Exchange and Power in Social Life* (New York: Wiley, 1964); Richard M. Emerson, "Power-Dependence Relations," *American Sociological Review*, 27, no. 1 (1962): 31–41; George C. Homans, "Social Behavior as Exchange," *American Journal of Sociology* 63, no. 6 (1958): 597–606; Linda D. Molm, *Coercive Power in Social Exchange* (New York: Cambridge University Press, 1997).

EDWARD POWERS

SOCIAL LEARNING THEORY. Social learning theory has been one of the most utilized explanations for the occurrence of violence in general and, more specifically, in intimate partner violence. Its chief architect, Albert Bandura, posited that humans model behavior to which they have been exposed.[1] Social learning theory argues that people learn from the observation of others, as well as from the consequences affecting the observed others, through a cognitive processing interface. By observing the outcomes of the actions of others, a person develops expectations that the performance of similar behaviors will result in similar rewards or punishers. In a famous study, Albert Bandura, Dorothea Ross, and Sheila Ross[2] found that children who watched a video of an adult being rewarded for displays of verbal and physical aggression against a Bobo doll were more likely to imitate the aggressive behaviors than if the model had received no consequences or negative consequences. The observational learning from others in social situations has been refined in a host of research studies over the past 30 years.

In the field of victimology, social learning theory provided an accepted evidence-based approach to understanding aggression and family violence. Social learning theory has provided a venue for assessing the role of intergenerational transmission of violence.[3] Numerous articles have concluded that witnessing family violence increases the probability of children later engaging in intimate partner violence.[4] One of the most significant of these was the National Family Violence Survey,[5] which found that the exposure of children, both male and female, to family violence was predictive of violence with future partners. Cathy Widom,[6] in a prospective study of juvenile delinquents, found that early child abuse and neglect predicted delinquency, adult crime, and violence.

Bandura and others had warned that television and media violence were likely to contribute to violence in society. Research has shown relationships between media portrayal of violence and aggressive behavior from such sources as video games,[7] television,[8] and film.[9]

NOTES

1. Albert Bandura, *Aggression: A Social Learning Analysis* (Englewood Cliffs, NJ: Prentice Hall, 1973).

2. Albert Bandura, Dorothea Ross, and Sheila Ross, "Imitations of Aggressive Film-Mediated Models," *Journal of Abnormal and Social Psychology* 66 (1963): 3–11.

3. James F. Anderson and Kimberly Kras, "Revisiting Albert Bandura's Social Learning Theory to Better Understand and Assist Victims of Intimate Personal Violence," *Women and Criminal Justice* 17, no. 1 (2006): 99–124.

4. Emma Bevan and Daryl J. Higgins, "Is Domestic Violence Learned? The Contribution of Five Forms of Child Maltreatment to Men's Violence and Adjustment," *Journal of Family Violence* 17, no. 3 (2002): 223–45; Deborah M. Capaldi and Sara Clark, "Prospective Family Predictors of Aggression toward Female Partners for At-Risk Young Men," *Developmental Psychology* 34, no. 6 (1998): 1175–88.

5. Murray Straus, "Ordinary Violence, Child Abuse, and Wife Beating: What Do They Have in Common?" in *Physical Violence in American Families: Risk Factors and Adaptations to Violence in 8,145 Families,* eds. Murray A. Straus and Richard J. Gelles (New Brunswick, NJ: Transaction, 1990).

6. Cathy S. Widom, "The Cycle of Violence," *Science* 244 (1989): 160–244.

7. Nicholas L. Carnagey and Craig A. Anderson, "The Effects of Reward and Punishment in Violent Video Games on Aggressive Affect, Cognition, and Behavior," *Psychological Science* 16, no. 11 (2005): 882–89.

8. John P. Murray, "Media Violence: The Effects Are Both Real and Strong," *American Behavioral Scientist* 51, no. 8 (2008): 1212–19.

9. Tilmann Betsch and Dorothee Dickenberger, "Why Do Aggressive Movies Make People Aggressive? An Attempt to Explain Short-Term Effects of the Depiction of Violence on the Observer," *Aggressive Behavior* 19, no. 2 (1993): 137–49.

SUGGESTED READING

Craig A. Anderson and Brad J. Bushman, "Effects of Violent Video Games on Aggressive Behavior, Aggressive Cognition, Aggressive Affect, Physiological Arousal, and Prosocial Behavior: A Meta-Analytic Review of the Scientific Literature," *Psychological Science* 12, no. 5 (2002): 353–59; Leonard Berkowitz et al., "The Effects of Justified and Unjustified Movie Violence on Aggression in Juvenile Delinquents," *Journal of Research in Crime and Delinquency* 11, no. 1 (1974): 16–24.

DAN L. PETERSEN

SOCIETY FOR THE PREVENTION OF CRUELTY TO CHILDREN

(SPCC). Established in 1874, the New York Society for the Prevention of Cruelty to Children (NYSPCC) represented the first organized effort to protect children from abuse and neglect.[1] Until this time, laws that had been enacted to prevent cruel and inhumane treatment protected animals, not children. This changed when Mary Ellen Wilson, a severely abused, eight-year-old girl, came to the attention of concerned citizens. The ensuing public outrage marked the "discovery" of child maltreatment.

Henry Bergh used "cruelty to animals" provisions to gain protective custody of Mary Ellen. Some ten years earlier, Bergh had founded the American Society for the Prevention of Cruelty to Animals (ASPCA).[2] Bergh's reform efforts on behalf of animals were firmly rooted in a fundamental, moral issue that crossed political, sectarian, and economic lines. Bergh relied on the same humanitarian appeal to address the plight of children.

Childhood, as a separate and protected status, is a relatively recent social development. Historically and legally, children represented chattel or property. This view, along with the short life expectancy of most children, engendered an economic and emotional "indifference" toward children.[3] Philippe Ariès notes that surviving children graduated immediately to adulthood, viewed and treated as "little adults." Social expectations and obligations forced children to work long hours in unsafe conditions. Society tolerated exploitive conditions for all adults, so children did not merit special treatment.

By the close of the nineteenth century, society assumed responsibility for the protection of children. The Society for the Prevention of Cruelty to Children (SPCC) set forth a comprehensive model for child protection and advocacy. Legislation provided for children's basic needs (food, clothing, shelter, medical care, and supervision), regulated children's employment, and restricted the sale of harmful products to minors. Other services in support of organized child protection efforts included investigations and housing for runaways or abandoned children and for maltreated children removed for their own protection. Inspections of private nurseries or foster placements prevented abuses or neglect by unscrupulous operators.

The SPCC united a cross-section of religious, humanitarian, philanthropist, political, and business activists. These reformers became the architects of the child protection and welfare reforms that continue to serve as a model throughout the nation and the world.

NOTES

1. New York Society for the Prevention of Cruelty to Children (NYSPCC), "History," NYSPCC, http://www.nyspcc.org/beta_history/index_history.htm.

2. American Society for the Prevention of Cruelty to Animals (ASPCA), "'Regarding Henry:' A 'Bergh's-Eye' View of 140 Years at the ASPCA," ASPCA, http://www.aspca.org/.

3. William Doerner and Steven Lab, *Victimology* (Newark: LexisNexis, 2008), 248.

SUGGESTED READING

Philippe Ariès, *Centuries of Childhood: A Social History of Family Life* (New York: Random House, 1965); J. Riis, "The Child-Saving Movement," in *Childhood in America*, eds. Paula S. Fass and Mary A. Mason (New York: New York University Press, 2000) 539–42; Eric A. Shelman and Stephen Lazoritz, *The Mary Ellen Wilson Child Abuse Case and the Beginning of Children's Rights in 19th Century America* (New York: McFarland & Company, 2005); American Society for the Prevention of Cruelty Animals (ASPCA), "History," ASPCA, http://www.aspca.org/.

LAURA PATTERSON

SOCIOBIOLOGY THEORY. A biological approach to the study of human behavior, sociobiology theories explain human behaviors in terms of genetics and the evolutionary process.[1] Sociobiologists maintain that culture and environmental factors alone cannot explain the totality of human behavior; therefore, they include evolutionary origins in behavioral analyses. They extend Charles Darwin's theory of natural selection (current behaviors in animals are those that enhanced their chances of survival) and apply this principle to human behavior—with controversial results.[2]

The application of this biological principle to human behavior is credited to Edward O. Wilson, the Harvard scientist who is famous for discovering the existence of pheromones. In his 1975 book, *Sociobiology: The New Synthesis,* Wilson defined sociobiology as "the systematic study of the biological basis of all social behavior."[3] The first 26 chapters of Wilson's massive book focused on the social systems of nonhuman species and were widely acclaimed, but the last chapter applied similar biological analyses to human behavior, and it sparked intense criticism.[4]

One premise of sociobiological theory incorporated the concepts of inclusive fitness and altruistic behavior. An organism can transmit its genes by either having its own offspring or by assisting relatives (who share its genes) to reproduce. Such altruism among nonhuman species is recognized, but sociobiologists extended this principle to humans as an explanation for the human tendency to favor relatives over non-relatives.[5] That is, we are more likely to protect from harm those with our same genetic makeup.

Catherine Malkin and Michael Lamb applied sociobiological principles to child abuse and neglect and predicted that children who live with a nonbiological custodian may be more at risk than the biological offspring.[6] Reciprocal altruism can then explain varying human relationships ranging from friendship to hostility.

The term *sociobiology* has given way to *evolutionary psychology*. The label became too publicly linked to the controversies of the past for researchers to continue research in evolutionary reasoning under that heading.[7]

NOTES

1. Francois Nielsen, "Sociobiology and Sociology," *Annual Review Sociology* 20 (1994): 267–303.

2. Bio-Medicine, "Sociobiological Theory," http://www.bio-medicine.org/biology-definition/Sociobiology.

3. Edward O. Wilson, *Sociobiology: The New Synthesis* (Cambridge, MA: Harvard University Press, 1975), 4.

4. Michael J. Novacek, "Lifetime Achievement: E. O. Wilson, American's Best; Science and Medicine, CNN/IME, http://www.cnn.com/SPECIALS/2001/americasbest/science.medicine/pro.eowilson.html.

5. Nielsen, "Sociobiology."

6. Catherine M. Malkin and Michael Lamb, "Child Maltreatment: A Test of Sociobiological Theory," *Journal of Comparative Family Studies* 25 (1994): 121–33.

7. Monique Borgerhoff Mulder and Carl McCabe, "Whatever Happened to Human Sociobiology?" Preprint of article appearing in *Anthropology Today* (March 28, 2006), http://www.hbes.com/HBES/mulder-AT-preprint.htm.

SUGGESTED READING

Leonard R. Brand and Ronald L. Carter, "Sociobiology: The Evolution Theory's Answer to Altruistic Behavior," *Origins* 19, no. 2 (1992): 54–71; David Sloan Wilson and Edward O. Wilson, "Rethinking the Theoretical Foundation of Sociobiology," *Quarterly Review of Biology* 82, no. 4 (2007): 327–48.

BARBARA HART

SOVEREIGN IMMUNITY. Sovereign immunity refers to the power reserved by a sovereign entity against suit in its own courts unless it expressly agrees to be sued. In the United States, sovereign immunity has been extended to both federal and state government officials and agencies.[1] The intent of sovereign immunity is to protect the government in its pursuit of legitimate responsibilities without fear of gratuitous litigation. However, immunity is not absolute; most state and federal bodies have agreed to waive the right of immunity in cases of negligence and other damages. Nonetheless, in the instance of government refusal to waive sovereign immunity, victims are left with little to no source of legal recourse. Sovereign immunity has been afforded to law enforcement agents who use excessive force or administer false arrests, prison officials who engage in abuse and even torture against detainees, and medical institution workers who do not protect residents or visitors. These diverse examples of state victimization against citizens bear witness of the suffering inflicted by state actors with no fear of being held accountable for their actions.

The case of *Petta v. Rivera*[2] provides an example of the breadth of the protection provided to government actors. In *Petta*, the Fifth Circuit denied compensation to two children (ages three and seven) victimized by a law enforcement official.[3] Even in the infamous and deadly case of the Virginia Tech shootings, the victims' families were prohibited from suing [Virginia Tech] in federal court. Their only option was to file negligence lawsuits in state court against the commonwealth of Virginia (with maximum penalties of $100,000).[4]

NOTES

1. Terence Centner, "Discerning Immunity for Government Entities: Analyzing Legislative Choices," *Review of Policy Research* 24, no. 5 (2007): 425–41.

2. *Petta v. Rivera*, 133 F.3d 330, 346–58 (5th Cir. 1998).

3. Denise Gilman, "Calling the United States' Bluff: How Sovereign Immunity Undermines the United States' Claim to an Effective Domestic Human Rights System," *Georgetown Law Journal* 95, no. 3 (2007): 591–652.

4. Sara Lipka and Amanda Foster, "Lessons from a Tragedy," *Chronicle of Higher Education* 53, no. 34 (2007): A12–A13.

SUGGESTED READING

Theodore Giuttarti, *The American Law of Sovereign Immunity: An Analysis of Legal Interpretation* (New York: Praeger, 1970).

TARA N. RICHARDS

STALKING. Stalking is the abnormal or persistent pattern of threat or unwanted pursuit directed at a specific individual. The pursuit may be physical or, in the case of cyberstalking, include the use of technology and identity theft for purposes of control. First criminalized in California, this crime is now recognized nationally and internationally as predatory in nature. Most states and countries now use a hybrid of civil and criminal sanctions that are only somewhat effective.

The victim may be a stranger, a non-stranger, or an acquaintance. The obsessive behavior may extend to the victim's family, friends, coworkers, and those who might offer support during the victimization. Stalking is maliciously calculated to frighten, cause emotional or physical harm, and control the target of the pursuit and the environment in which he or she lives and works. The obsession with the victim and the need to diminish the autonomy of the stalking victim may include verbal threats; unwanted surveillance, notes, and gifts; persistent use of technology to contact, threaten, or hamper the well being of the victim; physical or sexual assault; and homicide. In the workplace the trauma of stalking may result in loss of employment, either because of the victim's poor job performance or because the presence of the victim may pose a secondary threat to fellow employees.

Erotomania is the stalking of victims based on their employment or their status. In this instance, stalkers obsess over a constructed fantasy relationship with a high-profile victim. Madonna, Jennifer Garner, and David Letterman are victims of delusional erotomanic stalkers believing that they have a relationship with the victim or need to personally express their love to the victim. High-profile victims often employ private security to maintain their safety.

The fantasy-motivated stalker often misreads a casual "good morning" by an acquaintance as a declaration of intimacy. Consistent with this type of misinterpretation are those patients who see the care provided by a physician or nurse as a desire to establish a more intimate relationship. Similar scenarios are found in academics, counseling, and social service professions.

Stalking may be an act of revenge or retaliation for perceived wrongdoings, as in the discordant termination of a professional relationship, a marriage, an intimate relationship, or a friendship. The stalker's psychological issues may cause him to obsess about a stranger or acquaintance in which the stalker has constructed a relationship born out of fantasy and inappropriate reading of social niceties.

When the victim in any of the examples refuses the stalker, the resulting narcissistic rage leads the stalker to engage in behaviors that make the victim aware of the stalker's control and presence. The victim is aware of the stalker's persistence as a stalker often adopts a symbol or an act as a "signature." Beyond being frightening, the signature is considered by the stalker to be an intimate message of power over the victim.

Stalking victims experience psychological harm and extreme fear of physical assault and possible homicide. Most often stalkers are individuals with behavior disorders that have remained undiagnosed and untreated. Others are sociopaths who ignore the rights of the victims, as seen in domestic violence and termination of relationships. About 20% of stalkers are female, with same-sex stalking occurring as well. The stalking of potential victims of robbery, home invasion, sexual assault, or child molestation often includes calculated surveillance and casual interactions that will render the victims powerless to protect themselves or their families.

SUGGESTED READING

M. A. (Toni) DuPont-Morales, "The Female Stalker: International Perspectives and Environmental Scenarios," in *Current Issues in Victimology Research*, ed. Laura J. Moriarty and Robert A. Jerin, 2nd ed., (Durham, NC: Carolina Academic Press, 2007), 207–20; Troy McEwan, Paul E. Mullen, and Rosemary Purcell, "Identifying Risk Factors in Stalking: A Review of Current Research," *International Journal of Law Psychiatry* 30, no. 1 (2007): 1–9.

TONI DUPONT-MORALES

STATUTORY RAPE. Statutory rape is defined as a sexual act with a minor under the age of consent. Unlike other forms of rape, statutory rape typically refers to consensual sexual activity. Since the victim is not of the age of consent and is considered incapable of understanding the nature and consequences of the act, the offender is prosecuted under the presiding state's statutory rape law. Currently, the age of consent, depending on the state, ranges from 16 to 18 years of age in the United States. Even though there has been increasing media attention focusing on male statutory rape due to high-profile cases (i.e., teacher misconduct), females continue to represent the vast majority of victims; approximately 95% of all statutory rape victims are female.

Statutory rape laws are neither new nor innovative. Statutory rape laws date back to antiquity; however, such laws were not codified into English law until 1275. With the creation of the United States, these laws were simply merged into the American justice system. These laws, historically, have been used to dissuade individuals from having sex with young teenagers, in particular young females. The original logic behind statutory rape laws was the protection of "property;" however, the laws have evolved as a measure mainly to protect teenage girls from older men who psychologically manipulate their well-being, and to prevent teenage pregnancy. Although previous literature has alluded to the belief that young girls are partnering with older males, more recent studies have found that teenage girls are increasingly likely to engage in sexual relationships with teenage boys and young adult males. Statutory rape reports, however, attest that only 18% of offenders were under the age of 18; the median age difference between female victims and male offenders is approximately six years.

Age is undeniably the most influential factor in the probability of arrest and the prosecution of the offender. Victims who are 15 or younger are more likely to elicit arrests than girls 16 and older. In addition, an offender is more likely to be arrested and prosecuted if he is over the age of 18. States have begun to progressively pass more legislation enhancing the penalties for statutory rape. An increasing number of states have created mandatory minimums for offenders who are 10 or more years older than the victim. In addition, age gap provisions have been established in the majority of states. Age gap provisions establish that a statutory rape has been committed if the defendant is a specified number of years older than the victim. Hence, being a minor does not guarantee freedom from prosecution. For instance, Genarlow Wilson, who was 17 at the time of the incident, was sentenced in Georgia to a 10-year mandatory sentence for having oral sex with a 15-year-old girl. Although most states have established a four- to five-year age difference, some states maintain a two-year provision. Although Wilson's case is an example of a more punitive state law, the fact remains that having sex with a minor remains illegal.

SUGGESTED READING

Michelle Oberman, "Turning Girls into Women: Re-Evaluating Modern Statutory Rape Law," *Journal of Criminal Law and Criminology* 85, no. 1 (1994): 15–79; Karyl Troup-Leasure and Howard N. Snyder, "Statutory Rape Known to Law Enforcement," Office of Juvenile Justice and Delinquency Prevention of the U.S. Department of Justice, http://www.ncjrs.gov/pdffiles1/ojjdp/208803.pdf.

TAMMY GARLAND

STOCKHOLM SYNDROME. In August 1973, a bank in Stockholm, Sweden was robbed. During the robbery, a number of bank employees were held hostage. During the six-day hostage ordeal, instead of anger and hatred towards the robbers, some of the victims developed a sense of loyalty and devotion towards their captors. In fact, when the police attempted to intervene, some of the victim-hostages generated negative attitudes and feelings towards the police, as well as others attempting to offer assistance. Nils Bejerot, a criminologist, was one of those attempting to assist the police. It was Bejerot who coined the victim's reaction to the hostage-takers as the Stockholm Syndrome.

The Stockholm Syndrome occurs when a psychological connection develops between a victim and abuser. Furthermore, this connection is usually one of a power differential—not isolated to hostage situations. It is not uncommon for victims of domestic abuse, child abuse, elder abuse, and rape, to name a few, to develop signs and characteristics of the Stockholm Syndrome.

For example, a victim of abuse, be it physical or psychological, may experience an "emotional bond" with the abuser, including sympathy, empathy, and loyalty. Victims of abuse may also experience a sense of powerlessness and isolation. The victim's survival thereby becomes dependent upon the whim of the abuser. Identifying with the abuser serves as a defense mechanism against further abuse.

The Stockholm Syndrome is not an excuse for abuse, nor does it serve as a form of victim-blaming (i.e., blaming the victim). It merely explains a psychological phenomenon that serves to minimize the pain and suffering experienced by victims who have temporarily lost control and power in an abusive relationship.

SUGGESTED READING

Richard K. James, *Crisis Intervention Strategies*, 6th ed. (Belmont, CA: Thomson, 2008), 262, 509–10, 524; Anne Speckard et al., "Stockholm Effects and Psychological Responses to Captivity in Hostages Held by Suicide Terrorists," *Traumatology* 11 (2005): 121–40; Thomas Strentz, "The Stockholm Syndrome: Law Enforcement Policy and Ego Defenses of the Hostage," *Law Enforcement Bulletin* 48 (April, 1979): 1–11.

TOD BURKE

SUBCULTURE OF VIOLENCE. The subculture of violence theory grew out of an examination of homicide trends in Philadelphia.[1] Most of the homicide victims were young, black males from the lower class. Many of the homicides were committed over seemingly minor issues. The hypothesis used to explain this finding was that young, black males in inner cities shared a culture that supported the use of violence in a wider array of situations than would be permissible in the larger culture. The subculture of violence theory indicates that some groups of people see the use of violence as a positive and necessary trait in situations, although the general culture would not view such a reaction as appropriate.

The idea that groups of people share the belief that violence is a preferred method of conflict resolution has been tied to inner-city black males as well as young males in the southern and western United States, and also to lower-class males in general. This notion is also tied to the social construction of masculinity; some males learn that to be manly, one must be willing to use violence when challenged. Following this logic, if groups of young males respond to perceived slights with aggressive behavior, then higher rates of violent victimization would be expected where these young males are geographically concentrated. The problem of violent victimization is increased when violent incidents lead to an increase in defensive (or offensive) measures such as carrying handguns and other weapons. Such a context blurs the idea of guilty offenders and innocent victims. Instead, a series of aggressive and escalating interactions could result in either party becoming a homicide offender or victim.

Gangs are an example of a subculture of violence. Policing agencies in large cities have developed specific units to break up gangs through arrest and incarceration. The idea behind this approach is that the culture of violence can be reduced by weakening the bonds between members of that culture and removing the most violent members. However, research on the role of policing during a recent period of increased homicide trends indicated that the police did not have a significant effect on reducing violence. In fact, large numbers of arrests may have increased the destabilization of crack cocaine markets during the late 1980s and early 1990s and actually increased the homicide rates.[2]

Other public policies aimed at reducing the level of violence in inner cities include programs such as the Chicago area projects, the Boston mid-city project, and Mobilization for Youth (New York City).[3] These programs were theoretically driven and aimed to increase the number of positive role models for young males and provide opportunities for positive development. Unfortunately, the programs had only mixed success at best. Each of the programs met with political opposition and conflict among the community agencies involved.

NOTES

1. Marvin E. Wolfgang, *Patterns in Criminal Homicide* (Philadelphia, PA: University of Pennsylvania Press, 1958).

2. Benjamin Pearson-Nelson, *Understanding Homicide Trends: The Social Context of a Homicide Epidemic* (New York: LFB Scholarly Publishing, 2008).

3. Ronald L. Akers and Christine S. Sellers, *Criminological Theories: Introduction, Evaluation, and Application* (Cary, NC: Roxbury, 2003), 182–86.

SUGGESTED READING

Matthew R. Lee et al., "Revisiting the Southern Culture of Violence," *The Sociological Quarterly* 48, no. 2 (2007): 253–75; William Alex Pridemore, "A Test of Recent Sub-cultural Explanations of White Violence in the United States," *Journal of Criminal Justice* 34, no. 1 (2006): 1–16.

BENJAMIN PEARSON-NELSON

SUBINTENTIONAL DEATH. Subintentional death occurs when a person's own behavior partially or unconsciously causes his death. Examples of this type of death include a person who stops taking her medications, a depressed person who begins driving recklessly, or a person who consumes alcohol to excess on a regular basis. In addition to being self-destructive, these behaviors may make a person more vulnerable to victimization.

The person who commits a subintentional death often experiences emotions such as fear, anxiety, hate, and confusion toward his own death. People who are fearful or anxious of their deaths may try to hasten their death along in order not to worry about it any longer. Those who are confused about their own deaths may try various experimentations (such as increased drug and alcohol use, playing Russian roulette, participating in risk-taking behaviors, etc.) to alleviate the confusion by terminating their own lives. Those who have feelings of hate toward themselves may engage in self-punishing behaviors (mutilation, reckless driving, cessation of taking life-saving medications, etc.). In extreme cases, the person provokes another to kill him, for example when murderers have killed and then acted in such a way as to force law enforcement officials to use deadly force against them. This has been called "suicide by cop."

SUGGESTED READING

David Lester, "Suicidology: A Victimology Perspective," *Crisis: The Journal of Crisis Intervention and Suicide Prevention* 22, no. 3 (2001): 89–90; David Lester, *Why People Kill Themselves: A 2000 Summary of Research on Suicide*, 4th ed. (Springfield, IL: Charles C. Thomas, 2000); Mark Lindsay and David Lester, *Suicide by Cop:*

Committing Suicide by Provoking Police to Shoot You (Amityville, NY: Baywood, 2004).

ROBERT FERNQUIST

SUPPLEMENTARY HOMICIDE REPORT (SHR). The Supplementary Homicide Reports (SHRs) are part of the Federal Bureau of Investigation's Uniform Crime Reporting (UCR) Program. The UCR Program collects and publishes information on the number of crimes reported to the police each year. The UCR Program defines murder and nonnegligent manslaughter as "the willful (nonnegligent) killing of one human being by another." Excluded from this definition are deaths caused by negligence, suicides, accidents, justifiable homicides, and murder attempts. Local police departments are requested to complete a SHR for every murder that they report to the UCR Program.[1] The SHR data have been collected annually since 1961.[2]

The SHRs contain the following information about reported homicides: the jurisdiction, month, and year of occurrence; characteristics of the victim and offender including age, sex, and race; the number of offenders and victims; the type of weapon used in the murder (e.g., firearms, knives or cutting instruments, personal weapons such as hands and feet); the relationship between the victim and the offender (e.g., husband, wife, friend, acquaintance, neighbor, employee, etc.); and the circumstances surrounding the homicide (e.g., whether the murder was committed during the course of a felony such as a robbery, as part of a romantic triangle, etc.).[3]

The SHRs have several strengths. First, they provide annual national-level data on homicides. This allows researchers to study homicide trends. Second, the fact that the SHRs include the characteristics of victims and offenders permits researchers to analyze patterns in homicide and to develop policy recommendations.[4] Third, researchers have noted the "rich detail" provided on the nature of the victim-offender relationship which enables the examination of particular types of homicide, such as those that occur between intimates.[5]

Despite its strengths, the SHR also has several weaknesses. One weakness is that a SHR is not completed for every homicide that occurs in the U.S. There are several reasons for this. First, not all police departments file SHRs. In fact, according to Richard Gelles, "in some years, entire states fail to file reports."[6] Second, SHRs cannot be completed for homicides that are incorrectly classified. For instance, the police may incorrectly rule a homicide as an accident. This means that a SHR would not be completed for this homicide. Third, homicides committed on Indian reservations, military installations, and in federal prisons are not reported to the SHR.[7] Finally, any homicides that do not come to the attention of the police are not contained in the UCR or the SHRs.

A second weakness of the SHRs is missing data. One reason is that police departments may not provide complete information.[8] Another reason is because a suspect was not identified (i.e., the homicide is unsolved).[9] Without identification, police departments cannot provide information on the characteristics of the offender or classify the victim-offender relationship.

A third weakness of the SHRs is related to the types of information it solicits from police departments. Some researchers criticize the SHR forms for not asking for more information, such as the specific type of location (e.g., home, store, street).[10]

NOTES

1. Federal Bureau of Investigation, "Uniform Crime Report: Crime in the United States, 2007; Murder," http://www.fbi.gov/ucr/cius2007/documents/murdermain.pdf.

2. Lawrence A. Greenfeld et al., *Violence by Intimates: Analysis of Data on Crimes by Current or Former Spouses, Boyfriends, and Girlfriends* (Washington DC: U.S. Department of Justice, Office of Justice Programs, 1998).

3. Thomas D. Bazley and Thomas Mieczkowski, "Researching Workplace Homicide: An Assessment of the Limitations of the Supplementary Homicide Reports," *Journal of Criminal Justice* 32 (2004): 243–52; Federal Bureau of Investigation, "Uniform Crime Report."

4. Michael D. Maltz, "Bridging Gaps in Police Crime Data: A Discussion Paper from the BJS Fellows Program," http://www.ojp.usdoj.gov/bjs/pub/ascii/bgpcd.txt.

5. Greenfeld et al., *Violence by Intimates*, vii.

6. Richard J. Gelles, "Estimating the Incidence and Prevalence of Violence Against Women: National Data Systems and Sources," *Violence Against Women* 6, no. 7 (2000): 784–804, 788.

7. Bazley and Mieczkowski, "Researching Workplace Homicide."

8. Maltz, "Bridging Gaps."

9. Bureau of Justice Statistics, "Homicide Trends in the U.S.: Additional Information about the Data," http://www.ojp.usdoj.gov/bjs/homicide/addinfo.htm.

10. James A. Fox, "Missing Data Problems in the SHR: Imputing Offender and Relationship Characteristics," *Homicide Studies* 8, no. 3 (2004): 214–54.

SUGGESTED READING

Anthony A. Braga, Anne M. Piehl, and David M. Kennedy, "Youth Homicide in Boston: An Assessment of Supplementary Homicide Report Data," *Homicide Studies* 3, no. 4 (1999): 277–99; Federal Bureau of Investigation, *Uniform Crime Report: Crime in the United States, 2007: Methodology*, http://www.fbi.gov/ucr/cius2007/documents/methodology.pdf.

SHANNON A. SANTANA

SUPPORT GROUPS. When a person becomes a victim of crime, often there are psychological consequences. Many crime victims feel isolated and may develop post-traumatic stress disorder (PTSD) as a result of their victimization. The Sidran Foundation found that 49% of rape victims, 31.9% of physical assault victims, 15% of shooting or stabbing victims, and 7% of those witnessing murder are at risk for PTSD. Symptoms of PTSD include intrusive thoughts about the event, avoiding anything that might remind the victim of the event, and psychological and physical arousal which can manifest in the form of hyper vigilance, insomnia, nightmares, and irritability.[1] One method of treatment to address the effects of victimization is support groups.

There are a variety of support groups available for crime victims. Many support groups address issues related to sexual assault and domestic violence, but there are groups that focus on victims of homicide, robbery, burglary, and other crimes. Group topics will often include the identification of sources of support, dealing with the psychological symptoms of the victimization experience, and integrating their experience into their lives. Issues addressed in a sexual abuse support group can include discovering healthy sources of support, discussing the responsibility of the offender, coping with feelings of anger, loss, and guilt, and self-esteem training.[2] Groups provide support to victims through the process of communicating their story among other survivors who also share their experiences. Victims can find support groups in the community and, with the advent of technology, can now access them online.

The Office of Victims of Crime reports that many victims participate in support groups to alleviate psychological suffering as a result of their victimization. During 2005–2006,[3] 965,970 or 14% of victims received group treatment and support. This is an increase from 2003–2004, when 470,645 and 480,406[4] victims received similar group treatment, respectively. Other reports regarding the use of psychological services state that about 30% of women and 20% of men sought psychological services after stalking victimization.[5] These numbers are representative of victims who sought support through victim compensation services and do not reveal the number of crime victims who sought support through independent private practice not associated with the Office for Victims of Crimes.

The group process allows victims to share their stories, and in doing so realize they are not suffering alone. For example, one support group for domestic violence victims fostered trust and established supportive networks[6] that allowed the members an increase in their social capital. Victims of crime may have a physical disability, live in a rural area where services are limited, or desire more privacy. Online support groups allow individuals who may not be able to attend a support group to get the help they need and develop networks online.

NOTES

1. Sidran Foundation: Trauma Stress and Education Advocacy, "What is Post-Traumatic Stress Disorder?" http://www.sidran.org/sub.cfm?contentID=76&sectionid=4.

2. Crime Victim Services, "Domestic Violence Support Groups," http://www.crimevictim services.org/domviolence/supportgroup.php.

3. Office for Victims of Crime, "Report to the Nation 2007," U.S. Department of Justice, Office of Justice Programs, http://www.ojp.usdoj.gov/ovc/welcovc/reporttonation2007/welcome.html.

4. Office for Victims of Crime, "Report to the Nation 2005," U.S. Department of Justice, Office of Justice Programs, http://www.ojp.usdoj.gov/ovc/welcovc/reporttonation2005/welcome.html.

5. National Victimization Rights Week, "Overview of the Resource Guide, http://www.ojp.gov/ovc/ncvrw/2006/pdf/overview.pdf.

6. Lisa Young Larance and Maryann Lane Porter, "Observations from Practice: Support Group Membership as a Process of Social Capital Formation among Female Survivors of Domestic Violence," *Journal of Interpersonal Violence* 19, no. 5 (2004): 676–90.

SUGGESTED READING

Severin Haug, Jan Sedway, and Hans Kordy, "Group Processes and Process Evaluations in a New Treatment Setting: Inpatient Group Psychotherapy Followed by Internet-Chat," *International Journal of Group Psychotherapy* 58, no. 1 (2008): 35–53; Haim Weinberg, "Group Process and Group Phenomena on the Internet," *International Journal of Group Psychotherapy* 51, no. 3 (2001): 361–78.

DAWNA KOMOROSKY

SUPREME COURT CASES. The legal impetus for the modern victims' rights movement began in 1972 with the U.S. Supreme Court's decision in *Linda R.S.* v. *Richard D.*,[1] in which the plaintiff complained that the prosecutor's office discriminately applied a child support statute by failing to prosecute fathers of children born to unmarried women. The Court narrowly decided that a private citizen does not have a judicially cognizable interest in the prosecution or nonprosecution of another. At the same time, the Court created a legal basis for victims' rights by stating that Congress could enact statutes that provide legal rights to victims. Ten years later, the President's Task Force issued a report on the victims of crime. Since that time, various pieces of legislation and Supreme Court decisions have affected victims' right to participation in criminal justice proceedings, seek financial compensation and services (i.e., victims' access to financial resources), secure harsher sanction for perpetrations (i.e., victim impact statements), and, above all, limit the introduction of character evidence of victims in rape trials (i.e., rape shield laws).[2]

Rape Shield Laws

Rape shield laws were the result of lobbying efforts by feminist activists, lawyers, and legislators. Following the model of state rape shield laws, in 1978 the U.S. Congress enacted Rule 412 of the Federal Rules of Evidence, making it inadmissible to introduce any evidence intended to prove the victim's sexual predisposition in any civil or criminal proceeding.[3] The intent of the law was twofold: first, to ease the emotional burden of rape victims who testify in court; second, to disallow proof of prior unchastity as a character trait, from which the current consent could be inferred.[4] Current rape shield laws include victims of all sexual offenses and any evidence legislators considered might have a prejudicial effect on the victim.

Victim Impact Statements

Victim impact statements are usually introduced at the sentencing phase of a capital case as an aggravating factor, which the defendant cannot rebut. Often these statements are highly emotional, and, if the victims are articulate, tend to have a more profound impact on the sentencing authority rather than the severity of the crime. The U.S. Supreme Court decided on this issue of proportionality in *Booth,*[5] *Gathers,*[6] and *Payne,*[7] in which the defendants received the death penalty after the victim impact statement. In *Booth* v. *Maryland* (1987), the Supreme Court ruled by a five to four margin that a victim impact statement per se is unconstitutional, as it violated the Eighth Amendment's proportionality. In 1991, the Supreme Court reversed its earlier decisions in *Payne* v. *Tennessee* and shifted its focus from the Eighth Amendment to the Fourteenth Amendment's due process clause. The Fourteenth Amendment does not bar victim impact statements; thus a defendant can contest the admissibility of such statements as being unduly prejudicial to the point where the trial becomes fundamentally unfair.[8]

Sexual Harassment Issues

Title VII of the Civil Rights Act prohibits employment discrimination; however, it was not until 1981 that the Equal Employment Opportunity Commission (EEOC) forbade sexual harassment. In 1986, the U.S. Supreme Court, in *Meritor Savings Bank* v. *Vinson,*[9] held that an employer could be liable for sexual harassment committed by a supervisor if the employer knew but did not do anything to correct it. In 1993, the Court extended the protection against sexual harassment in *Harris v. Forklift Systems*[10] and ruled that a discriminatory work environment is unlawful when a reasonable person would find such an environment hostile or abusive, or when the victim subjectively perceives that the environment is abusive. More recent cases have provided protection to both genders as well as situations of same-sex harassment.

Victims' Access to Financial Resources

The first crime victim compensation program was started in 1965 in California. Today these programs are funded through fees and fines collected from those convicted of crimes, in addition to 20–25% of federal funds authorized by the Victims of Crime Act (1984). Those eligible under the program include victims of rape, assault, child sexual abuse, drunk driving, domestic violence, and the families of victims of homicide.[11] Despite the great strides achieved in this area, the Supreme Court, in *Simon & Schuster* v. *Crime Victims Board* (1991),[12] held that the New York State law that prevented convicted criminals from profiting from their crimes by publishing a book violated the First Amendment's right of free speech.

NOTES

1. *Linda R.S. v. Richard D.*, 410 U.S. 614 (1973).

2. National Crime Victim Law Institute, "History of Victims' Rights," http://www.ncvli .org/vrhistory.html.

3. Robert J. Meadows, "Rape Shield Laws: A Need for an Ethical and Legal Reexamination?" *Criminal Justice Studies* 17 (2004): 281–90.

4. Harriett R. Galvin, "Shielding Rape Victims in the State and Federal Courts: A Proposal for the Second Decade," *Minnesota Law Review* 70 (1986): 791–801.

5. *Booth v. Maryland*, 482 U.S. 496 (1987).

6. *South Carolina v. Gathers*, 490 U.S. 805 (1989).

7. *Payne v. Tennessee,* 501 U.S. 808 (1991).

8. Mark Stevens, "Victim Impact Statements Considered in Sentencing: Constitutional Concerns," *California Criminal Law Review* 2 (2000): ¶ 25, http://www.boalt.org/bjcl/v2/ v2stevens.pdf.

9. *Meritor Savings Banks v. Vinson,* 477 U.S. 57, (1986).

10. *Harris v. Forklift Systems,* 114 S. Ct. 367, 63 (1993).

11. National Association of Crime Victims Compensation Boards, "Crime Victim Compensation: An Overview," http://www.nacvcb.org/articles/Overview_prn.html.

12. *Simon & Schuster v. Crime Victims Board,* 502 U.S. 105 (1991).

SUGGESTED READING

Peggy M. Tobolowsky, *Crime Victim Rights and Remedies* (Durham, NC: Carolina Academic Press, 2001).

SESHA KETHINENI

SYMBOLIC RESTITUTION. Restitution refers to a "court-ordered sanction that involves payment of compensation by the defendant to the victim for injuries suffered as a result of the defendant's criminal act".[1] A victim may receive restitution for a number of reasons, including compensation for medical bills or lost wages, compensation to replace damaged property, or to add a punitive element to the offender's sentence. It may not always be possible, however, to repay victims for criminal offenses. Some crimes are committed against a large number of victims that individually only suffered a small amount of hardship (for example, financial crimes). Other crimes are considered "victimless" crimes, where society is the only identifiable victim (for example, drug offenses). And finally, some victims may be deceased or may refuse compensation.

Symbolic restitution seeks to provide a solution to the dilemma of paying restitution in situations where it may not be possible or beneficial, such as in the examples previously discussed. In these scenarios, substitute victims may be identified and compensated in place of the original victims. The compensation of substitute victims is symbolic restitution.[2] Examples of symbolic restitution include drug offenders sentenced to pay for drug education programs in middle schools, a convicted arsonist required to pay for a new fire truck for the community, and a violent offender funding improvements for the local nursing home after murdering an elderly couple with no family members.

NOTES

1. Harvey Wallace, *Victimology: Legal, Psychological, and Social Perspectives* (Boston: Pearson, 2007), 343.

2. Andrew Karmen, *Crime Victims: An Introduction to Victimology* (Belmont, CA: Thomson Wadsworth, 2007), 445.

SUGGESTED READING

M. Kay Harris, *Sentencing to Community Service* (Washington DC: American Bar Association, 1979).

SUZANNE GODBOLDT

T

TARGET HARDENING. Target hardening is a concept that is closely associated with crime prevention through environmental design (CPTED). Target hardening refers to the process by which criminal opportunities can be reduced through the incorporation of specific types of structural design elements and security features.[1] The concept of target hardening is based upon the assumption that criminal offenders will be deterred when it becomes more difficult to successfully complete a criminal act. The difficulty associated with a criminal act can be increased through design features and the use of physical security barriers, such as strengthened building materials, reinforced locks, lighting, and alarm systems.[2] Empirical evaluations have found that target hardening can reduce criminal offending, but that some types of target hardening are more effective than others.[3]

NOTES

1. Ronald V. Clarke, "Situational Crime Prevention: Its Theoretical Basis and Practical Scope," in *Crime and Justice: An Annual Review of Research*, vol. 4, eds. Michael Tonry and Norval Morris (Chicago: University of Chicago Press, 1983), 225–56.

2. Ibid.

3. Lawrence W. Sherman et al., *Preventing Crime: What Works, What Doesn't, What's Promising* (Washington DC: National Institute of Justice, 1998).

SUGGESTED READING

Paul J. Brantingham and Patricia L. Bratingham, eds. *Environmental Criminology* (Prospect Heights, IL: Waveland, 1991); Timothy Crowe, *Crime Prevention Through Environmental Design: Applications of Architectural Design and Space Management Concepts*, 2nd ed. (Burlington, MA: Elseview, 2000); C. Ray Jeffery, *Crime Prevention Through Environmental Design* (Thousand Oaks, CA: Sage, 1971); Oscar Newman, *Defensible Space: People and Design in the Violent City* (New York: MacMillan, 1973).

JASON JOLICOEUR

TERRORISM. Until the bombing of the Alfred P. Murrah building in Oklahoma City in 1995, "victims of terrorism" was a concept in America largely limited to those with relatives in Ireland or a few other countries. At this time, the influence of international terrorism was minimal even though the first attack on the World Trade Center had occurred two years prior. Most of the focus on terrorism prior to the turn of the twenty-first century was on domestic terrorist groups, and their victims were usually facilities such as gas pipelines. Following the second attack on the World Trade Center in 2001, the concept of being a victim of terrorism in the United States changed permanently.

There are two primary forms of terrorism—domestic and international. Domestic terrorism involves groups from within a country carrying out actions against that country, while international terrorism involves groups travelling to other countries for the actions, or attacking international targets within their own country. These distinctions are not related, however, to the type of attacks or their damage. The Irish Republican Army was a domestic terrorist group that carried out many devastating attacks and gained international attention. Typically, however, it is the international groups (the most famous currently being Al Qaeda) that cause the most concern for victims.

The principle goal of terrorism is to make change in a government (either a policy change or a complete overthrow) by turning public support against the government. The attacks may range from damaging whaling boats to massive bombs that kill hundreds of people. The nature of terrorism means that victims must be a part of the action (a government victim, a corporate victim, or people).

The primary influence of terrorism is to make people fear being victimized, and thus change their behavior. This was shown in the weeks following 9/11, when people were afraid to fly—and the U.S. government was afraid for people to fly. This fear changed the behavior of the people and thus changed the behavior of the government.

Often, the change in government from terrorism is not what the terrorist group wanted. For example, Al Qaeda's stated goal was for the United States to remove troops from the Middle East (particularly Saudi Arabia). The result was a massive increase in U.S. troops in the Middle East and the invasion of Afghanistan and

Iraq. As in this example, it is common for terrorist acts to be met with increased security. Victims and potential victims of terrorism have a heightened fear and want increased security. This typically comes in the form of increased security at places most vulnerable to attack. For example, airline security is almost always increased as a response to terrorism. As more bombings and attacks on hotels occur, it is likely security will be increased around them.

SUGGESTED READING

David Miers, "Rebuilding Lives: Operational and Policy Issues in the Compensation of Victims of Violent and Terrorist Crimes," *Criminal Law Review* August (2006): 695–721; Arvind Verma, "Terrorist Victimization: A Case Study from India," *International Journal of Offender Therapy and Comparative Criminology* 25 (2001): 183.

JEFF WALKER

THIRD-PARTY LIABILITY. Crime victims seek civil redress from business or property owners if it is proven that the owner was negligent in protecting them from criminal attack while they were on the property. In many instances, intruders entering property such as parking lots, schools, or other business establishments commit crimes because of opportunity. Whether the actual culprit is apprehended or not, the business or property owner may be liable for damages inflicted upon the victim. This is referred to as third-party liability. While owners and property managers are not the people who actually committed the crime, courts have ruled that the business or property conditions contributed to the factors that allowed the crime or crimes to occur by allowing certain conditions to exist.

In third-party lawsuits, the victim must establish that (1) the defendant (property owner) owed a legal duty to protect, but (2) breached that duty or failed to protect, and (3) the breach was the primary cause of the injury to the victim (the failure to protect was linked to the injury). It does not matter whether the owner or manager had knowledge or not of the security conditions; all that is necessary is to show that there was a foreseeable harm and that the owner or manager should have known of such dangers or conditions.

There are a number of cases where business and other properties have been liable as third-party defendants. The following are examples:

- In 2008, most families of victims of the mass shootings at Virginia Tech in 2007 agreed to an $11 million state settlement that will compensate families who lost loved ones, pay survivors' medical costs, and avoid a court battle. Seung-Hui Cho, a mentally disturbed student, killed 32 victims and wounded two at Virginia Tech on April 16, 2007, before committing suicide. The university officials were criticized for waiting about two hours before informing students and employees about the first shootings, which police initially thought were an act of domestic violence.

- A nurse was arriving for work at a hospital when she was abducted and sexually assaulted. The nurse sued the hospital for inadequate security, claiming that the facility had no perimeter security, no lot attendant, and no security guards, and that there was inadequate monitoring of CCTV cameras. The jury awarded the plaintiff $400,000.

Many of these civil suits are sending a message to public and private institutions about their liability for potential damages. Actions against third parties have been credited with changing security and safety practices in a number of businesses and institutions.

SUGGESTED READING

Department of Justice, "Civil Legal Remedies for Crime Victims," http://library.findlaw .com/1999/Mar/4/126733.html; The National Crime Victim Bar Association, "Helping Crime Victims Pursue Civil Justice," http://www/ncvc.org/vb/main.aspx?dbID= DB_CaseLaw495.

ROBERT J. MEADOWS

U

UNFOUNDING. Police officers possess a great amount of discretion, including unfounding an incident. Unfounding occurs when a police officer determines there is insufficient evidence that a crime has occurred, therefore an official crime report is unwarranted. As a result, unfounding may impact the victim.

There are a number of reasons why an officer may "unfound" an incident. First, when an officer arrives at a location, she must determine if a crime has occurred. Insufficient evidence of a crime results in unfounding the case. The victim often fails to understand the necessary elements of a crime and becomes confused and upset by the inaction of the officer. Informing the victim by the officer may serve to aid in a better understanding.

Second, the officer may determine there is insufficient evidence for a criminal conviction, bypassing the written report. The officer should consult with the district attorney prior to making this determination, and inform the victim as to the reasoning of the unfounding to prevent further misunderstanding.

Third, the officer may "unofficially" categorize the incident as "too minor to file an official report." This may be due to officer workload issues (e.g., "I should be concentrating on more serious crimes").

Fourth, officer bias may play a role in unfounding an incident. For example, this may occur when the victim facilitates her own victimization (e.g., a prostitute getting robbed).

Fifth, the officer may rationalize the incident (e.g., "Everybody smokes marijuana, so why bother writing a report?"). Since the victim reported the crime, the victim does not understand the lack of officer interest. While there may be nothing the officer can say to make amends to the victim, perhaps victim understanding of the reasoning behind the unfounding may suffice.

SUGGESTED READING

Jeffrey A. Bouffard, "Predicting Type of Sexual Assault Closure from Victim, Suspect, and Case Characteristics," *Journal of Criminal Justice* 28, no. 6 (2000): 527–42; Samuel Walker and Charles Katz, *Police in America*, 4th ed. (New York, NY: McGraw Hill, 2002), 164–66.

TOD BURKE

UNIFORM CRIME REPORT (UCR). The Uniform Crime Report (UCR) is an annual report assembled by the Federal Bureau of Investigation (FBI). In 1929, The International Association of the Chiefs of Police recommended this report format as a means of standardizing the measurement of criminal activity. In 1930, the FBI was charged with gathering, measuring, and assessing the nation's crime in the form of its annual report. Currently over 17,000 local, state, and federal law enforcement agencies voluntarily submit crime statistics for inclusion in the FBI database.

The UCR utilizes standardized definitions of criminal behavior, as provided within their guidebook, and collects information on the following offenses:

Part I (index offenses): homicide (murder and non-negligent manslaughter), forcible rape, robbery, aggravated assault, burglary, larceny-theft, auto theft, and arson.

Part II (other offenses): other assaults, forgery and counterfeiting, fraud, embezzlement, stolen property (buying, receiving, possessing), vandalism, weapons (carrying, possession), prostitution and commercialized vice, sex offenses, drug abuse violations, gambling, offenses against the family and children, driving under the influence, liquor laws, drunkenness, disorderly conduct, vagrancy, all other offenses (with exception of those previously listed and traffic offenses), suspicion, curfew and loitering laws, and juvenile runaways.

The UCR has been criticized for its neglect to gather or provide detailed information on or statistics regarding victims of crime. The UCR provides information on the criminal act but it does not gather or report extensive information on crime victims. The UCR also evidences definitional bias. For example, male victims of rape have been excluded because rape has historically been defined as "the carnal knowledge of a female forcibly and against her will." Similarly, the UCR is solely compiled on the basis of crimes that are reported to the police, leaving the dimension of criminal activity that is not reported to authorities unaccounted for (known as the "dark figure" of crime).

Neglect of victimization also occurs in the UCR classification and scoring system, or what is termed the Hierarchy Rule. The rule states that if more than one

Part I offense has occurred, only the most serious will be reported. For example, if an individual was a victim of forcible rape, robbery, and assault, only the charge of rape would be reported (homicide, motor vehicle theft, and arson are exceptions to the Rule). Lastly, the UCR does not measure corporate, occupational, or computer crime, neglecting crime for which individuals are most likely to become the victim.

SUGGESTED READING

Bureau of Justice Statistics, "The Nation's Two Crime Measures," U.S. Department of Justice, http://www.ojp.usdoj.gov/bjs/pub/html/ntcm.htm; Federal Bureau of Investigation, *Uniform Crime Reporting Handbook: Revised 2004* (Washington DC: U.S. Department of Justice, 2004); Federal Bureau of Investigation, "Uniform Crime Reports," http://www.fbi.gov/ucr/ucr.htm; Michael D. Maltz, "Crime Statistics: A Historical Perspective," *Crime & Delinquency* 23, no. 1 (1977): 32–40.

ALANA VAN GUNDY-YODER

V

VICARIOUS VICTIMIZATION. Vicarious victimization is characterized by the psychological, behavioral, and physiological impact of observing or learning of the violence or crime perpetrated upon others. Vicarious victimization has been used to explain the nature, extent, and causes of fear of crime in communities and among various multicultural groups with a history of victimization.[1] For example, V. Paul Poteat and Dorothy Espelage have used the term to describe the fear and traumatic stress that occurs in gay and lesbian students when homophobic victimization of some students occurs.[2] James Garofalo used the term to describe a model of determinants of the fear of crime.[3] He found that the fear of crime is not simply a function of risk or actual experiences as a crime victim. Others found evidence of vicarious victimization in children who witnessed violence in the home even when they were not directly abused.[4] Victimization symptoms have also been found in adults not directly affected by terrorist attacks in the Oklahoma City Bombing[5] and the New York City September 11th terrorist attacks.[6] Research on national samples in the United States also revealed that three to five days after the September 11th attack, 44% of Americans reported at least one symptom of post-traumatic stress disorder.[7] The crimes of serial rapists and serial murders are commonly believed to vicariously produce fear and anxiety on the part of people who live in communities impacted by such crimes.[8]

NOTES

1. Min S. Lee and Jeffery T. Ulmer, "Fear of Crime Among Korean Americans in Chicago Communities," *Criminology* 38, no. 4 (2006): 1173–206.

2. V. Paul Poteat and Dorothy L. Espelage, "Predicting Psychosocial Consequences of Homophobic Victimization in Middle School Students," *The Journal of Early Adolescence* 27, no. 2 (2007): 175–91.

3. James Garofalo, "Victimization and the Fear of Crime," *Journal of Research in Crime and Delinquency* 16, no. 1 (1979): 80–97.

4. K. L. Kilpatrick, M. Litt, and L. M. Williams, "Posttraumatic Stress Disorder in Child Witnesses to Domestic Violence," *American Journal of Orthopsychiatry* 67 (1997): 639–44.

5. Ginny Sprang, "Vicarious Stress: Patterns of Disturbance and Use of Mental Health Services by Those Indirectly Affected by the Oklahoma City Bombing," *Psychological Reports* 89, no. 2 (2001): 331–38.

6. Amy L. Ai et al., "The Traumatic Impact of the September 11, 2001, Terrorist Attacks and the Potential Protection of Optimism," *Journal of Interpersonal Violence* 21, no. 5 (2006): 689–700.

7. Mark A. Schuster et al., "A National Survey of Stress Reactions After the September 11, 2001, Terrorist Attacks," *New England Journal of Medicine* 345, no. 20 (2002): 1507–12.

8. Michael J. Herkov and Monica Biernat, "Assessment of PTSD Symptoms in a Community Exposed to Serial Murder," *Journal of Clinical Psychology* 53, no. 8 (1997): 809–15.

SUGGESTED READING

Sandro Galea et al., "Psychological Sequelae of the September 11 Terrorist Attacks in New York City," *New England Journal of Medicine*, Special Report 346 (2002): 982–87; J. Joseph, "Fear of Crime Among Black Elderly," *Journal of Black Studies* 27, no. 5 (1997): 698–717.

DAN L. PETERSEN

VICTIM BILL OF RIGHTS. By the 1970s, a victim rights movement had emerged in this country designed to provide a greater role for and recognition of crime victims in the criminal justice process. One of the goals of the victim rights movement has been the establishment of constitutional rights for victims of crime.[1] The most prominent initial support for this goal occurred in 1982 when the President's Task Force on Victims of Crime, convened by President Ronald Reagan, endorsed the amendment of the Sixth Amendment to the United States Constitution. In addition to the offender rights related to criminal prosecutions contained in the Sixth Amendment, the President's Task Force proposed a requirement that victims in criminal prosecutions have the right to be present and heard at all "critical stages" of judicial proceedings.[2] Although several constitutional amendment proposals regarding crime victim rights have been introduced in Congress since the President's Task Force made its recommendation, there has not yet been sufficient congressional support for an amendment to warrant a congressional vote.[3] Instead, Congress has enacted a variety of statutes designed to codify the rights of crime victims in the federal criminal justice system.[4]

Similarly, legislatures in every state have enacted some type of legislation regarding crime victim rights, and most states have additional statutes concerning victim restitution, compensation, and services.[5] Moreover, beginning with California in 1982, a majority of states adopted constitutional provisions affording constitutional status to a variety of crime victim rights. Currently, 33 states have such constitutional provisions.[6]

These constitutional provisions vary in scope. Of the 33 states with constitutional provisions, 29 states include some requirement of victim notification of criminal justice proceedings. Fewer states require victim notification of specified outcomes in the proceedings, such as an offender's arrest, release, escape, or conviction. Thirty-one states include a general or conditional victim right to be present at court proceedings or criminal justice proceedings. Twenty-eight states also include general or specific provisions that afford a victim the right to be heard regarding sentencing; fewer than 20 states have such general or specific provisions that encompass a victim's right to be heard regarding pleas or plea proceedings or parole release proceedings. Twenty states include a right to restitution in their constitutional provisions. Over 20 states provide a general victim right to respect, dignity, or fairness. Over 10 states include a victim constitutional right to a speedy disposition, consideration of victim safety, or both in their provisions. Only a few states provide any remedies for victim rights violations in their constitutional provisions. To the contrary, most states expressly preclude any cause of action or challenges to or changes in the results of proceedings due to victim rights violations.[7]

NOTES

1. Peggy M. Tobolowsky, *Crime Victim Rights and Remedies* (Durham, NC: Carolina Academic Press, 2001), 7–11.

2. President's Task Force on Victims of Crime, *Final Report* (Washington DC: GPO, 1982), 114–15; LeRoy L. Lamborn, "Victim Participation in the Criminal Justice Process: The Proposals for a Constitutional Amendment," *Wayne Law Review* 34 (1987): 125–28.

3. Victoria Schwartz, "Recent Development: The Victims' Rights Amendment," *Harvard Journal on Legislation* 42 (2005): 525–33.

4. E.g., 18 U.S.C.A. § 3771 (West Supp. 2008); Tobolowsky, *Crime Victim Rights*, 10–11.

5. Tobolowsky, *Crime Victim Rights*, 11.

6. Ibid, 205–26.

7. Ibid, 25–26, 45, 68–69, 84, 105, 114–15, 128, 205–26.

SUGGESTED READING

Douglas E. Beloof, "The Third Wave of Crime Victims' Rights: Standing, Remedy, and Review." *Brigham Young University Law Review* 2005 (2005): 255–370; U.S. Department of Justice, Office for Victims of Crime, *New Directions from the Field: Victims' Rights and Services for the 21st Century* (Washington DC: GPO, 1998).

PEGGY TOBOLOWSKY

VICTIM DISCOUNTING. Victim discounting refers to tendencies in the criminal justice system to punish those convicted of crimes against minority group members less severely than those who commit crimes against white victims. Using the application of the death penalty as an example of victim discounting, numerous studies show that homicide defendants are more likely to be sentenced to death if their victims were white rather than black. In fact, the Death Penalty Information Center reports that since 1977, about 80% of the people executed for capital murder were convicted of killing white victims, even though blacks and whites were the victims of murder in almost equal numbers.

Although the uneven exercise of the death penalty is the most extreme form of victim discounting, research on capital justice offers clear and consistent findings. Christina Swarns, as well as David Baldus, Charles Pulaski, and George Woodworth, identify several points at which racial bias infects the death penalty system. For one, chief prosecutors, who are overwhelmingly white, make critical decisions in the administration of the death penalty and are likely to assess cases, in part, according to the race of the victim. In fact, between 1995 and 2000, U.S. attorneys sought the death penalty for black defendants accused of murdering nonblack victims almost twice as often as they did for black defendants accused of killing black victims. In addition, juries appear to tolerate increased levels of aggravation before imposing the death penalty in cases involving a black victim as compared to cases with a white victim. Swarns asserts that in terms of the death penalty, "blackness is a proxy for worthlessness."[1]

In 1972, the U.S. Supreme Court declared the death penalty unconstitutional because it was imposed disproportionately on the poor, African Americans, and members of unpopular groups. The Court reviewed and reinstated the death penalty in 1976, concluding that race and class no longer played a pivotal role in its administration. Because evidence suggested that racial injustice continued to play a significant role in capital murder cases, Supreme Court Justice Harry Blackmun wrote in opposition to the death penalty in *Callins v. Collins*, stating "[E]ven under the most sophisticated death penalty statutes, race continues to play a major role in determining who shall live and who shall die."[2]

The unease over discrepancies in the application of the death penalty reflects a broader concern that victim discounting is pervasive in the criminal justice system. The fact that nationwide research indicates that the race and the ethnicity of the victim unduly affects the treatment of criminal offenders lends support to the claim that victim discounting continues to have an impact on the administration of justice.

NOTES

1. Christina Swarns, "The Uneven Scales of Capital Justice: How Race and Class Affect Who Ends Up on Death Row," *American Prospect* July (2004): A14.

2. *Callins v. Collins*, 510 US 1141 (1994).

SUGGESTED READING

David C. Baldus, Charles Pulaski, and George Woodworth, "Comparative Review of Death Sentences: An Empirical Study of the Georgia Experience," *Journal of Criminal Law and Criminology* 74, no. 3 (1983): 661–753; David Cole, *No Equal Justice: Race and Class in the American Criminal Justice System* (New York: New Press, 2000); Death Penalty Information Center Web site, http://www.deathpenaltyinfo.org.

DOUGLAS F. GEORGE

VICTIM IMPACT PANELS. A victim impact panel (VIP) is a forum for crime victims to tell their personal stories of criminal victimization to an audience of offenders. Panelists are typically adult speakers who describe the crime and its subsequent impact on their and loved ones' lives—physically, financially, emotionally, spiritually, mentally, and socially. Panel proponents believe that hearing the first-hand experiences of crime victims told in non-confrontational ways may enhance the awareness of offenders as to the potential for harm beyond the direct consequences meted out by the criminal justice system.

Panels are generally imbedded in the criminal justice system; offender participation is often a component of probation. As compared to other criminal justice responses, VIPs are relatively inexpensive and, by incorporating victims, are seen by many as promoting restorative justice principles.

The first victim impact panels were the brainchild of Judge David Admire of Redmond, Washington, who met Shirley Anderson while campaigning for election. Shirley, whose son Mark had been killed by a drunk driver, asked David his plans for dealing with those charged with DUI and some months after taking office, Judge Admire contacted Shirley to see if she and other drunk driving victims would be interested in sharing their stories with a group of drunk driving offenders. The first panel took place September 1983, and as word of the initiative spread, David and Shirley co-authored a booklet, *The Offender Meets the Victim*, to guide other communities interested in developing a panel program.

By the mid 1980s, the national office of Mothers Against Drunk Driving (MADD) had developed a detailed how-to guide and accompanying videotape in response to widespread interest in the program. A grant enabled MADD to expand the panel concept into juvenile correctional facilities, and other victim services organizations began experimenting with panels made up of victims of other types of crimes.

Today victim impact panel attendance is a standard component for first-time DUI offenders in many jurisdictions, and similar panel programs are utilized in other criminal justice contexts including prisons, treatment programs, and defensive driving classes. In addition to victims/survivors of drunk driving crashes, some DUI impact panels also include first responders such as police officers or EMTs, criminal justice professionals such as judges or probation officers, and reformed drunk driving offenders.

Research as to the efficacy of panels on subsequent offender attitudes and behavior has been limited. Some studies have found a modest reduction in subsequent offending, but others have found no difference among offenders who attended a VIP as compared to those who did not. Research published by MADD as to the benefit of panel participation for the panelists themselves suggest that positive benefits reported by panelists are supported by psychological testing and that as compared to non-panelist victims, panelists have higher measures of various positive outcomes.

SUGGESTED READING

Dorothy Mercer, Rosanne Lorden, and Janice Harris Lord, "Victim Impact Panels: A Healing Opportunity for Victims of Drunk Driving Crashes," *MADDVOCATE* (Winter, 1999): 8–9; Dean G. Rojek, James E. Coverdill, and Stuart W. Fors, "The Effect of Victim Impact Panels on DUI Rearrest Rates: A Five-Year Follow-Up," *Criminology* 41, no. 4 (2003): 1319–40.

STEPHANIE FROGGE

VICTIM IMPACT STATEMENT. Victim impact statements allow victims or the families of victims to express the details and impact of the victimization to the court. Originally, this was an area of contention, especially for those cases in which the victim was murdered. In the *Booth v. Maryland*[1] case of 1987, the United States Supreme Court stated that victim impact statements violate the Eight Amendment because evidence of harm inflicted on a deceased victim and the resulting harm to the family is arbitrary evidence and sways the verdict in the punishment phase of a capital crime so drastically that it can be deemed cruel and unusual punishment. Later, in the 1989 case of *South Carolina v. Gathers*,[2] the Supreme Court expounded upon the earlier decision made in *Booth* and decided that prosecutors are not allowed to present testimony or make comments in regard to victims' characteristics.

In the 1991 case of *Payne v. Tennessee*,[3] the Supreme Court held that it was constitutionally valid to allow victim impact statements to be made during the sentencing phase of capital crimes. In other words, victims could testify in regard to the impact and harm that the crime has had on their lives. If the case is a murder trial, then the family members of the deceased victim are given an opportunity to speak on behalf of the harm inflicted on the victim and the effect it has had on the members of the family as well. The ruling in *Payne* effectively overturned the previous decisions made in *Booth* and *Gathers*. Furthermore, the case of *Mosley v. State*[4] in 1998 found that victim impact statements were admissible as a rebuttal when the defense introduced evidence or testimony implying mitigating circumstances but did not speak to their validity in the punishment phase of the trial.

Despite the acceptance of victim impact statements in most states, they are not always used. Although some victims want to be highly involved in their case, some avoid making impact statements because it is a traumatizing experience that makes them relive the incidence and revictimizes them. In capital murder cases, it is common practice that families will make impact statements. However, administrators of criminal justice do not allow the admissibility of victim impact statements in some jurisdictions and for certain hearings.

Victim advocates claim that victim impact statements and victim involvement in the criminal justice processing of their case will enhance their view of substantive and procedural justice.[5] However, some researchers have found that the use of victim impact statements did not increase satisfaction with the criminal justice system or match victims' expectations of involvement in their case.[6] Laura Moriarty argues that although victim participation in the form of victim impact statements may only cause modest effects in satisfaction with the system, victims should be allowed to give a statement. If the victim impact statement option is denied to victims, their dissatisfaction with the criminal justice system would most likely increase.[7]

NOTES

1. *Booth v. Maryland*, 482 U.S. 496 (1987).

2. *South Carolina v. Gathers*, 490 U.S. 805 (1989).

3. *Payne v. Tennessee*, 111 U.S. 2597 (1991).

4. *Mosley v. State*, 983 S.W. 2d 249 (1998).

5. Edna Erez, "Who's Afraid of the Big Bad Victim? Victim Impact Statements as Victim Empowerment and Enhancement of Justice," *Criminal Law Review* (1999): 546–56.

6. Edna Erez, Leigh Roeger, and Frank Morgan, "Victim Harm, Impact Statements, and Victim Satisfaction with Justice," *International Review of Victimology* 5 (1997): 37–60.

7. Laura J. Moriarty, "Victim Participation at Parole Hearings: Balancing Victim, Offender, and Public Interest," *Criminology & Public Policy* 4, no. 2 (2005): 385–90.

SUGGESTED READING

Trina M. Gordon and Stanley L. Brodsky, "The Influence of Victim Impact Statements," *Journal of Forensic Psychology Practice* 7, no. 2 (2007): 45–52; Jennifer K. Wood, "Balancing Innocence and Guilt: A Metaphorical Analysis of the U.S. Supreme Court's Rulings on Victim Impact Statements," *Western Journal of Communication* 69, no. 2 (2005): 129–46.

MELINDA R. YORK

VICTIM INFORMATION AND NOTIFICATION EVERYDAY (VINE).

In December of 1993, on the day of her twenty-first birthday, Mary Byron was violently murdered by her ex-boyfriend, Donavan Harris, whom she believed was still in jail. Byron was unaware that Harris had been released on bail for charges of raping, assaulting, and stalking her a few weeks earlier. Harris confronted Byron in the parking lot of a local mall, where he shot her seven times. The criminal justice system failed to notify Byron of Harris's release even though they promised to do so.

Byron's violent murder spurred the creation of the Mary Byron Foundation, a public charity designed to stop domestic violence and fund innovative approaches to keeping victims safe. This foundation, based in Louisville, Kentucky, began looking for ways to notify victims when offenders were released from custody, and partnered with Appriss Inc. to implement new technology. What resulted was the creation of the Victim Information and Notification Everyday (VINE) system.

VINE is an automated process to notify and inform victims and other concerned individuals about the current status of offenders. VINE users can register to receive immediate notice when an offender escapes, transfers, or has been released from custody. Users of this system can choose to receive notices over the telephone or through e-mail. The VINE system also offers 24-hour technical support so victims can speak directly with a live operator if that need arises. The VINE system interfaces with jail and prison booking systems. When these systems indicate a change in a particular offender's status, a notification is triggered in the VINE system, causing an immediate notice to be sent out to all users who are registered for that offender. Notices continue until the victim enters a four-digit personal identification number (PIN) that is established at the time of registration. The purpose of the PIN is to ensure that the victim registered to receive the notification is in fact the person who received it.

While Kentucky was the first state to utilize the VINE system, now over two-thirds of the nation is using it to keep victims informed about offenders. Victim notification is a right protected by the constitution in many states. VINE helps to satisfy this legislative requirement. Appriss Inc., the largest criminal justice database in the nation, handles approximately 13 million offender transactions every month, resulting in nearly 700,000 monthly notification calls by VINE.

For more information about the VINE system, log onto http://www.vinelink .com or call Appriss Inc. at 1-866-APPRISS.

SUGGESTED READING

David Beatty and Trudy Gregorie, "Implementing Victims' Rights: Why Corrections Professionals Should Care," *Corrections Today Magazine* 65, no. 5 (2003): 78–82; Jo-Anne M. Wemmers, "Victim Notification and Public Support for the Criminal Justice System," *International Review of Victimology* 6, no. 3 (1999): 167–78.

KARLA BECK

VICTIMIZATION TRENDS. The most comprehensive source of information for victimization trends in the United States comes from the Bureau of Justice Statistics' (BJS) National Crime Victimization Survey (NCVS). The NCVS was designed to collect detailed data on crime victims and the consequences of crime. The advantage of the NCVS over the Federal Bureau of Investigation's (FBI) Uniform Crime Reporting Program (UCR) is that the NCVS provides a better picture of victimization rates, since it includes crimes that were not reported to the police.

The NCVS has been collecting annual data from a nationally representative sample since 1972.[1] Currently, approximately 76,000 households are surveyed, which accounts for around 135,000 individuals. Anyone in the household over the age of 12 is eligible for interviewing. People who participate in the survey are asked a series of questions to determine if they have been victimized by any of the following crimes: rape, sexual assault, robbery, assault, theft, household burglary, or motor vehicle theft. Crime victims are questioned about the frequency of victimization and the impact the crime had on their lives. The NCVS divides crimes into two categories: violent crimes and property crimes.

An annual distribution of categories of victimizations provides an illustration of the relative proportions of different kinds of victimizations. For example in 2006, U.S. residents age 12 or older were victimized by approximately 25 million crimes. Of these crimes, 1% were personal theft, 75% were property crimes, and 24% were violent crimes.[2]

Most victimizations are minor crimes. In 2006 the rate of serious violent crime victimizations per 1,000 people was: one rape, two assaults that included injury to the victim, three robberies, and 0.006 homicides (or around six victims per 100,000 people).[3]

Overall, violent victimization trends began a steep decline in 1994 and are now at a historically low point. However, the NCVS indicates that violent victimization varies by demographic category and that overall trends can mask the victimization rates of different groups. The NCVS provides publicly available data on the following categories: age, race, ethnicity, gender, annual household income, and marital status. Violent victimization includes: murder (which is drawn from the UCR), rape and sexual assault, robbery, and assault.

Younger Americans are more likely to be violently victimized than older Americans. The age groups most likely to be victimized are between 12 and 24 years. After age 24, there is a decline in the likelihood of victimization of various age groups. For example, in the year 2005 people age 12 to 15 had a rate of 44 violent crimes per 1,000, while those over 65 had a rate of just over two (2.4) per 1,000.[4]

Comparing the violent victimization rates of blacks and whites reveals that since 1973 black rates of violent victimization have generally been about twice the rates of white.[5] Between 2001 and 2005, the violent victimization rate of Native Americans was more than twice the rate of blacks and five times greater than the rate of Asians, who have the lowest rates.[6]

Males are much more likely to be violently victimized than females. From 1973 until 1991, males were about twice as likely to be victimized; however, since 1991 victimization rates by gender have grown closer. The most recent data indicate that males have victimization rates about 50% higher than females.[7]

Indigent Americans are more likely to be violently victimized than affluent Americans. In 2006, the rate of aggravated assaults for households with incomes less than $7,500 was 13 per 1,000, while the rate for incomes of $75,000 or greater was three per 1,000.[8] In the same year, divorced or separated people experienced slightly higher rates of violent victimization than other marital status categories.[9]

Property crime victimizations in the NCVS include: burglary, motor vehicle theft, and property theft. The elderly are disproportionately affected by property crimes. Between 1993 and 2002, more than nine out of ten crimes against those 65 and older were property crimes, while only four out of ten crimes against those aged 12 to 24 were property crimes.[10]

In 2006 the property crime rate was 212 per 1,000 for Hispanic households, 186 per 1,000 for black households, and 157 per 1,000 for white households. Also in 2006, motor vehicle theft rates per 1,000 households were 15 for blacks, 13 for Hispanics, and seven for whites.

The indigent are disproportionately affected by property crime. In 2006 the rate per 1,000 households for burglary was 56 for household incomes below $7,500 and 22 for household incomes of $75,000 or more.

NOTES

1. Bureau of Justice Statistics, "Crime and Victim Statistics," http://www.ojp.usdoj.gov/bjs/cvict.htm#Programs.

2. Bureau of Justice Statistics, "Criminal Victimization," http://www.ojp.usdoj.gov/bjs/cvictgen.htm.

3. Ibid.

4. Bureau of Justice Statistics, "Violent Victimization Rates by Age," http://www.ojp.usdoj.gov/bjs/glance/tables/vagetab.htm.

5. Bureau of Justice Statistics, "Victim Characteristics," http://www.ojp.usdoj.gov/bjs/cvict_v.htm.

6. Ibid.

7. Bureau of Justice Statistics, "Violent Victimization Rates by Gender," http://www.ojp.usdoj.gov/bjs/glance/tables/vsxtab.htm.

8. Bureau of Justice Statistics, "Victim Characteristics."

9. Ibid.

10. Ibid.

SUGGESTED READING

Kathleen J. Ferraro, *Neither Angels Nor Demons: Women, Crime, and Victimization* (Boston, MA: Northeastern University Press, 2006); Terance D. Miethe and Robert F. Meier, *Crime and Its Social Context: Toward an Integrated Theory of Offenders, Victims, and Situations* (Albany, NY: State University of New York Press, 1994).

BENJAMIN PEARSON-NELSON

VICTIMLESS CRIMES. Victimless crimes are those that do not directly harm other persons or their property. The contemporary interest in victimless crimes in the United States can be traced to Edwin Schur's 1965 treatment of the subject.[1] Crimes such as abortion, homosexuality, and drug addiction were included as central examples. Other crimes that have been identified as victimless include euthanasia, gambling, prostitution, pornography, public nudity, public drunkenness, drunk driving, seatbelt laws, and status crimes (crimes charged against juveniles that would not be crimes for adults, such as truancy or curfew violations).

The debate over victimless crimes revolves around the harm caused by such behavior. Those who oppose laws against victimless crimes argue that these laws waste public resources and enforce the moral rules of a limited population against everyone. Laws should instead focus more narrowly on the protection of people and property. The private and consensual actions of citizens should be allowed, as long as no one is harmed. Finally, the criminal justice response to victimless crimes causes more damage to individuals and society than the original behavior.

For example, marijuana users can be incarcerated and labeled as felons, which is more damaging than the effects of using the drug.

Those who support laws against victimless crimes argue that such behavior does harm others. The harm to others can include a general decline in the quality of community life and also a more direct effect on those who are close to the offender. For example, the family of someone who is addicted to drugs can suffer from the behavior. In the case of abortion, some of those who are opposed to the legalization argue that terminating a pregnancy is homicide.

The relative harm caused by victimless crimes has been central to political debate for decades. Abortion, gambling, and homosexuality were once illegal but have been legalized in the United States, although morality-based arguments are still levied against these behaviors. Furthermore, the extent to which these behaviors are permitted varies across time and by jurisdiction.

Prostitution provides an illustration of the difficulty of labeling crime "victimless." The exchange of sex for money could be entirely consensual, with both parties benefiting and no harm caused to either. However, prostitution has been associated with the exploitation of women by pimps and human traffickers. Men who frequent prostitutes may also become infected with sexually transmitted diseases, which could then be spread to others. On the other hand, arguments for legalization of prostitution point out that prostitutes who are victims of crime (from rape, for example), have difficulty accessing legal remedies. Furthermore, public health suffers when prostitutes have sex without protection or routine medical examination, both of which could be affected by legalization.

NOTE

1. Edwin M. Schur, *Crimes Without Victims: Deviant Behavior and Public Policy; Abortion, Homosexuality, Drug Addiction* (Englewood Cliffs, NJ: Prentice Hall, 1965).

SUGGESTED READING

Gilbert Geis, *Not the Law's Business? An Examination of Homosexuality, Abortion, Prostitution, Narcotics, and Gambling in the United States* (Skokie, IL: Rand-McNally, 1972); Robert F. Meier and Gilbert Geis, *Victimless Crime? Prostitution, Drugs, Homosexuality, Abortion* (Los Angeles, CA: Roxbury, 1997); Edwin M. Schur and Hugo Adam Bedau, *Victimless Crimes: Two Sides of Controversy* (Englewood Cliffs, NJ: Prentice-Hall, 1974).

BENJAMIN PEARSON-NELSON

VICTIM-OFFENDER RECONCILIATION PROGRAMS (VORPS).
Victim-Offender Reconciliation Programs (VORPs) are often identified as one of the longest-standing approaches to victim-offender dialogue in North America.

Steeped in the restorative justice perspective, VORPs are regarded as the prevailing form of restorative justice practice currently in operation in the United States. Restorative justice, a distinctive paradigm for understanding and responding to crime and victimization, holds offenders accountable to their victims.

The initial identifiable victim-offender reconciliation meeting, believed to have taken place in Canada in 1974, occurred after a crime spree by two young men in Ontario resulted in 22 vandalism victims. Representatives from probation and the community arranged a meeting with each victim for the offenders to accept responsibility for their actions, apologize, and arrange restitution. The result had such a positive impact that the parties involved developed a project called Victim-Offender Reconciliation Program (VORP) to continue the initiative.

Victim-Offender Reconciliation Programs (VORPs) are often confused with Victim-Offender Mediation Programs (VOMs). While these two endeavors are similar, there are distinct differences. The major objective of VOMs is to offer victims and offenders the prospect of meeting with a trained mediator to promote dialogue in discussing the crime, and to construct steps toward justice by encouraging mutual problem solving. The session is frequently preceded by one or more preparatory meetings.

VORPs utilize a preparatory process but accentuate movement toward reconciliation (i.e., settlement and understanding), a step that takes the objective further than problem solving. Reconciliation is the desired outcome because it is the central feature that allows the healing process to begin. Foundational to VORPs is the restorative justice perspective that the crime that occurred has not only violated the law but has caused a violation of a relationship between two or more people. Accordingly, encounter and understanding can initiate the healing process not only for individuals and communities as victims, but for offenders as well.

Some proponents of victim-offender dialogue take exception to the use of the word "reconciliation," since the dialogue can occur with valuable outcomes whether or not complete resolution is achieved. One key feature that VORPs highlight is the conflict resolution *process* that both parties perceive as fair.

In the United States, the majority of victim-offender reconciliation programs are run by nonprofit organizations and less than half are run by religious organizations. About half of all programs handle cases involving both juvenile and adult offenders. State and local governments often provide funding. Victims are voluntary participants and can leave the process at any stage. Offenders generally have been found guilty in court but may or may not have been sentenced when the reconciliation meeting takes place. Problems associated with operating victim-offender reconciliation programs include securing adequate funding, appropriate referrals, maintaining positive working relationships with agencies that promote retribution, and convincing angry victims to overcome initial resistance and to give this restorative justice initiative the opportunity to assist in initiating their healing process.

SUGGESTED READING

Clifford K. Dorne, *Restorative Justice in the United States* (Upper Saddle River, NJ: Prentice Hall, 2008); Gerry Johnstone and Daniel W. Van Ness, *Handbook of Restorative Justice* (Portland, OR: Willan, 2007); Daniel Van Ness and Karen Heetdevks Strong, *Restoring Justice*, 2nd ed. (Cincinnati, OH: Anderson, 2006); Howard Zehr, *The Little Book of Restorative Justice* (Intercourse, PA: Good Books, 2002).

DEBRA HEATH-THORNTON

VICTIMOLOGISTS. Victimologists typically focus on those people who have suffered physical, emotional, or financial harm at the hands of another. The criminal and victim play roles, the dynamics of which can resemble a winner or loser, predator and prey, or master and slave relationship. Victimologists explain relationships between victims and offenders and examine victim interactions with the police, courts, and correctional components of the criminal justice system, as well as other institutions, the media, and businesses. Unlike the mainstream population, victimologists steer away from blaming or defending the victim, but rather objectively assess what has gone on in the relationship between the victim and the perpetrator. As a result, victimologists can present a balanced view by examining all sides of the issue.

The trend towards studying both victims and offenders is about 70 years old. The term "victimology" was coined in 1947. During the 1960s the Department of Justice urged criminologists to begin studying crime victims (due to the increase in street crime). Studies occurring before victimologists became prominent primarily focused on the offender (i.e., who they were, why they committed the crime, and how they could be rehabilitated). By 1970, victimology had become a recognized area of study and a specialization under criminology.

Victimologists contribute to this area of study utilizing an interdisciplinary approach (e.g., social work, psychology and psychiatry, and criminal justice and criminology). Some victimologists are conservative in their approach toward crime victims and tend to restrict their analyses and education of crime victims on how not to become a victim of street crime. Others are liberal in their approach and extend their definition of victims to include all kinds of crime victims. Radical victimolgists include victims of hazardous waste, sexism, racism, poverty, fraudulent advertising, and pollution, to name a few. Liberal and radical victimologists study all kinds of harmful behavior to include victims of other social problems.

Victimologists, therefore, gather data about victims by conducting unfunded and funded research projects, identify the nature and extent of the crime problem, investigate how the criminal justice system responds to crime victims and offenders, as well as examine the societal response to the problem (e.g., the development and evaluation of self help programs and their groups, and the business owners' responses to what crime victims need).

Finally, victimologists also study the influence of the media. By examining the accuracy of media reports, victimologists can investigate the impact of the media on offenders and victims. Victimologists assess how ethical journalists are when reporting harm suffered by crime victims. They also examine how the media reports depict crime and the offenders who commit the crimes. Victimologists assess the vulnerability of a target, regardless of whether it is tangible or non-tangible, after which the goal focuses on strategies for reducing crime and victimization risks through prevention.

SUGGESTED READING

Andrew Karmen, *Crime Victims: An Introduction to Victimology*, 6th ed. (Belmont, CA: Thompson / Wadsworth, 2007).

CHARISSE COSTON

VICTIMOLOGY. Linguistically the word victimology is a combination of two parts, *victim* and *-ology*. The word *victim* comes from the Latin word *victima*, which referred to a person or animal sacrificed in a religious ceremony. The *-ology* comes from the Greek word *logos*, which meant *speech, word,* or *reason,* and was especially associated with divine wisdom, reason, doctrine, theory, and science.[1] Today the word *victimology* is defined from the victim's perspective as the discipline which scientifically studies, as objects of investigation, all types of victims, especially crime victims.[2] It includes the theories and research used to explain all aspects of victimization; victim behaviors prior to, during and after the victimization; and the analysis of laws, policies, psychological interventions and programs used to help victims cooperate with government systems and recover from their physical, psychical, social, economical, and legal injuries. Since victimology comes from the word victim, logically victimology should be about victim characteristics rather than being qualified by the many forces that cause victimization. It is the status, condition, and plight of victims that form the essence of what victimology studies.

The very early origins of victimology can be found in somewhat unrelated writings of a few insightful persons in: a novel about murder victims by Franz Werfel in 1920;[3] a small chapter on victims in an American criminology textbook by Edwin Sutherland in 1924; a Cuban book about protecting crime victims by J. R. Figueroa, D. Tejera, and F. Plá in 1929; a major chapter about victims in a criminology book by Hans von Hentig in 1948; a sentence about the need for "a science of victimology" in a book on violence by an American psychiatrist, Fredric Wertham in 1948;[4] and a speech on victimology in Romania by Beniamin Mendelsohn in 1958.[5] Then came the first full book on victim restitution based in the English language by Hungarian criminologist Stephen Schafer in 1960; a dissertation on victimology published as a Japanese book by Koichi Miyazawa in 1965;[6] and, finally, the first victimology textbook, also by Stephen Schafer, in 1968.[7]

The conceptualization of victimology as a formal discipline was born in the mind of the Romanian defense attorney Beniamin Mendelsohn. He began his interest with victims and their relationships with offenders when trying to defend persons accused of crimes. He became aware of how important it was to understand the victim-offender interaction for determining degrees of offender blame. Eventually going beyond victim and offender interaction, Mendelsohn recognized that victims were largely ignored, disrespected, and even abused by the system. Thus, he began to seek ways to protect and help victims by proposing the creation of victim assistance clinics, international organizations, and special research institutes. Because of his early writings, his persistent campaigning on behalf of victim rights, and his prolific writings about victimology, he earned the title "The Father of Victimology." Like most of his contemporaries, Mendelsohn's early work with victimology was mostly about crime victims and their relationship with their offenders; however, as he began to develop his ideas, his focus centered more on just the victim. This orientation reached its peak with the realization that victimology logically should be about the concern for all types of victims, from crimes, traffic accidents, disasters, etc. He referred to this broader type of victimology as "general victimology."[8] Today there are roughly three types of victimologists: those whose focus is limited to crime victims (specific), those whose focus is on human rights victims (which includes crime victims), and those whose focus is on all victims regardless of the cause (general). Victimology today is an interdisciplinary field drawing especially from law, criminology, psychology, sociology, anthropology, and political science.

NOTES

1. *Webster's Ninth New Collegiate Dictionary* (Springfield, MA: Merriam-Webster Inc., Publisher, 1991).

2. John Dussich, Thomas Underwood, and Dan Petersen, "New Definitions for Victimology and Victim Services: A Theoretical Note," *The Victimologist* 7, no. 2 (2003): 1.

3. Hans Schneider, *Viktimologie: Wissenschaft vom Verbrechensopfer* (Tübingen, Germany: J. C. B. Mohr UTB, Paul Siebeck, 1975).

4. Fredric Wertham, *The Show of Violence* (Garden City, NY: Doubleday and Company, 1948), 259.

5. Gerd Kirchhoff, *What is Victimology?* Monograph Series No.1, Tokiwa International Victimology Institute (Tokyo, Japan: Seibundo Publishing Co., Ltd., 2005).

6. Koichi Miyazawa, *The Basic Theory of Victimology* (Tokyo: Seibundo, 1965).

7. Stephen Schafer, *Restitution to Victims of Crime* (London: Stevens & Sons Limited, 1960).

8. Emilio C. Viano, "Conclusions and Recommendations: International Study Institute on Victimology Bellagio, Italy, July 1–12, 1975," in *Victim and Society*, ed. Emilio C. Viano (Washington DC: Visage Press Inc., 1976).

SUGGESTED READING

Steven Schafer, *Victimology: The Victim and His Criminal* (Reston, VA: Reston Publishing, 1977).

JOHN DUSSICH

VICTIM'S RIGHTS CONSTITUTIONAL AMENDMENT. The effort to amend the U.S. Constitution to include a provision regarding crime victims' rights formally began with a recommendation by the President's Task Force on Victims of Crime in 1982. In addition to dozens of statutory and implementation proposals designed to improve the treatment of crime victims in the criminal justice system, the Task Force, convened by President Ronald Reagan, proposed that the Sixth Amendment to the Constitution be amended to require that victims in criminal prosecutions have the right to be present and heard at all "critical stages" of judicial proceedings.[1] Rather than undertake action on a federal constitutional amendment at that time, victims' rights advocates initially pursued the adoption of victims' rights constitutional amendments at the state level.[2]

In 1996, the first federal crime victims' rights constitutional amendment was introduced in the U.S. Congress. The proposed amendment enumerated specified victims' rights to notice, to be present and heard, and to receive restitution from the offender; and to have victim safety and interest in the avoidance of unreasonable delay considered. During the next four years, hearings were held in committees of the U.S. Senate and House of Representatives on the initial amendment proposal and subsequently introduced modifications of it. Although the proposed amendment had significant support in Congress, concerns were also raised regarding its effect on established offender constitutional rights and other issues.[3]

The proposed victims' rights amendment received its most significant consideration in Congress in 1999–2000. Following approval of the then-current proposal in the Senate Judiciary Committee in late 1999 concerning victims of violent crime, the proposed amendment was debated on the floor of the Senate in 2000. Its sponsors withdrew the proposal from consideration, however, when it became clear that there was insufficient support for a successful resolution in the Senate.[4]

Subsequent versions of the constitutional amendment were introduced in 2002 and 2003 and as recently as 2007. These versions of the amendment also limit the proposed constitutional rights to victims of violent crime. The proposed rights include the rights to notice of public proceedings regarding the crime and the offender's release or escape; to be present at these public proceedings; to be heard at public proceedings regarding the offender's release, plea, sentencing, reprieve, and pardon; and to have the victim's interest in safety, the avoidance of unreasonable delay, and restitution considered in adjudicative decisions. The specified victim rights are not to be restricted unless required by compelling necessity or a substantial interest in the administration of justice or public safety.[5]

Congress has not voted on any of these constitutional amendment proposals.[6] Instead, in 2004, Congress enacted a new statute regarding the rights of crime victims in federal proceedings that generally included, and even expanded, the rights specified in the previous amendment proposals.[7]

NOTES

1. President's Task Force on Victims of Crime, *Final Report* (Washington DC: GPO, 1982), 114–15; LeRoy L. Lamborn, "Victim Participation in the Criminal Justice Process: The Proposals for a Constitutional Amendment," *Wayne Law Review* 34 (1987): 125–28; Victoria Schwartz, "Recent Development: The Victims' Rights Amendment," *Harvard Journal on Legislation* 42 (2005): 525–27.

2. Lamborn, "Victim participation," 128–34; Schwartz, "Recent Development," 526.

3. National Victims' Constitutional Amendment Passage Web site, http://www.nvcap.org; Schwartz, "Recent Development," 525–28.

4. National Victims' Constitutional Amendment Passage; Schwartz, "Recent Development," 529.

5. National Victims' Constitutional Amendment Passage; Schwartz, "Recent Development," 529–33; Lori A. Stiegel and Ellen M. Klemm, "Recent Victims' Rights Legislation," *The Crime Victims Report* 12, no. 3 (2008): 43.

6. National Victims' Constitutional Amendment Passage.

7. 18 U.S.C.A. § 3771 (West Supp. 2008).

SUGGESTED READING

Paul G. Cassell, "Barbarians at the Gates? A Reply to the Critics of the Victims' Rights Amendment," *Utah Law Review* 1999 (1999): 479–544; Robert P. Mosteller, "The Unnecessary Victims' Rights Amendment," *Utah Law Review* 1999 (1999): 443–77.

PEGGY TOBOLOWSKY

VICTIMS' RIGHTS LEGISLATION. The crime victims' rights movement began in the 1960s as a reaction to offenders receiving greater protections from the criminal justice system and a newfound emphasis for individual civil rights versus the power of governmental officials. The initial movement was a response to the first victimization surveys that uncovered the massive amounts of unreported crime victimization which was occurring and the harm it was creating.

Slowly since the 1960s, crime victims have been able to establish certain rights or privileges within the criminal justice system.

The new victims' rights legislation impacts three concerns of crime victims. The first concern is providing government-sponsored services and programs for victims. These programs include compensation programs and victim/witness programs. The second concern is the right of victims to be informed of and participate in the criminal justice process. The last concern is for the protection of current and potential crime victims.[1]

The first legislation to establish rights for victims was the passage of California's victim compensation program in 1965. The program sought to provide crime victims with an insurance policy against the expense of physical injury due to criminal acts. By the end of the 1960s, five additional states (New York, Massachusetts, Maryland, Hawaii, and Georgia) had established their own programs.[2] By the end of the 1970s, the number of states had grown to 30, and by the end of the 1980s, all but two states (Maine and South Dakota) had such programs. On April 6, 1992, Maine became the last state to provide a crime victim compensation program for crimes occurring within its borders.[3] These programs were not without problems. Many programs had severe restrictions on the qualifications of the victims to receive compensation, and the programs differed from state to state. Many programs also did not have enough funds to provide compensation to all of the victims who did qualify. The rescue of victim compensation programs occurred in 1984 with the passage of the federal Victims of Crime Act (VOCA). This federal legislation established consistent guidelines for states as to levels of compensation and qualifications for compensation. It also provided states with an additional funding source from the federal government for their compensation programs, as well as other victim assistance programs.

The establishment of advocates in government agencies for crime victims was the next right crime victims acquired. Advocates have been instrumental in keeping crime victims informed of the proceedings within the criminal justice system. Beginning in 1973, the first victim/witness programs were created using funding from the federal Law Enforcement Assistance Administration (LEAA). The initial funding provided for the establishment of 10 programs.[4] Today, all federal prosecutors' offices are required to have a victim/witness program staffed with advocates. Most states also have some type of victim/witness program in their prosecutors' offices, staffed with individuals whose job it is to help crime victims negotiate the criminal justice system. Additionally, victim services programs are also located in local police and sheriffs' departments.

The right of participation of crime victims within the criminal justice system is occurring with the passage of crime victims' bills of rights and state constitutional amendments. This legislation specifically addresses procedures that criminal justice systems must follow. The first allowance by the criminal justice system to provide a way for crime victims to participate is the use of victim impact statements (VIS). In 1973, the first VIS was created by James Rowland, the Chief probation officer in Fresno, California. A VIS allows the victim or the surviving family members to address the court before sentencing or the parole board before parole is granted. The VIS can be given orally or can be in written form and provides information as to the impact of the crime on the survivors of the crime. It may be the only time the victims have any input if there has been a plea bargain.

On the federal level, the President's Task Force on Victims of Crime[5] attempted to change the U.S. Constitution by adding a sentence to the Sixth Amendment, which would have guaranteed victims the right to be heard throughout their judicial proceedings. This attempt failed; however, today most states have enacted their own constitutional amendment or a state statute that provides for victims' rights or guidelines for the treatment of crime victims by the criminal justice system. This began in 1977, with Wisconsin passing the first crime victims' bill of rights statute.[6] Today every state has a set of legal rights for crime victims within its code of laws, often called a victims' bill of rights. The model for crime victims' rights can be found in the federal Crime Victims' Rights Act, Section 3771 (a).[7] However, the major limitation of almost all of the victims' rights laws is that victims are severely limited in making sure the rights are followed through.[8]

The last major concern is the protection of the crime victim. This concern focuses upon how crime victims are treated within the criminal justice process and the establishment of laws to prevent victimization. This concern derives from the way victims of rape and domestic violence were being treated by the criminal justice system. In many ways they were being held responsible for their own victimization. The first protection victims were provided came from the enactment of Rape Shield Laws in the 1970s. These laws protect women from having their sexual histories put on display in court. Another protection was the passage of mandatory domestic violence arrest statutes. Widespread inaction by police agencies concerning domestic violence crimes forced states to demand that police treat domestic violence as they would any other assault. Finally, victims were provided with protection against intimidation initially through the passage of the 1982 Federal Victim and Witness Protection Act. The provision also provided for restitution by offenders. Restitution, provided for in all 50 states, is the provision of monies or services to the community or crime victim directly by the offender. Restitution had very little acceptance until the passage of the 1982 Federal Victim and Witness Protection Act.[9]

NOTES

1. National Organization for Victim Assistance, *Victims' Rights and Services: A Legislative Directory 1988/1989* (Washington DC: National Organization for Victim Assistance, 1990).

2. G. Ramker and M. Meagher, "Crime Victim Compensation: A Survey of State Programs," *Federal Probation* 5 (1982): 68–72.

3. National Organization for Victim Assistance, "Impact Statement Not Having Much Effect," *Nova Newsletter* 16 (1992), 2.

4. Robert A. Jerin and Laura J. Moriarty, *The Victims of Crime* (Upper Saddle River, NJ: Prentice Hall, 2009).

5. President's Task Force on Victims of Crime, *Final Report* (Washington DC: Government Printing Office, 1982).

6. National Organization for Victim Assistance, "Victims'Rights."

7. Crime Victims' Rights Act

8. Ibid.

9. Omnibus Victim and Witness Protection Act (Public Law No. 97–291, 96 Stat. 1248)

SUGGESTED READING

Ellen K. Alexander and Janice H. Lord, *Impact Statements: A Victim's Right to Speak, a Nation's Responsibility to Listen* (Washington DC: U.S. Department of Justice, 1994).

ROBERT JERIN

VICTIM VS. SURVIVOR. The terms "victim" and "survivor" are both used in the multidisciplinary and multisystem field of victimology. While oftentimes the terms are used interchangeably to reference a person who has been harmed, language can reflect an ideology,[1] and the dominant use of a term may reflect a power struggle between competing ideologies.[2]

A traditional perspective of "victim" offers a perception of one who is weak, overpowered by an external source, and possibly even at some level of fault or blame, thus suggesting a lack of resources, power, or a dependence on others. The term "survivor" has been favored by a feminist framework,[3] especially as it relates to sexual abuse, to suggest an internal strength and empowerment to cope for recovery. Recognizing the early grassroots responses to victims of domestic violence and sexual assault, the term survivor is commonly used by community-based service organizations such as domestic violence shelters and rape crisis programs.

In this context, the terms "victim" and "survivor" are often considered on a continuum, with the term "victim" as the negative and the term "survivor" as the positive. In other words, the conceptualization is that an individual moves, transcends, or evolves from the negative to the positive. This conceptualization views both terms in a psychological framework, but it is more appropriate to consider the term "victim" from a sociological framework. "Victim" is a social construct,[4] and the victimization event infers a social status, albeit not one that people strive to obtain.

NOTES

1. Thomas Underwood, "Concepts of Victim Assistance," in *Victim Assistance: Exploring Individual Practice, Organizational Policy, and Societal Responses*, eds. Thomas Underwood and Christine Edmunds (New York: Springer, 2002), 1–20.

2. Sharon Lamb, *New Versions of Victims: Feminist Struggle with the Concept* (New York: New York University Press, 1999).

3. Laura Anderson and Karen Gold, "I Know What It Means But It's Not How I Feel: The Construction of Survivor Identity in Feminist Counseling," *Women and Therapy* 15 (1994): 5–17.

4. Paul Rock, "On Becoming a Victim," in *New Visions of Crime Victims*, eds. Carolyn Hoyle and Richard Young (Portland, OR: Hart, 2002), 1–22.

SUGGESTED READING

Anne McLeer, "Saving the Victim: Recuperating the Language of the Victim and Reassessing Global Feminism," *Hypatia* 13, no. 1 (1998): 41–55.

THOMAS UNDERWOOD

VICTIM/WITNESS ASSISTANCE PROGRAMS (VWAPS). In many counties in the United States, the district attorney's office is the agency that prosecutes major crimes. In most offices, there are advocates who work directly with the victim, witnesses, and others associated with a major crime.

Historically, the focus on victims' rights has been neglected. The focus was purely on prosecuting the offender. Beginning in the 1970s, more attention began to focus on victims' rights. A study conducted by Frank Cannavale that revealed the top reason for prosecution failure was that once-cooperative witnesses decided to stop helping. They felt that the justice system did not support their basic needs. However, during the 1970s many high-profile organizations formed (e.g., Families and Friends of Missing Persons, Parents of Murdered Children, Justice for Victims) and advocates as well as victims became more outspoken regarding the importance of crime victim care. The victim/witness state programs were formed as a result of the President's Task Force on Violent Crime and the Victim and Witness Protection Act of 1982. Each district attorney's office was given Victims of Crime Act (VOCA) funds (primarily made up of offender penalties, fines, forfeitures, and special assessments) to assign a victim assistance coordinator to each office and to hire advocates to assist in providing direct service to crime victims and witnesses.

The role of a victim/witness advocate is multifaceted. Many times, they serve as middlemen between the prosecutor and a victim or family. They are a secondary contact in the prosecutor's office, and often can be easier to reach than the prosecuting attorney. The victim/family can call the advocate instead of the prosecutor to discuss the case, vent frustration, or just look for a shoulder to lean on. The advocate can also serve as a liaison to the prosecutor on behalf of the family and vice versa, as well as informing the victim/family of court date changes or disposition changes. The advocate can also explain the court process and answer any questions that the victim may have.

Advocates can provide many other services as well. They can provide information and referral, such as finding the victim community resources, counseling, etc. They will also help the victim fill out crime victim compensation paperwork and any other forms for assistance for which victims might be eligible. Finally, the advocates also may provide follow-up after the case is over.

SUGGESTED READING

District of Nevada, "Victim Witness Program," http://www.justice.gov/usao/nv/home/about_us/vwp.htm; Office of Victims of Crime, "The History of the Crime Victims' Movement in the United States," http://www.ojp.usdoj.gov/ovc/ncvrw/2005/pg4c.html#i; Shasta County District Attorney's Office, "History of Victim Witness Programs," http://www.da.co.shasta.ca.us/vicwit.shtml#history.

CINDY LINDQUIST

VON HENTIG, HANS. Hans von Hentig (1887–1974) earned his Juris Doctorate from Munich in 1912. A veteran of World War I, he began studying the criminal personality in 1925; he taught at the University of Kiel (1931–1934), and was a professor of law and criminology in Bonn from 1934 until dismissed in 1935 for failing to engage in the Hitler salute. He migrated to the United States in 1936 and lectured at Yale on the causes of war. The University of California awarded him the prestigious Hitchcock Chair in 1937, where his "Detection and Suppression of Crime" lecture reflected his continued criminological research. Von Hentig was appointed as an expert assistant to the U.S. Attorney General in Washington DC in 1942. He was a professor at the University School of Law in Boulder, Colorado in 1943 and 1945. While there he published the *Degrees of Parole Violation and Graded Remedial Measures* (1943) and *The Delinquency of the American Indian* (1945), and directed the Colorado Crime Survey.

In 1944 he went to the University of Iowa, where he proposed a "Police in Occupied Countries" military training program. While he was there, a neo-conservative Christian group charged him with being a Communist and hinted at sedition. Von Hentig thanked Iowa University President Hancher for his support but returned to Colorado, only to move to the University of Kansas City in 1946. While there he published two texts: *Crime: Causes and Conditions* (1947) and *The Criminal and His Victim* (1948). This last work noted that the criminal and the victim do not interact in isolation, and became a theoretical basis in victimology research.

SUGGESTED READING

Hans von Hentig, "Degrees of Parole Violation and Graded Remedial Measures," *The Journal of Criminal Law and Criminology* 33 (1943): 363–72; Hans von Hentig, "The Delinquency of the American Indian," *Journal of Criminal Law and Criminology* 36 (1945): 75–84.

TONI DUPONT-MORALES

VON HENTIG'S TYPOLOGIES. Hans von Hentig based his theoretical typology on research of the time, the presence of consistent factors, and the intricacies of the perpetrator and victim interaction disregarded by criminal law. He proposed thirteen categories, postulating that in a crime there were always two partners, the perpetrator and the victim. He penned his theory after his work on the Colorado Crime Survey and *Crime: Causes and Conditions* (1947), noting factors which shape criminal behavior. Von Hentig's *The Criminal and His Victim: Studies in the Sociobiology of Crime* (1948) developed the foundation for studying the causes of crime and what factors combine to make individuals into victims. Von Hentig's typology recognizes that the criminal and the victim may come from two different worlds, but the perpetrator and the victim often bring equal weight to the mechanics of the crime. He found that the behaviors of the victim and offender may be enumerated by three factors (psychological, social, and biological) which help define the criminal act and possible consequences.

The young, the female, the old, and the mentally defective and mentally deranged reflect all three factors to varying degrees. The very young and the very old may be victimized by combined psychological, social, and biological factors. Their psychological and biological status may result in ignorance or risk taking leading to sexual assault or homicide, while increased age may make them eligible for fraud. The mentally defective and mentally deranged fail to comprehend the presence of threats and are placed in danger. *Immigrants, minorities, and dull normals* are victimized because of their social status and the lack of a voice in political society. Thus, they are both victimized and unfairly blamed for all sorts of actions while labeled as dull because of a nexus of psycho-socio-biological factors. Von Hentig experienced this in his own time when his immigration status raised suspicion about potential sedition.

The depressed, the acquisitive, the wanton, and the lonesome and heartbroken experience the combined impact of bio-social factors that are emphasized by the psychological. In the reaction to a lost relationship, the quest for companionship, or the excesses of greed, the victim places himself in situations where he fails to respond to signs of danger. The instinct for self-preservation is diminished, and the consequences may be severe. *The tormentor and the blocked, exempted, and fighting victim* are found in those cases where the victim has ignored the dangerousness of provocation and avarice. Consider the abusive husband or father who later may be killed by his wife or son; the lifelong bully; or the criminal who seeks suicide by provoking police. The blocked, exempted, and fighting victim is one who has been so enmeshed in poor decisions that he has no defense for his victimization, nor the opportunity to seek assistance. Finally, the blackmail victim, the store owner who commits fraud, or criminals who pay off law enforcement cannot expect help from the legal system without encountering more consequences.

SUGGESTED READING

Hans von Hentig, *Crime: Causes and Conditions* (New York: McGraw-Hill, 1947); Hans von Hentig, *The Criminal and His Victim: Studies in the Sociobiology of Crime* (New Haven, CT: Yale University Press, 1948).

TONI DUPONT-MORALES

WIDENING THE NET. The phrase "widening the net" has traditionally applied to the increased number of offenders processed in the formal criminal justice system due to the expanding availability of intermediate sanctions.[1] In other words, having the option of less severe punishments available for criminal sanctions allows the criminal justice system to process offenders that may have otherwise been removed from the system. This phenomenon has also appeared in services for the victims. As victim services are expanded in local communities, more crime victims are being helped. However, increasing the availability of services to crime victims also has some negative consequences for those seeking help.

Reporting a crime to the police not only gets criminal justice officials involved in the offender's life, it also invites those officials into the victim's life. As a result, victims often experience a level of personal invasion they did not expect. For example, criminal background checks are performed on victims during the initial investigation at the scene of the crime. Also, domestic violence victims staying at a shelter may be required to attend counseling sessions, perform household duties, or secure employment in exchange for a safe place to live.[2] Emi Koyama and Lauren Martin developed a "power and control" wheel to illustrate how shelter rules can contribute to the further victimization of the residents who live there.[3] The wheel includes using the children of victims against the women, increased isolation due to the secrecy of the shelter's location, threats and intimidation used against women to enforce house rules, and financial burdens introduced due to curfew or confidentiality rules interfering with employment.[4]

The advantage of a wider net for victims' services is that more crime victims are being helped through various agencies and programs. The disadvantage is that the victims seeking these services must often surrender control of personal information and lifestyle to receive the services. The ultimate concern regarding widening the net in victims' services is that crime victims will feel re-victimized by the system. If victims feel burdened by the criminal justice system and service providers, they may stop reporting crimes to the police and stop taking advantage of the services available to crime victims.

NOTES

1. Larry H. Gaines and Roger L. Miller, *Criminal Justice in Action* (Belmont, CA: Thomson Wadsworth, 2009).

2. Clackamas Women's Services, "Information on Domestic Violence," http://www.cwsor.org/description.htm.

3. Emi Koyama and Lauren Martin, "Abusive Power and Control within the Domestic Violence Shelter," Survivor Project, http://eminism.org/readings/pdf-rdg/wheel-sheet.pdf.

4. Koyama and Martin, "Abusive Power."

SUGGESTED READING

Linda Olsen, "Shelter Rules: The Good, the Bad, and the Ugly," Washington State Coalition Against Domestic Violence, http://www.wscadv.org/pages.cfm?aId=CFEA5CF2-C298-58F6-03334DDA03E687D9.

SUZANNE GODBOLDT

WILSON, MARY ELLEN. The 1874 case of Mary Ellen Wilson sparked a transformation of the child protection movement in the United States. Abandoned by her impoverished mother at age two, Mary Ellen was turned over to New York City's Department of Charities. The Department eventually placed her with Mary and Thomas McCormick, who claimed to be Mary Ellen's biological father. Shortly thereafter, Thomas died and his widow married Francis Connolly, who moved the new family to a tenement. Soon after, Mary Connolly began mistreating Mary Ellen, repeatedly beating and neglecting her.

On several occasions a neighbor, Mary Smitt, observed a frail, ill-clad Mary Ellen shivering outside her apartment and heard her painful screams during apparent beatings by her stepmother. Finally, Mary Smitt contacted Etta Angell Wheeler, a Methodist mission worker, who personally observed a dirty and malnourished Mary Ellen with numerous bruises and scars on her arms and legs. Ms. Wheeler then explored possible legal interventions and protection for Mary Ellen, but New York City authorities refused to intervene. Not knowing where to turn, Ms. Wheeler's niece suggested she contact Henry Bergh, founder of the American Society for the Prevention of Cruelty to Animals (ASPCA). Mr. Bergh intervened as a private citizen, sent a New York SPCA investigator to substantiate Mary Ellen's condition, and persuaded his good friend, Elbridge T. Gerry, an ASPCA attorney, to file a petition to remove Mary Ellen from her home. Henry Bergh also contacted several *New York Times* reporters, who attended Mary Ellen's court hearings and provided numerous detailed accounts of her physical abuse and neglect. Ultimately, presiding Judge Lawrence issued a *writ de homine replagiando*, which gave the court temporary custody of Mary Ellen. Subsequently, Mary Ellen was placed in the Sheltering Arms Children's Home and later was cared for by Etta Wheeler's mother, Sally Angell, in northern New York. Mary Connolly was subsequently convicted of felonious assault and received a one-year prison sentence.

Mary Ellen's plight began a national movement to combat child maltreatment. Extensive newspaper coverage raised public awareness of child abuse and motivated numerous public and private organizations and agencies to speak out for new laws that would rescue and protect abused children. Led by Elbridge Gerry, the Society for the Prevention of Cruelty to Children (SPCC) was established in New York in 1875. The New York SPCC was soon duplicated in Chicago, Philadelphia, Boston, and many other large cities. These chapters intervened in cases of child abuse and neglect, advocated for child protection, and sponsored shelters for impoverished women and children and victims of domestic violence. The Boston SPCC chapter promoted treating the entire family (i.e., family rehabilitation), which eventually became the major philosophy of U.S. child protection agencies and the centerpiece of the 1909 White House Conference on Dependent Children. This conference led to the establishment of both the Children's Bureau in 1912 and the Child Welfare League of America. Although these societies and organizations were largely non-governmental, and it would take until the 1960s before specific legislation against child abuse was common in the United States, the case of Mary Ellen Wilson was a key component in initiating this process.

SUGGESTED READING

Eric A. Shelman and Stephen Lazoritz, *Out of the Darkness: The Story of Mary Ellen Wilson* (Los Angeles: Dolphin Moon, 2003); S. A. Watkins, "The Mary Ellen Myth: Correcting Child Welfare History," *Social Work* 35, no. 6 (1990): 500–503.

THOMAS KELLEY

WOLFGANG, MARVIN E. Marvin E. Wolfgang (1924–1998) was a highly influential American criminologist and pioneer in theoretical and methodological analyses of violent crime. As an indication of his reputation, the *British Journal* *of Criminology* in 1994 named him "the most influential criminologist in the English-speaking world."[1]

Wolfgang's early work[2] was a landmark in violence and victimology scholarship, illustrating flaws in common assumptions about the nature and circumstances surrounding homicide. The author observed that most homicides are committed not by strangers, but by acquaintances of the victim. He also stated that victims frequently provoke and exacerbate arguments, generally with overtly aggressive behavior, thereby contributing to the escalation from trivial to serious physical threats. Thus, victims range from unwitting accomplices to deliberately culpable for their own demise.

Wolfgang later speculated that victim provocation in homicide cases could be related to the victim's unconscious desire to commit suicide,[3] a notion which has recently reemerged with the study of "suicide by cop." Wolfgang also presented a "subcultural" approach to violence, in which individuals subscribing to certain norms regard honor, respect, and status above safety and prudence.[4] Under this formulation, individuals whose honor is threatened have no choice but to react with aggressive posturing and requisite violence, as these responses are the ones validated and reified by the subculture itself. These findings, though groundbreaking, are also controversial, implying that victims control their own fate rather than having victimization forced unwillingly upon them.

NOTES

1. Ellen G. Cohn and David P. Farrington, "Who Are the Most Influential Criminologists in the English-Speaking World?" *British Journal of Criminology* 34, no. 2 (1994): 204–25.

2. Marvin E. Wolfgang, *Patterns in Criminal Homicide* (Philadelphia: University of Pennsylvania Press, 1958).

3. Marvin E. Wolfgang, "A Sociological Analysis of Criminal Homicide," *Federal Probation* 23 (1961): 48–55.

4. Marvin E. Wolfgang and Franco Ferracuti, *The Subculture of Violence: Towards an Integrated Theory in Criminology* (London: Tavistock, 1967).

SUGGESTED READING

Marvin E. Wolfgang, *Delinquency in a Birth Cohort* (Chicago: University of Chicago Press, 1979).

MATT R. NOBLES

WORKPLACE VICTIMIZATIONS. According to the U.S. Department of Justice,[1] workplace violence accounts for 18% of all violent crime. Most of these incidents are aggravated or simple assault. While homicide accounts for less than

1% of workplace violence, it is the third leading cause of fatal occupational injury. Less than half of all workplace violence incidents are reported to police.

Victimization at the workplace can be categorized in one of four types. Stranger violence may be the most commonly considered by the general public. This is when the offender has no legitimate relationship to the workplace or the victim and usually enters the workplace to commit a criminal act, such as a robbery. The second type is job function-related, whereby the offender is the recipient of an object or service, such as when a police officer, the occupational group with the highest rates of workplace violence,[2] is hit while making an arrest. The third type is employment-related, where the offender has a direct employment relationship with the workplace, such as when a supervisor is threatened by an employee or when one employee makes sexually suggestive remarks to another. The last type is domestic-related, where an offender had or has a relationship with the victim but has never been an employee, such as when a husband enters a workplace to confront his wife or when the victim receives harassing phone calls at work from a former girlfriend. A survey by the Family Violence Prevention Fund[3] found that 91% of corporate executives believe that domestic violence affects both the private lives and working lives of their employees.

There are many contributors to workplace violence. The state of the economic climate may be associated with the propensity for violence.[4] Outsourcing, reduced benefits, layoffs, and other organizational responses to economic conditions lead to greater employee stress and frustration. The organizational response to enhance productivity via use of surveillance, such as video camera and e-mail monitoring, is a relatively recent phenomenon that may cause disorganizing conditions, including real or perceived workplace injustices.[5] While diversity is generally embraced as a social value, differences of gender, race, ethnicity, religion, and sexual orientation in the workforce may also lend themselves to conflicts in that prejudices and biases in the community spill over to the workplace. Substance abuse is another factor that contributes to workplace violence. Even though most organizations have clear policies and programs regarding substance use and abuse, the availability and acceptability of alcohol and other drugs affect the potential for workplace violence, especially the types of stranger, job-related, and domestic violence.

The impact of workplace violence on the individual victim and the organization can be significant. Victims of workplace violence who return to work are forced to revisit the "scene of the crime" every day they go to work. In addition, if the victimization is employment related, that is the offender is another employee, the victim may be exposed to the offender. At the very least, victims may be exposed to others who remind them of the offender (customers, other employees, etc). This constant reminder of the victimization may make it difficult to return to work or, if the victim does return, to be productive, thereby compromising his potential on the job.

The organization is also affected, even when a victimization is directed to only one employee. Co-workers may be secondary victims and experience psychological and physiological trauma reactions. Co-workers may feel vulnerable, recognizing that they too may be victims of violence in the future. Co-workers may also have negative feelings toward the victim out of resentment for being placed at risk by a victim who may have violated protocol or due to increased workload in order to cover for victim down time. All of this may cause decreased productivity due to low morale, absenteeism, and fewer resources with greater demands. There may also be a real cost to the organization due to recruitment and training caused by staff turnover, worker compensation to cover medical and mental health care, and the potential for civil liability.

NOTES

1. Detis Duhart, "National Crime Victimization Survey: Violence in the Workplace, 1993–1999," (Washington DC: U.S. Department of Justice, Bureau of Justice Statistics, NCJ 190076, 2007).

2. Ibid.

3. Family Violence Prevention Fund, "Corporate Awareness of Domestic Violence," http://www.endabuse.org.

4. Robert Elliot and Deborah Jarrett, "Violence in the Workplace: The Role of Human Resource Management," *Public Personnel Management* 23 (1994): 287–99.

5. Vern Baxter and Anthony Margavio, "Assaultive Violence in the U.S. Post Office," *Work and Occupations* 23 (1996): 277–96.

SUGGESTED READING

Gina Respass and Brian K. Payne, "Social Services Workers and Workplace Violence," *Journal of Aggression, Maltreatment & Trauma* 16, no. 2 (2008): 131–43.

THOMAS UNDERWOOD

WORLD SOCIETY OF VICTIMOLOGY (WSV). The conceptual roots of the World Society of Victimology are represented in the early works of Beniamin Mendelsohn, who in 1958 published six goals he wanted for the field of victimology: focus on all victims' suffering and treatment in a scientific way; publish a victimology journal; create an institute; create an international society; conduct periodic symposia; and establish victimological clinics.[1] A number of other criminologists who had started presenting papers and publishing about victims at national and international conferences agreed to come together under the direction of Israel Drapkin and conduct an international symposium on victimology in Jerusalem, Israel in 1973. Some of the early victimologists who participated were

Stephen Schafer, Koichi Miyazawa, Simha F. Landau, Emilio Viano, Paul Zvonimir Šeparović, Ann Wolbert Burgess, Lynda Lytle Holmstrom, Annette Pearson, Menahem Amir, John Dussich, Kauko Aromaa, and Ezzat Abdel-Fattah. These pioneers became the backbone of what was then referred to as "the victimology movement." Three years later Stephen Schafer organized the Second International Symposium on Victimology; however, he passed away shortly before he could see his symposium take place, and his colleagues and students coordinated the symposium. Three years after that the Third International Symposium on Victimology was organized by Hans-Joachim Schneider in Münster, Germany. It was at this event that the World Society of Victimology (WSV) was formed and elected Hans-Joachim Schneider as President, John Dussich as Secretary General, and Gerd Ferdinand Kirchhoff as Newsletter Editor in 1979. This organization was registered in Mönchengladbach, Germany and became the vehicle that has continued organizing a victimology symposium every three years. Since 1979 the symposia have been held in: 1982, Tokyo/Kyoto, Japan; 1985, Zagreb, Croatia; 1988, Jerusalem, Israel; 1991, Rio de Janeiro, Brazil; 1994, Adelaide, Australia; 1997, Amsterdam, The Netherlands; 2000, Montreal, Canada; 2003, Stellenbosch, South Africa; 2006, Orlando, USA; 2009, Mito, Japan.

The WSV is driven by members who come from a wide variety of fields: sociology, criminology, law, victim assistance, government, psychology, political science, social work, psychiatry, nursing, medicine, and others. Every three years the members in good standing elect the Executive Committee which governs the society. The WSV is a non-government, not-for-profit organization that has Special Category Consultative Status with the UN Economic and Social Council and with the Council of Europe. The WSV also maintains affiliations with other organizations across the globe, especially national victim-focused organizations. The motto of the WSV is "Advancing research, services and awareness for victims." The purpose is "To advance victimological research and practices around the world; to encourage interdisciplinary and comparative work and research in this field, and to advance cooperation between international, national, and local agencies and other groups who are concerned with the problems of victims."[2]

One of the most significant accomplishments of the WSV was the coordination of the UN General Assembly Resolution which was unanimously passed in 1985 and was named The Declaration of Basic Principles of Justice for Victims of Crime and Abuse of Power. This international instrument has been translated into all seven of the UN official languages, and has been used as a guide for countries to reform their practices, policies, and laws on behalf of victims of crime and abuse of power. In order to solidify an international resolve, the WSV is currently working to bring together support from nations that would culminate in the passage of a United Nations Convention for Victims of Crime and Abuse of Power.

NOTES

1. Hanoch Hoffmann, "What Did Mendelsohn Really Say?" in *International Faces of Victimology*, eds., Sarah Ben David and Gerd Ferdinand Kirchhoff (Mŏnchengladbach, Germany: WSV, 1992).

2. World Society of Victimology Web site, http://www.worldsocietyofvictimology.org/index.html.

SUGGESTED READING

World Society of Victimology, "Archived Copies of *The Victimologist*: Official Newsletter of the World Society of Victimology," http://www.worldsocietyofvictimology.org/publications.html.

JOHN DUSSICH

Resource Guide

SELECTED BIBLIOGRAPHY

A selection of recently published books that can provide a broad look at the field of victimology is provided. For more specific offerings, please refer to the suggested reading sections at the end of each entry.

Davies, Pamela M., Peter Francis, and Chris Greer, eds. *Victims, Crime and Society*. London: Sage, 2007.

Davis, Robert C., Susan J. Herman, and Arthur J. Lurigio, eds. *Victims of Crime*. 3rd ed. Thousand Oaks, CA: Sage, 2007.

Doak, Jonathan. *Victim Rights, Human Rights and Criminal Justice: Reconceiving the Role of Third Parties*. Oxford: Hart, 2008.

Doerner, William G., and Steven P. Lab. *Victimology*. 5th ed. Newark, NJ: LexisNexis Matthew Bender, 2008.

Jerin, Robert A., and Laura J. Moriarty. *The Victims of Crime*. Upper Saddle River, NJ: Prentice Hall, 2009.

———. *Victims of Crime: Understanding Victimology, Victimization and Victim Services*. 2nd ed. Los Angeles: Roxbury, 2006.

Karmen, Andrew. *Crime Victims: An Introduction to Victimology*. 7th ed. Belmont, CA: Wadsworth, 2009.

Kennedy, Leslie W., and Vincent F. Sacco. *Crime Victims in Context*. Cary, NC: Oxford University Press, 2007.

Meadows, Robert J. *Understanding Violence and Victimization*. 5th ed. Upper Saddle River, NJ: Prentice Hall, 2008.

Moriarty, Laura J., ed. *Controversies in Victimology.* 2nd ed. Newark, NJ: Anderson, 2008.

Moriarty, Laura J., and Robert A. Jerin, eds. *Current Issues in Victimology Research.* 2nd ed. Durham, NC: Carolina Academic Press, 2007.

Oliveira, Edmundo. *Victimology and Criminal Law: Crime Precipitated or Programmed by the Victim.* Lanham, MD: University Press of America, 2007.

Sgarzi, Judith M., and Jack McDevitt. eds. *Victimology: A Study of Crime Victims and Their Roles.* Upper Saddle River, NJ: Prentice Hall, 2002.

Shichor, David, and Stephen G. Tibbetts, eds. *Victims and Victimization: Essential Readings.* Prospect Heights, IL: Waveland, 2002.

Spalek, Basia. *Crime Victims: Theory, Policy and Practice.* New York: Palgrave Macmillan, 2006.

Turvey, Brent E., and Wayne Petherick. *Forensic Victimology: Examining Violent Crime Victims in Investigative and Legal Contexts.* St. Louis, MO: Elsevier Science & Technology Books, 2008.

Wallace, Harvey. *Victimology: Legal, Psychological, and Social Perspectives.* 2nd ed. Boston: Allyn and Bacon, 2006.

JOURNALS

Readers will find additional research on crime victims in these selected journals.

Child Abuse & Neglect

Child Abuse Review

Child Maltreatment

Family Relations

Homicide Studies

International Journal of Criminal Justice Sciences

International Journal of Cyber Crimes and Criminal Justice

International Perspectives in Victimology

International Review of Victimology

Journal of Aggression, Maltreatment & Trauma

Journal of Child & Adolescent Trauma

Journal of Child Sexual Abuse

Journal of Elder Abuse & Neglect

Journal of Emotional Abuse

Journal of Family Violence

Journal of Interpersonal Violence

Journal of School Violence

Sexual Abuse

Trauma, Violence, & Abuse

Victims & Offenders

Violence Against Women
Violence and Victims

WEB SITES

Numerous Web sites provide information ranging from victimization statistics and organizational membership opportunities to victim services and legal remedies. A selection of these Web sites is provided.

American Society of Victimology: http://american-society-victimology.us
> This is the national organization for victimologists in the United States.

Amnesty International: http://www.amnesty.org
> Members of this organization campaign internationally for human rights.

Bureau of Justice Statistics, Victim Statistics: http://www.ojp.usdoj.gov/bjs/cvict.htm
> This U.S. Department of Justice site provides statistics on criminal victimizations, including reports from the National Crime Victimization Survey.

Campaign to Rescue and Restore Victims of Human Trafficking: http://www.acf.hhs.gov/trafficking/index.html
> This U.S. Department of Health & Human Services agency provides for public awareness campaigns and outreach activities to identify victims of human trafficking.

Domestic Violence and Sexual Assault Data Resource Center: http://www.jrsainfo.org/dvsa-drc/index.html
> This Center, funded by the Bureau of Justice Statistics, provides state and local data on domestic violence and sexual assault.

International Victimology Web site: http://www.victimology.nl
> This site provides a global meeting place to share information for those working in the field of victimology.

National Association of Crime Victim Compensation Boards: http://www.nacvcb.org/index.html
> This site provides statistics on victim compensation, as well as training opportunities.

National Center for Missing & Exploited Children: http://www.ncmec.org
> The mission of this agency is to help prevent child abduction and sexual exploitation, as well as assist in finding missing children.

National Center for Victims of Crime: http://ncvc.org
> This organization provides direct services to victims of crime, as well as advocating for policy and legal changes expanding the rights of victims.

National Center on Domestic and Sexual Violence: http://www.ncdsv.org/index.html
> This organization works with professionals and criminal justice system agencies in training, consulting, and advocacy.

National Center on Elder Abuse: http://www.ncea.aoa.gov/ncearoot/main_site/index.aspx
> Established by the U.S. Administration on Aging, this center provides resources for the prevention of the mistreatment of the elderly.

National Coalition Against Domestic Violence: http://www.ncadv.org

> This agency works to educate about domestic violence and impact public policy at the local, state, and national levels.

National Crime Prevention Council: http://www.ncpc.org

> Members of this Council are committed to taking action to prevent crime by fostering partnerships and supporting programs, including McGruff the Crime Dog, to educate the public.

National Crime Victims' Rights Week: http://www.ovc.gov/ncvrw

> This site identifies various scheduled events to be held nationwide during the National Crime Victims' Rights Week.

National Criminal Justice Reference Service: http://www.ncjrs.gov

> This U.S. Department of Justice office offers a wide range of information, including numerous reports on victimization and additional links to victim-related Web sites.

National Organization for Victim Assistance: http://www.trynova.org

> The mission of this agency includes the promotion of rights and services for crime victims, as well as training and education activities.

Office for Victims of Crime: http://www.ojp.usdoj.gov/ovc

> This is the U.S. Department of Justice Web site charged with overseeing programs that provide support to crime victims.

Office for Victims of Crime Online Directory of Crime Victim Services: http://ovc.ncjrs.gov/findvictimservices

> This searchable directory helps locate crime victim services in the United States and abroad by location, type of victimization, service needed, and agency type.

Office on Violence Against Women: http://www.ovw.usdoj.gov

> This U.S. Department of Justice Web site provides resources on domestic violence, dating violence, sexual assault, and stalking.

Rape, Abuse & Incest National Network: http://www.rainn.org

> This organization offers services to victims of sexual assault, partners with agencies, and advocates for changes in public policy.

Victim-Assistance Online: http://www.vaonline.org

> This site provides for networking and information sharing for those interested in the field of victimology.

VictimLaw: http://www.victimlaw.info/victimlaw

> This site provides a searchable database of victims' rights laws.

Victim Offender Mediation Association: http://www.voma.org

> This site provides information and services to those working from a model of restorative justice.

World Society of Victimology: http://www.worldsocietyofvictimology.org

> This is an international organization for victimologists.

Index

Page numbers in **bold** type refer to main entries in the handbook.

ABC-X model of family stress, 90
Abuse: active and passive, **3–4**
Acquaintance rape, **5–6**
Adam Walsh Child Protection and
    Safety Act, 129
Adam Walsh Sex Offender Registration
    and Notification Act, 248
Administration on Aging (AoA),
    83–84
Adult abuse. *See* Elder abuse
Adult Protective Services (APS), **6–7**,
    77–78, 83–84
Advocates, **7–8**
  burnout, 32
  professionalism, 127
*Against Our Will: Men, Women and
    Rape* (Brownmiller), 119
Agent provocateur, **8–9**, 112
Alcohol and victimization, **9–10**. *See
    also* Victim impact panels
Alfred P. Murrah building, 278
Allocution, **11–12**. *See also* Victim
    impact statement
Al Qaeda, 278

Alternative Dispute Resolution (ADR),
    12–13
AMBER Alert, **13–15**, 153
American Society for the Prevention of
    Cruelty to Animals (ASPCA),
    260, 313
Amir, Menachem, **15**, 27–28
Anatomically correct dolls. *See*
    Anatomically detailed dolls
Anatomically detailed dolls, **16**, 44
Antiterrorism and Effective Death
    Penalty Act, 126
Arbitration, 12
Arson, **17–18**
Assault, **18–19**, 240
  aggravated assault, 173

"Bad Samaritan" laws, 101
Barr, Roseanne, 37
Battered child syndrome, **21–22**, 116
  Kempe, C. Henry, 151–52
Battered husband syndrome, **23–24**
Battered wife syndrome. *See* Battered
    woman syndrome

Battered woman syndrome, 24–25
Battered Woman, The (Walker), 119
Battery, 25–26
Belief in a Just World, 26–27
Berk, Richard, 168
Berkowitz, David, 184
*Bethel School District No. 403 v.
    Fraser*, 251
Bias crime. *See* Hate crime
Blaming the victim, 27–28, 112
Blue Knight, The (Wambaugh), 197
BMW of North America, Inc. v. Gore,
    212
Bobo doll, 258
Booth v. Maryland, 126, 273, 290–91
British Crime Survey (BCS), 224, 246
*Brown v. Board of Education of
    Topeka, Kansas*, 114, 117
Bullying, 28–30, 239–40
Bureau of Justice Statistics (BJS): and
    the National Crime Victimization
    Survey (NCVS), 175, 293
Burglary, 30–31
Burnout, 32–33
Bush, George W., 14, 128, 131
Byron, Mary, 292
Bystander effect, 33–34

Caffey, John, 252
Callins v. Collins, 288
Campus victimizations, 35–37
    Jeanne Clery Act, 36
Capital punishment. *See* Death penalty
Carjacking, 171–72, 231
Celebrity offender
    Simpson, O.J., 184
    Smith, Michael Kennedy, 5
    Tyson, Michael, 5
Celebrity victim, 37–38
    Barr, Rosanne, 37
    Garner, Jennifer, 264
    Lennon, John, 184
    Letterman, David, 264
    Lindbergh, Charles, 37
    Madonna, 264
    Pressly, Anne, 37
    Versace, Gianni, 37–38
Child Abduction Convention (CAC), 89

Child abuse, 38–40, 80
    active abuse, 3, 38
    financial exception, 4
    neglect, 38
    passive abuse, 3–4, 38
    prevention, 22
    religious exception, 3–4
    treatment programs for abusive par-
        ents, 39–40
    See also Incest; Neglect; Pedophilia
Child Abuse Prevention and Treatment
    Act (CAPTA), 121, 179
Child lures, 40–42
Child Protection and Sexual Predator
    Punishment Act, 126
Child Protective Services (CPS), 42–43,
    179
Child witness, 43–44
Civil litigation, 44–46. *See also*
    Third–party liability
Civil Rights Act, 114, 251, 273
Civil rights movement, 114, 117
Clery, Jeanne Ann, 35
Code Adam, 153
Code of Hammurabi, 109
Coercion: acquaintance rape, 5
Columbine massacre, 29
Community service, 46–47
Compensation programs, 47–49, 126,
    303
Compensatory damages, 49–50. *See
    also* Punitive damages
Conflict Tactics Scales, 39, 50–51
Consent
    acquaintance rape, 5
    hazing, 107–8
    statutory rape, 265
Correctional officials, community and
    victim involvement, 51–53
Corruption, 53–54
Costs of crime, 54–56, 110
Court Appointed Special Advocate
    (CASA), 56–58
Courtroom workgroup, 74
Creative restitution, 58–59. *See also*
    Restitution
Crime prevention, 59–61. *See also* Crime
    Prevention Through Environmen-

tal Design (CPTED); Defensible space; McGruff Campaign

Crime Prevention Through Environmental Design (CPTED), **61–62**

Crime Victims with Disabilities Act, 126

Criminal and His Victim, The (von Hentig), 8–9, 307, 308

Criminal-victim dyad, 8–9

Criminology (Sutherland), 110

Critical Victimology, **62–64**

CyberAngels.org, **64–65**

Cyberbully, 29, 66

Cybercrime, **65–67**

Cyberstalking, **67–69**

Cycle of violence, **69–70**

Dark figure of crime, **71–72**, 282

Date rape. *See* Acquaintance rape

Death notification, **72–73**

Death penalty
    and victim discounting, 288–89
    and victim impact statement, 290–91

Declaration of Basic Principles of Justice for Victims of Crime and Abuse of Power, 123–24, 317

Defended neighborhoods, 244

Defense attorneys, **73–74**

Defensible space, **75–76**

Defounding, **76–77**

Deinstitutionalization movement, 210

Direct victim. *See* Primary victimization

Dispatcher. *See* Operators

District attorneys. *See* Prosecuting attorneys

Domestic elder abuse, **77–78**

Domestic minor sex trafficking, **78–79**, 143

Domestic violence, **79–80**
    marital rape, 163

Domestic violence myths, **81–82**

"Double jeopardy" of women, 69

Drew, Lori, 68

Duke University lacrosse team, 88

Eglash, Albert, 58, 228

Elder abuse, 80, **83–85**
    active abuse or neglect, 4

domestic, 77–78

institutional, 138

passive abuse or neglect, 4

Emergency Broadcast System (EBS), 14

Erotomania, 264

Ethnoviolence. *See* Hate crime

Evolutionary psychology. *See* Sociobiology Theory

Facebook, 41, 67

Facilitation, **87–88**, 222

Failure to thrive syndrome, nonorganic, 3

Fair and Accurate Credit Transactions Act (FACTA), 134

False allegations, 88

Family abduction, **88–90**. *See also* Kidnapping

Family reunification, 135

Family Stress Theory, **90–91**; ABC-X model, 90

Family violence court, **91–93**

Fantasy-motivated stalker, 264

Father of victimology, 166, 300

Fear of crime, **94–96**
    elderly levels of, 84, 94
    See also Vicarious victimization

Federal Bureau of Investigation (FBI)
    and National Incident-Based Reporting System (NIBRS), 177–78
    and Uniform Crime Report (UCR), 282–83, 293

Federal Victim and Witness Protection Act, 304

Feminine Mystique, The (Friedan), 117

Feminist movement, 96–97

Feminist perspectives on victimization, **96–98**
    use of "survivor," 305

Feminist victimology. *See* Feminist perspectives on victimization

Filicide, 136

Financial abuse, **98–99**
    and the elderly, 83, 98

Firearms: and murder, 172

Franklin v. Gwinnett County Public Schools, 251

Freud, Sigmund, 223
Friedan, Betty, 117
Fry, Margery, 47, **99–100**

Garner, Jennifer, 264
Gender symmetry debate, 23–24
General victimology, 300
Genovese, Catherine (Kitty), 33
Gideon v. Wainwright, 118
Good Samaritan, **101–2**
Guardian Ad Litem, 56, **102–3**
Guns. *See* Firearms

Hacking, 65
Hagerman, Amber, 13, 153
Harris v. Forklift Systems, 273–74
Hate crime, **105–7**
Hate Crime Statistic Act, 105
Hate Crimes Sentencing Enhancement
    Act, 105
Hazing, **107–8**
Hentig, Hans von, 8–9, 111–12, 299,
    307–8, 308–9

Hidden crime. *See* Dark figure of crime
Hierarchy Rule, 282–83
History of Victimology
    Pre-1940s, **108–11**
    1940s, **111–13**
    1950s, **113–16**
    1960s, **116–19**
    1970s, **119–22**
    1980s, **122–25**
    1990s, **125–28**
    2000 to today, **128–30**
Homicide. *See* Murder
Hostile environment, 251
Human trafficking, **130–32**, 143. *See*
    also Domestic minor sex
    trafficking
Husband battering. *See* Battered hus-
    band syndrome

Identity theft, 66, 67, 87, **133–34**
Identity Theft and Assumption Deter-
    rence Act, 126, 133
Incest, **134–36**
Index offenses, 282

Indirect victim. *See* Secondary victim-
    ization
Infanticide, **136–37**
Innocent victim, 167, 222, 238
Institutional elder abuse, **138–39**
Insurance policies, **139–40**
International Crime Victim Survey
    (ICVS), 124, **141–43**
International Criminal Court (ICC), 144
International Parental Kidnapping
    Crime Act, 89
International victimizations, **143–45**
Internet
    child lures, 40–41
    crimes against children, 200
    CyberAngels.org, 64–65
    cybercrime, 66
    cyberstalking, 67
    pornography, 199
Internet Crimes against Children (ICAC),
    200
Intimate partner violence, 23–24, 80,
    145–46. *See also* Same-sex part-
    ner abuse
Intimate terrorism, 23
Irish Republican Army, 278

Jacob Wetterling Act, 248
Jeanne Clery Act, 36
Jeffery, C. Ray, 61
Jim Crow laws, 113–14
Judges, **147–48**
Juries, **148–49**, 191
Jury nullification, 149
"Just deserts," 229
Justice for All Act, 129

Kant, Immanuel, 229
Keeping Children and Families Safe Act,
    179
Kempe, C. Henry, 21, 116, **151–52**.
    See also Battered child
    syndrome
Kidnapping, **152–53**. *See also* Family
    abduction

Larceny-theft, **155–56**, 239
Law-and-order movement, 118, 122

Law Enforcement Assistance Administration (LEAA), 120–21
and the National Crime Survey (NCS), 118, 175–76
and victim/witness programs, 303
Learned helplessness, **156–58**
Letterman, David, 264
Lex talionis, 111
Lifestyle Theory, **158–59**
Linda R.S. v. Richard D., 272
Lindbergh, Charles, 37
Lynching, 243–44

Madonna, 264
Male rape, **161–63**. *See also* Prison Rape
Mapp v. Ohio, 118
Marital exemption for rape, 120, 163
Marital rape, **163–64**
Maryland v. Craig, 43
Mass media, 13–14, 38, 245
coverage of infanticide, 136–37
Matza, David, 182
McGruff Campaign, **164–65**
Mediation, 12, **165–66**
Megan's Law, 126, 248
Mendelsohn, Beniamin, **166**, 167, 316, 299–300
Mendelsohn's Typologies, **166–68**
Meritor Savings Banks v. Vinson, 273
Minneapolis Domestic Violence Experiment, **168–69**, 197
Miranda v. Arizona, 118
Mosley v. State, 291
Mothers Against Drunk Driving (MADD), **169–71**, 290
Motor vehicle theft, 87, **171–72**
Mugging, 230
Murder, **172–73**
school fatalities, 240
See also Supplementary Homicide Report (SHR)
MySpace, 41, 68

National Association for the Advancement of Colored People (NAACP), 117
National Center for Missing and Exploited Children (NCMEC), 14

National Center for Shaken Baby Syndrome (NCSBS), 252
National Center on Child Abuse and Neglect (NCCAN), 114, 121
National Crime Survey (NCS). *See* National Crime Victimization Survey (NCVS)
National Crime Victimization Survey (NCVS), 119, **175–77**
average dollar loss, 139
dark figure of crime, 71
hate crime, 106
rape, 215
reporting rates, 224–25
series victimizations, 246
versus the Uniform Crime Report (UCR), 175–76
victimization trends, 293–94
National Family Violence Surveys, 23, 39, 50, 258
National Incidence Studies of Missing, Abducted, Runaway and Throwaway Children (NISMART), 152
National Incident-Based Reporting System (NIBRS), **177–79**
National Organization for Women (NOW), 117
National Prison Rape Elimination Commission (NPREC), 207
National Victim Assistance Academy (NVAA), 127, 130
National Violence Against Women Survey, 215–16
National Youth Survey, 246
Neglect, **179–80**
child abuse, 38–39
elder abuse; financial exception, 4
passive, 4
religious exception, 3–4
Negligent, third-party liability, 279
Neighborhood watch programs, **180–81**
Neutralization Theory, **182–83**
Newman, Oscar, 75
No-drop policies, 183
Notoriety for profit laws, **183–85**
Nursing Home Quality Protection Act, 138

Office for Victims of Crime (OVC), 126

Office of Violence Against Women (OVW), 36, 129

Oklahoma City bombing, 126, 203, 278

Older Americans Act, 138

Operators, 911, **187–88**

Order of protection, **188–89**

Overcharging, 208

Pain and suffering compensation, **191–92**

Parens patriae, 115

Parental abduction. *See* Family abduction

Parents Anonymous® Inc., **192–93**

Parole boards, **193–94**

Part I offenses, Uniform Crime Report, 282

Part II offenses, Uniform Crime Report, 282

Patterns in Forcible Rape (Amir), 15, 28

Payne v. Tennessee, 11, 126, 273, 291

Pecuniary damages, **194–95**

Pedophilia, **195–96**

People v. Jovanovic, 219

Petta v. Rivera, 263 n.2

Philip Morris USA v. Williams, 211–12

Phishing, 65–66

Piracy, 66

Plea bargaining, **196–97**

Plessy v. Ferguson, 114

Police officers, **197–99**, 233
   and domestic violence, 120
   See also Defounding; Unfounding

Pornography, **199–201**. *See also* Domestic minor sex trafficking

Post-Traumatic Stress Disorder (PTSD), 55–56, **201–2**, 271
   battered child syndrome, 22

Precipitation, 27–28, 158, **202–3**, 222

President's Family Justice Center Initiative (PFJCI), 128–29

President's Task Force on Victims of Crime, *Final Report*, 123, **203–5**, 286–87, 301, 304

Presidents
   Bush, George W., 14, 128, 131
   Reagan, Ronald, 123, 203, 286, 301

Pressly, Anne, 37

Primary victimization, **205–6**, 228

Prison rape, **206–8**

Prison Rape Elimination Act, 207

Prosecuting attorneys, **208–9**

Prostitution, 296

Provocation, 158, **209–10**, 222

Pseudo-victim, 222

Psychopathology Theory, **210–11**

Punitive damages, 49, **211–13**

Quid pro quo harassment, 251

Rape, **215–17**
   acquaintance, 5–6
   stranger, 5
   See also Acquaintance rape; Incest; Male rape; Marital rape; Pedophilia; Prison rape; Sexual assault; Statutory rape

Rape myths, 216, **217–18**, 250

Rape shield laws, **218–20**, 273, 304

Rape trauma syndrome, **220–21**. *See also* Post-Traumatic Stress Disorder (PTSD)

Rational Choice Theory, **221–23**

Reagan, Ronald, 123, 203, 286, 301

Recovered memories of sexual abuse, **223–24**

Rehabilitative justice, 228

Religious exception, child abuse and, 3–4

Rene Guyon Society, 195

Repeat victimization. *See* Series victimizations

Reporting rates, 71, **224–26**
   acquaintance rape, 5
   male rape, 161
   rape, 216
   workplace victimizations, 315

Restitution, **226–27**
   alternative dispute resolution, 13, 226
   community service, 46, 226

See also Creative restitution; Symbolic restitution
Restorative justice, **227–29**
  and neutralization theory, 182
  and victim-offender reconciliation programs (VORPs), 297
Restraining order. *See* Order of protection
Retributive justice, 228, **229–30**
Rideout, John, 163
Robbery, **230–32**
Routine Activity Theory, **232–33**
Rule of thumb, **233–34**

Same-sex partner abuse, **235–36**
Schafer, Stephen, **236–38**, 238–39, 317, 299–300
Schafer's Typologies, **238–39**
School victimizations, **239–41**. *See also* Bullying; Campus victimizations
Secondary victimization, 32, 205, 228, **241–43**
  of co-workers, 316
Security On Campus, Inc., 35
Self-defense, 24–25. *See also* Self-help justice
Self-help justice, **243–44**
Sensationalism, **245**
September 11th attacks, 203, 278, 285
Series victimizations, 225, **246–47**
Sex offender registration, **247–49**
Sexual assault, **249–50**. *See also* Incest; Domestic minor sex trafficking; Human trafficking; Male rape; Marital rape; Pedophilia; Prison rape; Rape
Sexual harassment, 251–52, 273
Sexual predators, 40–41
Shaken baby syndrome, **252–54**
Shelters, 119–20, **254–55**
Sherman, Lawrence, 168
Sibling abuse, **255–56**
  incest, 134–35
Simon & Schuster v. NY Crime Victims Board, 274. *See also* Notoriety for profit laws
Simpson, O.J., 184

Situational couple violence, 23–24
Sixth Amendment: proposed reform, 286–87, 301, 304
Social Exchange Theory, **256–58**
Social Learning Theory, **258–59**
Social movements
  antiwar movement, 118
  civil rights movement, 114, 117
  deinstitutionalization movement, 210
  feminist movement, 96–97
  law-and-order movement, 118, 122
  victims' rights movement, 118, 122, 286–87
  women's rights movement, 117, 119–20
Society for the Prevention of Cruelty to Children (SPCC), **259–61**, 313
Sociobiology Theory, **261–62**
"Son of Sam" laws. *See* Notoriety for profit laws
South Carolina v. Gathers, 126, 273, 290–91
Sovereign Immunity, **262–63**
Spanking, 3
Specific deterrence, 168
Spousal exemption. *See* Marital exemption
Stalking, **263–64**. *See also* Cyberstalking
Stranger rape, 5
State Farm Mutual Automobile Insurance Co. v. Campbell et al., 212
State of New Mexico v. Stephen F., 219
State Victim Assistance Academy (SVAA), 127, 130
Statutory rape, **265–66**. *See also* Domestic minor sex trafficking; Pedophilia
Stitch rule, 233
Stockholm Syndrome, **266**
Student Right to Know and Campus Security Act, 35–36
Subculture of violence, **267–68**
Subintentional death, **268–69**
"Suicide by cop," 268, 314
Supplementary Homicide Report (SHR), **269–70**

Support groups, 271–72
Supreme Court cases, 117–18, **272–74**
Survivor, 305
Sutherland, Edwin, 109–10
Sykes, Gresham, 182
Symbolic restitution, 275. *See also*
    Restitution

Target hardening, **277–78**
Techniques of neutralization, 182
Terrorism, 144, **278–79**
Third-party liability, 44, **279–80**
Thurman v. City of Torrington, 233
Title VII of the Civil Rights Act, 251,
    273
Trafficking Victims Protection Act, 78,
    129

Unfounding, **281–82**
    sexual assault, 249
Uniform Crime Report (UCR), **282–83**
    hate crime, 106
    rape, 215
    versus the National Crime Victim-
        ization Survey (NCVS), 175–76
    victimization trends, 293–94
    See also National Incident-Based
        Reporting System (NIBRS); Sup-
        plementary Homicide Report
        (SHR)
United Nations, 123–24, 131, 317
*United States of America v. Miami
    University of Ohio*, 36
U.S. Census Bureau, 175–76

Versace, Gianni, 37–38
Vicarious victimization, **285–86**
Victim and His Criminal, The
    (Schafer), 237, 238
Victim and Witness Protection Act,
    123
Victim Bill of Rights, **286–88**
Victim-blaming, 26–28, 112
Victim discounting, **288–89**. *See also*
    Sensationalism
Victim impact panels, **289–90**
Victim impact statement, 126, 273,
    290–92, 304. *See also* Allocution

Victim Information and Notification
    Everyday (VINE), **292–93**
Victim ombudsman, 7
Victim Rights Week, 123
Victimization-fear paradox, 94
Victimization trends, **293–95**
Victimless crimes, **295–96**
Victim-Offender Mediation Programs
    (VOMs), 297
Victim-Offender Reconciliation
    Programs (VORPs), **296–98**
Victimologists, **298–99**
Victimology, 166, **299–301**
Victims of Crime Act (VOCA), 48,
    123, 126, 303
Victims' rights Constitutional amend-
    ment, 127, 286–87, **301–2**, 304
Victims' rights legislation, **302–5**
Victims' rights movement, 118, 122,
    286–87
Victim versus survivor, **305–6**
Victim/Witness Assistance Programs
    (VWAPs), **306–7**
Vigilantism, 229. *See also* Self-help
    justice
Violence Against Women Act (VAWA),
    68, 125, 128
Violent Crime Control and Law
    Enforcement Act, 126
Virginia Tech shooting, 263, 279
von Hentig, Hans, 8–9, 111–12, 299,
    307–8, 308–9
von Hentig's Typologies, 9, 112,
    308–9

Walker, Lenore, 119, 157
Walsh, Adam, 153
White v. Illinois, 44
Widening the net, **311–12**
Wilson, Mary Ellen, 260, **312–13**
Wolfgang, Marvin E., 27, **313–14**
Women's rights movement, 117,
    119–20
Workplace victimizations, **314–16**
    stalking, 263
World Society of Victimology (WSV),
    316–18
World Trade Center attacks, 278

About the Editor and Contributors

JANET K. WILSON is an associate professor and former chair of the Department of Sociology at the University of Central Arkansas. Her research interests include victim rights and the Supreme Court cases that extend those rights. Dr. Wilson has published in the *American Sociological Review* and *Sociological Inquiry*. She is the editor of *The Praeger Handbook of Victimology*.

RIFAT AKHTER is an assistant professor of sociology at the University of Central Arkansas. Her research interests are globalization, gender, violence against women, and maternal and child health. Dr. Akhter has published in *Advances in Gender Research, The Global Studies Journal,* and *Critical Sociology.*

KARLA BECK is the director of Police Social Services, a unique law enforcement-based victim assistance program in Lafourche Parish, Louisiana. This program won the 2008 IACP International Award for Excellence in Victim Services. Lt. Beck is a licensed professional counselor and marriage and family therapist.

MICHELLE BEMILLER is an assistant professor of sociology at Kansas State University. Her research focuses on child custody cases that involve allegations of abuse, and domestic and sexual assault advocates' experiences with burnout. Dr. Bemiller has published in the *Journal of Family Issues, Sociological Focus,* and *Sociology Compass.*

ROBERT BING is an associate professor and former chair of the Department of Criminology and Criminal Justice at the University of Texas at Arlington. His research interests include corrections, plea bargaining, and crime and public policy. Dr. Bing has over 27 publications, including articles in *The Journal of Criminal Justice Education* and the *Journal of African American Studies*. He is also the recent author/editor of *Race, Crime and the Media* (McGraw-Hill).

ASHLEY G. BLACKBURN is an assistant professor of criminal justice at the University of North Texas. Her research interests include sexual victimization, family violence, and female offenders. Dr. Blackburn has published in *Youth Violence and Juvenile Justice* and *The Prison Journal*.

HOAN N. BUI is an associate professor of sociology at the University of Tennessee at Knoxville. Her research interests examine how resettlement experiences of immigrants influence crime offending, domestic violence, and help-seeking behavior among female victims. Dr. Bui has published in many academic journals including *Violence Against Women* and the *Journal of Crime and Justice*.

JACKSON BUNCH is a sociology doctoral candidate at the University of Georgia. His research examines routine activities and victimization.

TOD W. BURKE, a former Maryland police officer, is a professor of criminal justice at Radford University. His research interests include issues in policing and forensic science. Dr. Burke has published approximately 100 articles, book chapters, encyclopedia entries, etc.

DAWN C. CARR is a doctoral candidate in sociology and gerontology at Miami University. Her research looks at the impact of aging on the life course and demographic change.

JODY CLAY-WARNER is an associate professor of sociology at the University of Georgia. Her research focuses on the gendered nature of emotional and behavioral responses to criminal events. Dr. Clay-Warner has published in *Violence Against Women* and *Violence and Victims*.

HEITH COPES is an associate professor of justice studies at the University of Alabama at Birmingham. His primary research interest is the criminal decision-making process. Dr. Copes has published in the *British Journal of Criminology, Deviant Behavior,* and *Justice Quarterly*.

JAY CORZINE is a professor and chair of the Department of Sociology at the University of Central Florida. His research interests include homicide and violent crime, crime and inequality, and the relationships between neighborhood characteristics and crime. Dr. Corzine is a former co-editor of *Homicide Studies*. He has published in *Social Forces, Criminology,* and *Sociological Inquiry.*

CHARISSE COSTON is an associate professor of criminal justice at the University of North Carolina at Charlotte. Her research focuses on high-risk targets of criminal victimization both nationally and internationally. Dr. Coston also coordinates a study abroad program at Kingston University in London, England. She serves as a teaching affiliate in Africana studies, international studies, women's studies, the PhD program in public policy, and the honors college. Dr. Coston currently serves as the coordinator of her department's learning community for transfer students.

ANGELA CROSSMAN is an associate professor of psychology at John Jay College of Criminal Justice-City University of New York. Her research interests include child memory, suggestibility, credibility, and the development of deception. Dr. Crossman has published in *Behavioral Sciences and the Law,* the *Journal of Forensic Psychiatry and Psychology,* and *Applied Developmental Science.*

JOAN CROWLEY is an assistant professor of criminal justice at New Mexico State University. Her research areas include victimology, family violence, and sex crimes. Dr. Crowley has served as president of the Southwest Association of Criminal Justice, and as Region 4 Trustee for the Academy of Criminal Justice Sciences. She has published in the *Journal of Criminal Justice* and the *Journal of Social History.*

ELIZABETH QUINN DEVALVE is an assistant professor of criminal justice at Fayetteville State University. Her research interests include crime victims and the criminal justice system, repeat victimization, and females and criminal justice. She has published articles and book chapters on victimization experiences, female wardens, and drug-facilitated sexual assault. Dr. DeValve has published in *Applied Psychology in Criminal Justice* and *The Prison Journal.*

TONI DUPONT-MORALES joined the victimology faculty in the Department of Criminology at California State University, Fresno, after an academic career at Penn State where she earned emerita status. Her topics of research include domestic violence, stalking, and victim services. Dr. DuPont-Morales has published in *Controversies in Victimology, Humanity and Society,* and the *Journal of Criminal Justice Education.*

JOHN DUSSICH is a professor of victimology at California State University, Fresno. Dr. Dussich entered victimology by presenting the Victim Ombudsman concept at the First Symposium on Victimology in 1973. He launched the National Organization of Victim Assistance in 1976. Dr. Dussich is president of the World Society of Victimology, and he serves on the executive board of the American Society of Victimology.

ROBERT FERNQUIST is a professor of sociology at the University of Central Missouri. He studies sociological aspects of suicidal behavior. Dr. Fernquist has published in *Suicide and Life-Threatening Behavior, Archives of Suicide Research,* and *Adolescence.*

CONNIE D. FREY is an assistant professor of sociology at Southern Illinois University Edwardsville. Her research interests include the history of sociology and criminology, particularly how Jane Addams shaped the development of both. Dr. Frey has published in the *Journal of Higher Education* and *Nature Geoscience.*

STEPHANIE FROGGE is an adjunct instructor of social work at the University of Texas at Austin. She is the former national director of victim services for the organization Mothers Against Drunk Driving. Ms. Frogge also serves on the executive board of the American Society of Victimology.

TINA FRYLING, a practicing attorney, is an associate professor and chair of the Department of Criminal Justice at Mercyhurst College. Her primary areas of practice are criminal law, bankruptcy law, and domestic relations. Ms. Fryling has published in the *University of Dayton Law Review, Criminal Justice Review*, and *Elder Abuse: A Public Health Perspective.*

TAMMY S. GARLAND is an assistant professor of criminal justice at the University of Tennessee at Chattanooga. Her research emphasis includes the victimization of women, victimization of the homeless, popular culture and crime, and drug policy issues. Dr. Garland has published in *Criminal Justice Studies* and *The Southwest Journal of Criminal Justice.*

DOUGLAS F. GEORGE is an assistant professor of sociology at the University of Central Arkansas. His research interests include racial and cultural integration, multiculturalism, and American universalism. Dr. George has published in the *Journal of Comparative Family Studies, Sociological Focus,* and *Sociological Imagination.*

SUZANNE M. GODBOLDT is an assistant professor of criminal justice at Mercyhurst College. Her research and teaching interests include family violence, victimology, and juvenile delinquency. Dr. Godboldt has published in *Criminal Justice and Behavior.*

JAMES W. GOLDEN is a professor of criminal justice at the University of Arkansas at Little Rock and co-director of the Center for the Study of Environmental Criminology. His research utilizes GIS technology to map the location and displacement of crime. Dr. Golden has published in *Justice Research and Policy.*

PENNY HANSER is a gerontology master's candidate at the University of Louisiana at Monroe. Ms. Hanser has worked with victims of elder abuse and has published on issues related to geriatrics and the criminal justice system.

ROBERT D. HANSER is director of the Institute of Law Enforcement at the University of Louisiana at Monroe. He is a licensed professional counselor in the states of Texas and Louisiana, and has worked with victims of domestic violence and sexual assault. Dr. Hanser has published in the *International Journal of Restorative Justice* and *The Prison Journal.*

BARBARA L. HART is an associate professor and former chair of the Department of Social Sciences at the University of Texas at Tyler. Dr. Hart specializations in neuropsychology and counseling psychology, with expertise in serial violent behavior, risk assessment, and racial profiling.

DEBRA HEATH-THORNTON is a professor of criminal justice and chair of the Department of Sociology, Social Work, and Criminal Justice at Messiah College. She is a former county criminal justice system administrator. Her research interests include restorative justice and victimology. Dr. Heath-Thornton has contributed to *Teaching to Justice,* the *Encyclopedia of Crime and Punishment,* and *War against Domestic Violence.*

JESSICA P. HODGE is an assistant professor of criminal justice and criminology at the University of Missouri-Kansas City. Her research interests include bias crime legislation, gender issues in criminal justice, and juvenile justice and delinquency. Dr. Hodge has published in the *Journal of Ethnicity in Criminal Justice* and *Law Enforcement Executive Forum.*

LIN HUFF-CORZINE is a professor of sociology at the University of Central Florida. Her research examines the influences of weapon used, victim-offender relationship, immigration, and victim and offender characteristics on lethal violence. Dr. Huff-Corzine has published in *Social Forces, Homicide Studies,* and the *American Journal of Criminal Justice.*

HOLLY JACOBS is a criminal justice master's candidate at the University of Missouri-Kansas City. Her research examines gender issues in the criminal justice system, racial profiling, and rape.

KATIE JAMES is a sociology master's candidate at the University of Georgia. She studies social psychology and is particularly interested in gender and justice in paid and unpaid labor.

PAMELA JENKINS is a professor of sociology and faculty in the Women's Studies Program at the University of New Orleans. She is a founding and associate member of UNO's Center for Hazard Assessment, Response, and Technology. Her research interests post-Katrina include documenting the response to Katrina as part of a national research team on hurricane Katrina evacuees. Dr. Jenkins has published on first responders, faith-based communities, response to the storm, and the experiences of elderly during and after Katrina.

ROBERT A. JERIN is a professor of criminal justice at Endicott College. In 2005, he was the recipient of the John P. J. Dussich award from the American Society of Victimology. Dr. Jerin is a member of the steering committee for the Massachusetts' Victims' Assistance Academy. In addition, he is a lifetime member of both the World Society of Victimology and the National Organization for Victim Assistance. Dr. Jerin is the co-author of numerous books including the recently published *The Victims of Crime* (Prentice Hall).

MATTHEW JOHNSON is an assistant professor of criminal justice at East Carolina University. His research interests include the etiology of victimization, criminological theory, and quantitative methods. Dr. Johnson has published in the *Journal of Criminal Justice, Journal of Interpersonal Violence,* and *Deviant Behavior.*

JASON JOLICOEUR is an assistant professor of criminal justice at the University of Texas at Tyler. He is a doctoral candidate at the University of Missouri–St. Louis. His research interests include the relationship between religion and deviance, as well as law enforcement training practices.

CASEY JORDAN is an attorney and professor of justice and law administration at Western Connecticut State University. Her areas of specialization are gender and victimization, sexual assault and homicide patterns, policy analysis, and forensic consulting. Dr. Jordan has served as a legal analyst for numerous television shows including *CNN, Fox News,* and *Good Morning America.*

THOMAS KELLEY is an associate professor of criminal justice at Wayne State University. Dr. Kelley is a licensed clinical psychologist. His research areas include child abuse and neglect, as well as juvenile justice and delinquency. Dr. Kelley is the author of 35 journal articles and one book, *Falling in Love with Life.*

M. ALEXIS KENNEDY is an assistant professor of criminal justice at the University of Nevada, Las Vegas. With a law degree and a PhD in forensic psychology, she examines child abuse, sexual assault, and prostitution. Dr. Kennedy's dissertation on cross-cultural perceptions of child abuse won two American Psychological Association awards (Divisions 37 and 41).

SESHA KETHINENI is a professor of criminal justice at Illinois State University. Her research focuses on homicides, domestic violence, and juvenile justice in India; protective orders in domestic violence cases; youth-on-parent battering; juvenile justice in the U.S.; and international human rights issues. Dr. Kethineni has published in the *International Journal of Comparative and Applied Criminal Justice*, *International Criminal Justice Review*, *International Journal of Offender Therapy and Comparative Criminology*, *Journal of Family Violence*, *Youth Violence and Juvenile Justice*, and *Asian Journal of Criminology*.

DAWNA KOMOROSKY is an assistant professor of criminal justice administration at California State University East Bay. She has counseled and advocated for rape survivors and victims of domestic violence. Dr. Komorosky has published in *American Jail*, *Criminal Justice Review*, and the *Journal for Juvenile Justice and Detention Services*.

ANNA KOSLOSKI is a sociology doctoral candidate at Iowa State University. Her research interests include life course offenders, gender and crime, and human trafficking crimes.

PETER C. KRATCOSKI is a professor emeritus and former chair of the Department of Justice Studies at Kent State University, and is currently adjunct professor of justice studies at Kent State University's Stark Campus. His areas of research include juvenile justice, victimology, policing, and corrections. Dr. Kratcoski was formerly editor of the *Journal of Crime and Justice* and has published in the *International Review of Victimology* and *Criminal Justice Review*.

CHRYSANTHI LEON is an assistant professor of sociology and criminal justice at the University of Delaware. With a law degree and PhD in Jurisprudence and Social Policy, she examines sex crimes and punishments, as well as the sociology of law. Dr. Leon has published in the *Berkeley Journal of Criminal Law* and *Criminal Law Bulletin*.

TOYA Z. LIKE is an assistant professor of criminal justice and criminology at the University of Missouri-Kansas City. Her research interests include the assessment of risks for violent victimization, as well as racial and ethnic variations in victimization. Dr. Like has contributed to *The Many Colors of Crime* and *Images of Color/Images of Crime,* 2nd ed.

TERRY GLENN LILLEY is a sociology doctoral candidate at the University of Delaware. His research interests include intersectionality and social movements.

SARAH LINDAHL-PFIEFFER, has a certificate in victim assistance from Washburn University and California State University-Fresno. She led an undergraduate course titled "Women in the Criminal Justice System" for her Master's practicum and was also an intern at the Central Minnesota Sexual Assault Center. Ms. Lindahl-Pfieffer is currently a court manager in Minnesota.

CINDY LINDQUIST is currently employed with United Way Twin Cities. In addition, Ms. Lindquist is on the executive board of the American Society of Victimology. Previously, she was the state victim assistance coordinator for Mothers Against Drunk Driving in New Jersey and Indiana.

SUSAN LIPKINS is a psychologist with expertise in conflict and violence on high school and college campuses. She is the author of *Preventing Hazing: How Parents, Teachers and Coaches Can Stop the Violence, Harassment and Humiliation.* Dr. Lipkin's Web site, http://www.insidehazing.com, is a resource for news and educational information on hazing.

JASON MANDELBAUM is a forensic psychology doctoral candidate at John Jay College of Criminal Justice-City University of New York. He studies eyewitness identifications, jury decision making, lie detection, and the development of lying behaviors in children.

RAY MARATEA is a sociology doctoral candidate at the University of Delaware. He studies how the Internet is affecting the process of social problem construction and the emergence of the blogosphere as a claims-making arena.

ROBERT J. MEADOWS is a professor and chair of the Department of Criminal Justice and Legal Studies at California Lutheran University. His research interests are in violence and victimization, and the legal/policy responses of the justice system. Dr. Meadows is author of *Understanding Violence and Victimization,* 5th ed. (Prentice Hall).

BRIAN A. MONAHAN is an assistant professor of sociology at Iowa State University. His research interests are in the areas of deviance, crime, mass media, and social problems. Dr. Monahan has published in *Deviant Behavior* and the *Journal of Contemporary Ethnography*.

BERNADETTE MUSCAT is an associate professor of criminology at California State University, Fresno. Her areas of expertise include violence against women, child abuse, trauma response, elder abuse, victims with disabilities, workplace violence, and campus crimes. She has published in *International Perspectives in Victimology* and *Women & Criminal Justice*. Dr. Muscat serves on the executive board of the American Society of Victimology.

GLENN W. MUSCHERT is an associate professor of sociology at Miami University. His research focuses on social control through surveillance and the mass media coverage of crime and delinquency. Dr. Muschert has published in the *Annual Review of Law and Social Science* and *Youth Violence and Juvenile Justice*.

MATT R. NOBLES is an assistant professor of political science at Washington State University. His research interests include violent and interpersonal crimes, gun policy, GIS and spatial econometrics, criminological theory, and quantitative methods. Dr. Nobles has published in *Justice Quarterly, Criminal Justice and Behavior,* and *Security Journal*.

STEPHEN OWEN is an associate professor of criminal justice at Radford University. His areas of interest include corrections, crime prevention, interpersonal violence, and criminal justice pedagogy. Dr. Owen has published in the *Journal of Criminal Justice Education, The Prison Journal,* and *Social Justice Research*.

MARY PARKER is a professor and chair of the Department of Criminal Justice at the University of Arkansas at Little Rock. Dr. Parker is a member of the Arkansas Board of Corrections. Her research areas include juvenile law and constitutional rights.

LAURA PATTERSON is an assistant professor of criminal justice at Shippensburg University. Recently, she was a grant administrator for STOP Violence Against Women and Court-Ordered Special Advocates for Cumberland County, Pennsylvania. Dr. Patterson has published in *Criminology* and the *Journal of Criminal Law and Criminology*.

BENJAMIN PEARSON-NELSON is an assistant professor of public and environmental affairs at Indiana University-Purdue University Fort Wayne. His research areas are homicide and suicide trends, as well as sexual assault. Dr. Pearson-Nelson is the author of *Understanding Homicide Trends*.

DAN L. PETERSEN is the associate dean in the School of Applied Studies at Washburn University. He is on the executive board of both the Joint Center on Violence and Victim Studies and the American Society of Victimology. Dr. Petersen's research examines the victimization of persons with disabilities and the impact of trauma.

PETER W. PHILLIPS was recently awarded emeritus status in the Department of Criminal Justice at the University of Texas at Tyler. A 25-year veteran of state and federal law enforcement, he is a former assistant director for the Federal Law Enforcement Training Center and Special Agent for the Bureau of Alcohol, Tobacco, Firearms, and Explosives.

MARGARET L. POLINSKY conducts evaluation studies, develops and validates data collection tools, implements and monitors data collection, and produces publications for the Parents Anonymous® Inc. National organization. Dr. Polinsky's research examines child maltreatment prevention, family strengthening, and quality of life.

EDWARD POWERS is an associate professor of sociology at the University of Central Arkansas. His research focuses on the intersections between cultural change, social networks, and crime/delinquency. Dr. Powers has published in *Sociological Inquiry* and contributed to the *Encyclopedia of Juvenile Violence*.

CHITRA RAGHAVAN is an associate professor of psychology and director of the BA/MA Scholars program at John Jay College of Criminal Justice-City University of New York. Her research focuses on the interaction among community-level and individual-level factors to explain partner violence in low-income and ethnic minority populations. Dr. Raghavan has published in the *Journal of Interpersonal Violence, Violence Against Women,* and *Journal of Traumatic Stress*.

LAURA RAPP is a sociology doctoral candidate at the University of Delaware. Her research focuses on gender and racial stratification.

LAUREN REARDON is a forensic psychology master's candidate at John Jay College of Criminal Justice-City University of New York. Her research interests include cyberstalking, intimate partner violence, and sexual assault.

XIN REN is a professor of criminal justice at California State University, Sacramento, and serves as a board member of the Executive Committee of the World Society of Victimology. Her research interests include trafficking in women and children, prostitution and sex trafficking in Asia, recidivism of sex offenders in California, and juvenile justice systems in non-Western societies.

CLAIRE M. RENZETTI is a professor of sociology at the University of Dayton. She is editor of the journal *Violence Against Women*; co-editor of the Oxford University Press *Interpersonal Violence* book series; and editor of the Northeastern University Press series on *Gender, Crime, and Law*. She has authored or edited 16 books and numerous book chapters and journal articles on various aspects of intimate partner violence.

TARA RICHARDS is a criminology doctoral candidate at The University of South Florida. Her research interests include violence against women and human trafficking.

MICHELLE Y. RICHTER is a criminal justice doctoral candidate at Sam Houston State University. Her research interests include victim studies, hate crimes, and the impact of media and popular culture on perceptions of criminal justice, criminology, and forensics.

DUANE RUTH-HEFFELBOWER is an attorney and director of graduate programs for the Center for Peacemaking and Conflict Studies at Fresno Pacific University. His expertise is in the area of alternative dispute resolution and conflict resolution. He serves on the executive board of the American Society of Victimology. Dr. Ruth-Heffelbower has published over 50 books and articles.

SHANNON A. SANTANA is an assistant professor of sociology and criminology at the University of North Carolina Wilmington. Her research interests include violence against women, the use of self-protective behaviors in violent victimizations, and workplace violence. Dr. Santana has published in *Violence and Victims, Justice System Journal,* and *Security Journal.*

JENNIFER SCROGGINS is a sociology doctoral candidate at the University of Tennessee. She examines the effect of media images and social capital on the punishment of filicidal parents, women's reentry, and inequalities in the criminal justice system.

DAISY A. SEGOVIA is a forensic psychology doctoral candidate at John Jay College of Criminal Justice-City University of New York. Her research interests include accuracy and credibility of children's testimony, suggestibility, deception, and false memory reports.

LESLIE GORDON SIMONS is an associate professor of child and family development at the University of Georgia. Her research focuses on parenting, the intergenerational transmission of violence, and adolescent problem behaviors such as delinquency, drug use, risky sex, and dating violence. Dr. Simons has published in *Criminology, Journal of Marriage and Family, Deviant Behavior, Violence and Victims,* and *Family Issues.*

ALAN E. STEWART is an associate professor of counseling at the University of Georgia. His research interests include death notification, environmental psychology, and the psychology of weather and climate. He serves on the executive board of the American Society of Victimology. Dr. Stewart has published in *Death Studies* and the *Journal of Traumatic Stress.*

MOLLY SWEEN is a sociology doctoral candidate at Iowa State University. Her area of interest examines identity formation and development among members of deviant subcultures.

BRENT TEASDALE is an assistant professor of criminal justice at Georgia State University. His research focuses on mental illness and violence, drug and alcohol abuse prevention, and the community contexts of crime. Dr. Teasdale has published in *Social Problems*, *Law and Human Behavior*, and the *Journal of Research in Crime and Delinquency.*

RICHARD TEWKSBURY is a professor of justice administration at the University of Louisville. His areas of research include institutional corrections and sex offender registration. Dr. Tewksbury is editor of *Justice Quarterly*, former editor of the *American Journal of Criminal Justice*, and author of over 200 articles, chapters, and reports.

PEGGY TOBOLOWSKY is a professor and chair of the Department of Criminal Justice at the University of North Texas. Her areas of expertise include criminal law and procedure, victim rights and remedies, and capital punishment. Professor Tobolowsky is the author of *Crime Victim Rights and Remedies*, the editor of *Understanding Victimology,* and the author of several articles on crime victim rights and remedies.

TRACY FAYE TOLBERT is an assistant professor of criminal justice at California State University, Long Beach. Her research examines the facilitators and barriers affecting the way women report sex crimes. Dr. Tolbert is the author of *The Sex Crime Scenario* (Kendall/Hunt).

THOMAS UNDERWOOD is the executive director of the Joint Center on Violence and Victim Studies at Washburn University. He serves as treasurer of the American Society of Victimology. Dr. Underwood has developed a variety of professional and academic courses, conducted research and program evaluations, and has authored several books and journal articles related to crime victim issues.

ALANA VAN GUNDY-YODER is an assistant professor and coordinator of the Criminal Justice Program at Miami University Hamilton. Her research focuses on female criminality and the civil and ethical accountability of law enforcement. Dr. Van Gundy-Yoder has published in *Agenda for Social Justice, Gender and Society,* and *Women, Crime, and Criminal Justice.*

JEFFERY T. WALKER is a professor of criminal justice at the University of Arkansas at Little Rock. He has written six books and over 40 journal articles and obtained over $9 million in grants. He is a former president of the Academy of Criminal Justice Sciences. Dr. Walker has published in *Justice Quarterly, Journal of Quantitative Criminology,* and *Journal of Criminal Justice Education.*

JEFFREY A. WALSH is an assistant professor of criminal justice sciences at Illinois State University. His research examines family violence, predatory violence, and victimization. Dr. Walsh has published in the *Journal of Interpersonal Violence, Journal of Family Violence,* and *Journal of Research in Crime and Delinquency.*

KAREN WEISS is an assistant professor of sociology at West Virginia University. Her research areas are sexual victimization and victim blame. She has forthcoming articles on sexual victimization in *Violence Against Women* and *Men and Masculinities.*

MICHELLE WEST is a clinical forensic psychology doctoral candidate at John Jay College of Criminal Justice-City University of New York. Her research interests include psychopathy, stigma in patients with major mental illnesses, development of lying, and malingering.

JENNIFER WINGREN is an assistant professor of criminal justice at Metropolitan State University. Her research interests include domestic violence, corrections, and fear of crime. Dr. Wingren has published in *Challenge: A Journal of Research on African American Men.*

MELINDA YORK is an adjunct instructor and criminal justice doctoral candidate at Washington State University. Her areas of interest include courts, gender, race, and justice.

MELISSA YOUNG-SPILLERS is a sociology doctoral candidate at Purdue University. Her research areas include social policy, the family, and social inequality.

TASHA YOUSTIN is a criminal justice doctoral candidate at John Jay College of Criminal Justice-City University of New York. Her research interests include sexual offending, theory testing, situational crime prevention, and spatial analysis of crime.

YAN ZHANG is an assistant professor of criminal justice at Sam Houston State University. Her research interests include the social ecological contexts of delinquency, crime and victimization, sentencing policies and outcomes, and spatial temporal interaction of crime. Dr. Zhang has published in the *Journal of Criminal Justice, Violence Against Women,* and *Journal of Drug Issues.*